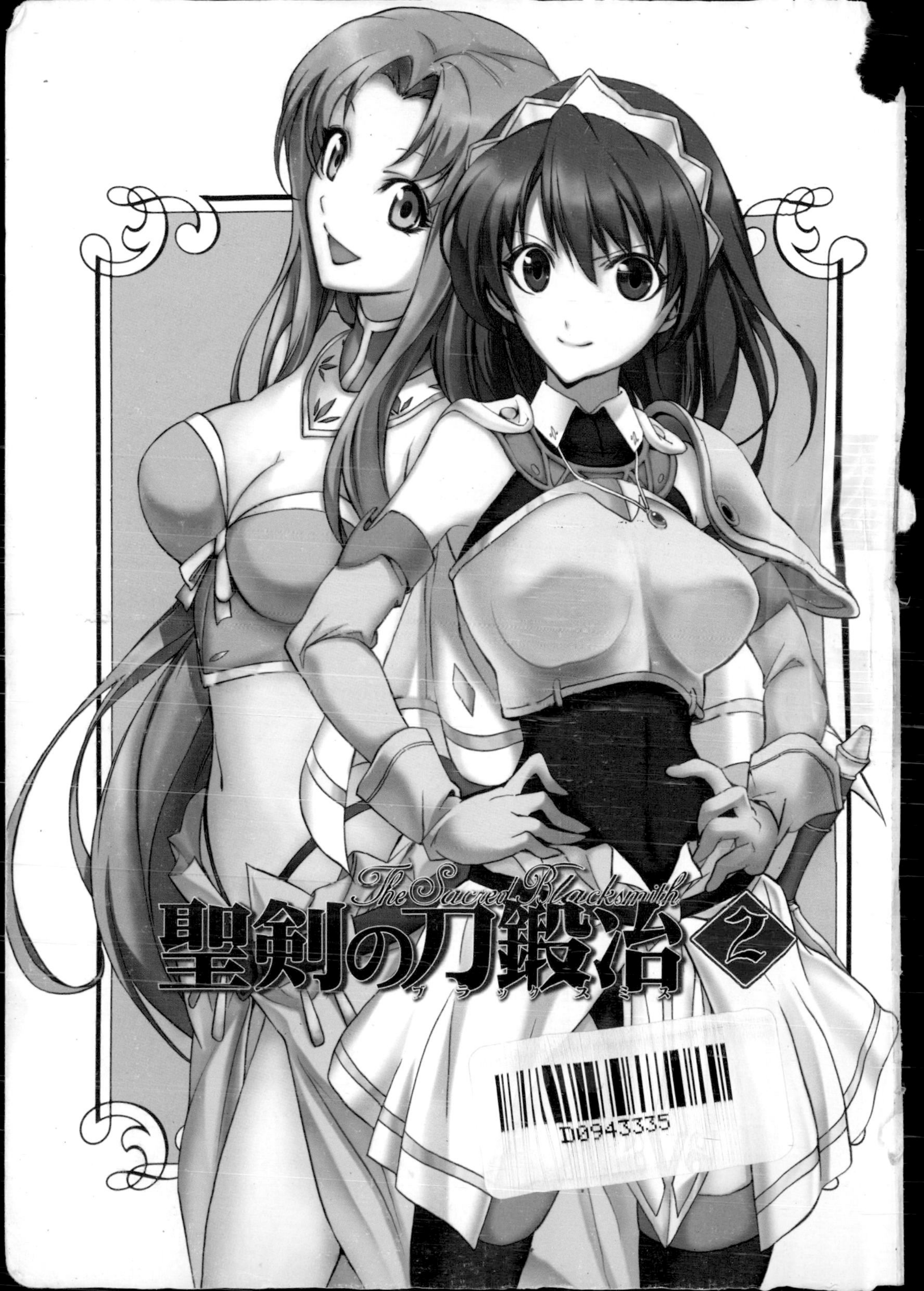
The Sacred Blacksmith
聖剣の刀鍛冶(ブラックスミス) 2

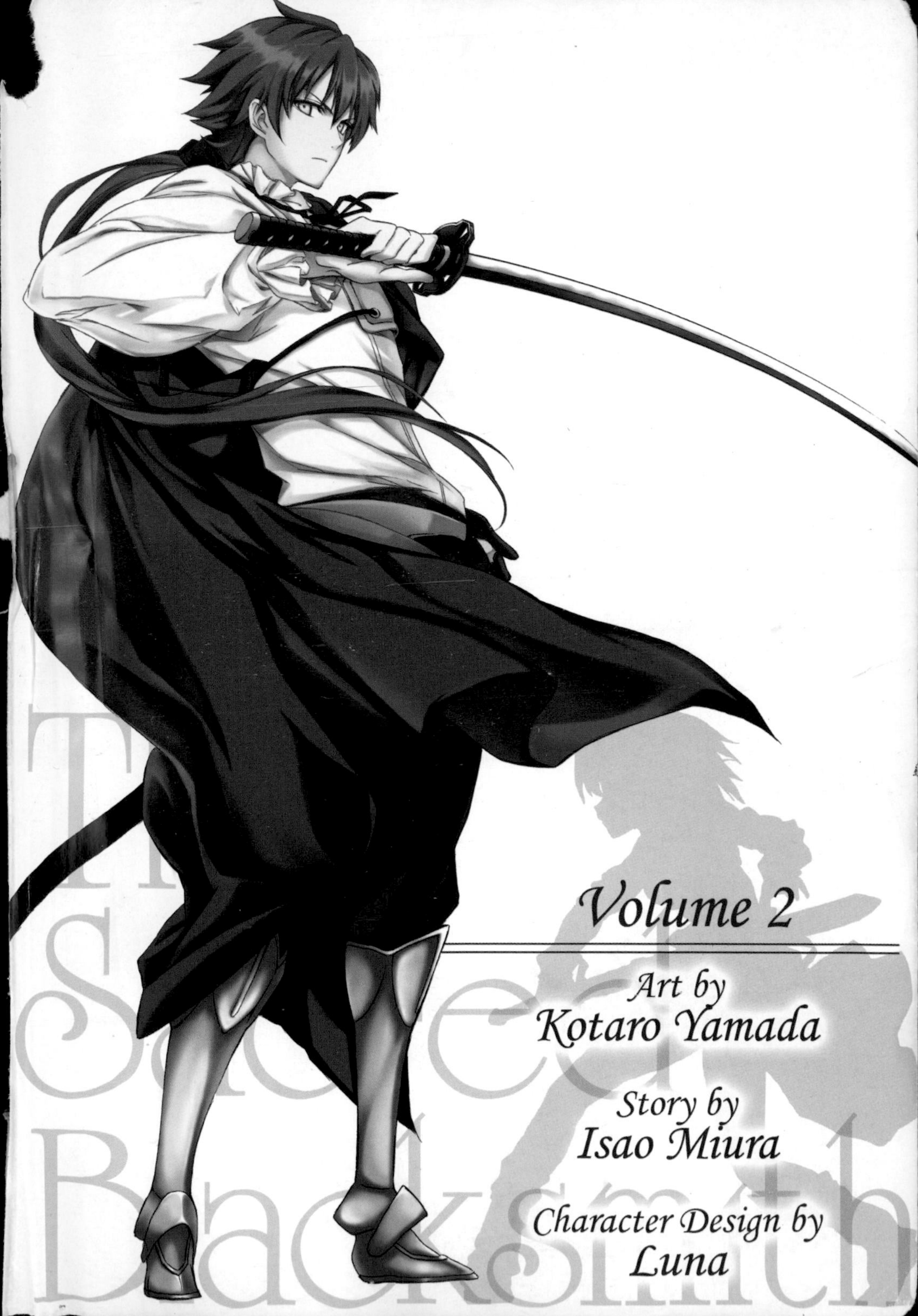

Volume 2

Art by
Kotaro Yamada

Story by
Isao Miura

Character Design by
Luna

登場人物紹介 *Character*

Luke Ainsworth
ルーク・エインズワース
A proficient swordsman who uses an unusual blade called a "katana." Pessimistic and world-weary, he runs his own smithy.

Cecily Campbell
セシリー・キャンベル
A young lady knight who is part of the Knight Guard, charged with defending the independent trade city of Housman. Ex-nobility, she has a strong sense of justice.

Aria
アリア
The "Demon Blade." She is part of the auction goods that the bandit gang captured by Cecily and Luke was after.

Lisa
リサ
Luke's assistant, who lives and works at his smithy. Innocent and carefree, she loves talking with everyone.

other characters
Hannibal Quasar
ハンニバル・クエイサー
Captain of the Third District Knight Guard, and Cecily's commander.

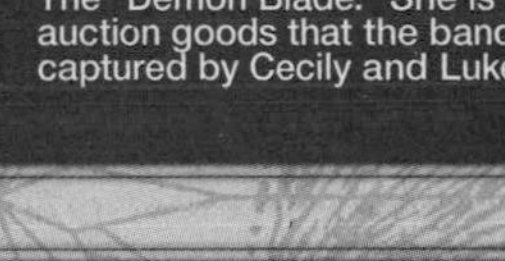

These are the characters introduced so far...

聖剣の刀鍛冶 The Sacred Blacksmith

That sentiment stems from one single thing—the Demon Pacts.
Their use eant that men did not fight other men. Instead, they ought demons nd hell-beasts. Thus it was named "The albanill War."

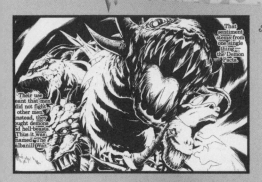

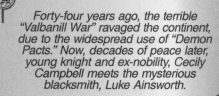

Forty-four years ago, the terrible "Valbanill War" ravaged the continent, due to the widespread use of "Demon Pacts." Now, decades of peace later, young knight and ex-nobility, Cecily Campbell meets the mysterious blacksmith, Luke Ainsworth.

A BLADE.

MY NAME IS CECILY CAMPBELL
I AM A MEMBER OF THE INDEPENDENT TRADE CITIES' KNIGHT GUARD, THIRD DISTRICT CORPS!!

GRAAAAH
CLENCH
DON'T WORR MISS CECILY. EVERY-THING'L BE OKA NOW.
KE HAS NALLY ECIDED
POK

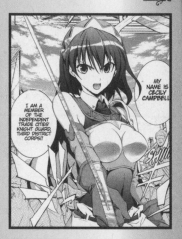

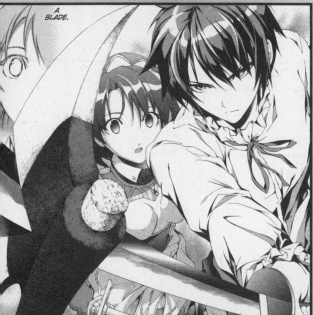

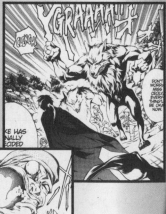

Cecily is entranced by the odd blade that Luke wields, a "katana." Wanting him to make one for her, she invites Luke and Lisa to join her on an excursion to capture bandits, to see if she is worthy to own one herself. But what their excursion finds isn't bandits, but inhumans and demons.

あらすじ Story

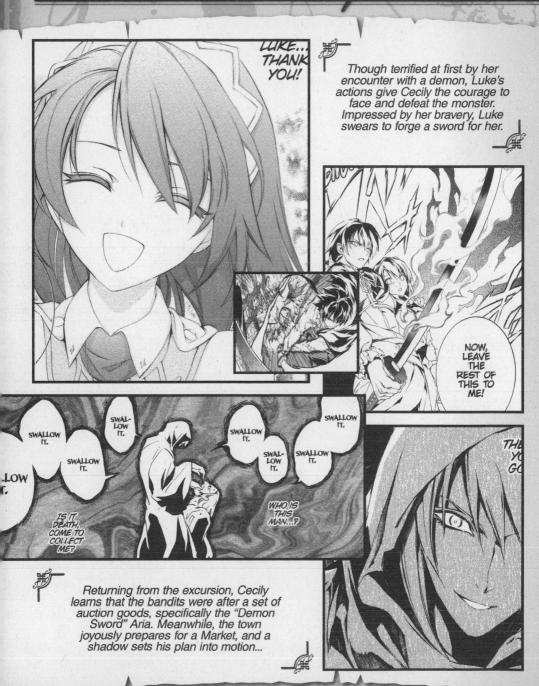

Though terrified at first by her encounter with a demon, Luke's actions give Cecily the courage to face and defeat the monster. Impressed by her bravery, Luke swears to forge a sword for her.

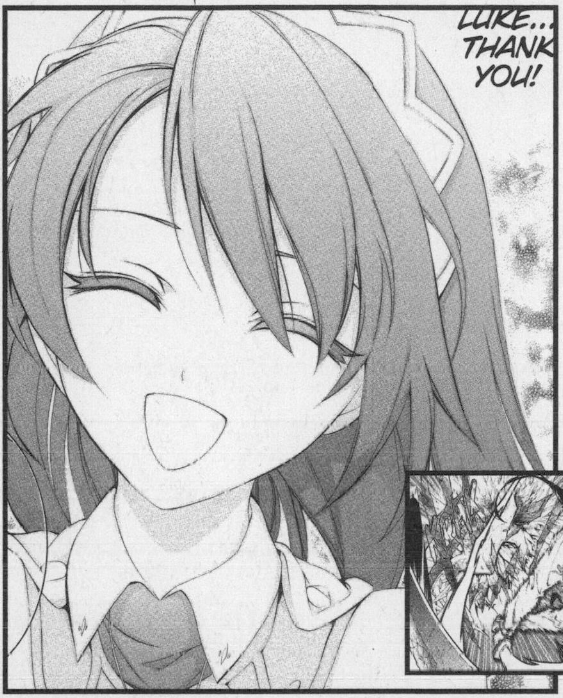
LUKE... THANK YOU!

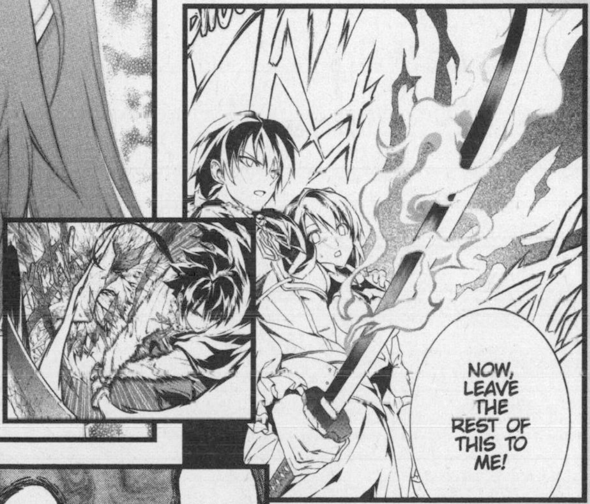
NOW, LEAVE THE REST OF THIS TO ME!

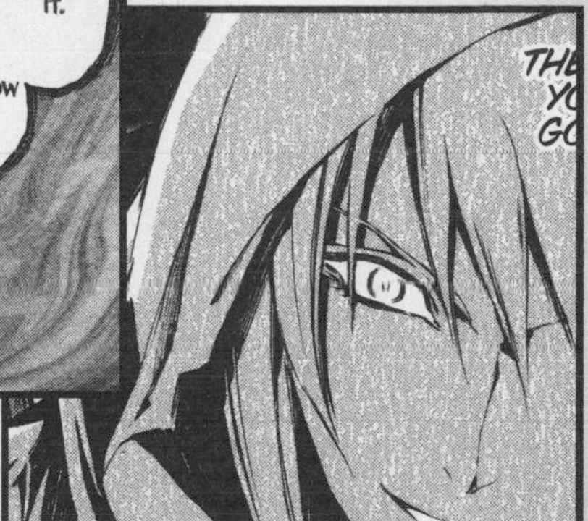

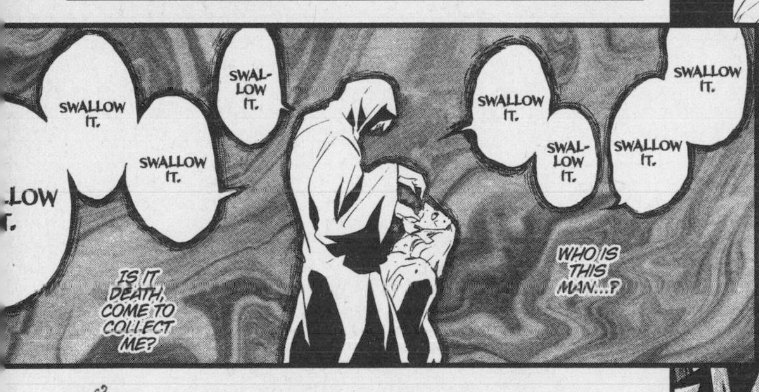
SWALLOW IT.
SWALLOW IT.
SWAL-LOW IT.
SWALLOW IT.
SWAL-LOW IT.
SWALLOW IT.
SWALLOW IT.
WHO IS THIS MAN...?
IS IT DEATH, COME TO COLLECT ME?

Returning from the excursion, Cecily learns that the bandits were after a set of auction goods, specifically the "Demon Sword" Aria. Meanwhile, the town joyously prepares for a Market, and a shadow sets his plan into motion...

The Sacred Blacksmith

聖剣の刀鍛冶

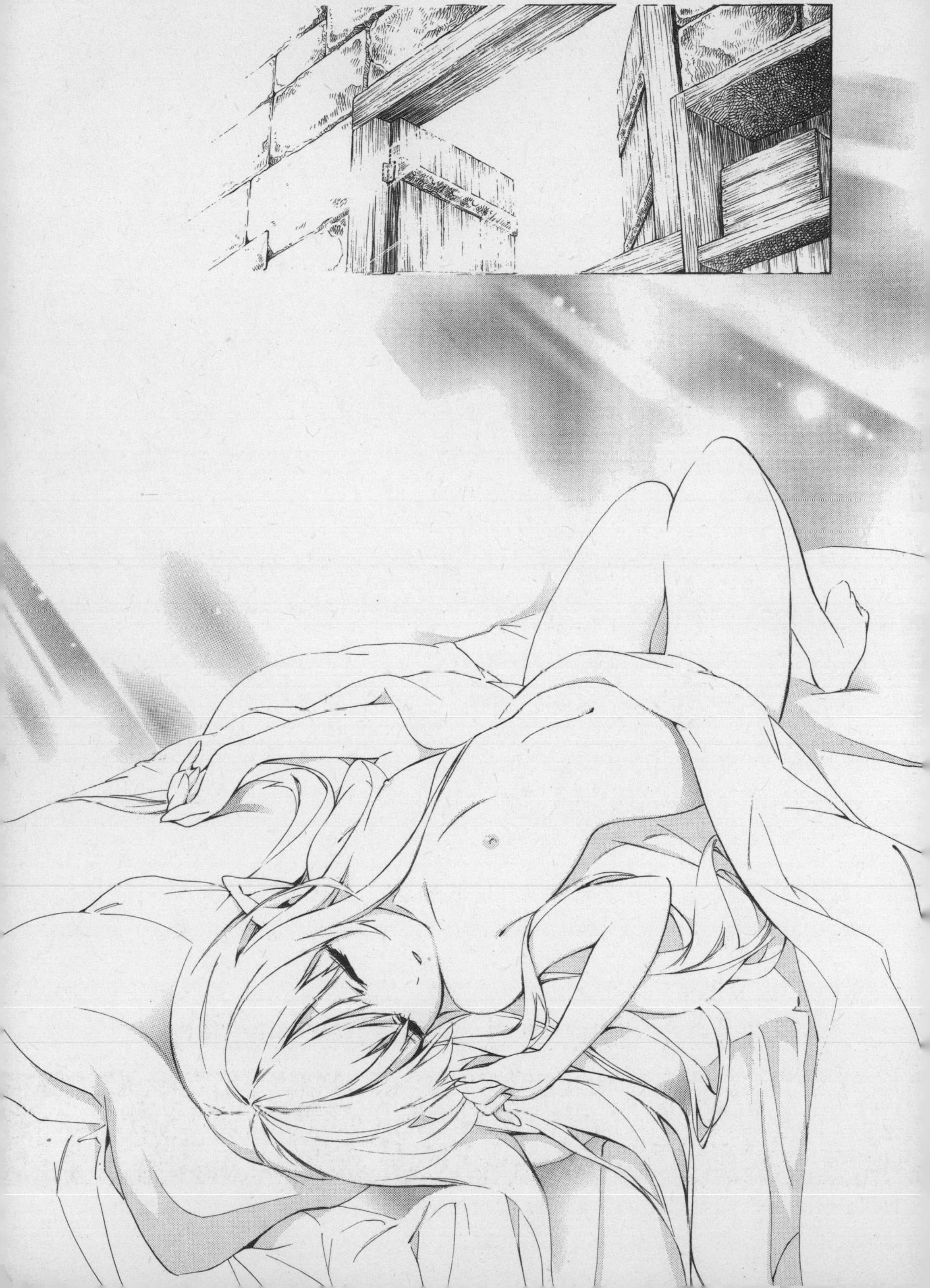

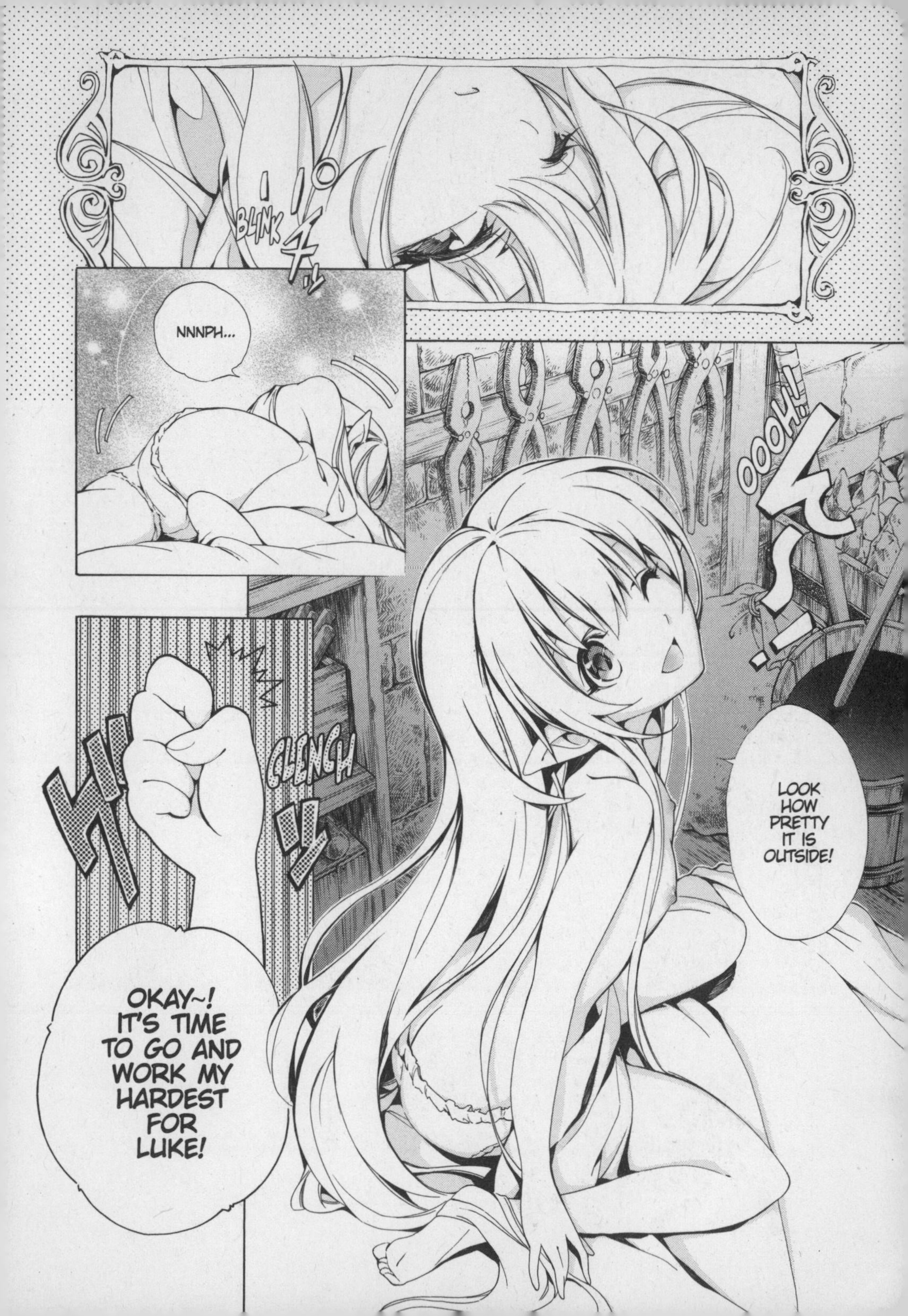
BLINK
OOOH!
LOOK HOW PRETTY IT IS OUTSIDE!
NNNPH...
CLENCH
OKAY~! IT'S TIME TO GO AND WORK MY HARDEST FOR LUKE!

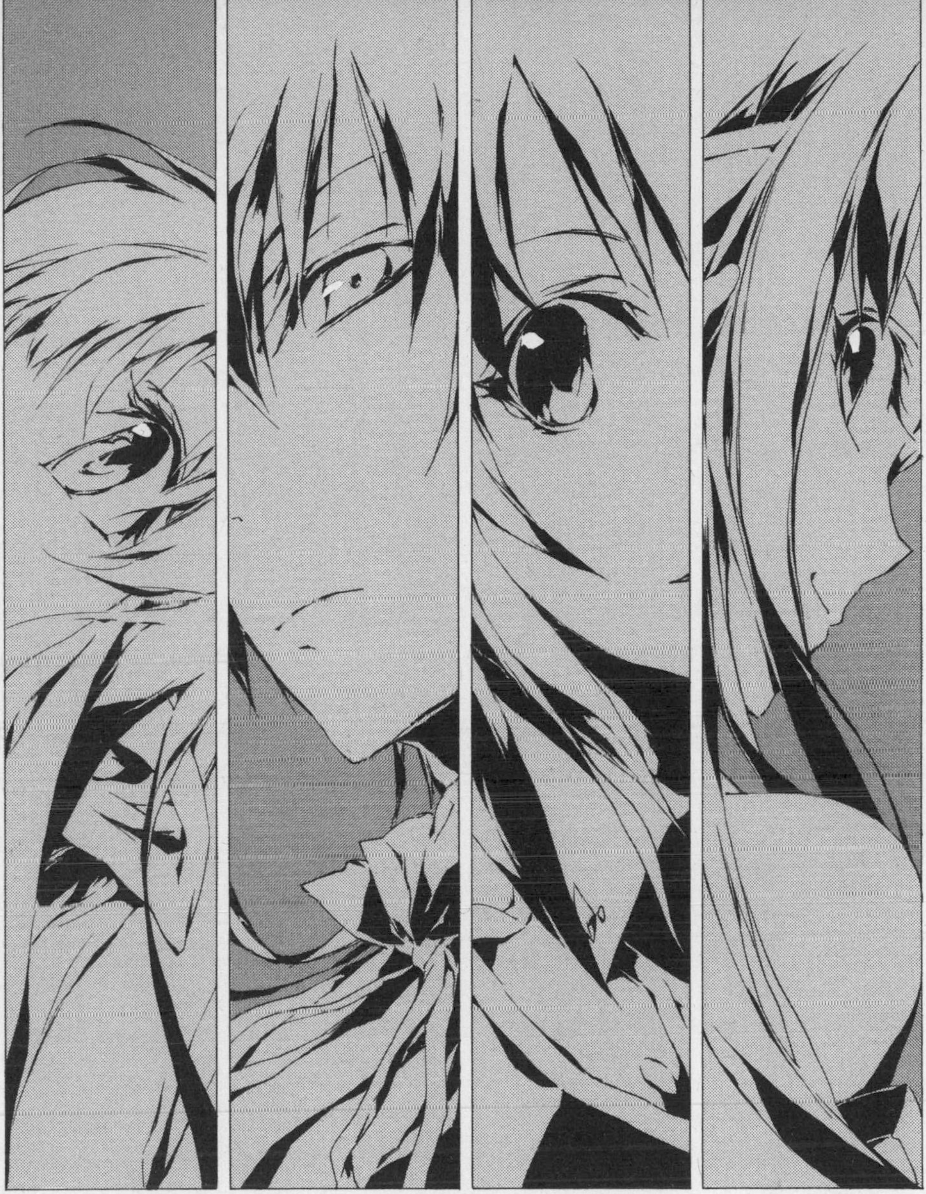

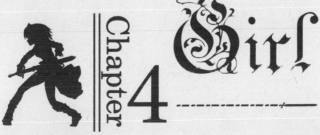

Chapter 4 Girl

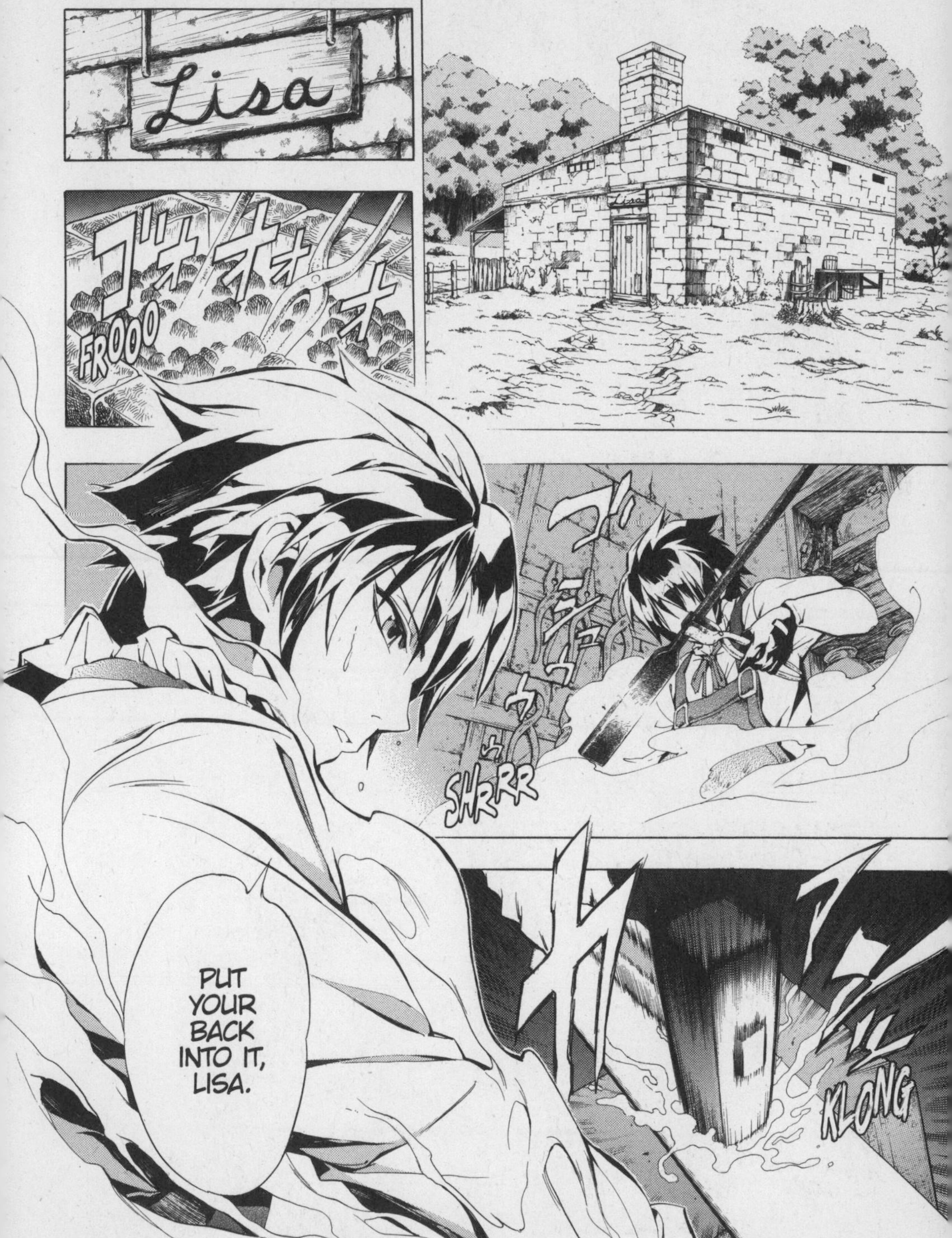
Lisa
Lisa
FROOO
SHRRR
PUT YOUR BACK INTO IT, LISA.
KLONG

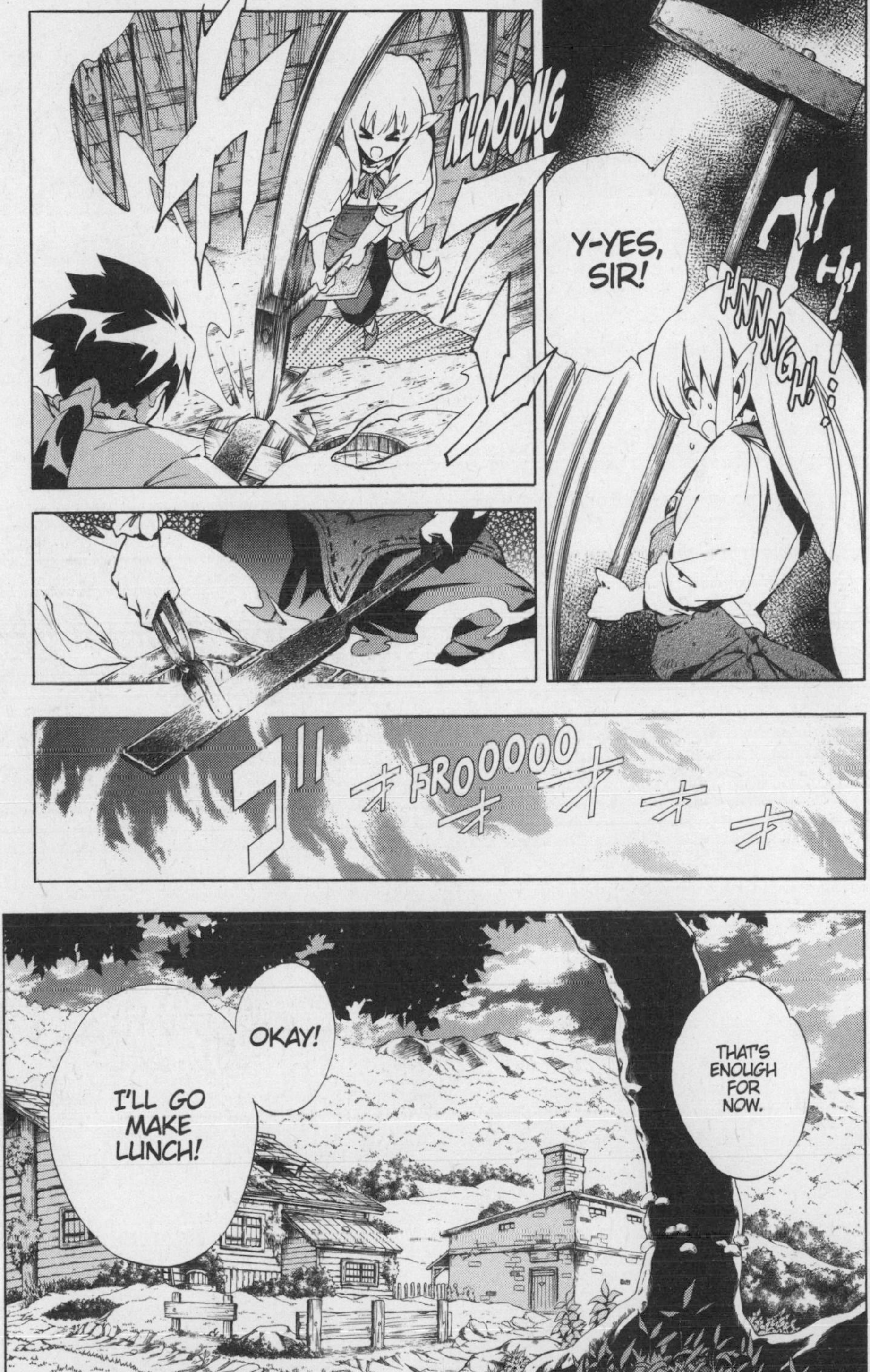
Y-YES, SIR!
HNNNGH!!
KLOOONG
FROOOOO
THAT'S ENOUGH FOR NOW.
OKAY!
I'LL GO MAKE LUNCH!

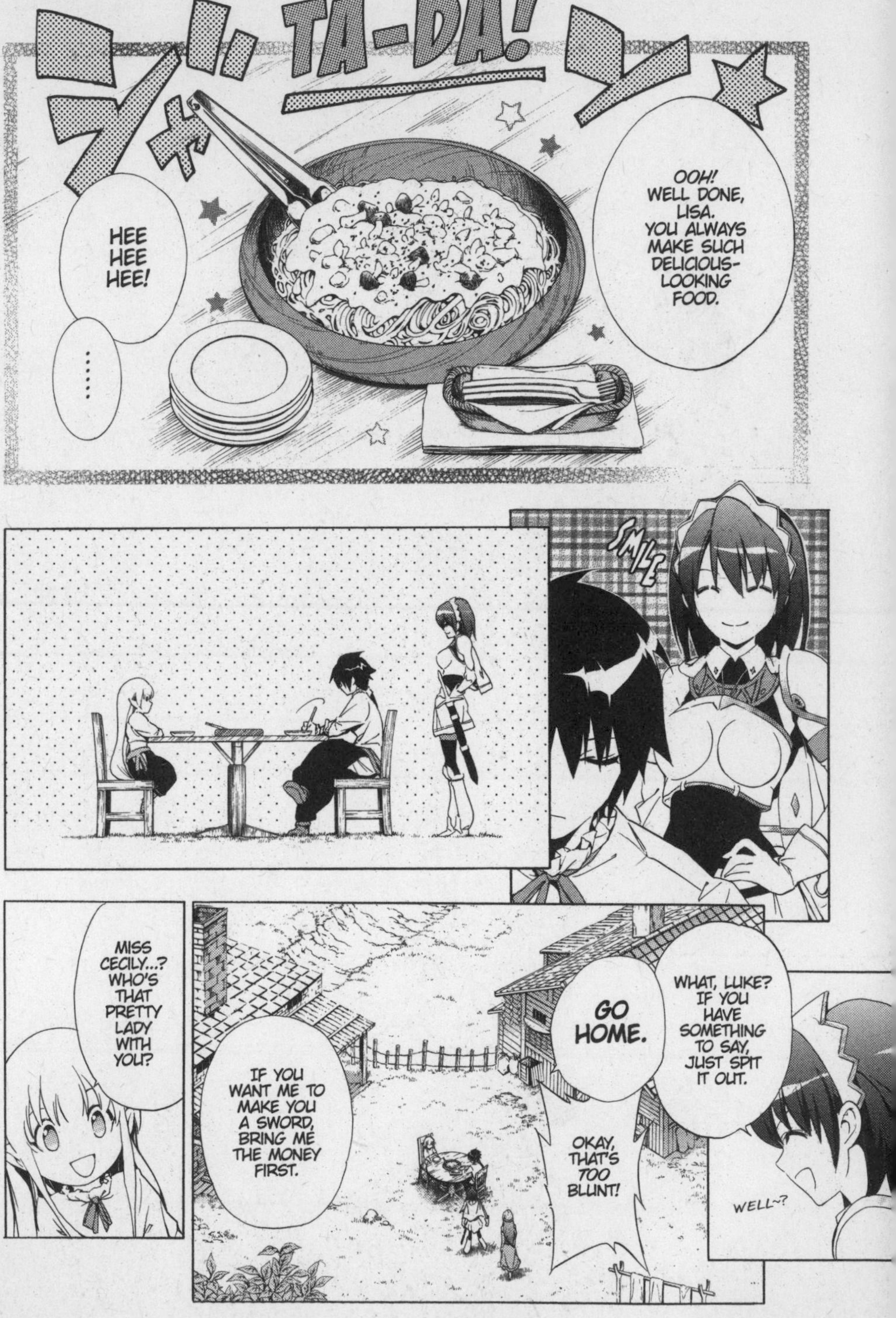
TA-DA!
OOH! WELL DONE, LISA. YOU ALWAYS MAKE SUCH DELICIOUS-LOOKING FOOD.
HEE HEE HEE!
......
SMILE
WHAT, LUKE? IF YOU HAVE SOMETHING TO SAY, JUST SPIT IT OUT.
WELL~?
GO HOME.
IF YOU WANT ME TO MAKE YOU A SWORD, BRING ME THE MONEY FIRST.
OKAY, THAT'S *TOO* BLUNT!
MISS CECILY...? WHO'S THAT PRETTY LADY WITH YOU?

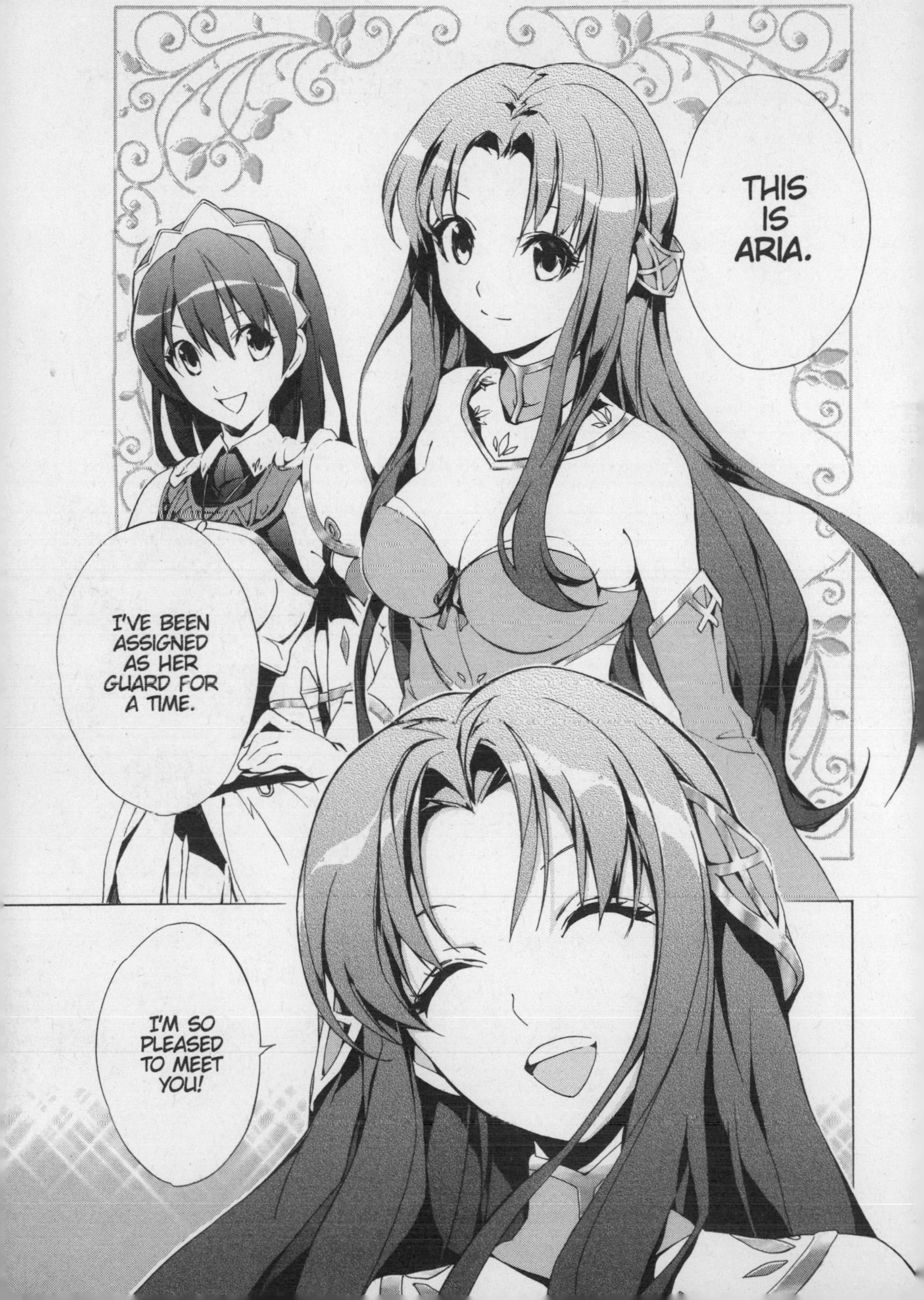
THIS IS ARIA.
I'VE BEEN ASSIGNED AS HER GUARD FOR A TIME.
I'M SO PLEASED TO MEET YOU!

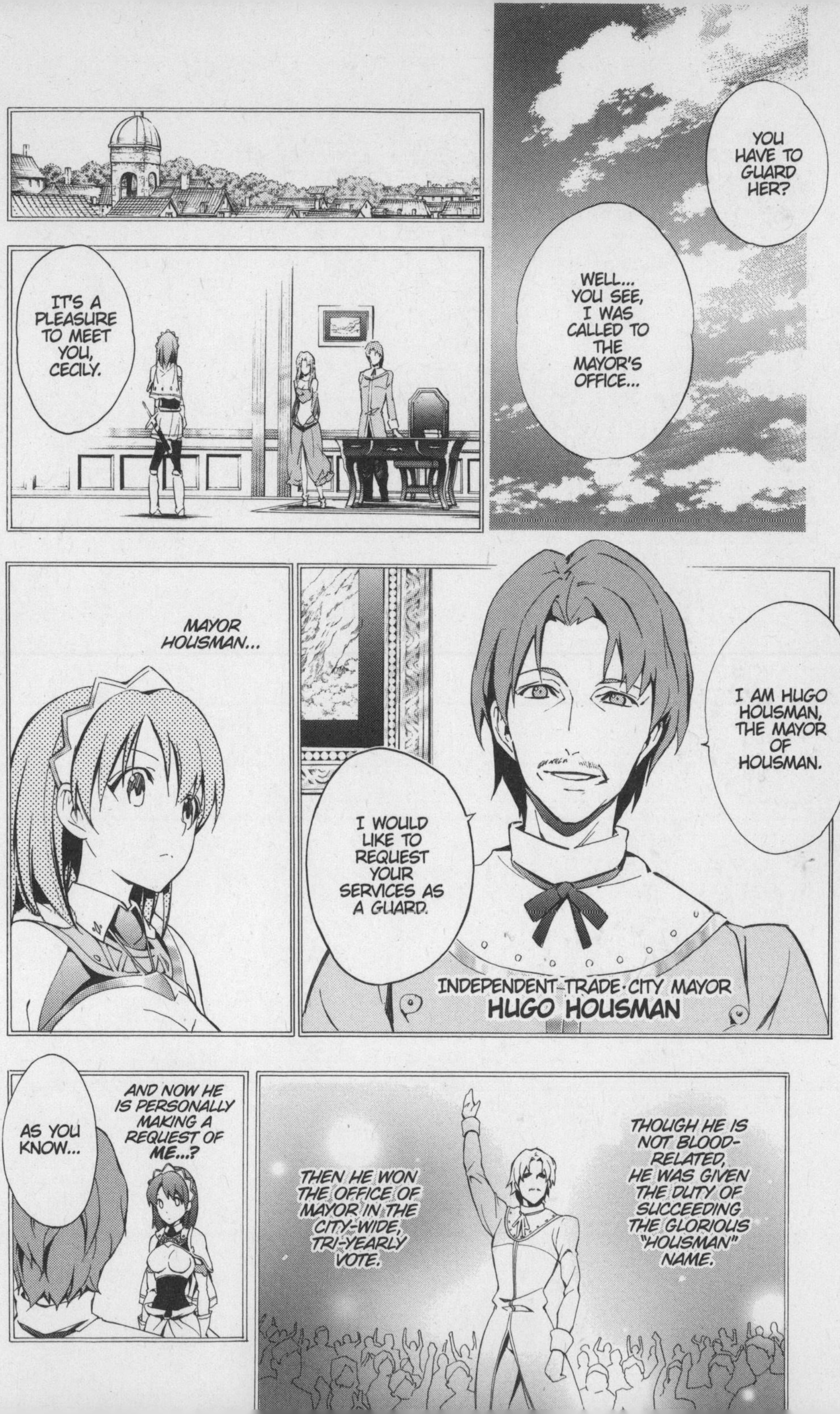
YOU HAVE TO GUARD HER?
WELL... YOU SEE, I WAS CALLED TO THE MAYOR'S OFFICE...
IT'S A PLEASURE TO MEET YOU, CECILY.
I AM HUGO HOUSMAN, THE MAYOR OF HOUSMAN.
I WOULD LIKE TO REQUEST YOUR SERVICES AS A GUARD.
INDEPENDENT TRADE CITY MAYOR
HUGO HOUSMAN
MAYOR HOUSMAN...
THOUGH HE IS NOT BLOOD-RELATED, HE WAS GIVEN THE DUTY OF SUCCEEDING THE GLORIOUS "HOUSMAN" NAME.
THEN HE WON THE OFFICE OF MAYOR IN THE CITY-WIDE, TRI-YEARLY VOTE.
AND NOW HE IS PERSONALLY MAKING A REQUEST OF ME...?
AS YOU KNOW...

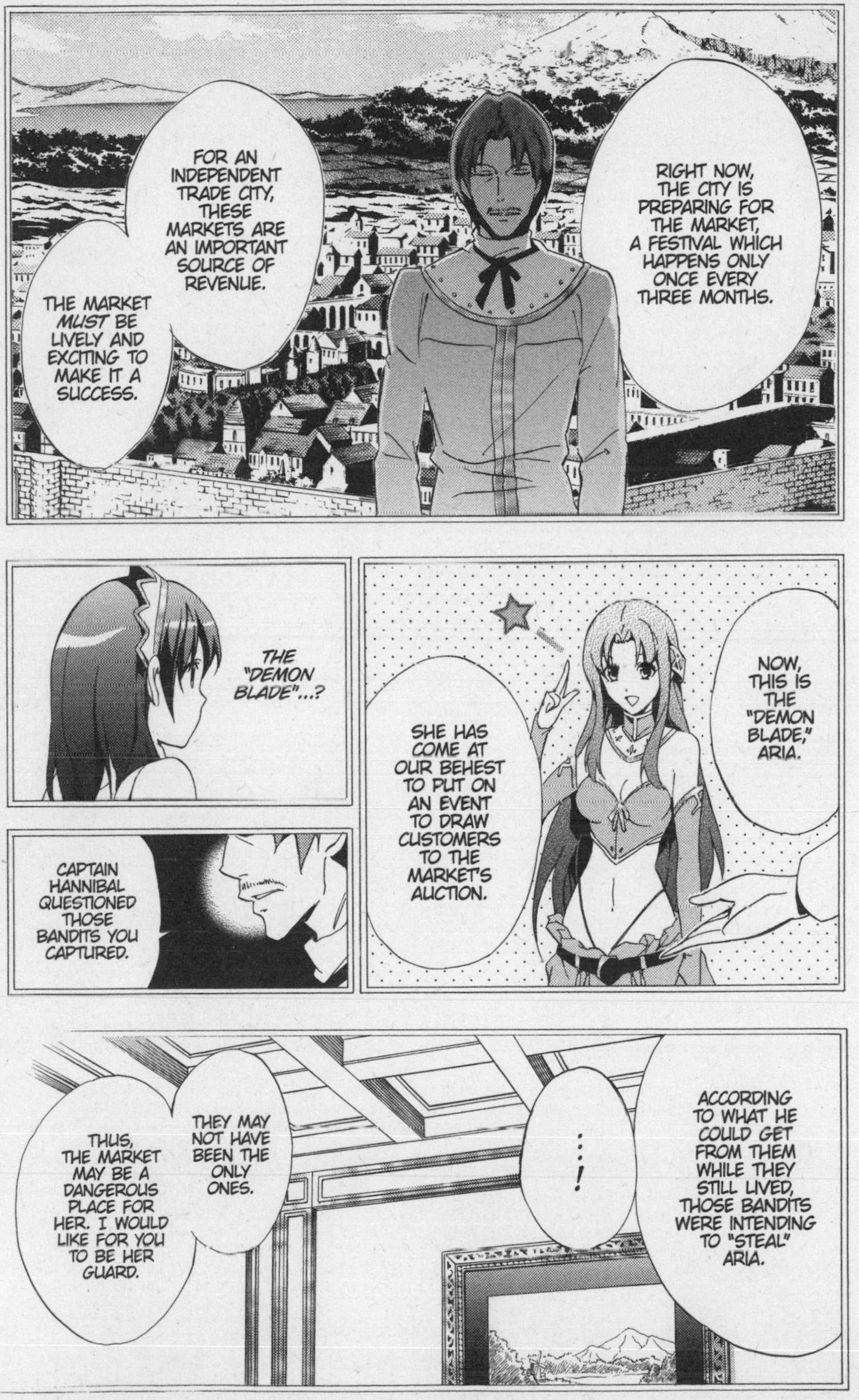
RIGHT NOW, THE CITY IS PREPARING FOR THE MARKET, A FESTIVAL WHICH HAPPENS ONLY ONCE EVERY THREE MONTHS.
FOR AN INDEPENDENT TRADE CITY, THESE MARKETS ARE AN IMPORTANT SOURCE OF REVENUE.
THE MARKET *MUST* BE LIVELY AND EXCITING TO MAKE IT A SUCCESS.
NOW, THIS IS THE "DEMON BLADE," ARIA.
SHE HAS COME AT OUR BEHEST TO PUT ON AN EVENT TO DRAW CUSTOMERS TO THE MARKET'S AUCTION.
THE "DEMON BLADE"...?
CAPTAIN HANNIBAL QUESTIONED THOSE BANDITS YOU CAPTURED.
ACCORDING TO WHAT HE COULD GET FROM THEM WHILE THEY STILL LIVED, THOSE BANDITS WERE INTENDING TO "STEAL" ARIA.
...!
THEY MAY NOT HAVE BEEN THE ONLY ONES.
THUS, THE MARKET MAY BE A DANGEROUS PLACE FOR HER. I WOULD LIKE FOR YOU TO BE HER GUARD.

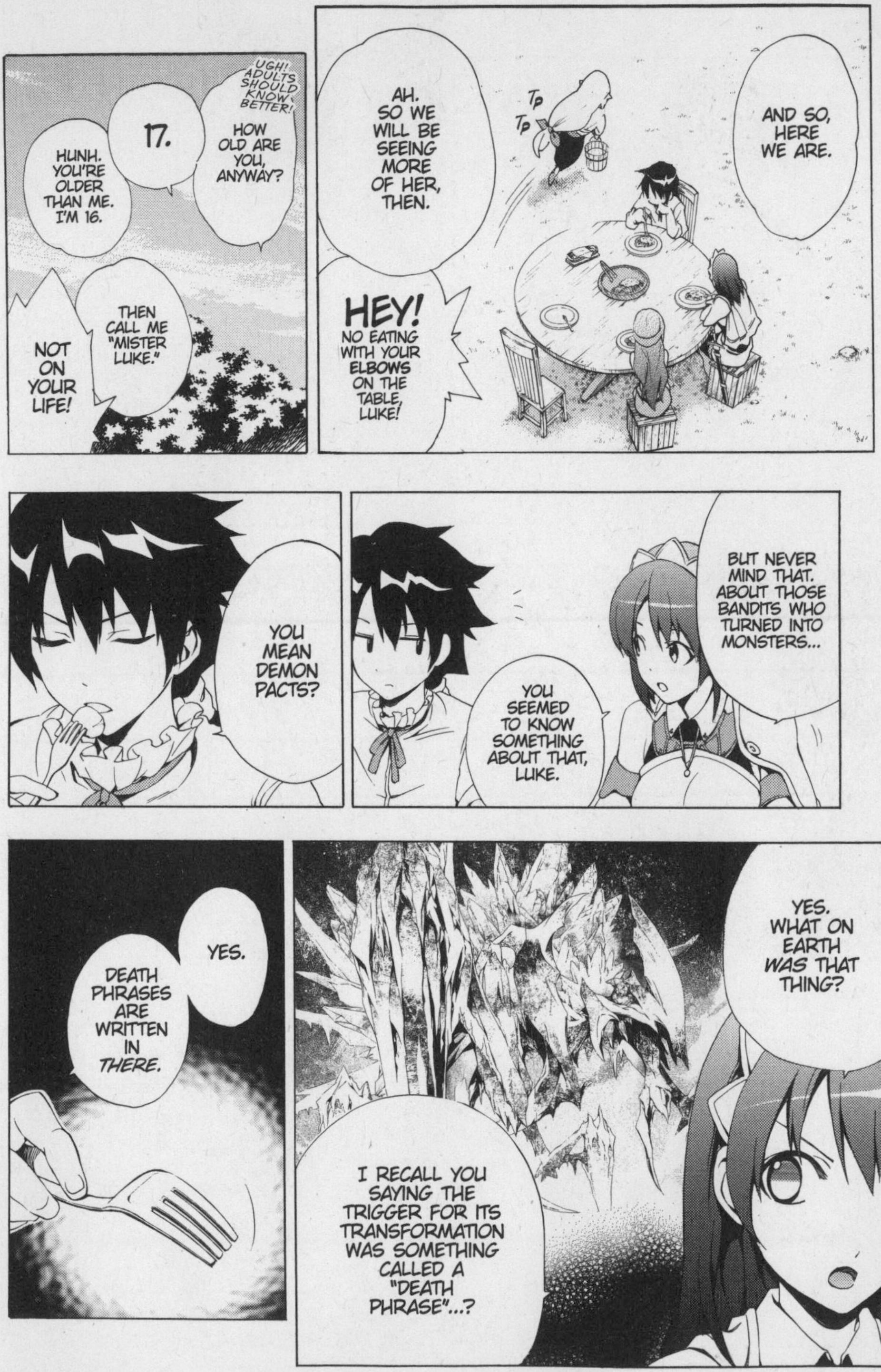
AND SO, HERE WE ARE.
AH. SO WE WILL BE SEEING MORE OF HER, THEN.
TP TP
HEY! NO EATING WITH YOUR ELBOWS ON THE TABLE, LUKE!
UGH! ADULTS SHOULD KNOW BETTER!
HOW OLD ARE YOU, ANYWAY?
17.
HUNH. YOU'RE OLDER THAN ME. I'M 16.
THEN CALL ME "MISTER LUKE."
NOT ON YOUR LIFE!
BUT NEVER MIND THAT. ABOUT THOSE BANDITS WHO TURNED INTO MONSTERS...
YOU SEEMED TO KNOW SOMETHING ABOUT THAT, LUKE.
YOU MEAN DEMON PACTS?
YES. WHAT ON EARTH *WAS* THAT THING?
I RECALL YOU SAYING THE TRIGGER FOR ITS TRANSFORMATION WAS SOMETHING CALLED A "DEATH PHRASE"...?
YES.
DEATH PHRASES ARE WRITTEN IN *THERE*.

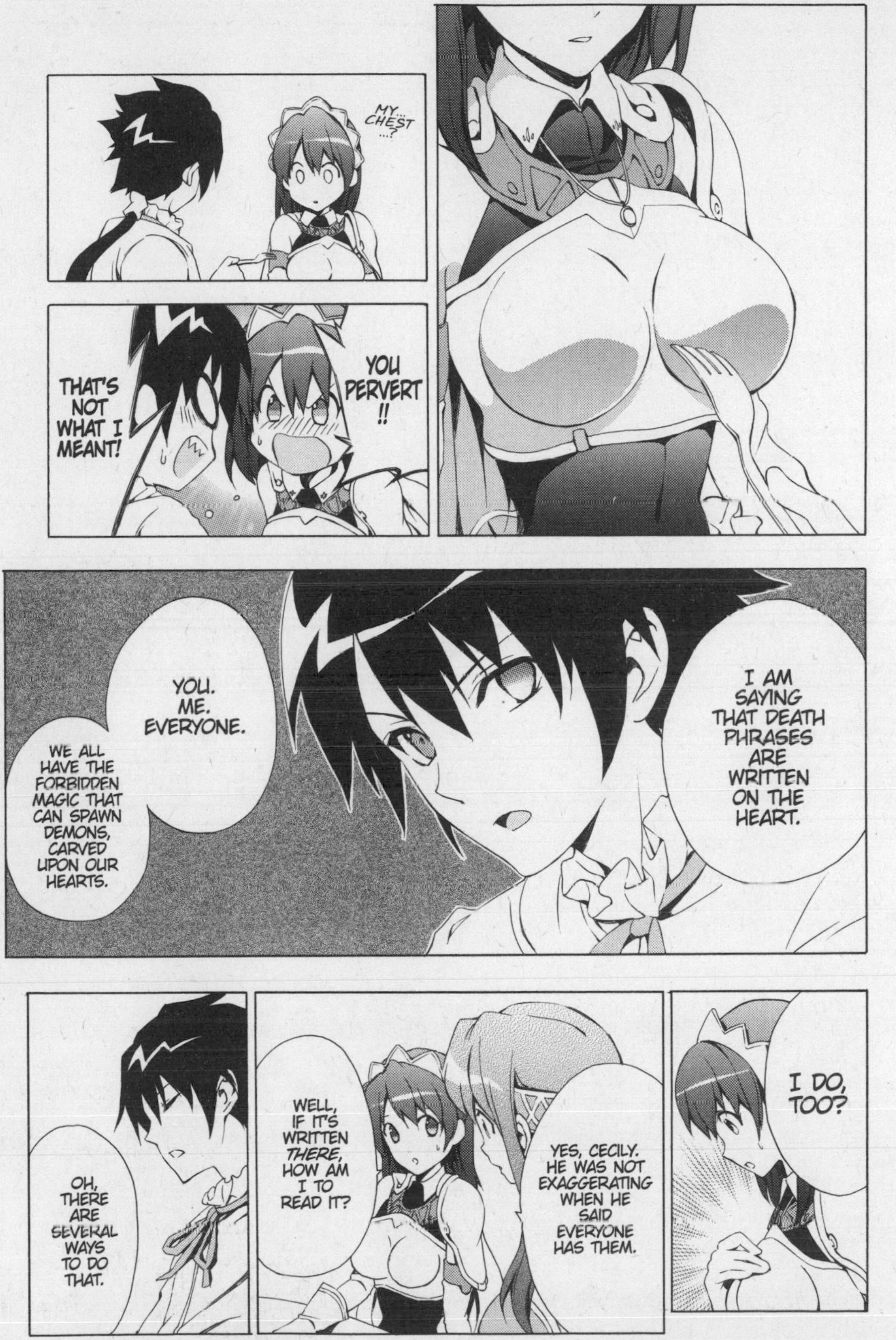
MY... CHEST ...?
YOU PERVERT!!
THAT'S NOT WHAT I MEANT!
I AM SAYING THAT DEATH PHRASES ARE WRITTEN ON THE HEART.
YOU. ME. EVERYONE.
WE ALL HAVE THE FORBIDDEN MAGIC THAT CAN SPAWN DEMONS, CARVED UPON OUR HEARTS.
I DO, TOO?
YES, CECILY. HE WAS NOT EXAGGERATING WHEN HE SAID EVERYONE HAS THEM.
WELL, IF IT'S WRITTEN *THERE*, HOW AM I TO READ IT?
OH, THERE ARE SEVERAL WAYS TO DO THAT.

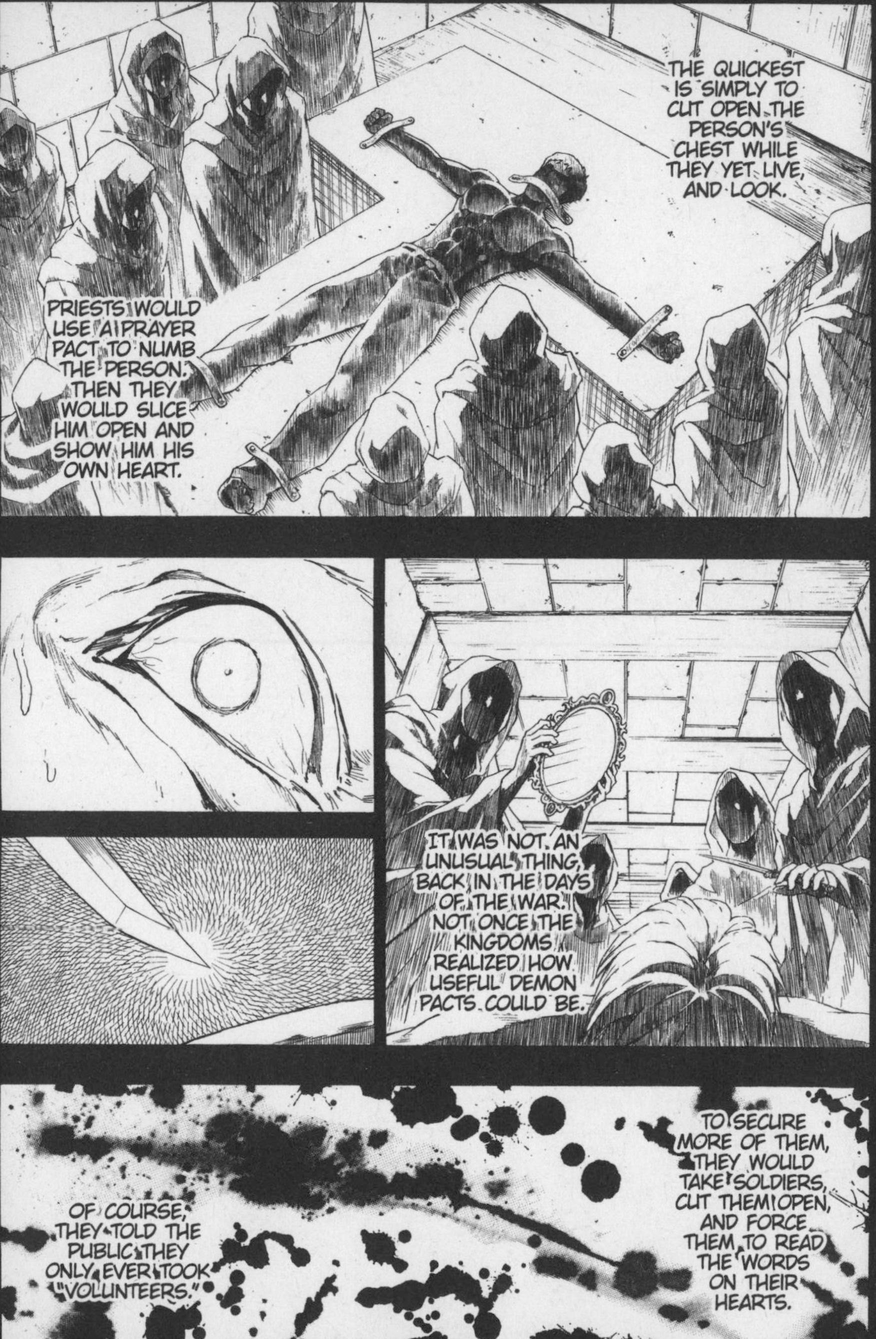
THE QUICKEST IS SIMPLY TO CUT OPEN THE PERSON'S CHEST WHILE THEY YET LIVE, AND LOOK.
PRIESTS WOULD USE A PRAYER PACT TO NUMB THE PERSON. THEN THEY WOULD SLICE HIM OPEN AND SHOW HIM HIS OWN HEART.
IT WAS NOT AN UNUSUAL THING, BACK IN THE DAYS OF THE WAR. NOT ONCE THE KINGDOMS REALIZED HOW USEFUL DEMON PACTS COULD BE.
TO SECURE MORE OF THEM, THEY WOULD TAKE SOLDIERS, CUT THEM OPEN, AND FORCE THEM TO READ THE WORDS ON THEIR HEARTS.
OF COURSE, THEY TOLD THE PUBLIC THEY ONLY EVER TOOK "VOLUNTEERS."

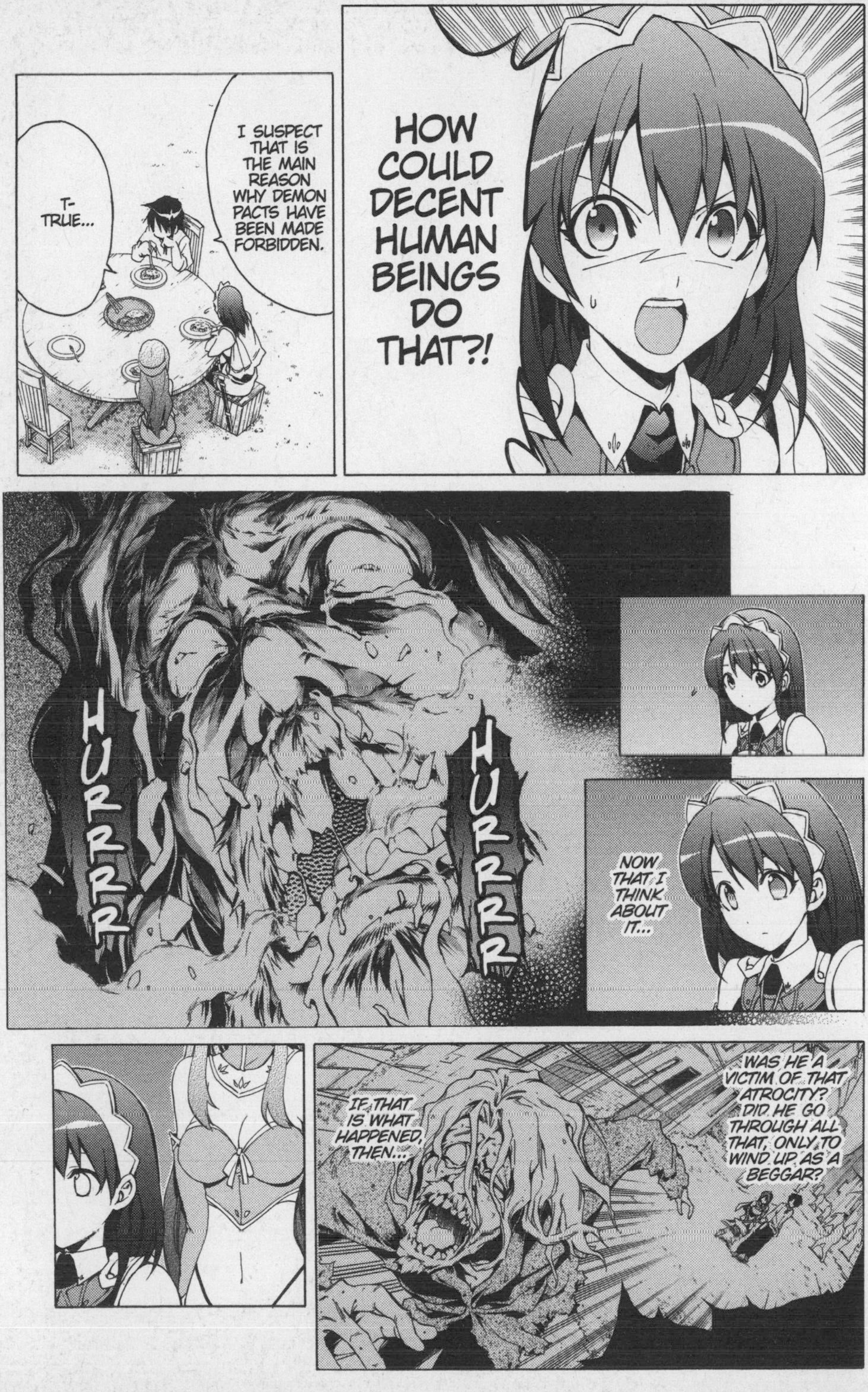
HOW COULD DECENT HUMAN BEINGS DO THAT?!
I SUSPECT THAT IS THE MAIN REASON WHY DEMON PACTS HAVE BEEN MADE FORBIDDEN.
T-TRUE...
NOW THAT I THINK ABOUT IT...
HURRRR
HURRRR
WAS HE A VICTIM OF THAT ATROCITY? DID HE GO THROUGH ALL THAT, ONLY TO WIND UP AS A BEGGAR?
IF THAT IS WHAT HAPPENED, THEN...

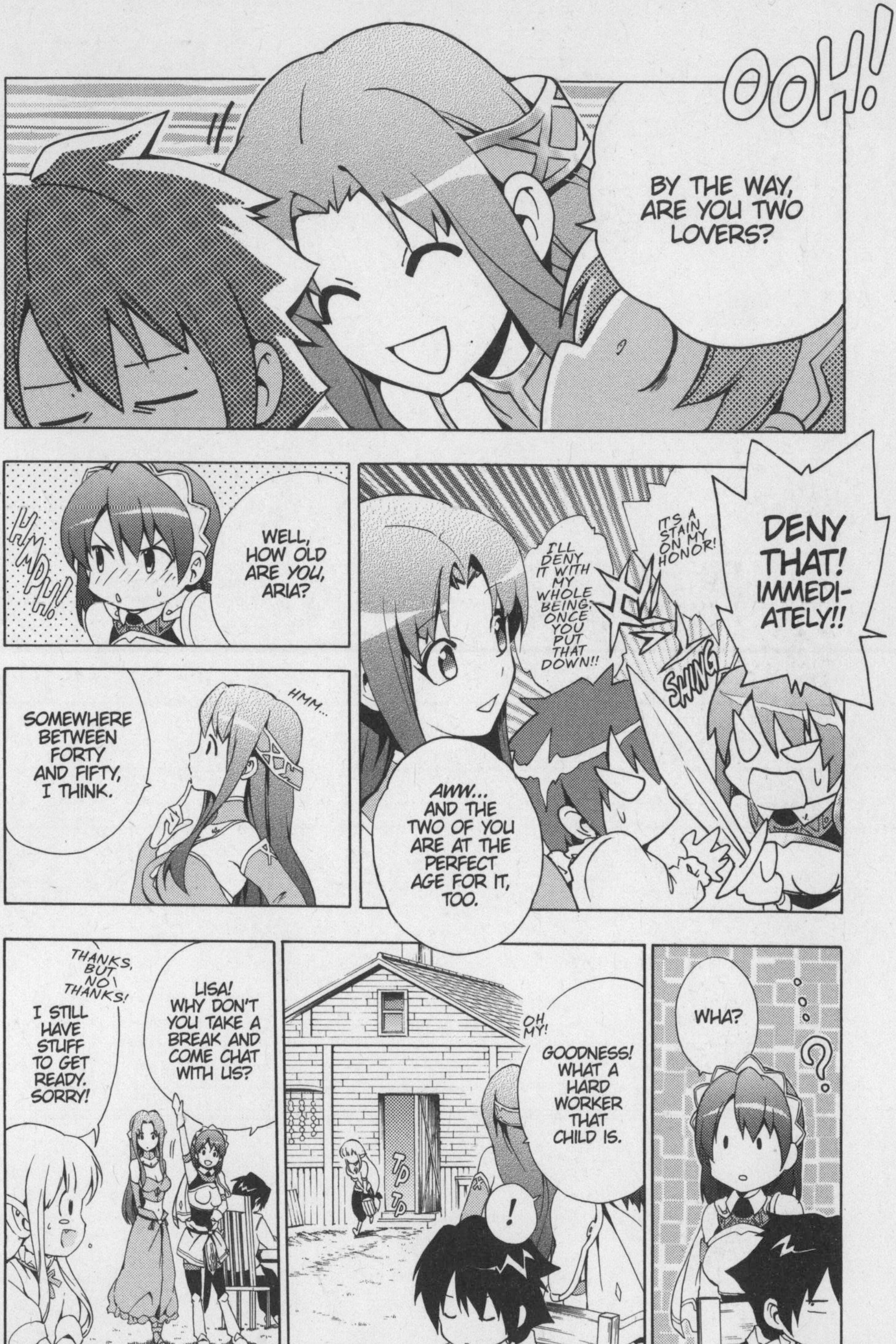
OOH!
BY THE WAY, ARE YOU TWO LOVERS?
DENY THAT! IMMEDIATELY!!
IT'S A STAIN ON MY HONOR!
SHING
I'LL DENY IT WITH MY WHOLE BEING, ONCE YOU PUT THAT DOWN!!
AWW... AND THE TWO OF YOU ARE AT THE PERFECT AGE FOR IT, TOO.
WELL, HOW OLD ARE YOU, ARIA?
HMPH!
HMM...
SOMEWHERE BETWEEN FORTY AND FIFTY, I THINK.
WHA?
?
!
OH MY!
GOODNESS! WHAT A HARD WORKER THAT CHILD IS.
TP TP
LISA! WHY DON'T YOU TAKE A BREAK AND COME CHAT WITH US?
THANKS, BUT NO THANKS!
I STILL HAVE STUFF TO GET READY. SORRY!

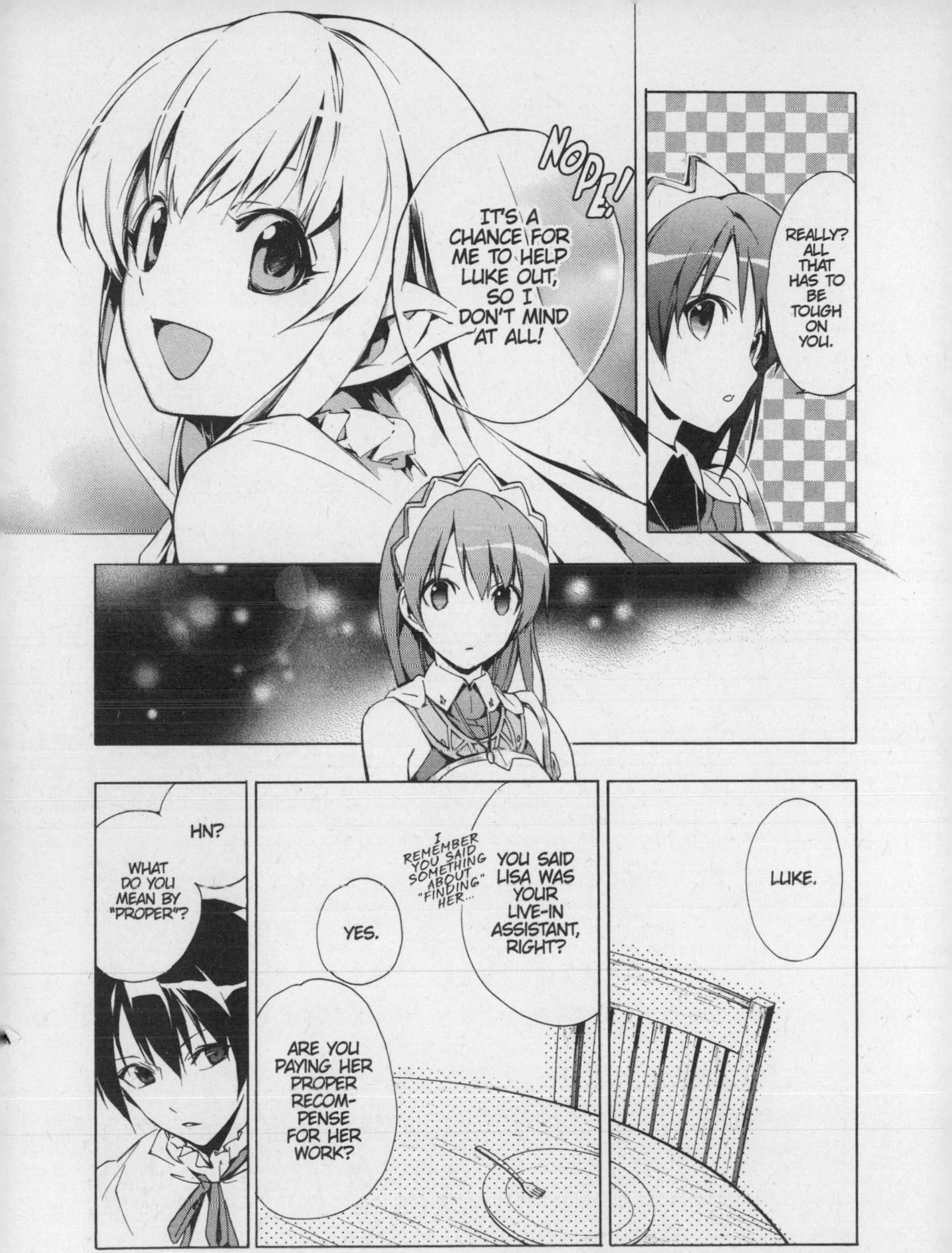
REALLY? ALL THAT HAS TO BE TOUGH ON YOU.
NOPE!
IT'S A CHANCE FOR ME TO HELP LUKE OUT, SO I DON'T MIND AT ALL!
LUKE.
YOU SAID LISA WAS YOUR LIVE-IN ASSISTANT, RIGHT?
I REMEMBER YOU SAID SOMETHING ABOUT "FINDING" HER...
YES.
ARE YOU PAYING HER PROPER RECOMPENSE FOR HER WORK?
HN?
WHAT DO YOU MEAN BY "PROPER"?

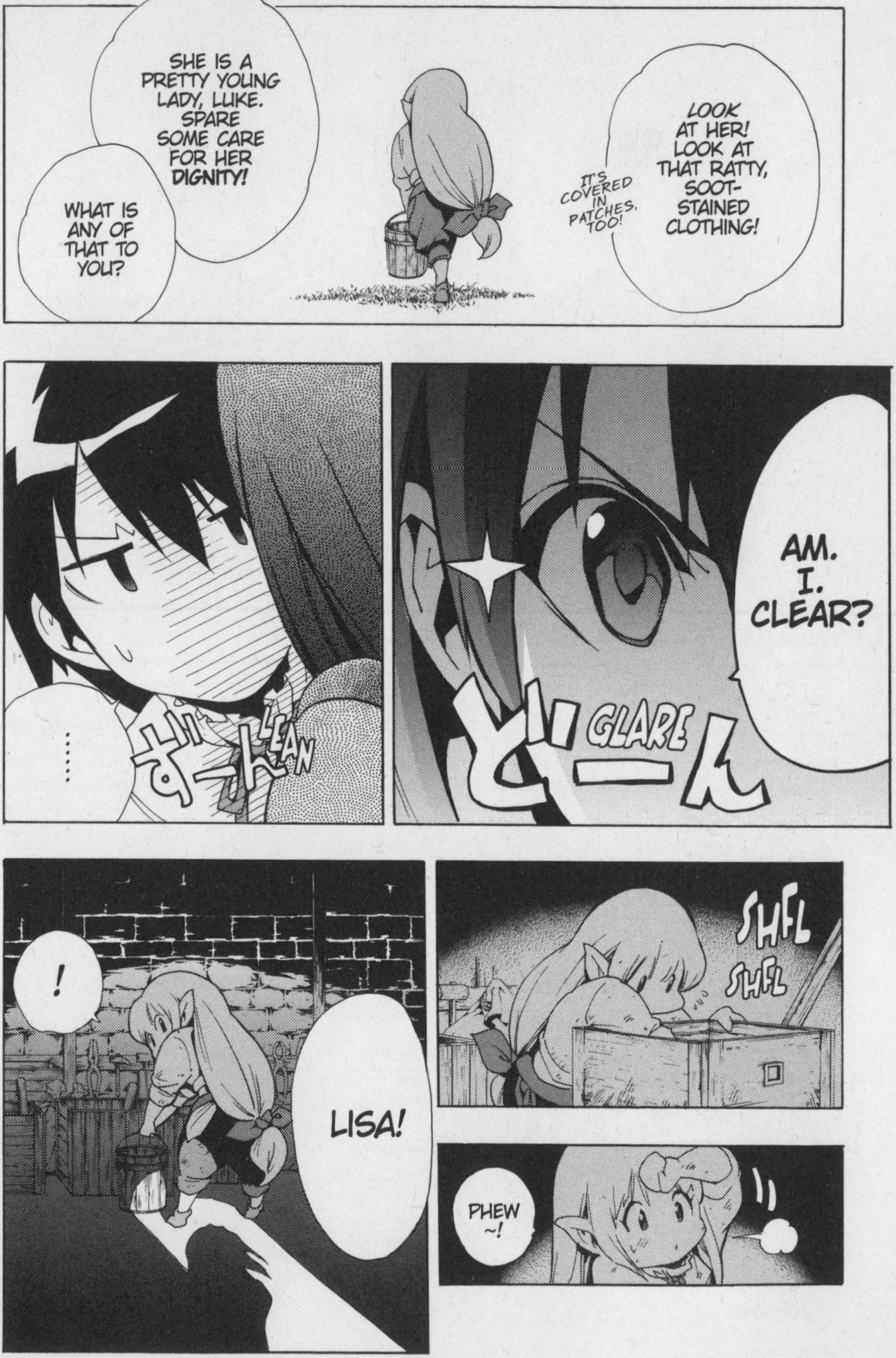
LOOK AT HER! LOOK AT THAT RATTY, SOOT-STAINED CLOTHING!
IT'S COVERED IN PATCHES, TOO!
SHE IS A PRETTY YOUNG LADY, LUKE. SPARE SOME CARE FOR HER DIGNITY!
WHAT IS ANY OF THAT TO YOU?
AM. I. CLEAR?
GLARE
……
LEAN
SHFL
SHFL
PHEW ~!
!
LISA!

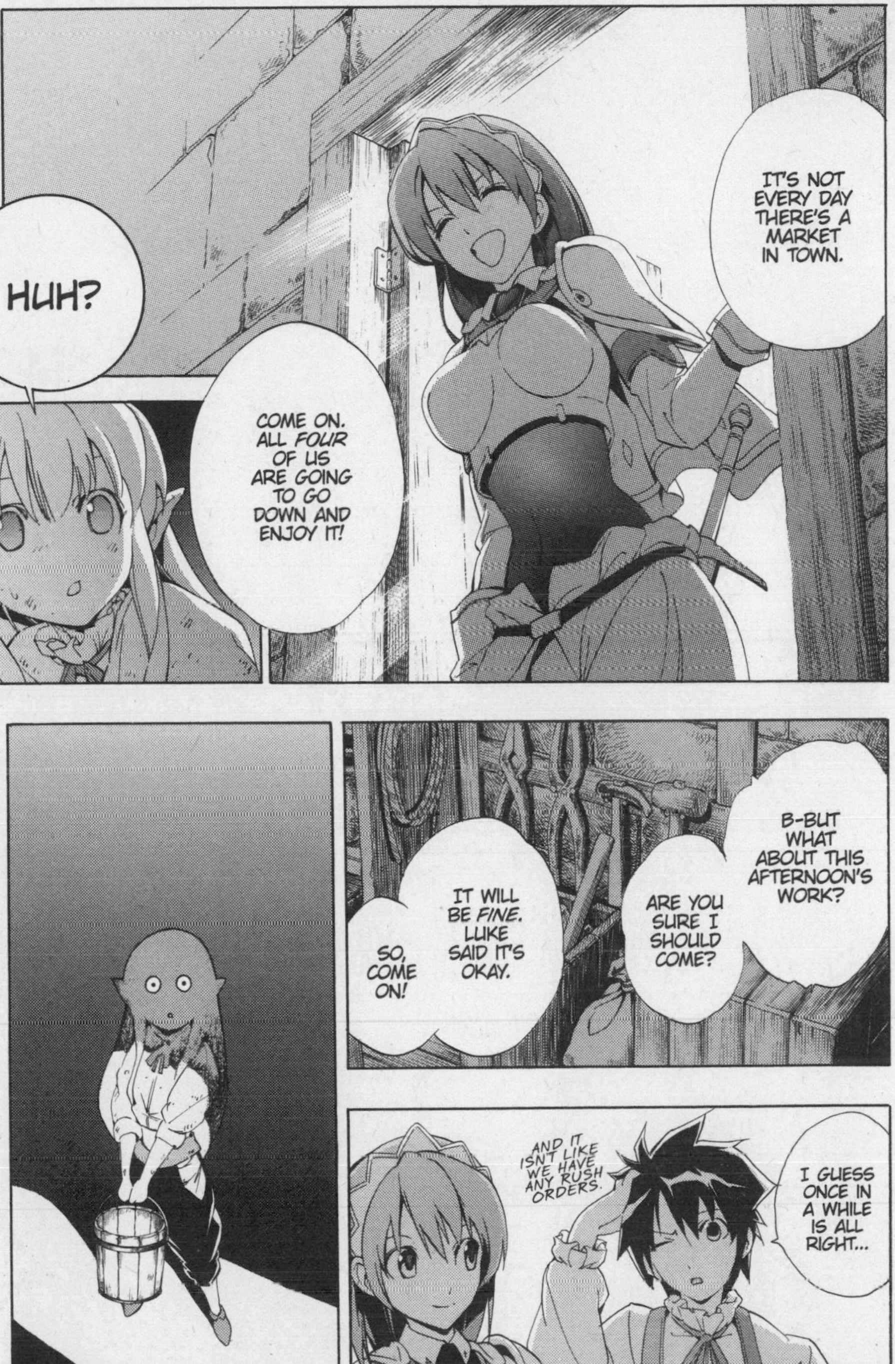
IT'S NOT EVERY DAY THERE'S A MARKET IN TOWN.
COME ON. ALL *FOUR* OF US ARE GOING TO GO DOWN AND ENJOY IT!
HUH?
B-BUT WHAT ABOUT THIS AFTERNOON'S WORK?
ARE YOU SURE I SHOULD COME?
IT WILL BE *FINE*. LUKE SAID IT'S OKAY.
SO, COME ON!
I GUESS ONCE IN A WHILE IS ALL RIGHT...
AND IT ISN'T LIKE WE HAVE ANY RUSH ORDERS.

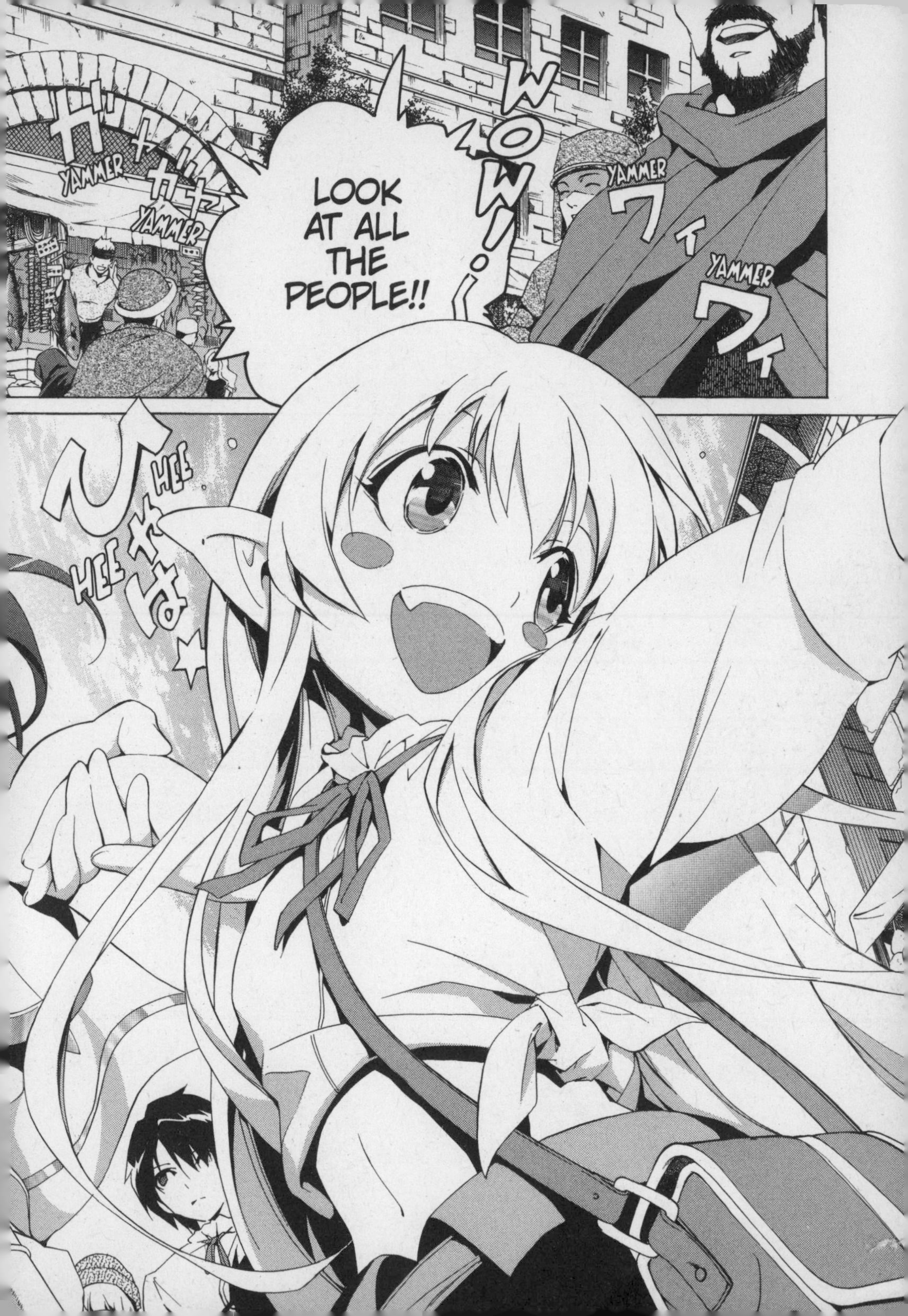
ワイ
YAMMER
ワイ
YAMMER
WOW!!
LOOK AT ALL THE PEOPLE!!
ガヤ
YAMMER
ガヤ
YAMMER
ひゃは
HEE HEE

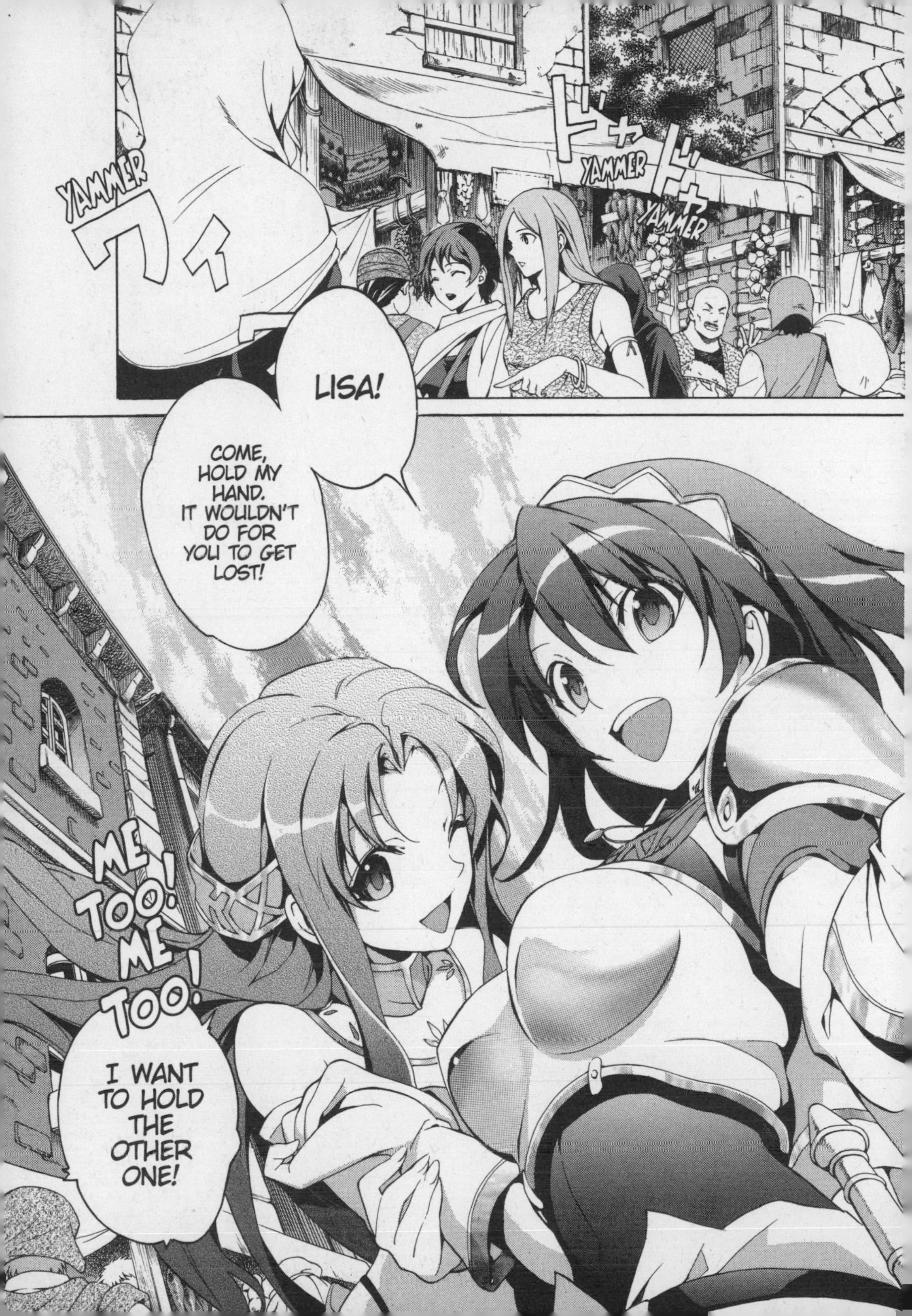
YAMMER
YAMMER
YAMMER
LISA!
COME, HOLD MY HAND. IT WOULDN'T DO FOR YOU TO GET LOST!
ME TOO! ME TOO!
I WANT TO HOLD THE OTHER ONE!

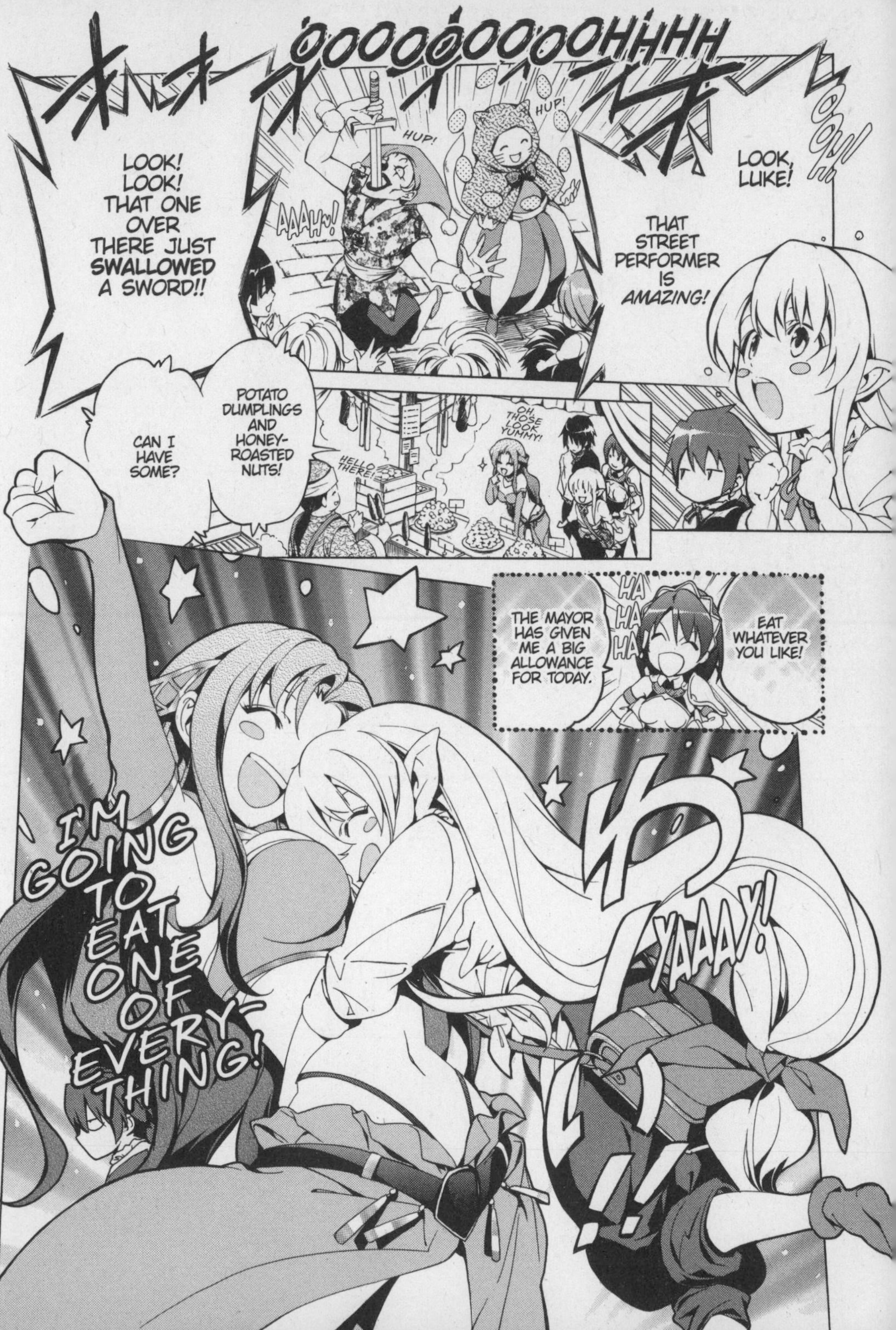
OOOOOOOOOOOHHHH
LOOK, LUKE!
THAT STREET PERFORMER IS AMAZING!
HUP!
HUP!
AAAAH~!
LOOK! LOOK! THAT ONE OVER THERE JUST SWALLOWED A SWORD!!
OH, THOSE LOOK YUMMY!
HELLO THERE!
POTATO DUMPLINGS AND HONEY-ROASTED NUTS!
CAN I HAVE SOME?
EAT WHATEVER YOU LIKE!
HA HA HA HA
THE MAYOR HAS GIVEN ME A BIG ALLOWANCE FOR TODAY.
YAAAY!
I'M GOING TO EAT ONE OF EVERYTHING!

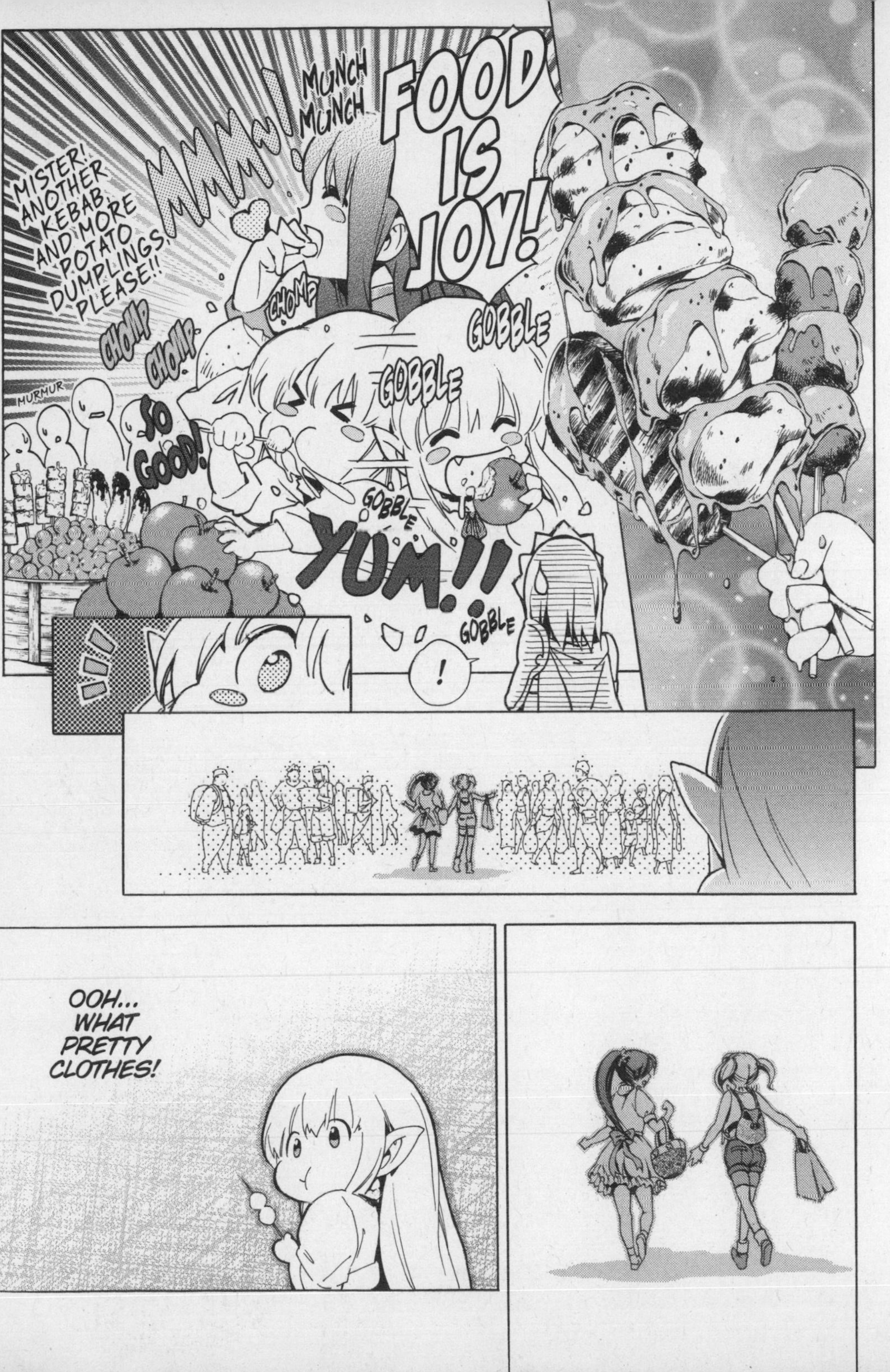
FOOD IS JOY!
MUNCH MUNCH
MMM~!
MISTER! ANOTHER KEBAB AND MORE POTATO DUMPLINGS, PLEASE!!
CHOMP
GOBBLE
GOBBLE
CHOMP CHOMP
SO GOOD!
MURMUR
GOBBLE
YUM!!
GOBBLE
!
!!!
OOH... WHAT PRETTY CLOTHES!

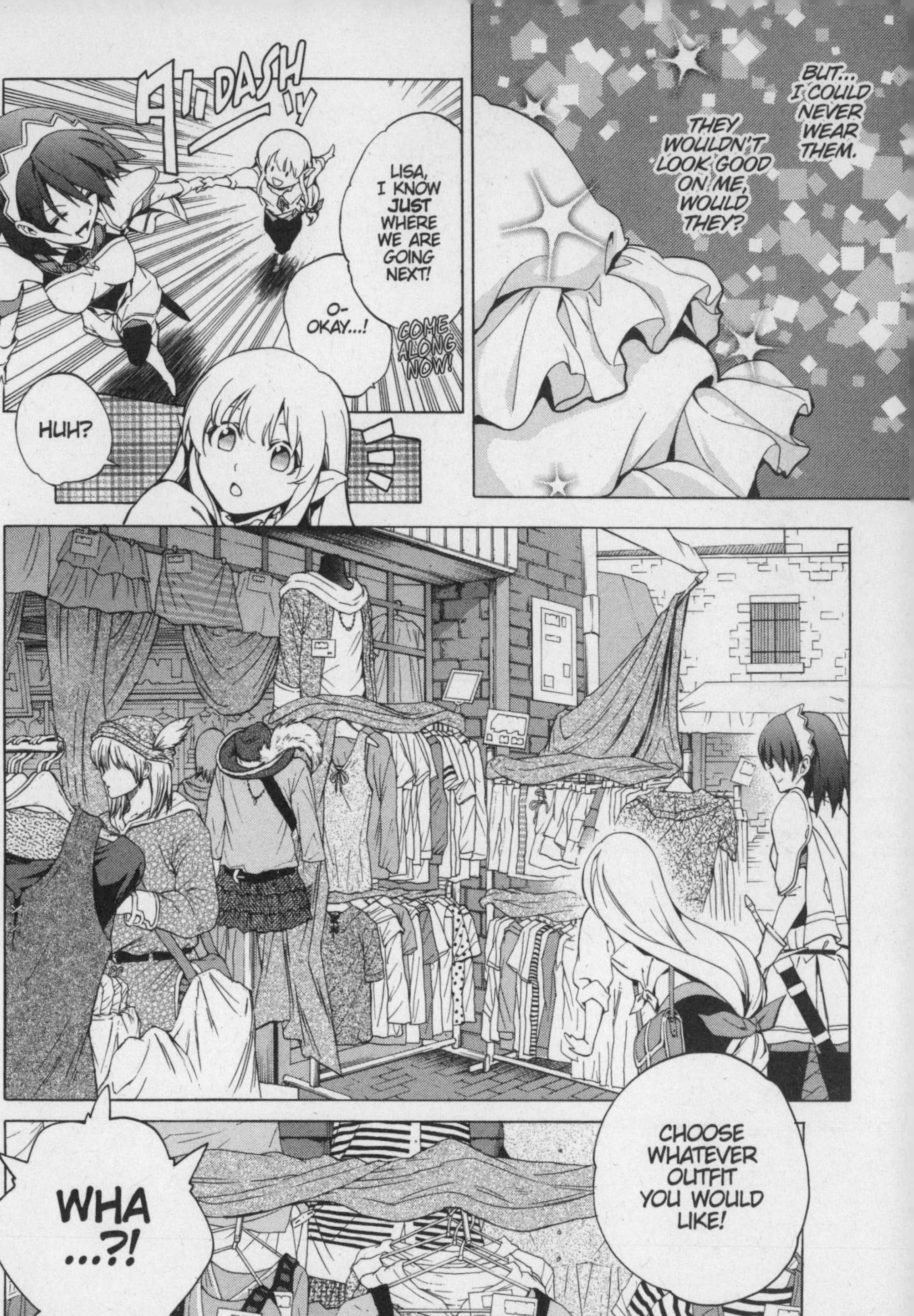
BUT... I COULD NEVER WEAR THEM.
THEY WOULDN'T LOOK GOOD ON ME, WOULD THEY?
DASH
LISA, I KNOW JUST WHERE WE ARE GOING NEXT!
COME ALONG NOW!
O-OKAY...!
HUH?
CHOOSE WHATEVER OUTFIT YOU WOULD LIKE!
WHA ...?!

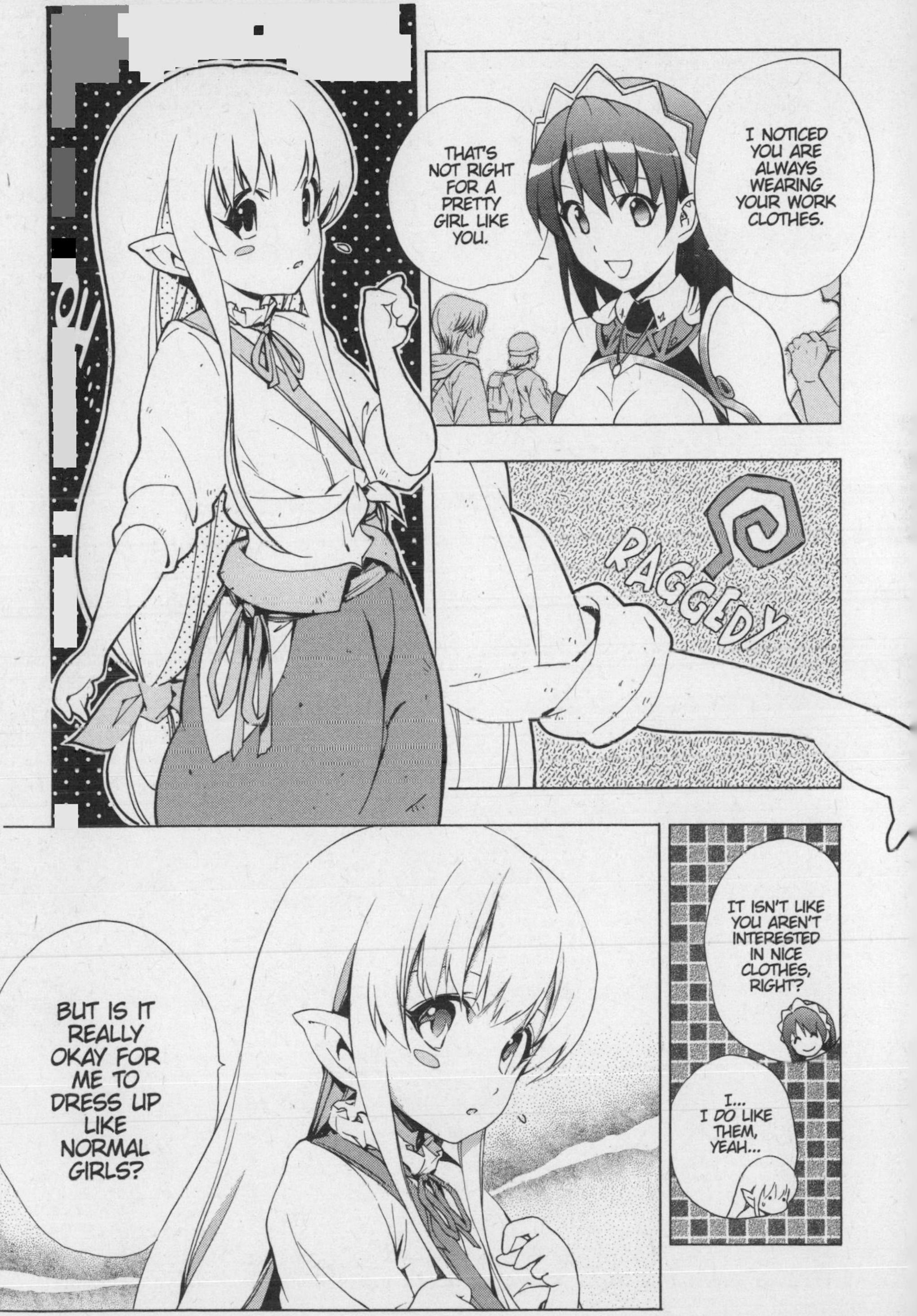
I NOTICED YOU ARE ALWAYS WEARING YOUR WORK CLOTHES.
THAT'S NOT RIGHT FOR A PRETTY GIRL LIKE YOU.
RAGGEDY
IT ISN'T LIKE YOU AREN'T INTERESTED IN NICE CLOTHES, RIGHT?
I... I DO LIKE THEM, YEAH...
BUT IS IT REALLY OKAY FOR ME TO DRESS UP LIKE NORMAL GIRLS?

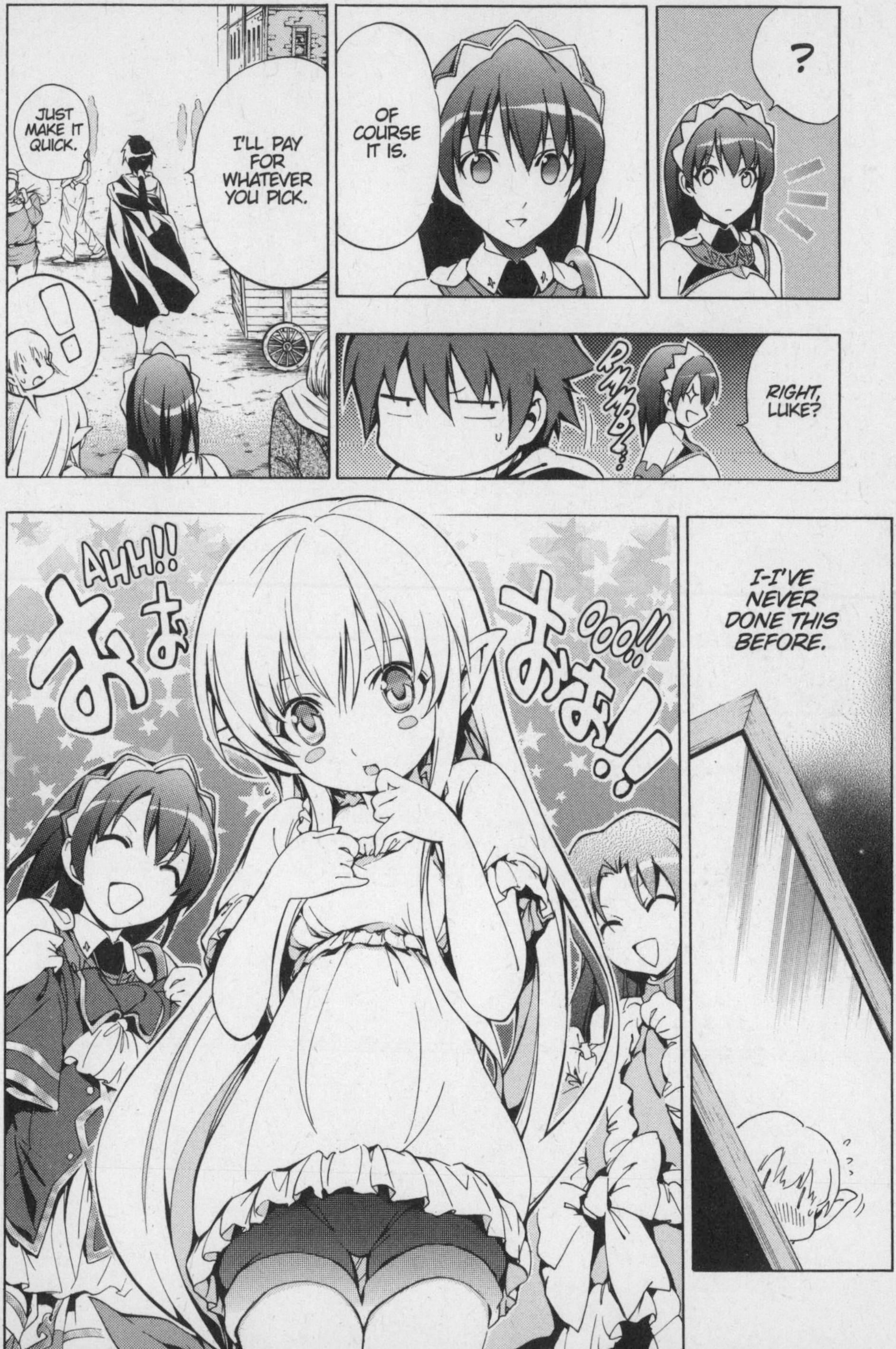
?
OF COURSE IT IS.
RMMBL...
RIGHT, LUKE?
I'LL PAY FOR WHATEVER YOU PICK.
JUST MAKE IT QUICK.
!
I-I'VE NEVER DONE THIS BEFORE.
AHH!!
おぉ
OOO!!
おぉ!!

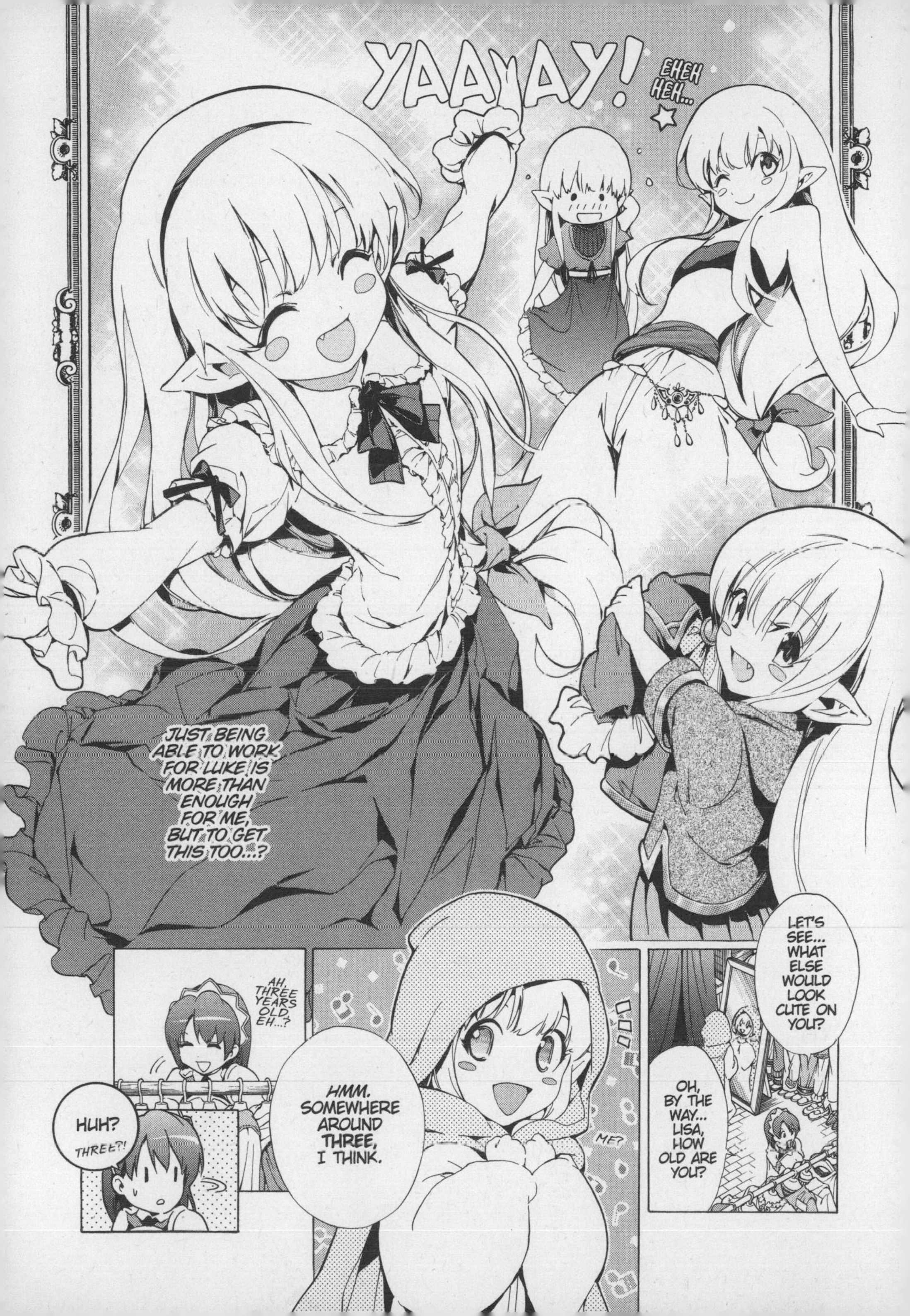
YAAAAY!
EHEH HEH...
JUST BEING ABLE TO WORK FOR LUKE IS MORE THAN ENOUGH FOR ME, BUT TO GET THIS TOO...?
LET'S SEE... WHAT ELSE WOULD LOOK CUTE ON YOU?
OH, BY THE WAY... LISA, HOW OLD ARE YOU?
ME?
HMM. SOMEWHERE AROUND THREE, I THINK.
AH, THREE YEARS OLD, EH...?
HUH?
THREE?!

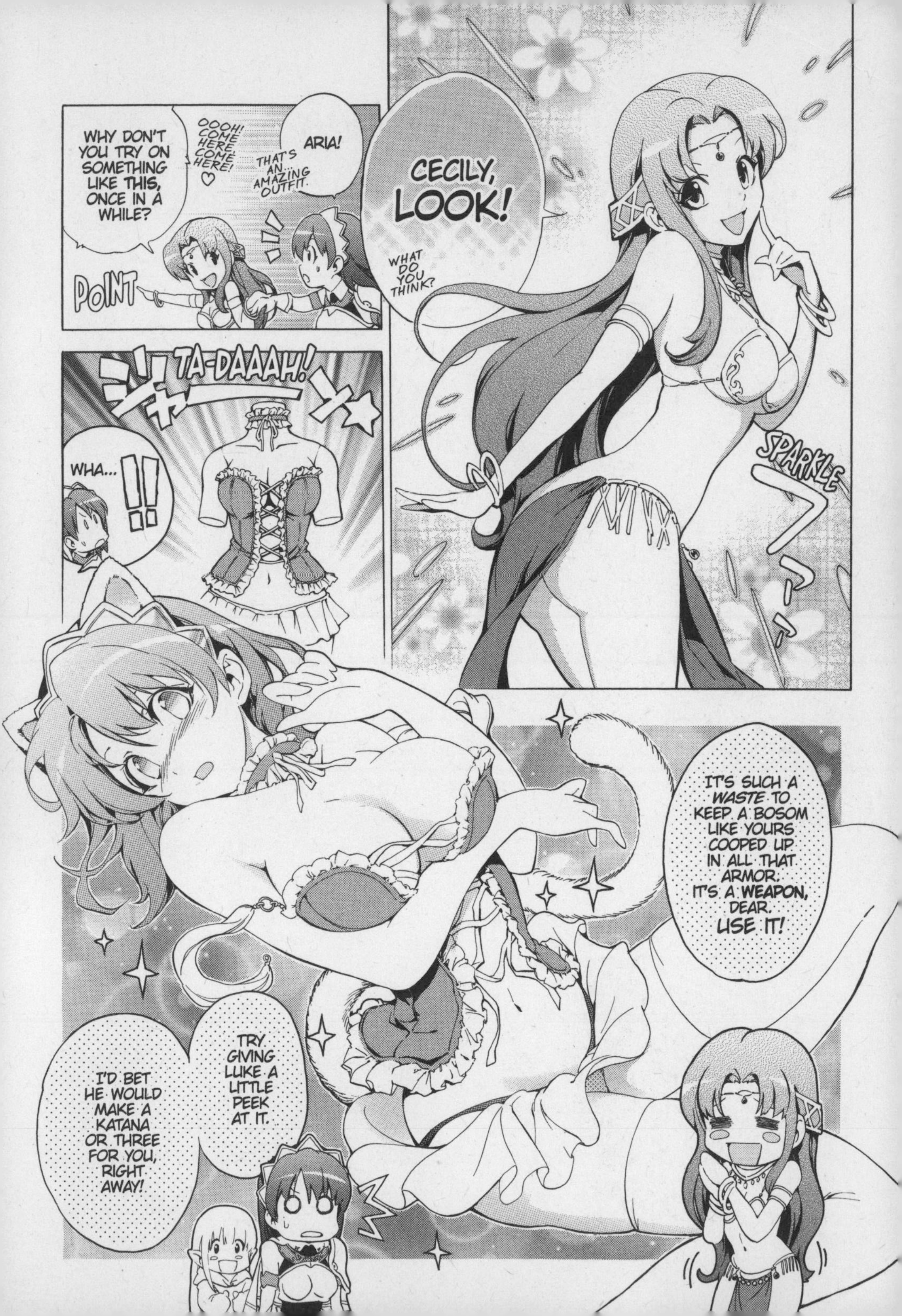
CECILY, LOOK!
WHAT DO YOU THINK?
SPARKLE
ARIA!
THAT'S AN... AMAZING OUTFIT.
OOOH! COME HERE COME HERE! ♡
WHY DON'T YOU TRY ON SOMETHING LIKE THIS, ONCE IN A WHILE?
POINT
TA-DAAAH!
WHA... !!
IT'S SUCH A WASTE TO KEEP A BOSOM LIKE YOURS COOPED UP IN ALL THAT ARMOR. IT'S A WEAPON, DEAR. USE IT!
TRY GIVING LUKE A LITTLE PEEK AT IT.
I'D BET HE WOULD MAKE A KATANA OR THREE FOR YOU, RIGHT AWAY!

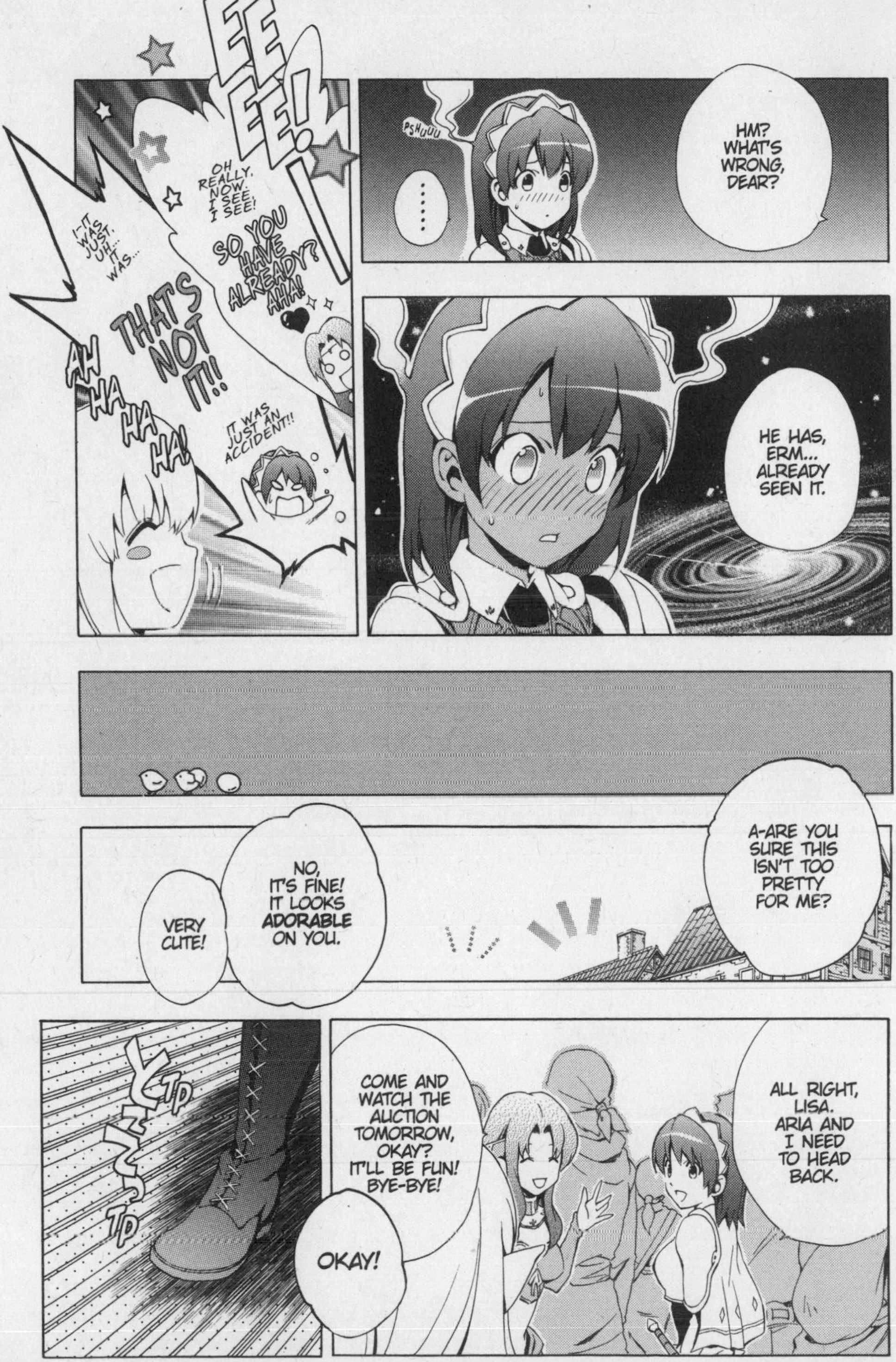
HM? WHAT'S WRONG, DEAR?
PSHUUU
......
HE HAS, ERM... ALREADY SEEN IT.
EEEEE!!
OH REALLY. NOW. I SEE, I SEE!
SO YOU HAVE ALREADY? AHA!
I-IT WAS. JUST... UH... IT WAS...
THAT'S NOT IT!!
AH HA HA HA HA!
IT WAS JUST AN ACCIDENT!!
A-ARE YOU SURE THIS ISN'T TOO PRETTY FOR ME?
NO, IT'S FINE! IT LOOKS ADORABLE ON YOU.
VERY CUTE!
ALL RIGHT, LISA. ARIA AND I NEED TO HEAD BACK.
COME AND WATCH THE AUCTION TOMORROW, OKAY? IT'LL BE FUN! BYE-BYE!
OKAY!
TP
TP

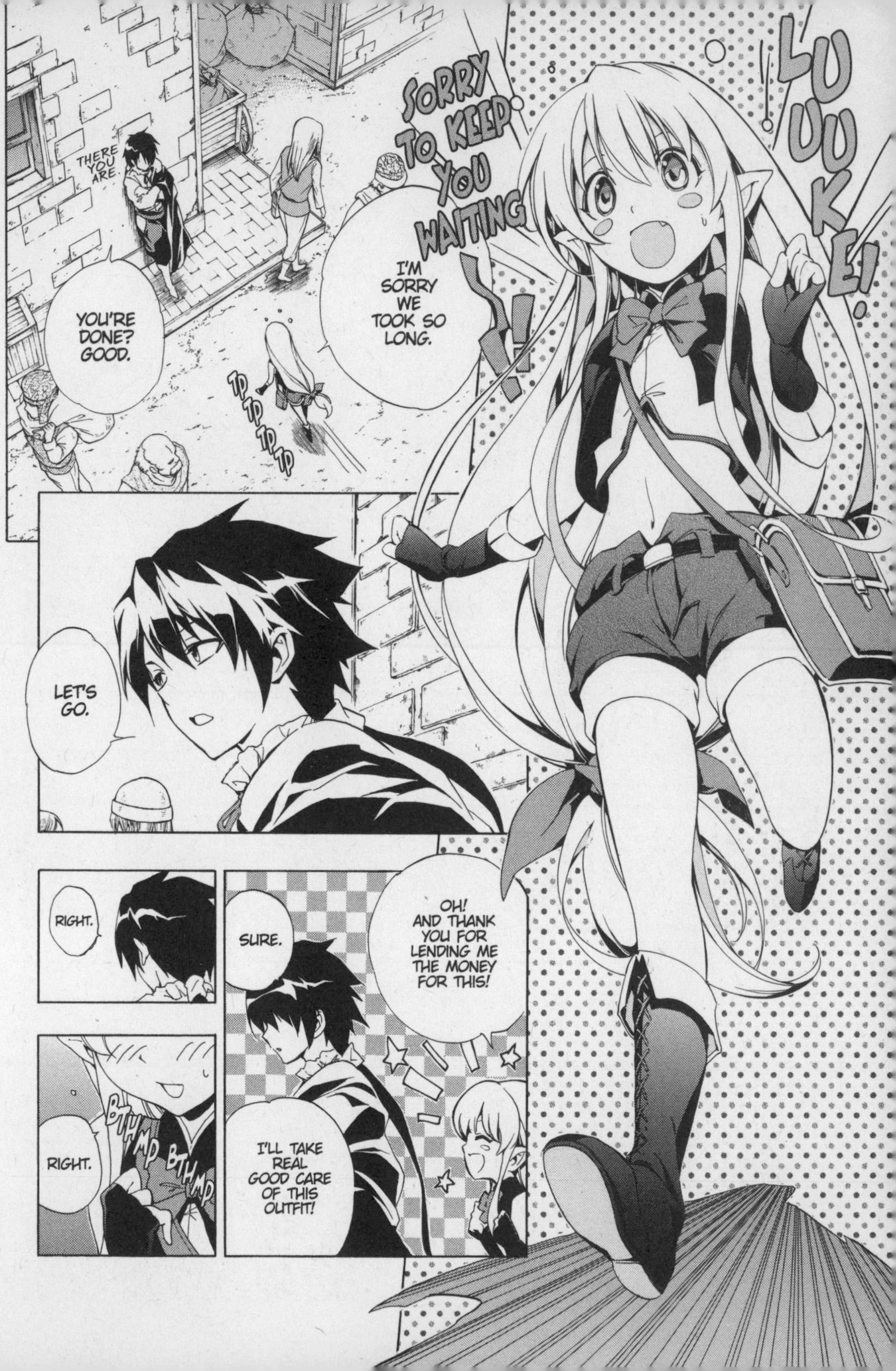
LUUUKE!
SORRY TO KEEP YOU WAITING
!!
THERE YOU ARE.
I'M SORRY WE TOOK SO LONG.
TP TP TP TP
YOU'RE DONE? GOOD.
LET'S GO.
OH! AND THANK YOU FOR LENDING ME THE MONEY FOR THIS!
SURE.
RIGHT.
I'LL TAKE REAL GOOD CARE OF THIS OUTFIT!
BTHMP BTHMP
RIGHT.

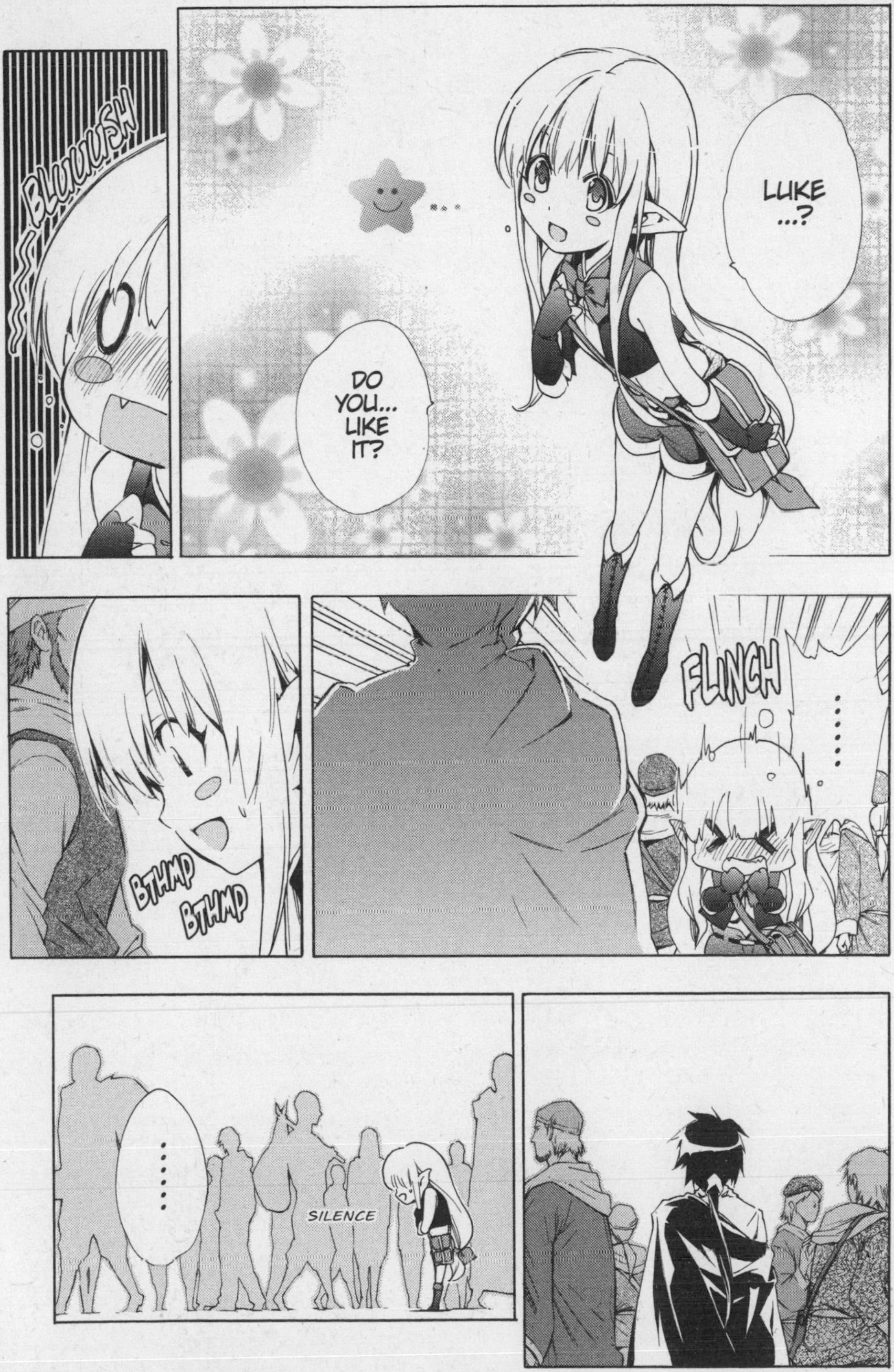
LUKE ...?
...
DO YOU... LIKE IT?
BLUUUUSH
FLINCH
......
BTHMP
BTHMP
......
SILENCE

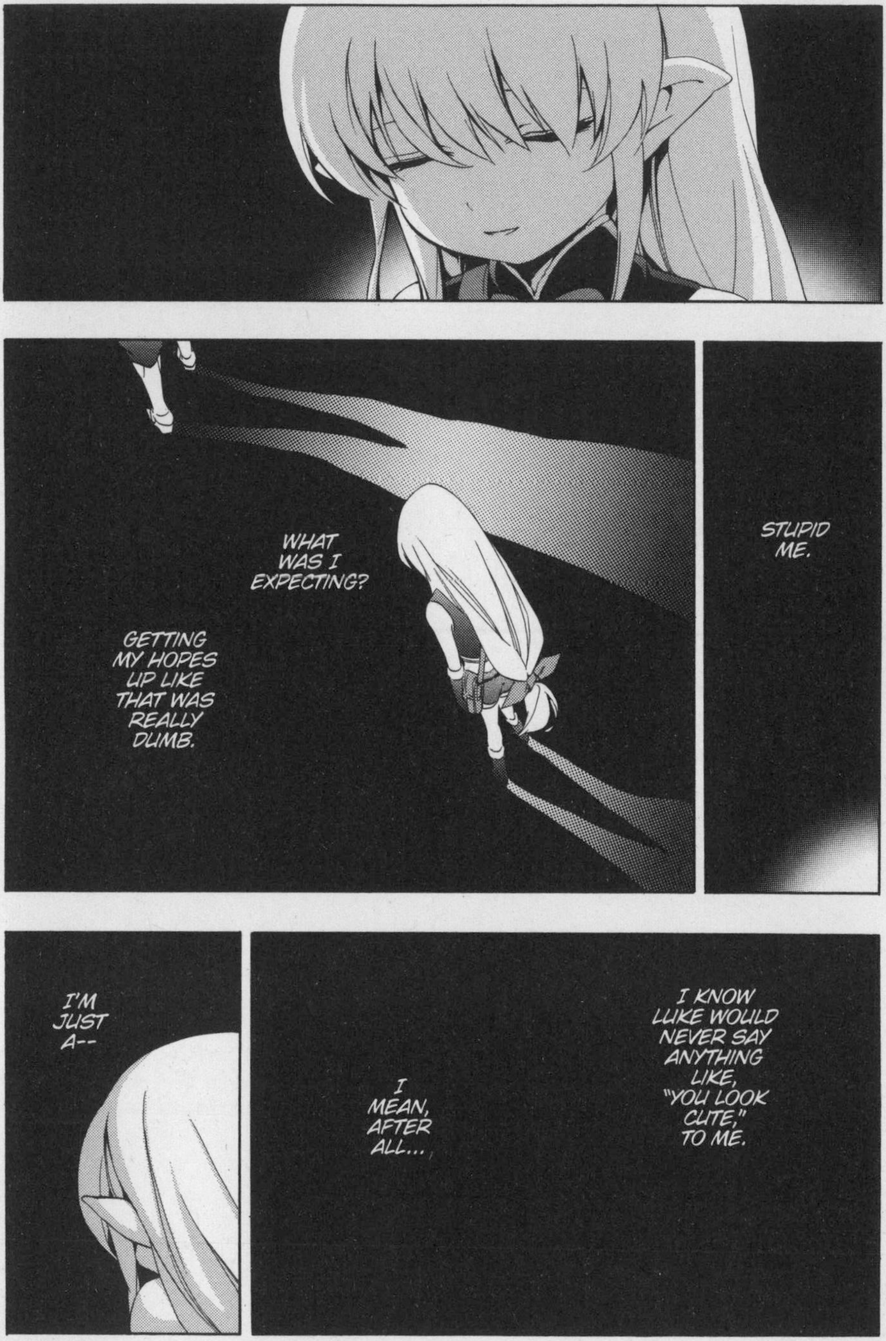
STUPID ME.
WHAT WAS I EXPECTING?
GETTING MY HOPES UP LIKE THAT WAS REALLY DUMB.
I KNOW LUKE WOULD NEVER SAY ANYTHING LIKE, "YOU LOOK CUTE," TO ME.
I MEAN, AFTER ALL...
I'M JUST A--

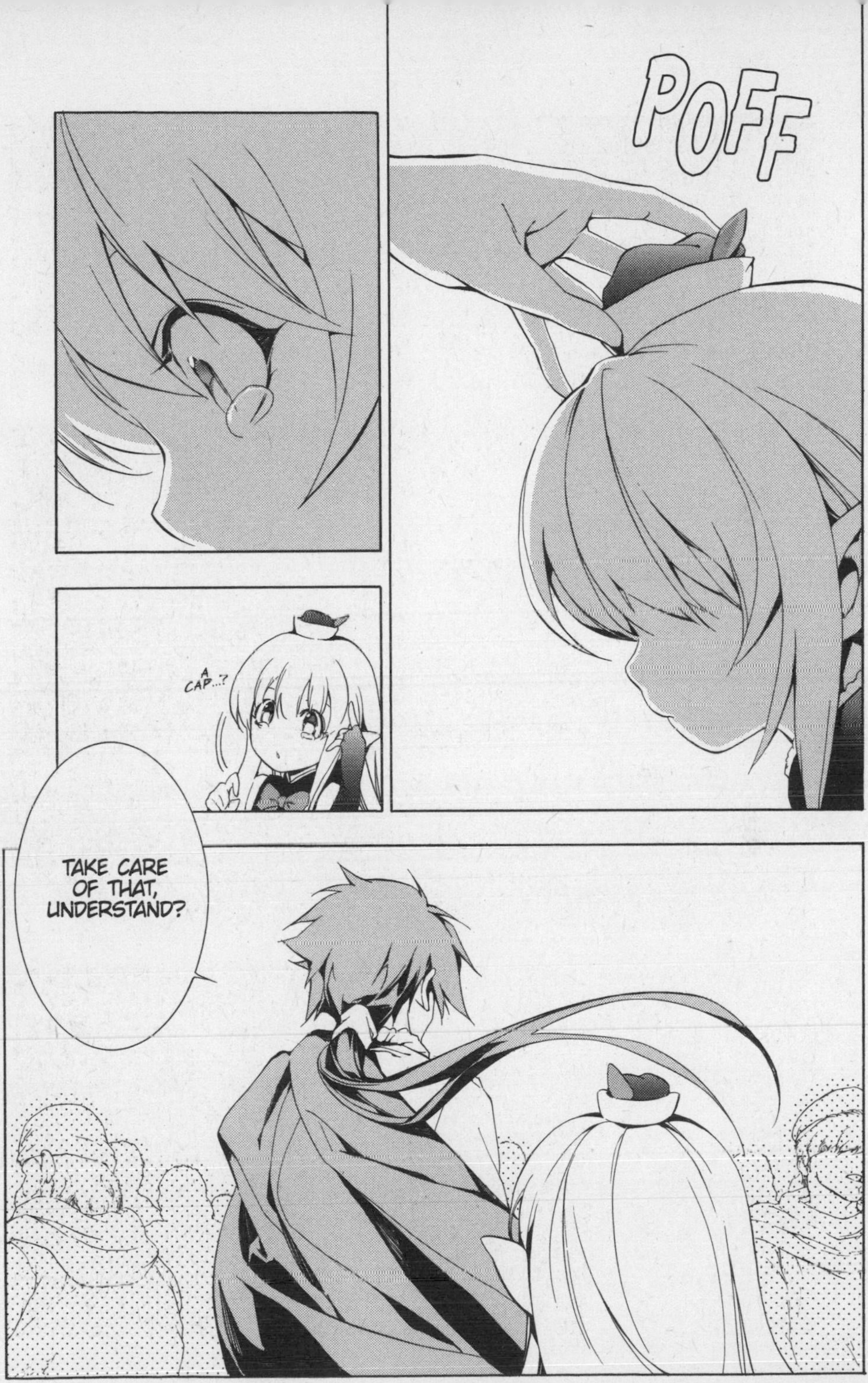
POFF
A CAP...?
TAKE CARE OF THAT, UNDERSTAND?

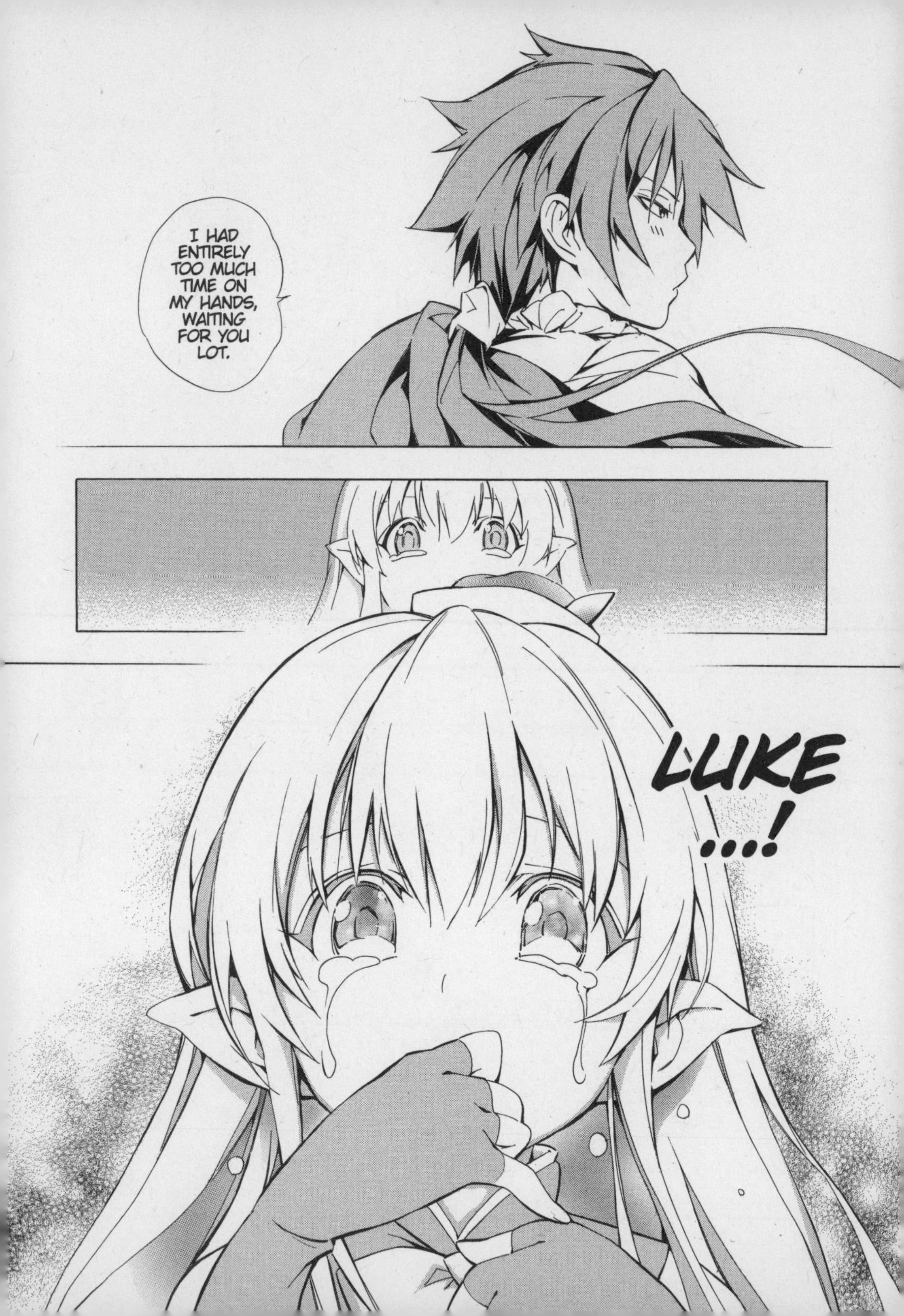
I HAD ENTIRELY TOO MUCH TIME ON MY HANDS, WAITING FOR YOU LOT.
LUKE ...!

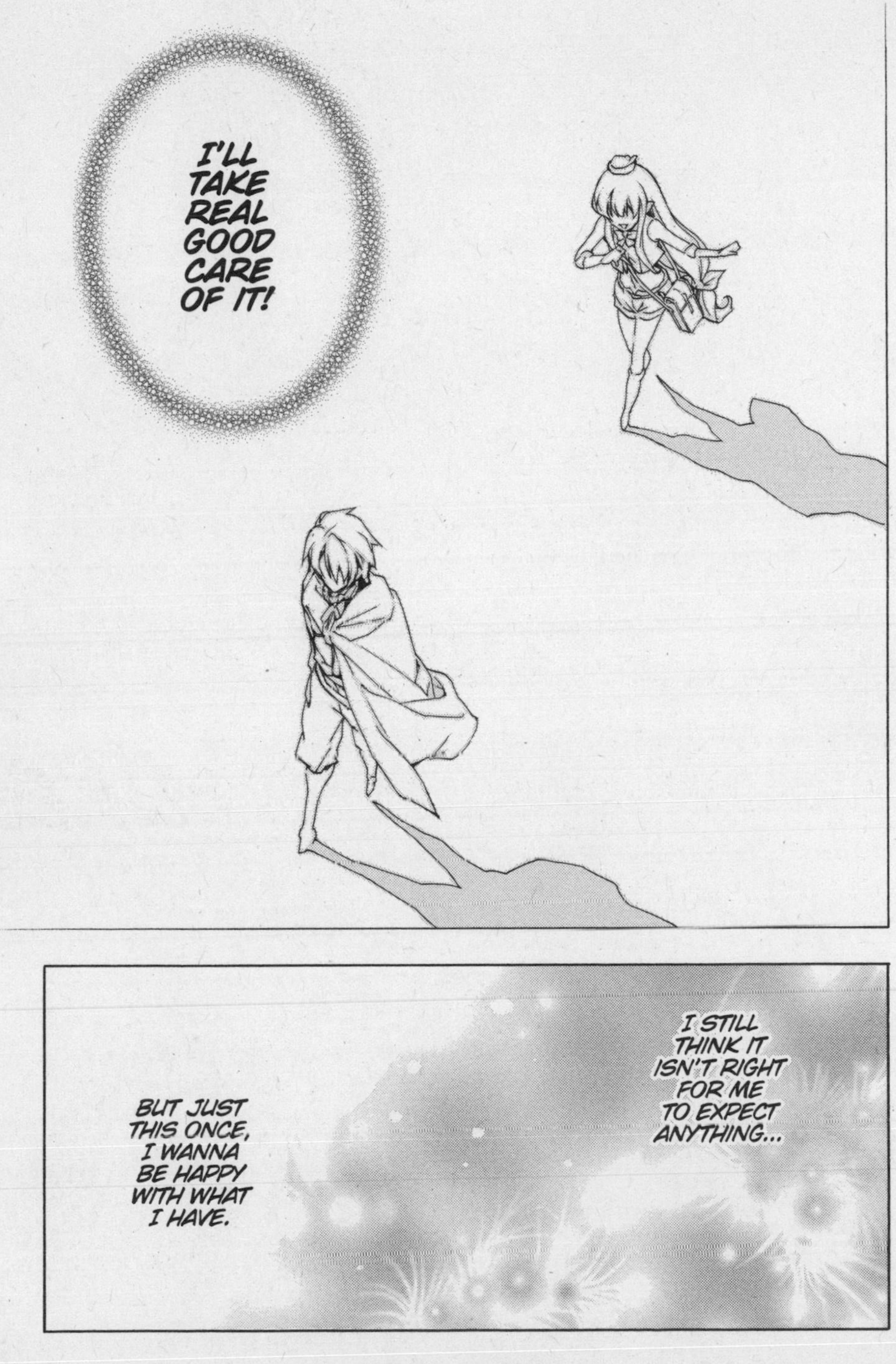
I'LL TAKE REAL GOOD CARE OF IT!
I STILL THINK IT ISN'T RIGHT FOR ME TO EXPECT ANYTHING...
BUT JUST THIS ONCE, I WANNA BE HAPPY WITH WHAT I HAVE.

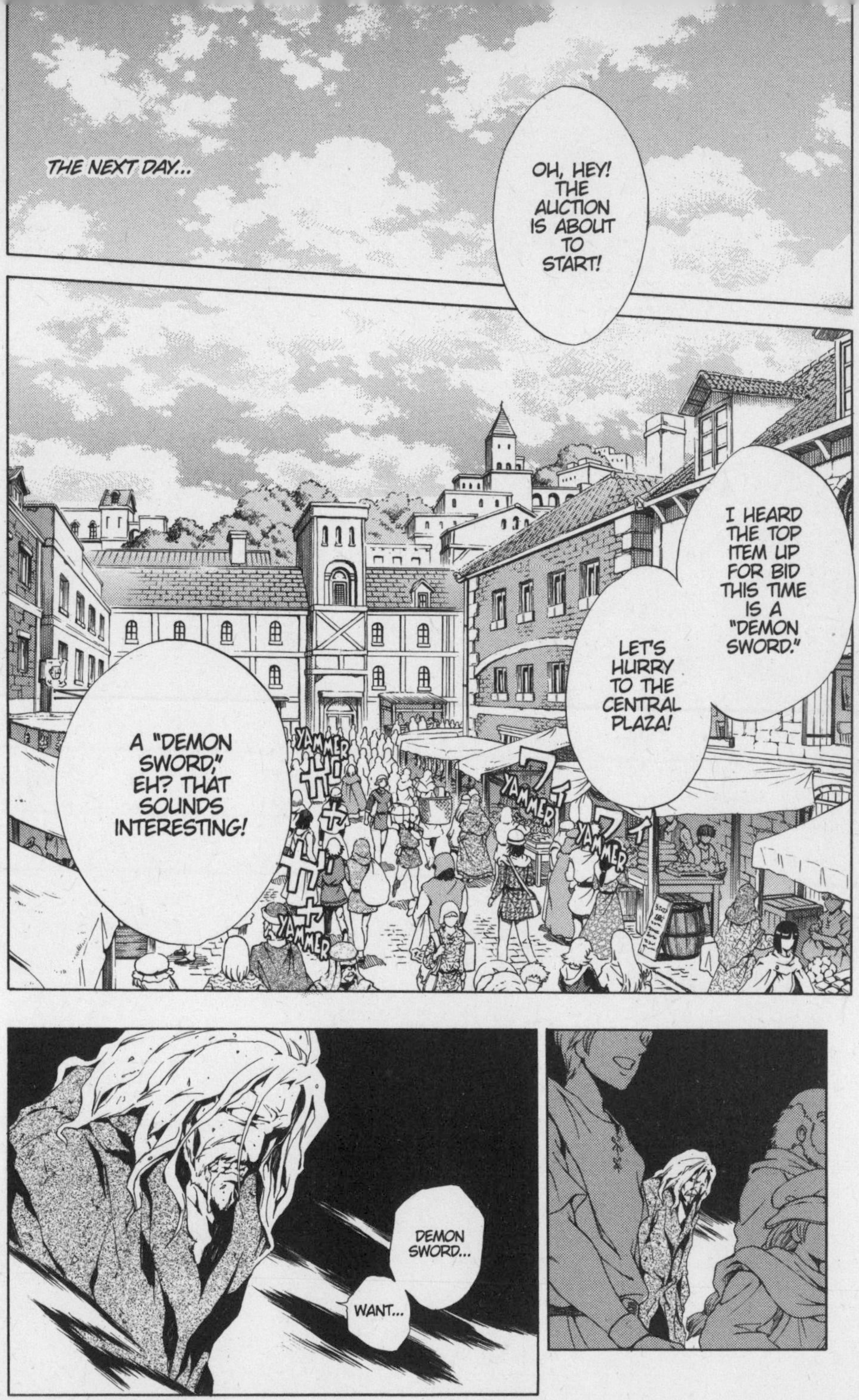
THE NEXT DAY...
OH, HEY! THE AUCTION IS ABOUT TO START!
I HEARD THE TOP ITEM UP FOR BID THIS TIME IS A "DEMON SWORD."
LET'S HURRY TO THE CENTRAL PLAZA!
YAMMER
YAMMER
A "DEMON SWORD," EH? THAT SOUNDS INTERESTING!
YAMMER
YAMMER
DEMON SWORD...
WANT...

✳ *Lisa* ✳

The Sacred Blacksmith

聖剣の刀鍛冶

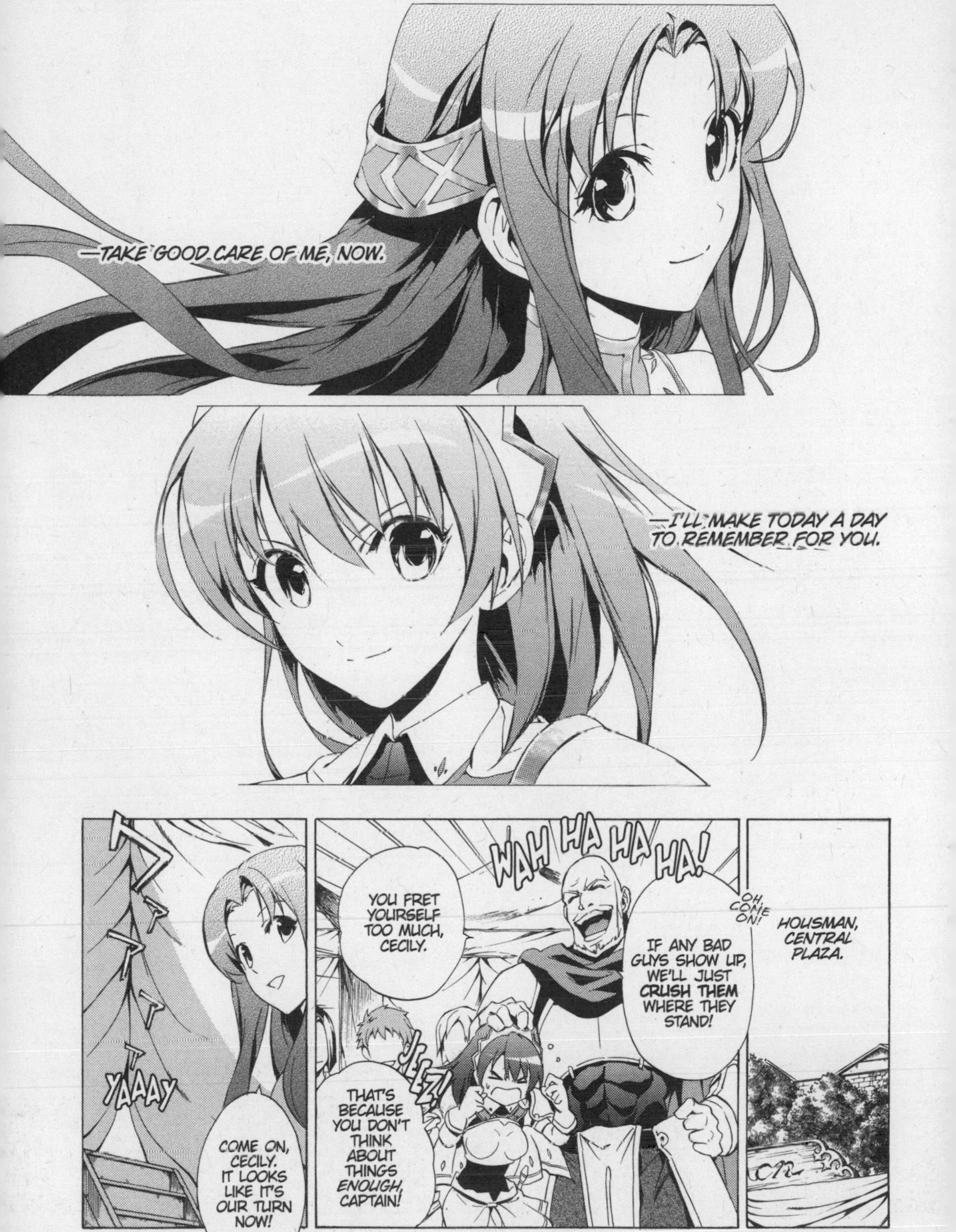
—TAKE GOOD CARE OF ME, NOW.
—I'LL MAKE TODAY A DAY TO REMEMBER FOR YOU.
HOUSMAN, CENTRAL PLAZA.
WAH HA HA HA!
YOU FRET YOURSELF TOO MUCH, CECILY.
OH, COME ON!
IF ANY BAD GUYS SHOW UP, WE'LL JUST CRUSH THEM WHERE THEY STAND!
JEEZ!
THAT'S BECAUSE YOU DON'T THINK ABOUT THINGS *ENOUGH*, CAPTAIN!
YAAAY
COME ON, CECILY. IT LOOKS LIKE IT'S OUR TURN NOW!

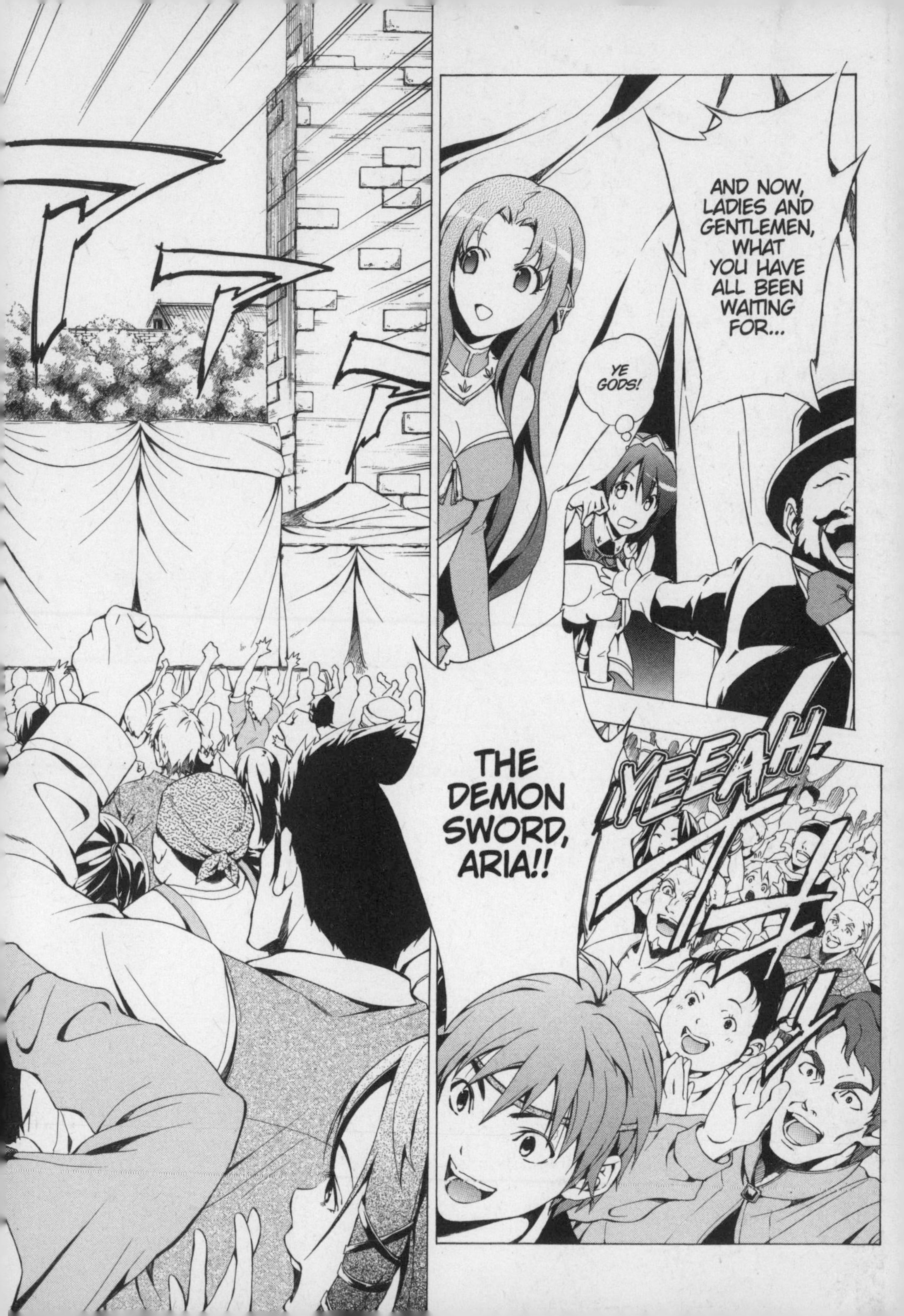
AND NOW, LADIES AND GENTLEMEN, WHAT YOU HAVE ALL BEEN WAITING FOR...
YE GODS!
THE DEMON SWORD, ARIA!!
YEEAH

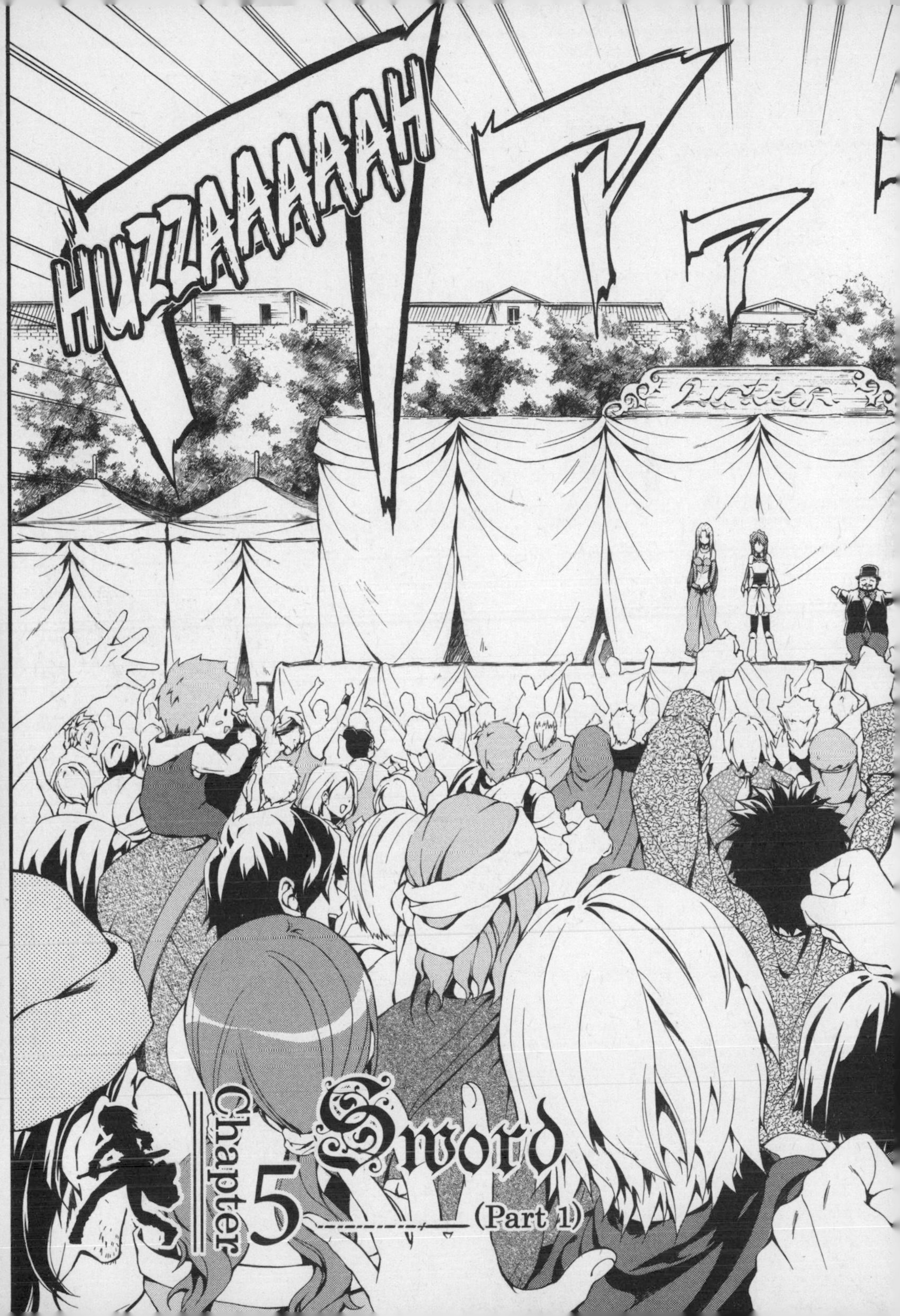
HUZZAAAAAH
Chapter 5 Sword (Part 1)

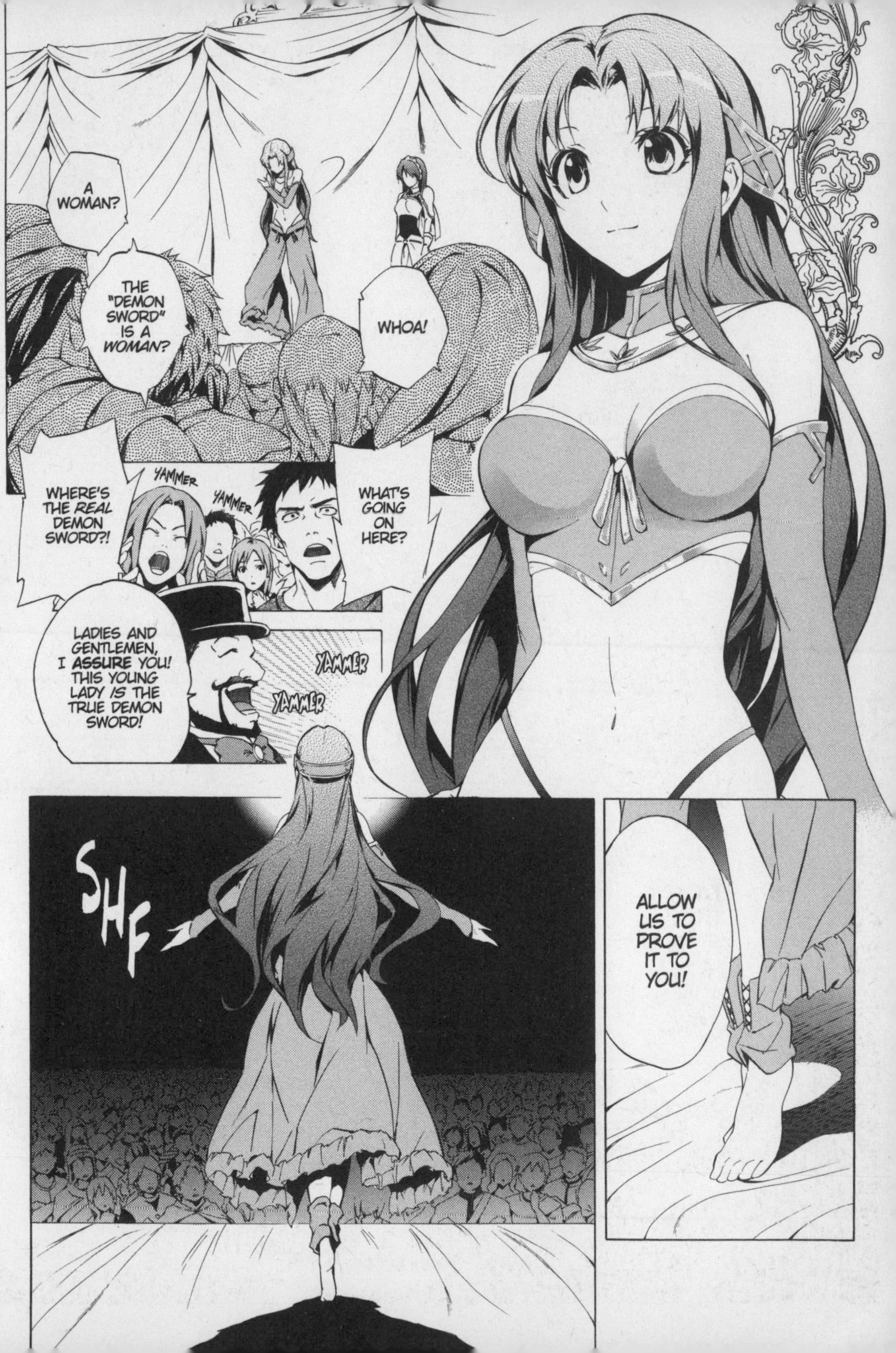
WHOA!
A WOMAN?
THE "DEMON SWORD" IS A WOMAN?
WHAT'S GOING ON HERE?
YAMMER
YAMMER
WHERE'S THE REAL DEMON SWORD?!
LADIES AND GENTLEMEN, I ASSURE YOU! THIS YOUNG LADY IS THE TRUE DEMON SWORD!
YAMMER
YAMMER
ALLOW US TO PROVE IT TO YOU!
SHF

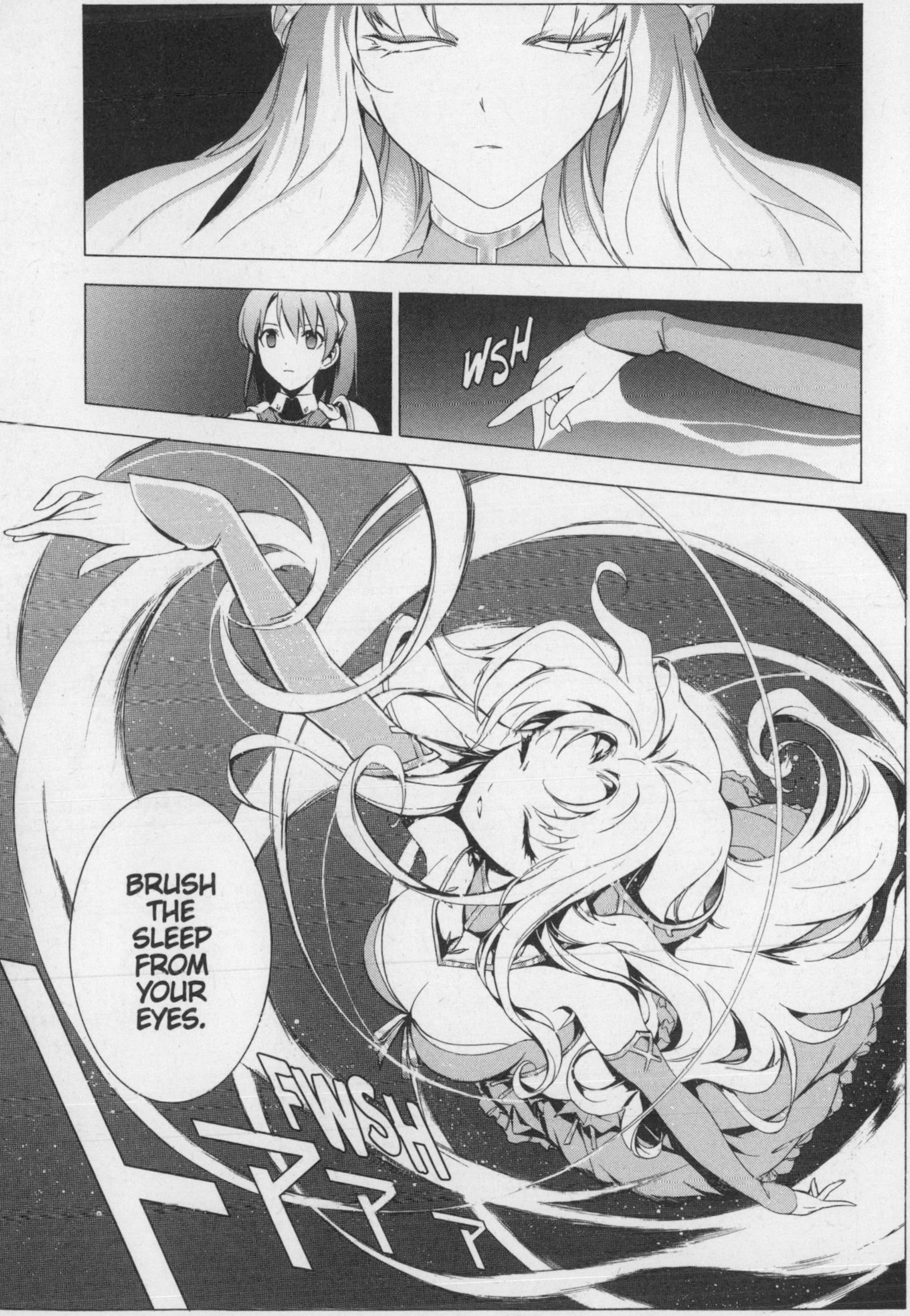
WSH
BRUSH THE SLEEP FROM YOUR EYES.
FWSH

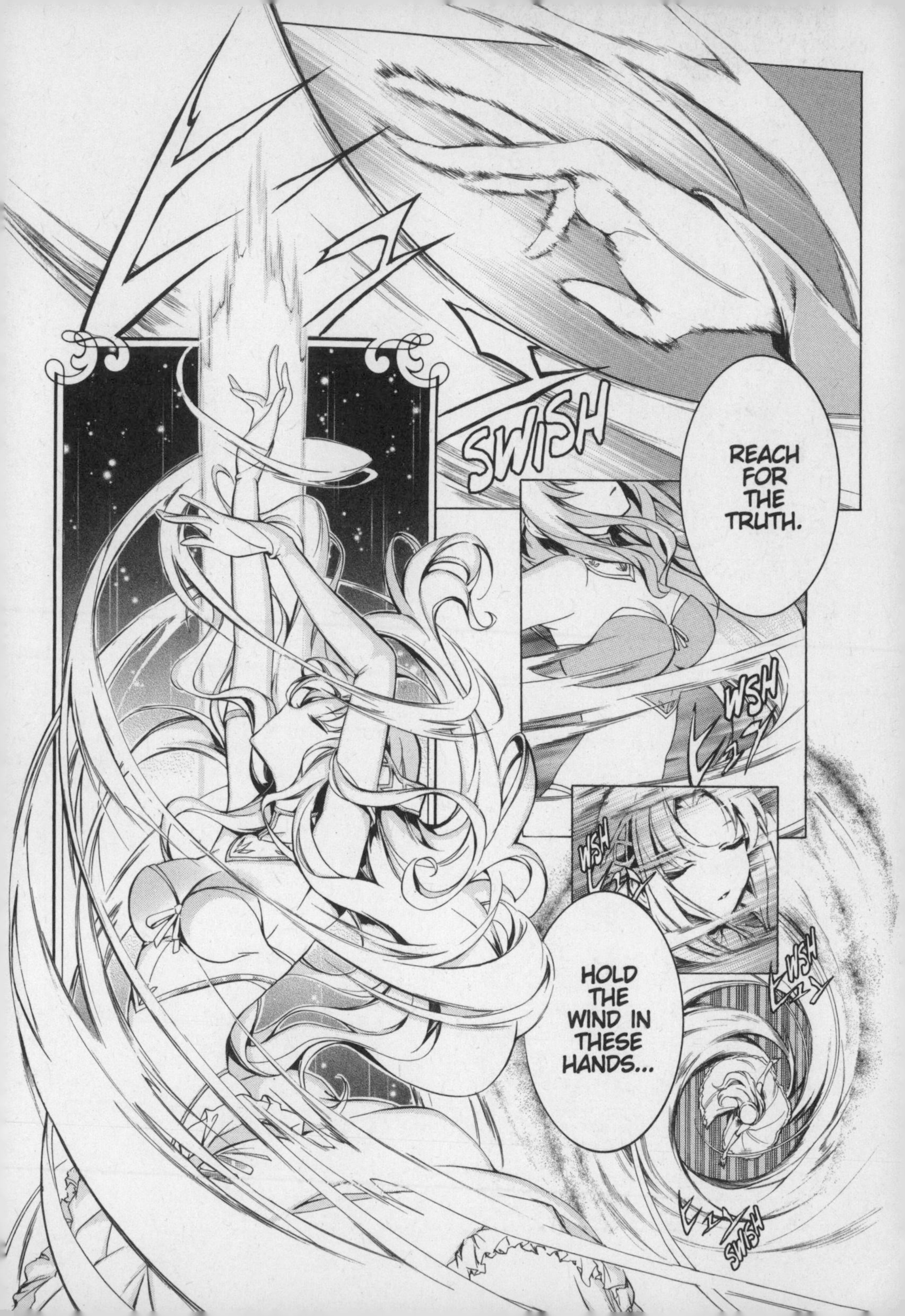
SWISH
REACH FOR THE TRUTH.
WSH
WSH
HOLD THE WIND IN THESE HANDS...
WSH
SWISH

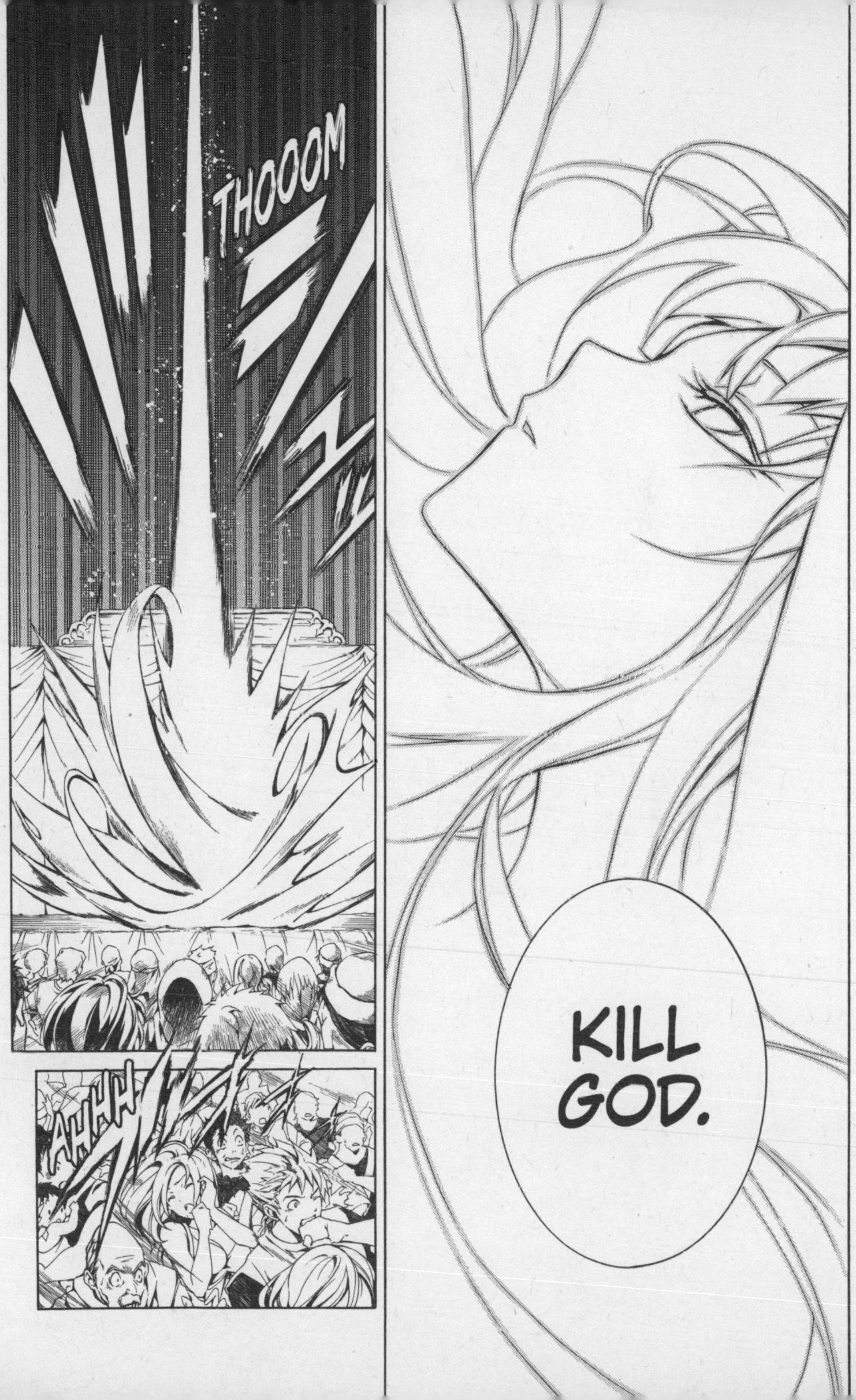
KILL GOD.
THOOOM
AHHH

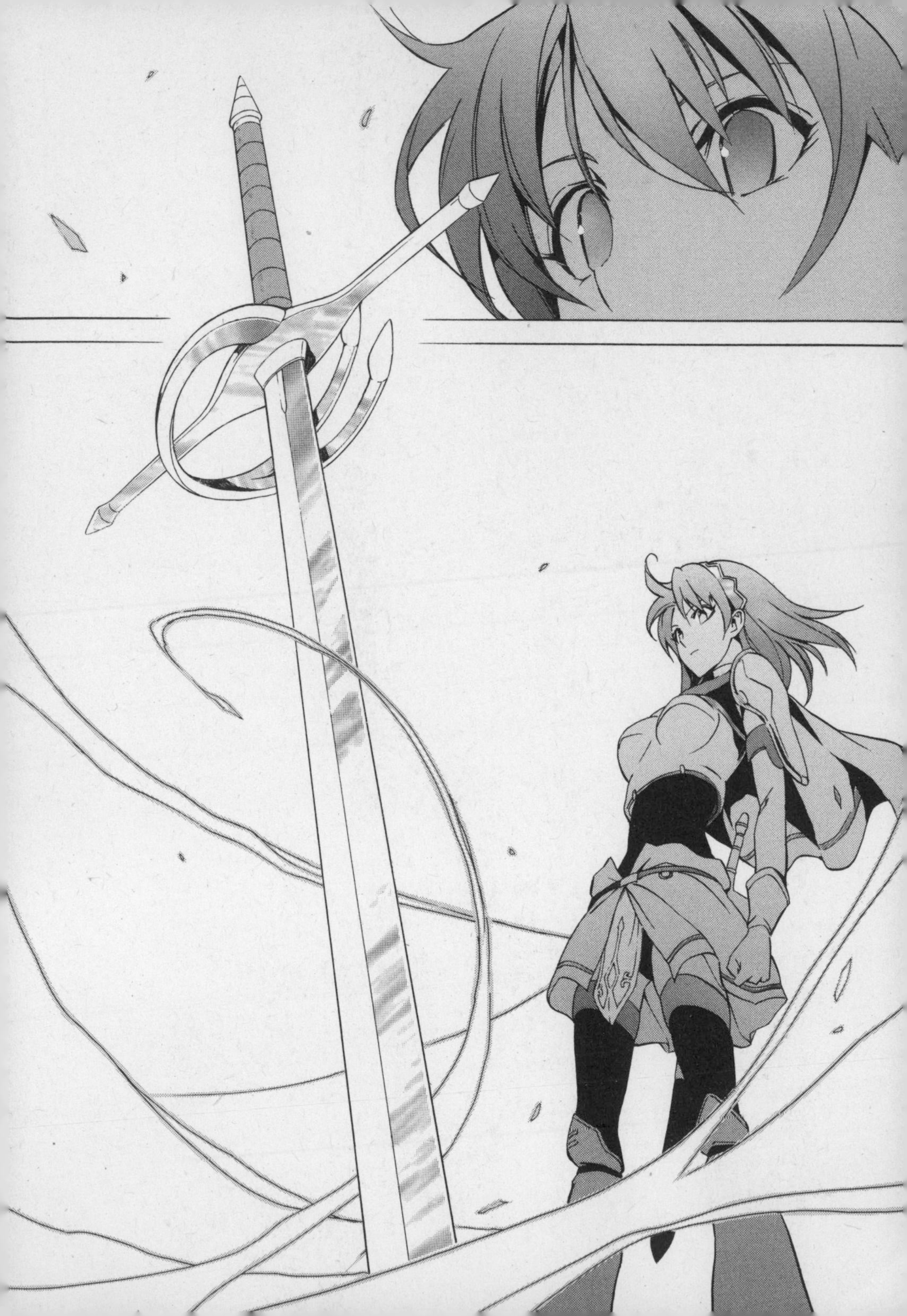

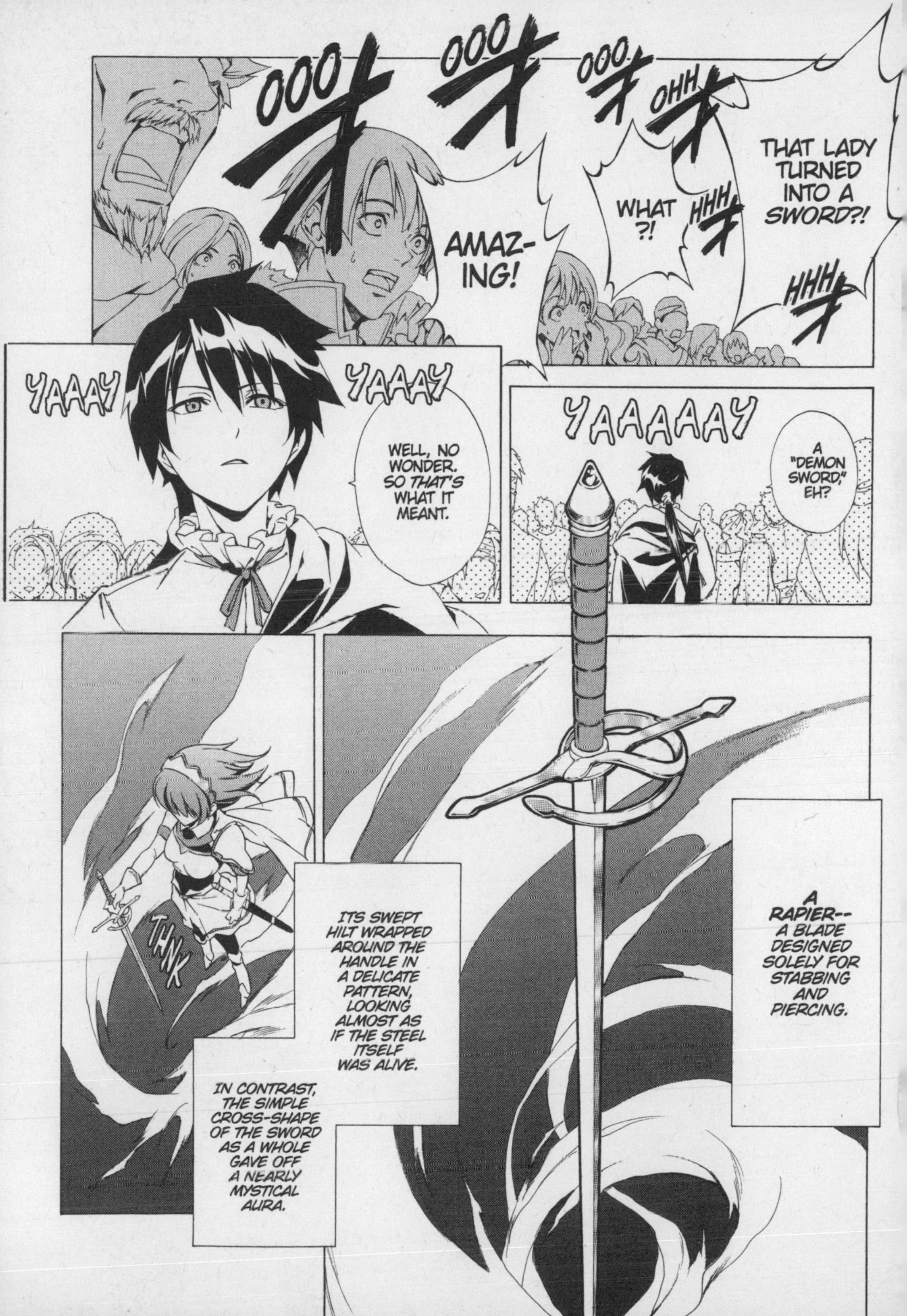
THAT LADY TURNED INTO A SWORD?!
HHH
WHAT?!
OHH
OOO-
OOO-
OOO
AMAZ-ING!
YAAAAAY
A "DEMON SWORD," EH?
YAAAY
WELL, NO WONDER. SO THAT'S WHAT IT MEANT.
YAAAY
A RAPIER-- A BLADE DESIGNED SOLELY FOR STABBING AND PIERCING.
ITS SWEPT HILT WRAPPED AROUND THE HANDLE IN A DELICATE PATTERN, LOOKING ALMOST AS IF THE STEEL ITSELF WAS ALIVE.
IN CONTRAST, THE SIMPLE CROSS-SHAPE OF THE SWORD AS A WHOLE GAVE OFF A NEARLY MYSTICAL AURA.
THNK

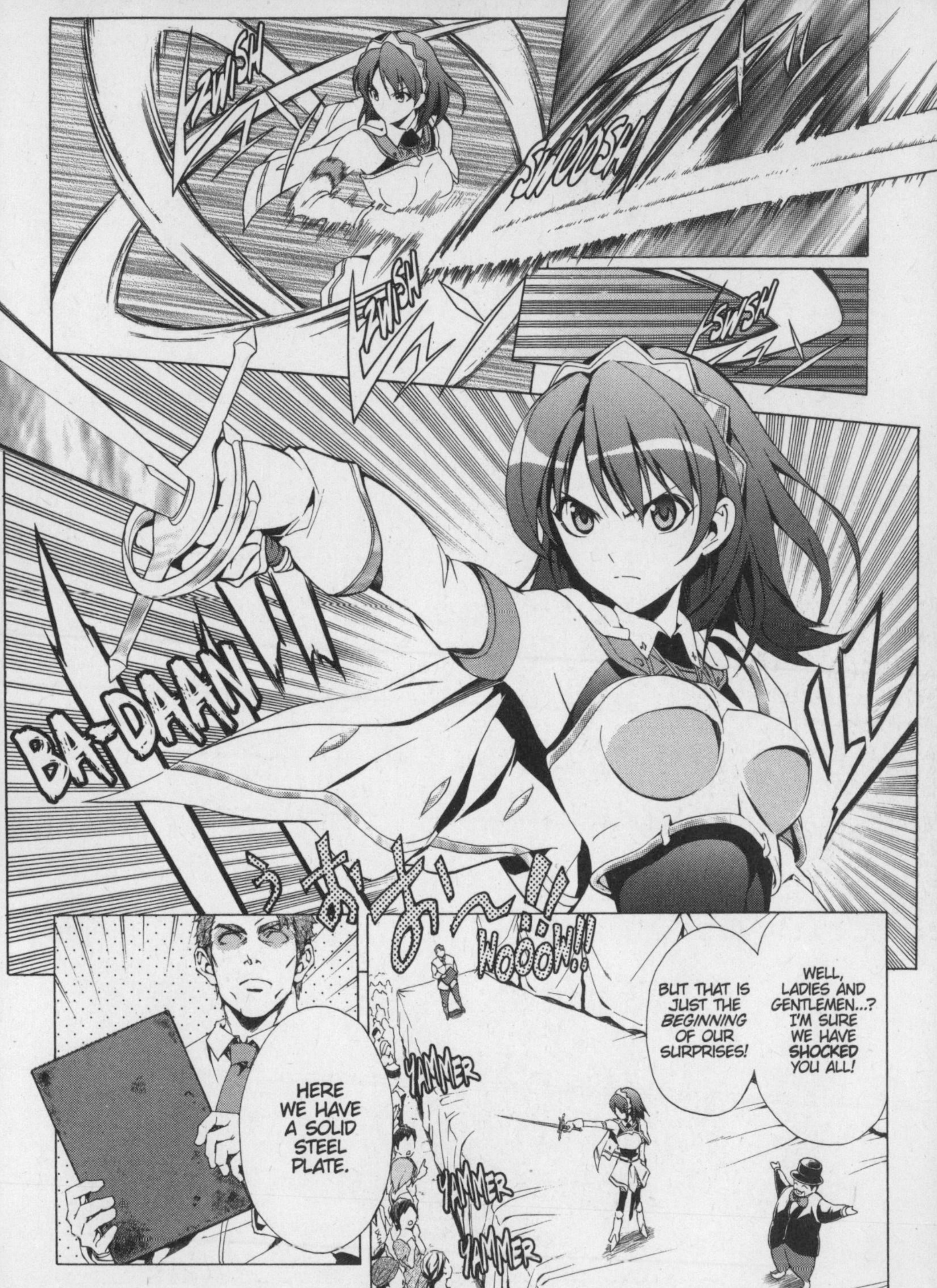
SWOOSH
ZWISH
SWISH
ZWISH
BA-DAAN!!
うおお～!!
WOOOW!!
WELL, LADIES AND GENTLEMEN...? I'M SURE WE HAVE SHOCKED YOU ALL!
BUT THAT IS JUST THE BEGINNING OF OUR SURPRISES!
YAMMER
YAMMER
YAMMER
HERE WE HAVE A SOLID STEEL PLATE.

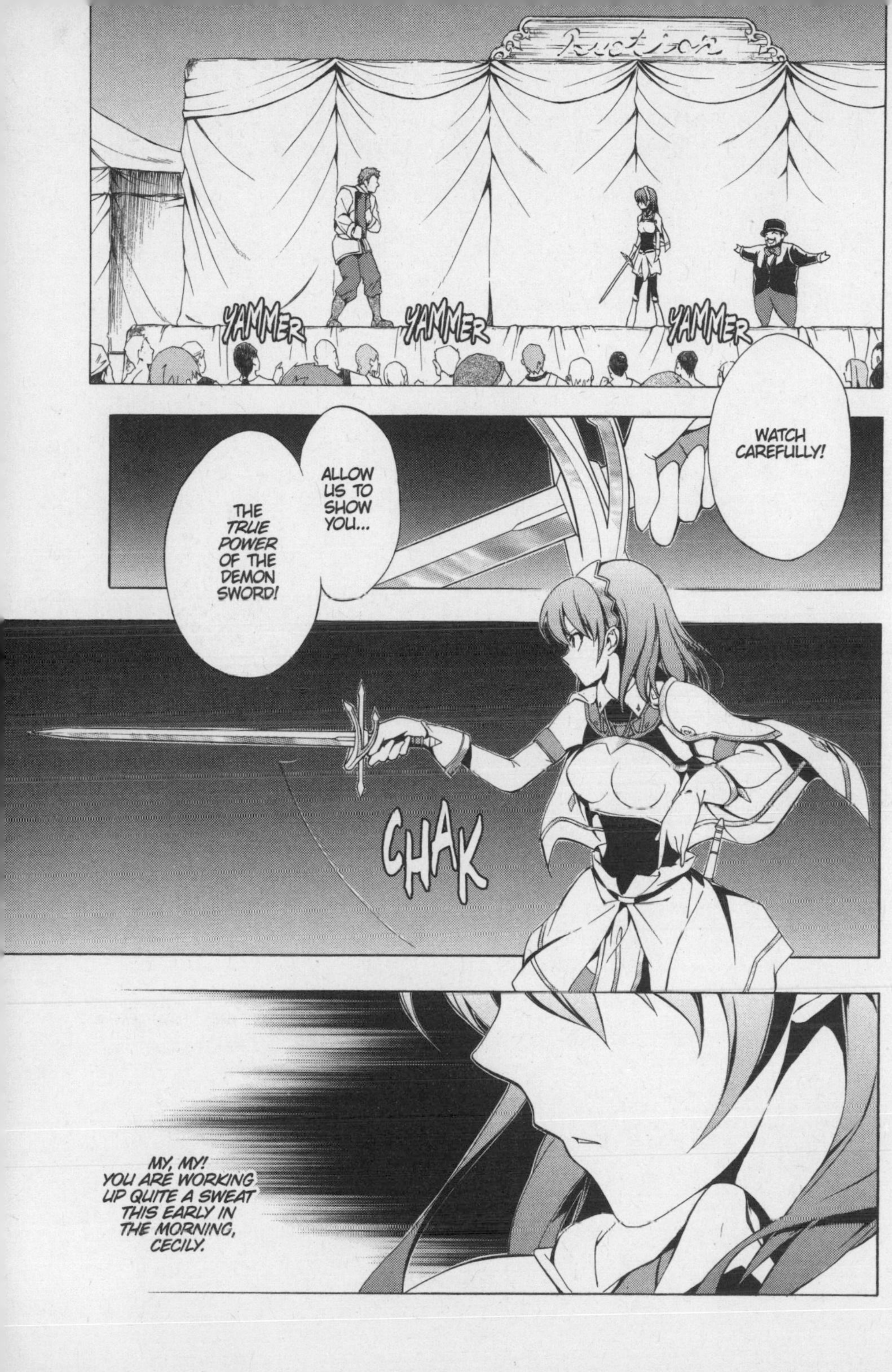
YAMMER
YAMMER
YAMMER
WATCH CAREFULLY!
ALLOW US TO SHOW YOU...
THE TRUE POWER OF THE DEMON SWORD!
CHAK
MY, MY! YOU ARE WORKING UP QUITE A SWEAT THIS EARLY IN THE MORNING, CECILY.

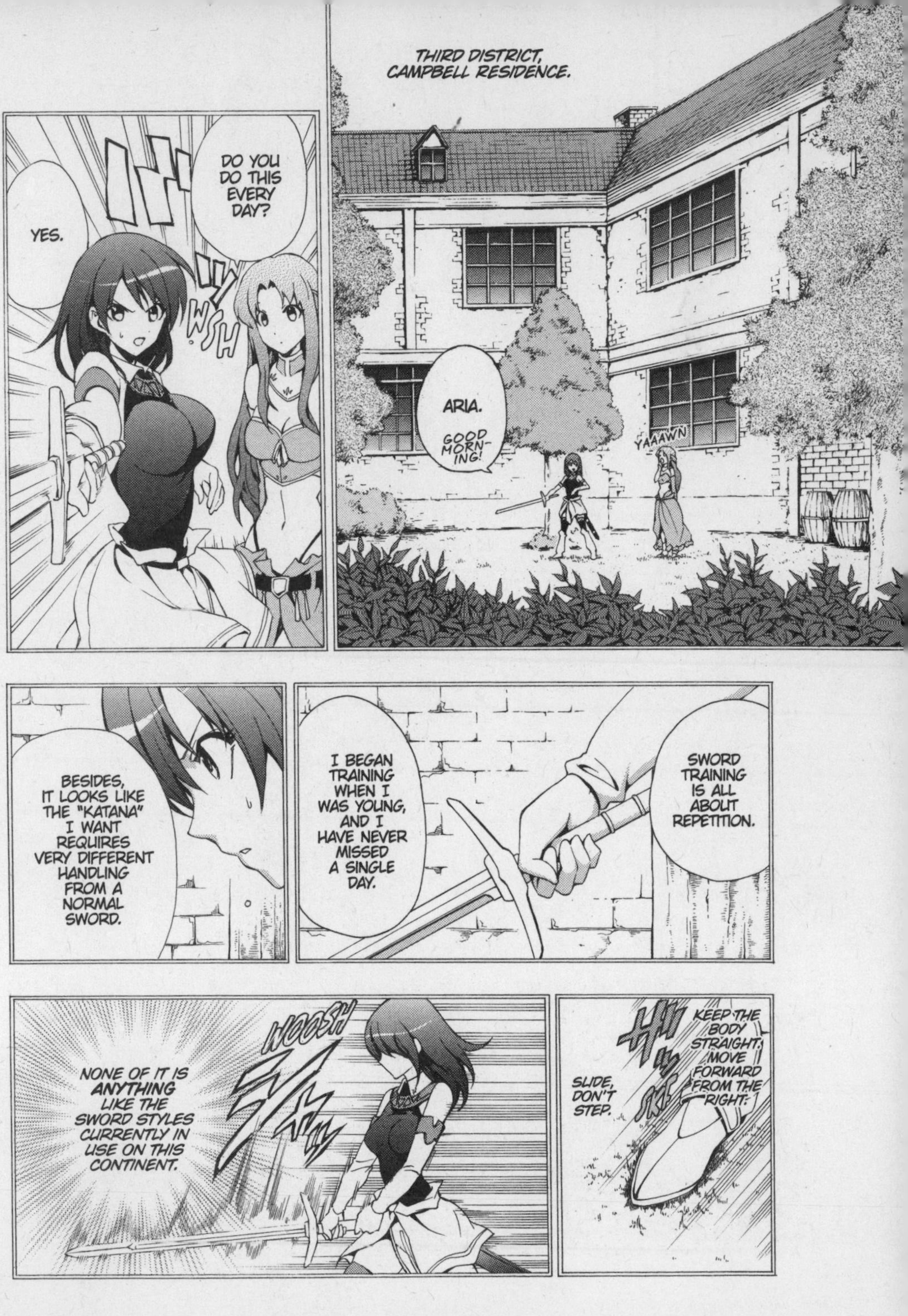
THIRD DISTRICT, CAMPBELL RESIDENCE.
ARIA.
GOOD MORNING!
YAAAWN
DO YOU DO THIS EVERY DAY?
YES.
WSH
SWORD TRAINING IS ALL ABOUT REPETITION.
I BEGAN TRAINING WHEN I WAS YOUNG, AND I HAVE NEVER MISSED A SINGLE DAY.
BESIDES, IT LOOKS LIKE THE "KATANA" I WANT REQUIRES VERY DIFFERENT HANDLING FROM A NORMAL SWORD.
KEEP THE BODY STRAIGHT; MOVE FORWARD FROM THE RIGHT.
SLIDE, DON'T STEP.
WOOSH
NONE OF IT IS ANYTHING LIKE THE SWORD STYLES CURRENTLY IN USE ON THIS CONTINENT.

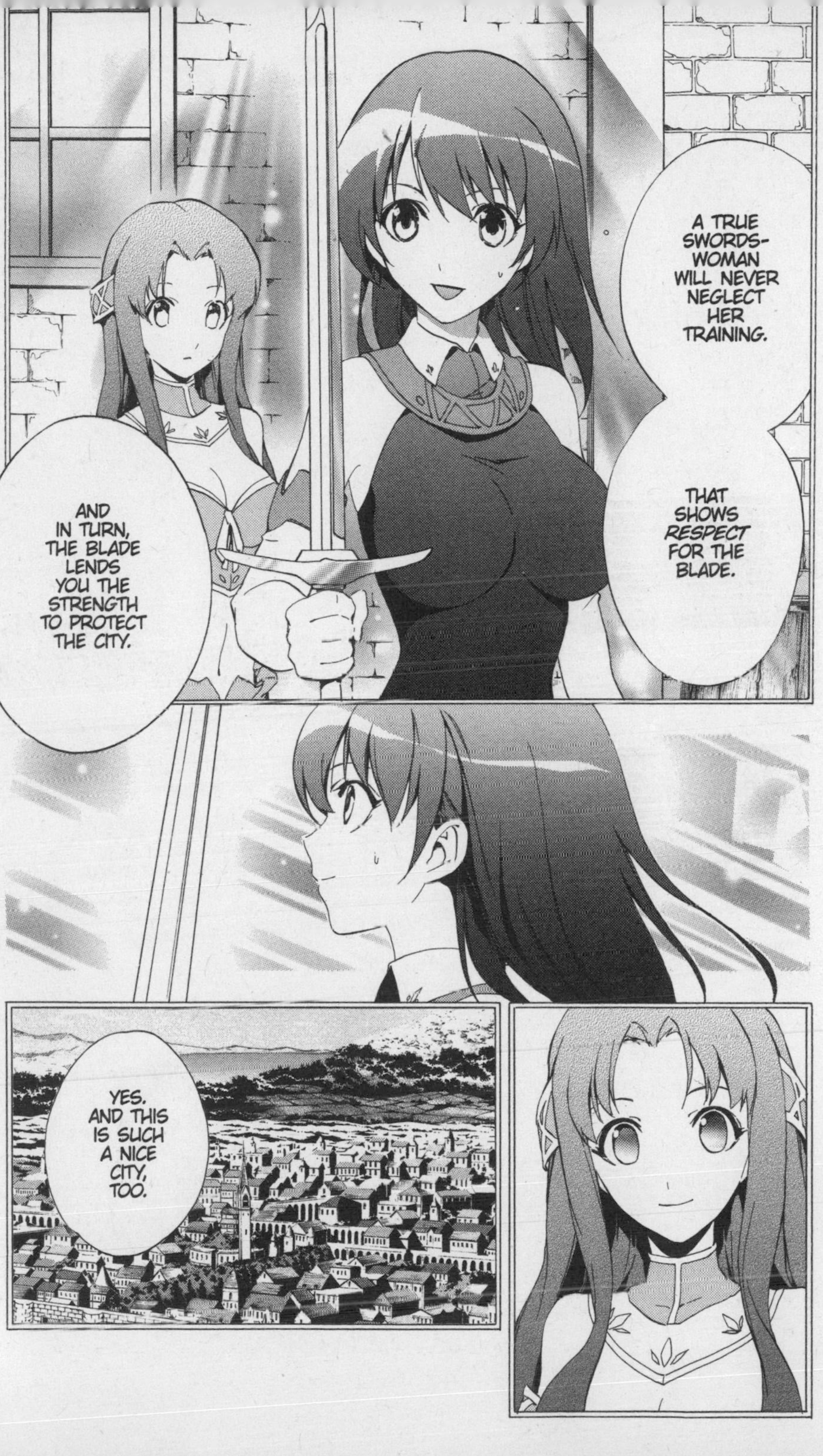
A TRUE SWORDS-WOMAN WILL NEVER NEGLECT HER TRAINING.
THAT SHOWS RESPECT FOR THE BLADE.
AND IN TURN, THE BLADE LENDS YOU THE STRENGTH TO PROTECT THE CITY.
YES. AND THIS IS SUCH A NICE CITY, TOO.

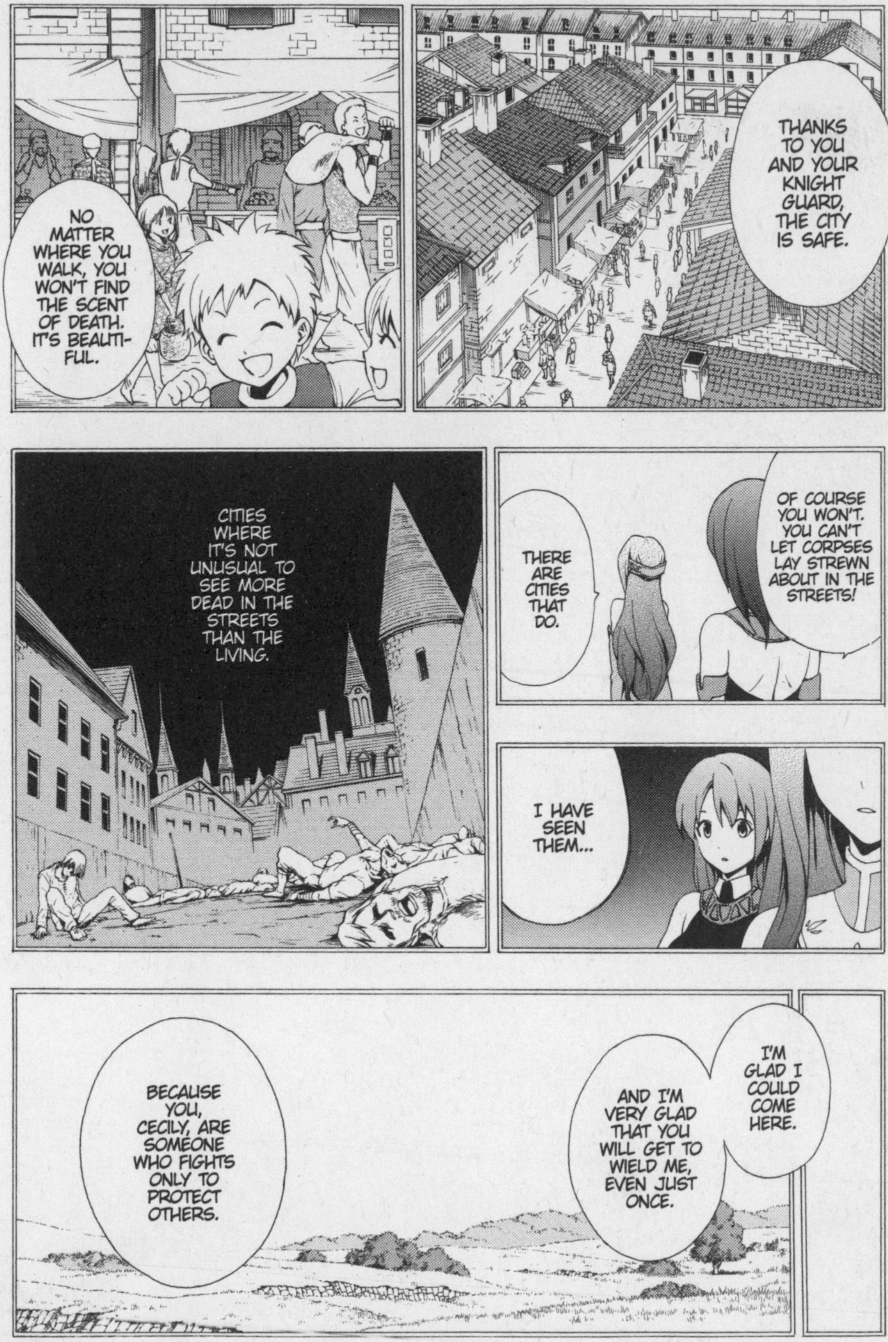
THANKS TO YOU AND YOUR KNIGHT GUARD, THE CITY IS SAFE.
NO MATTER WHERE YOU WALK, YOU WON'T FIND THE SCENT OF DEATH. IT'S BEAUTIFUL.
OF COURSE YOU WON'T. YOU CAN'T LET CORPSES LAY STREWN ABOUT IN THE STREETS!
THERE ARE CITIES THAT DO.
I HAVE SEEN THEM...
CITIES WHERE IT'S NOT UNUSUAL TO SEE MORE DEAD IN THE STREETS THAN THE LIVING.
I'M GLAD I COULD COME HERE.
AND I'M VERY GLAD THAT YOU WILL GET TO WIELD ME, EVEN JUST ONCE.
BECAUSE YOU, CECILY, ARE SOMEONE WHO FIGHTS ONLY TO PROTECT OTHERS.

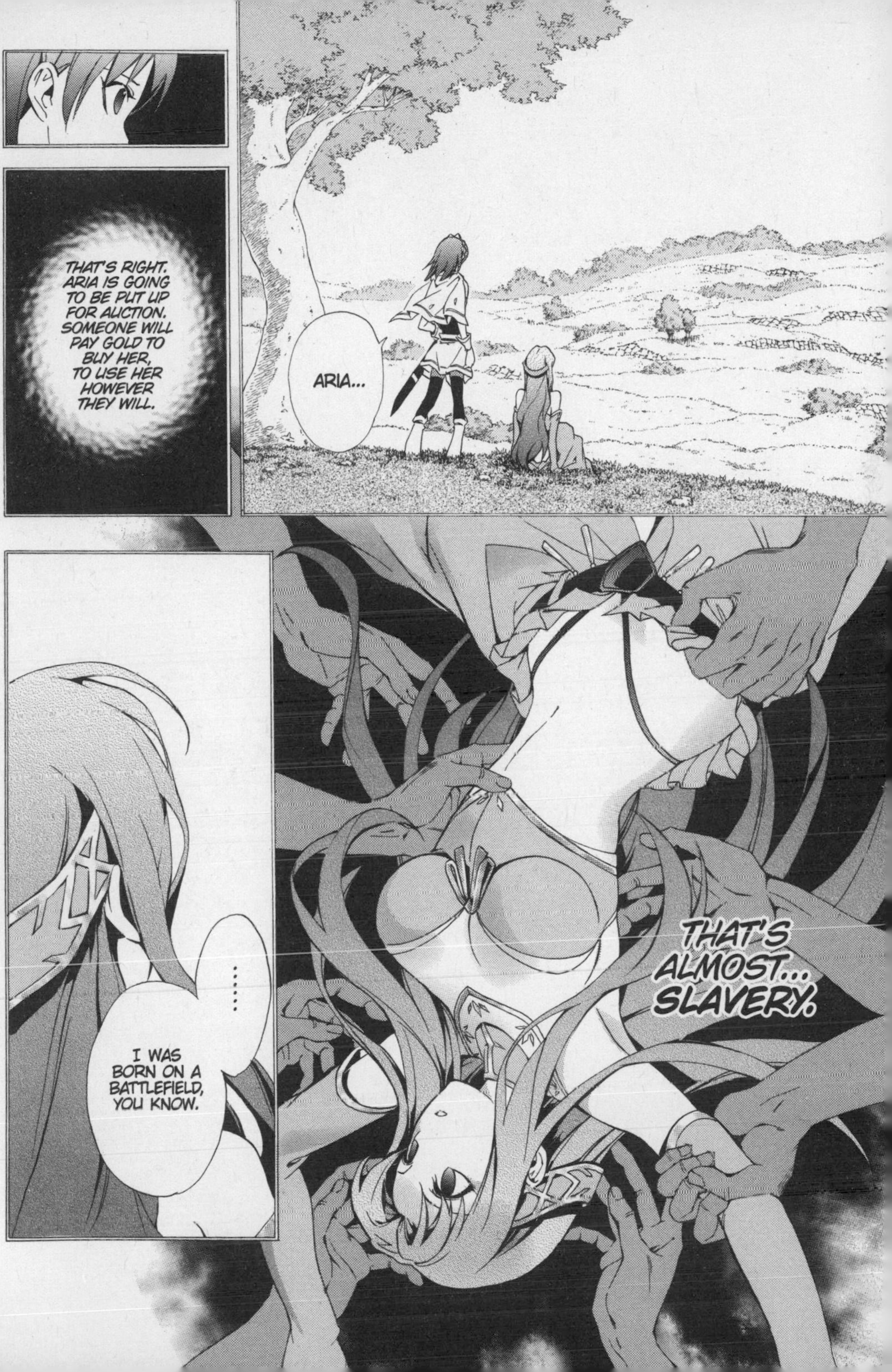
ARIA...
THAT'S RIGHT. ARIA IS GOING TO BE PUT UP FOR AUCTION. SOMEONE WILL PAY GOLD TO BUY HER, TO USE HER HOWEVER THEY WILL.
THAT'S ALMOST... SLAVERY.
......
I WAS BORN ON A BATTLEFIELD, YOU KNOW.

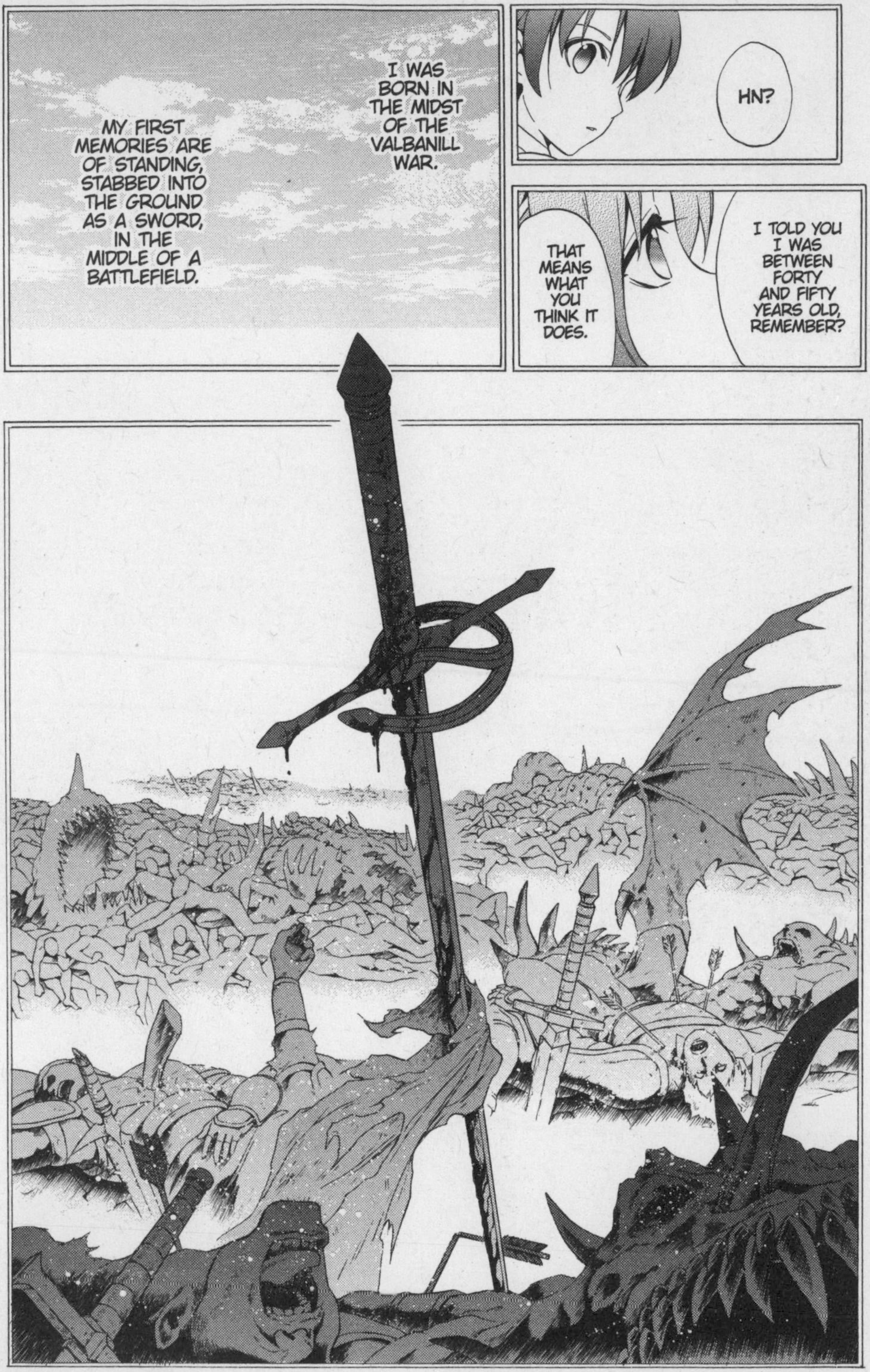
HN?
I TOLD YOU I WAS BETWEEN FORTY AND FIFTY YEARS OLD, REMEMBER?
THAT MEANS WHAT YOU THINK IT DOES.
I WAS BORN IN THE MIDST OF THE VALBANILL WAR.
MY FIRST MEMORIES ARE OF STANDING, STABBED INTO THE GROUND AS A SWORD, IN THE MIDDLE OF A BATTLEFIELD.

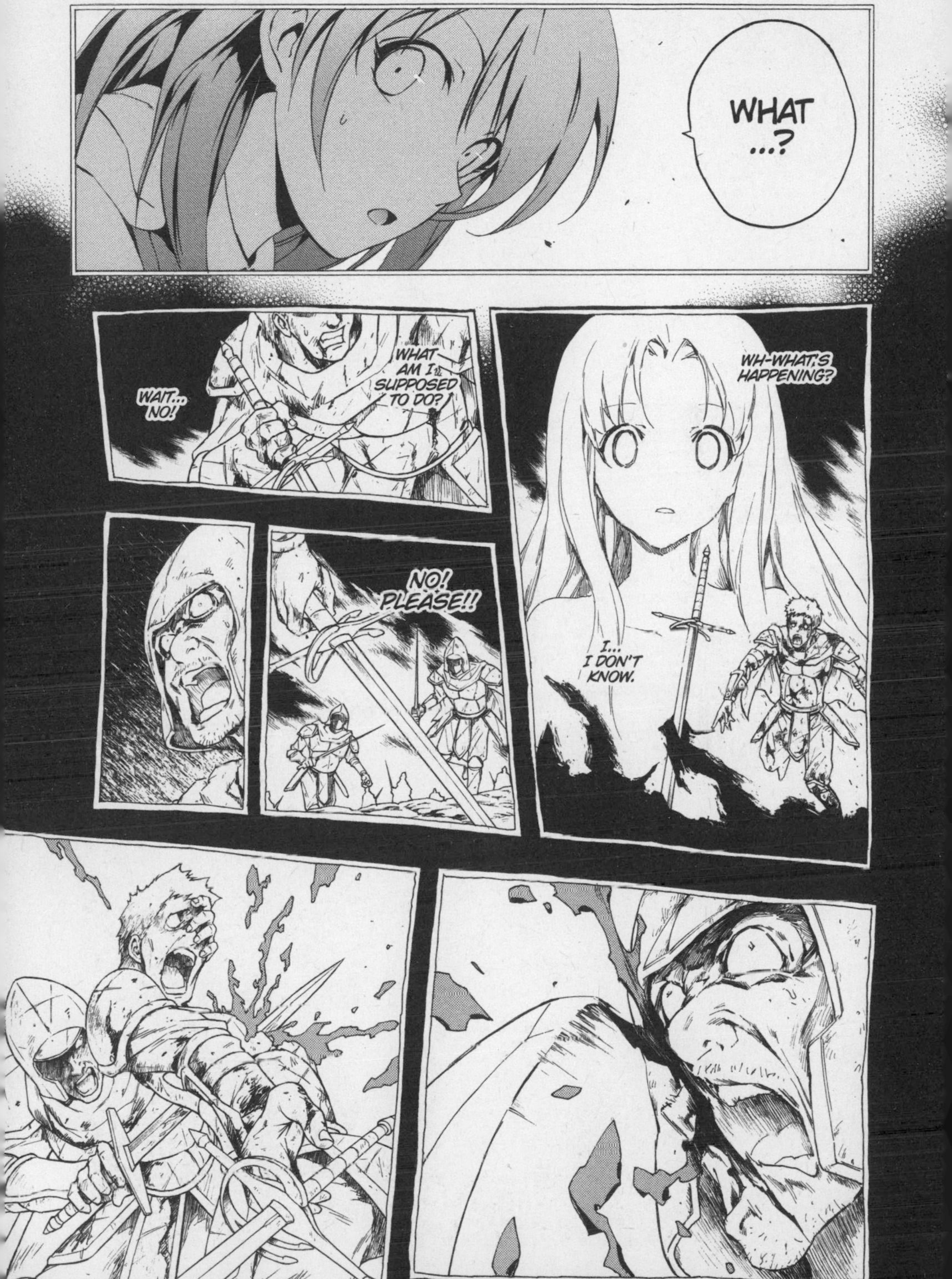
WHAT ...?
WH-WHAT'S HAPPENING?
I... I DON'T KNOW.
WHAT AM I SUPPOSED TO DO?
WAIT... NO!
NO! PLEASE!!

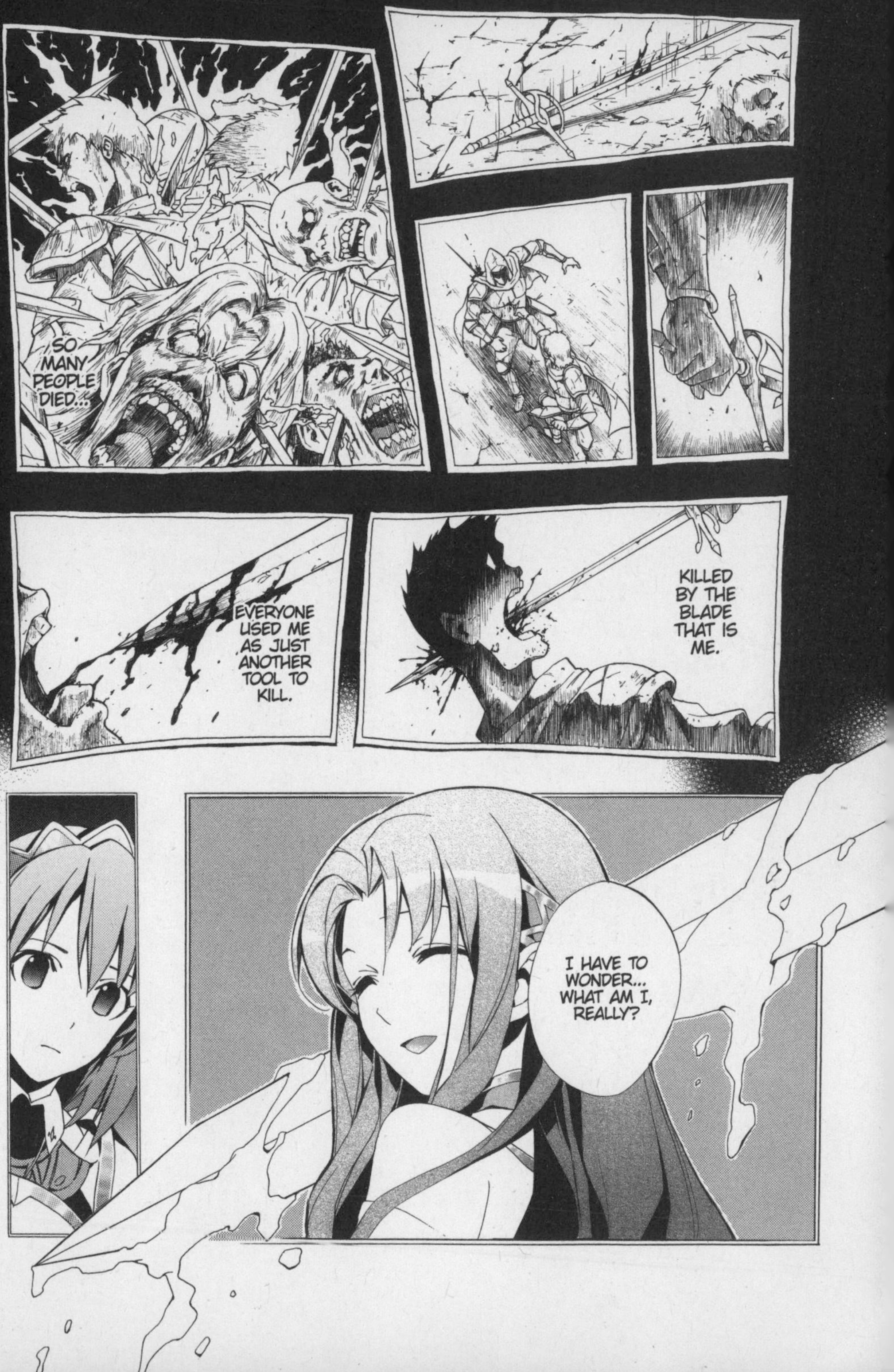
SO MANY PEOPLE DIED...
KILLED BY THE BLADE THAT IS ME.
EVERYONE USED ME AS JUST ANOTHER TOOL TO KILL.
I HAVE TO WONDER... WHAT AM I, REALLY?

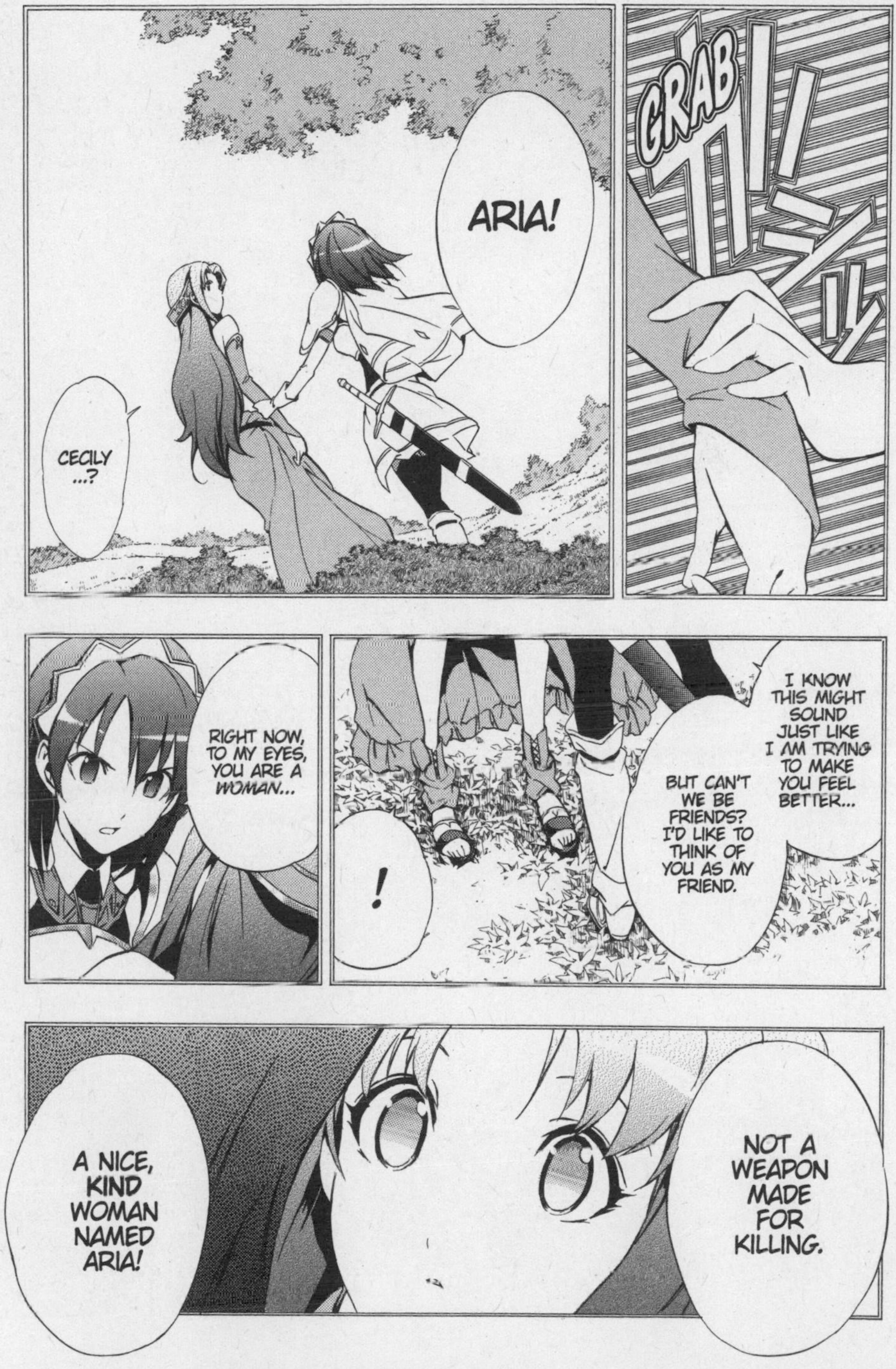
GRAB
ARIA!
CECILY ...?
I KNOW THIS MIGHT SOUND JUST LIKE I AM TRYING TO MAKE YOU FEEL BETTER...
BUT CAN'T WE BE FRIENDS? I'D LIKE TO THINK OF YOU AS MY FRIEND.
!
RIGHT NOW, TO MY EYES, YOU ARE A *WOMAN*...
NOT A WEAPON MADE FOR KILLING.
A NICE, KIND WOMAN NAMED ARIA!

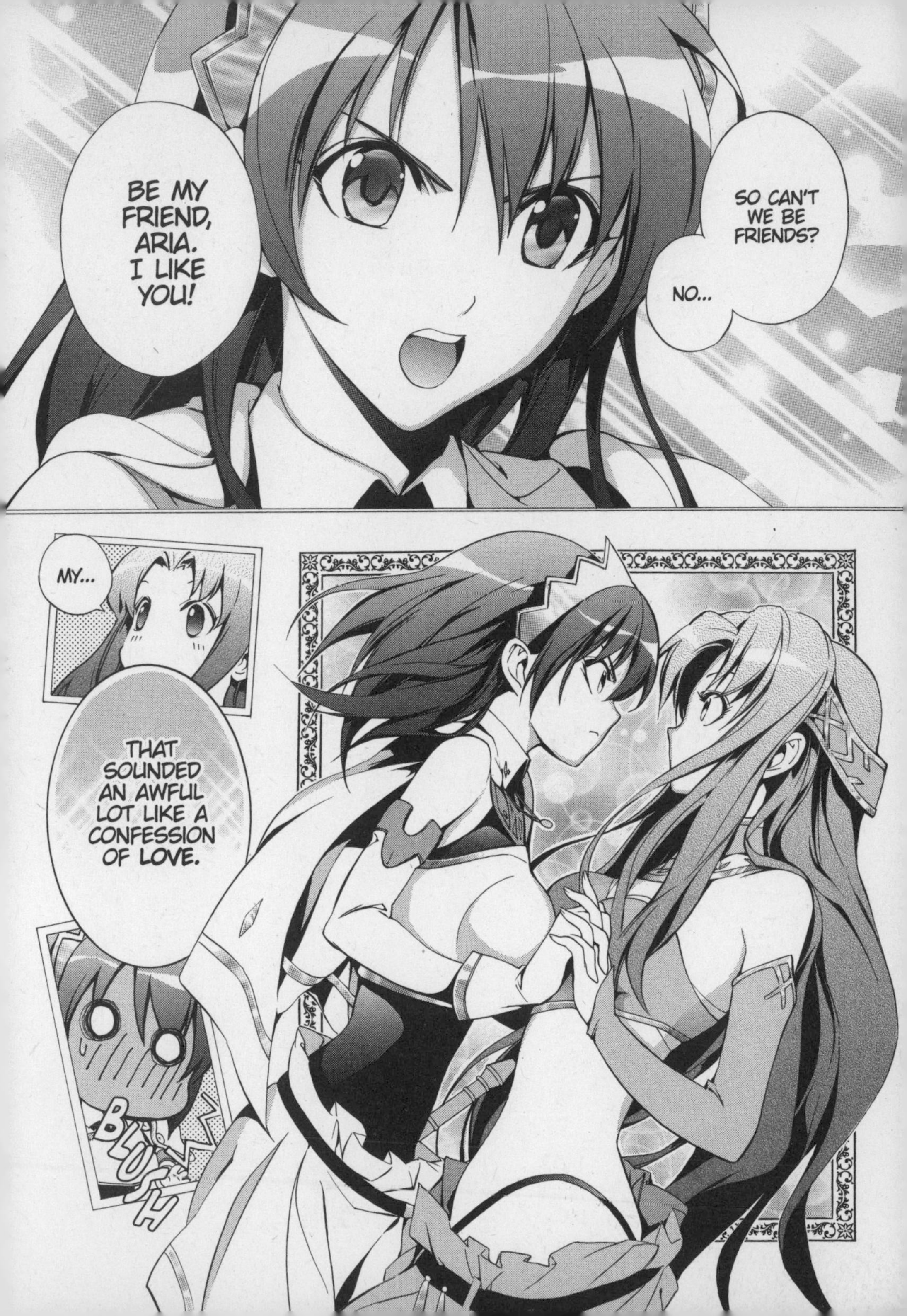
SO CAN'T WE BE FRIENDS?
NO...
BE MY FRIEND, ARIA. I LIKE YOU!
MY...
THAT SOUNDED AN AWFUL LOT LIKE A CONFESSION OF LOVE.
BLUSH

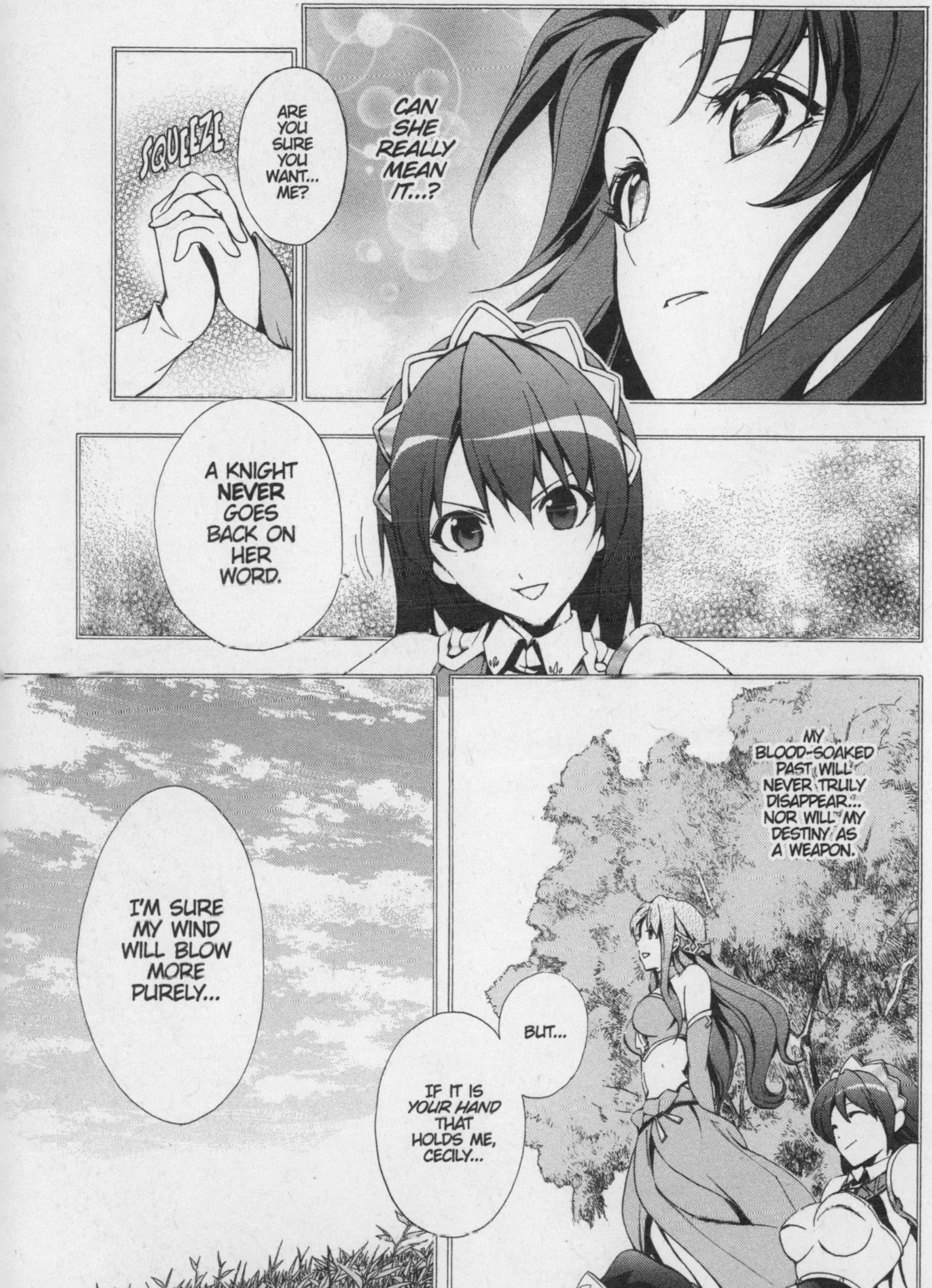
CAN SHE REALLY MEAN IT...?
SQUEEZE
ARE YOU SURE YOU WANT... ME?
A KNIGHT NEVER GOES BACK ON HER WORD.
MY BLOOD-SOAKED PAST WILL NEVER TRULY DISAPPEAR... NOR WILL MY DESTINY AS A WEAPON.
BUT...
IF IT IS YOUR HAND THAT HOLDS ME, CECILY...
I'M SURE MY WIND WILL BLOW MORE PURELY...

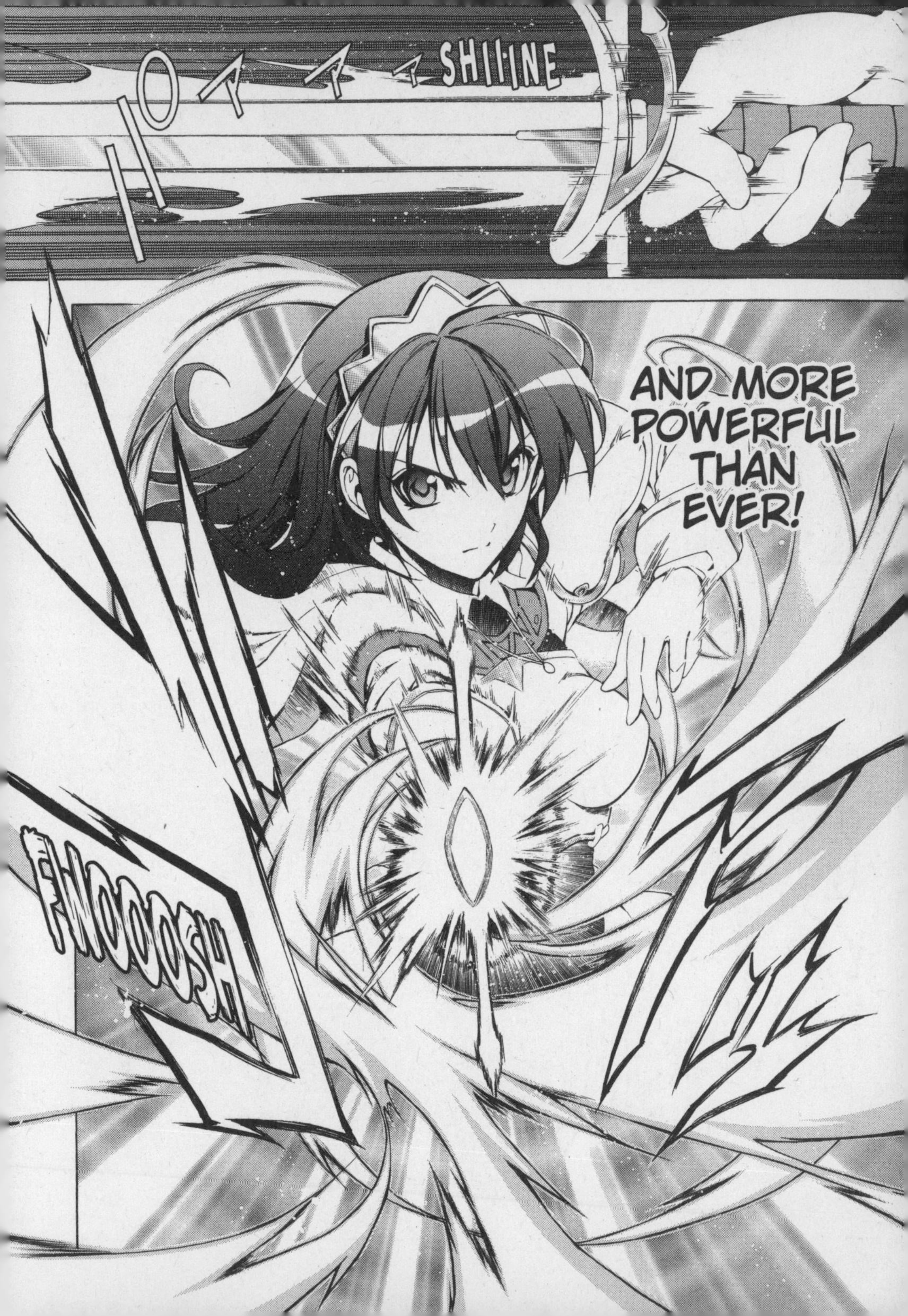
SHIIINE
AND MORE POWERFUL THAN EVER!
FWOOOSH

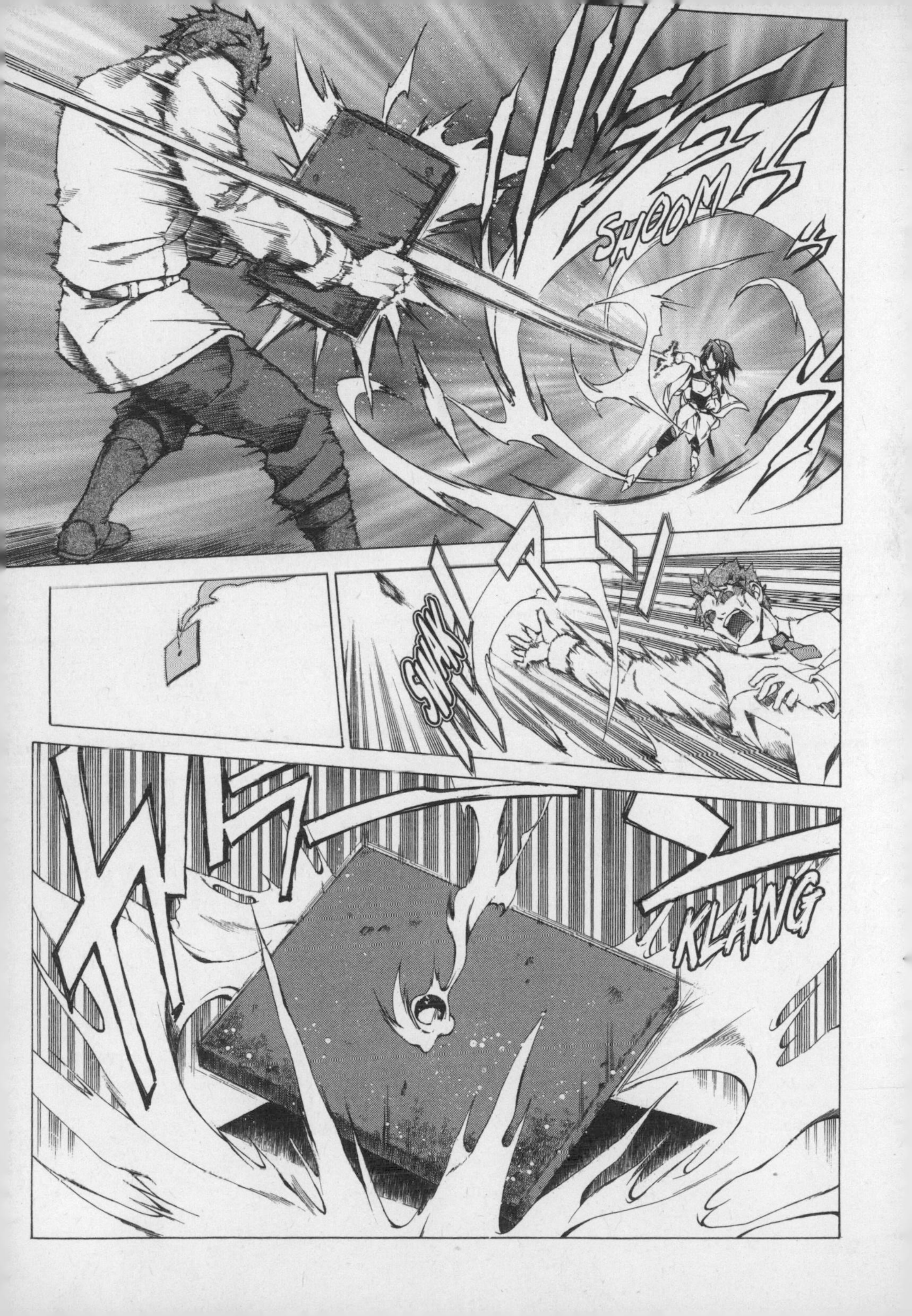
SHOOM
SWAK
KLANG

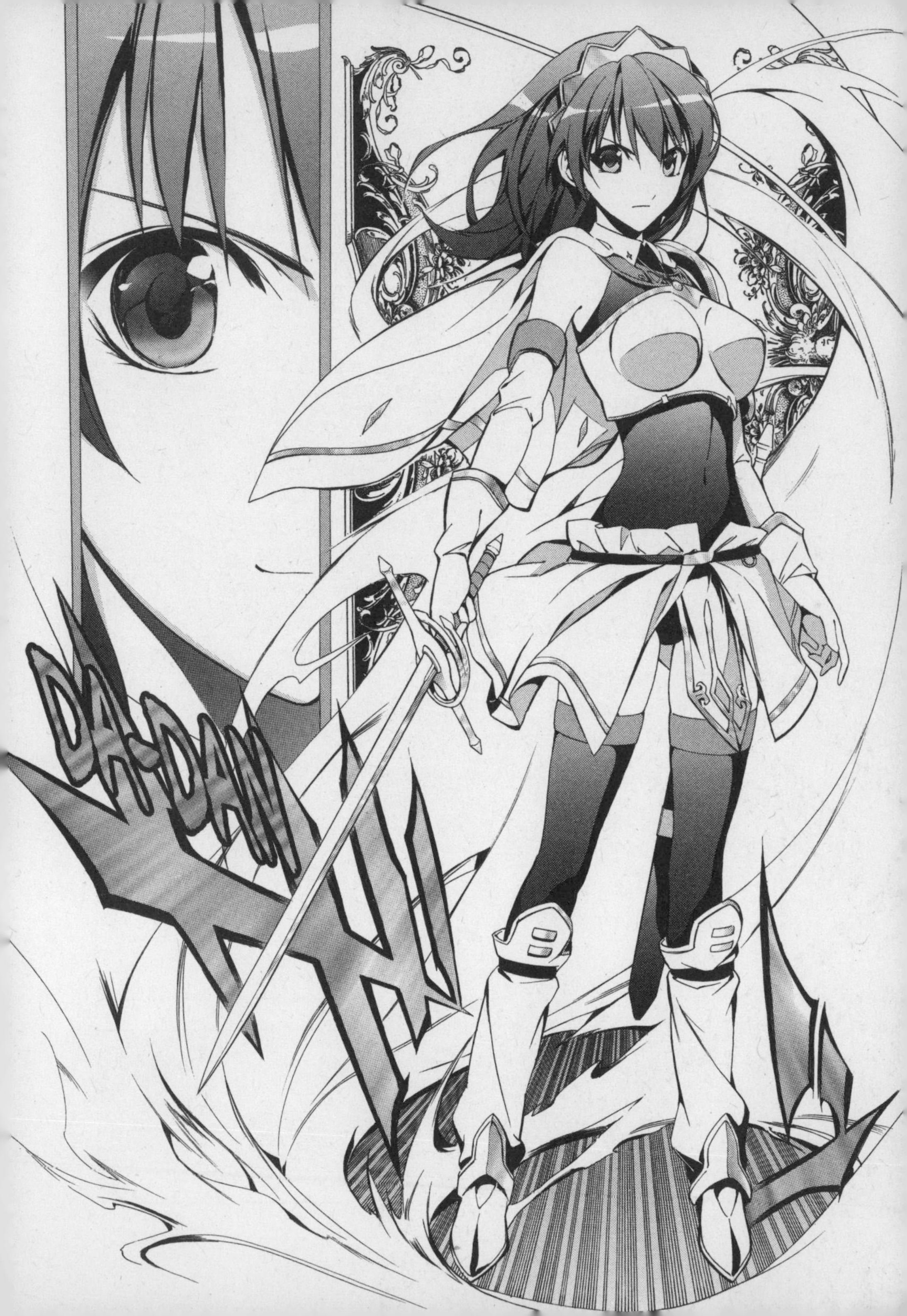
DA-DAN!!

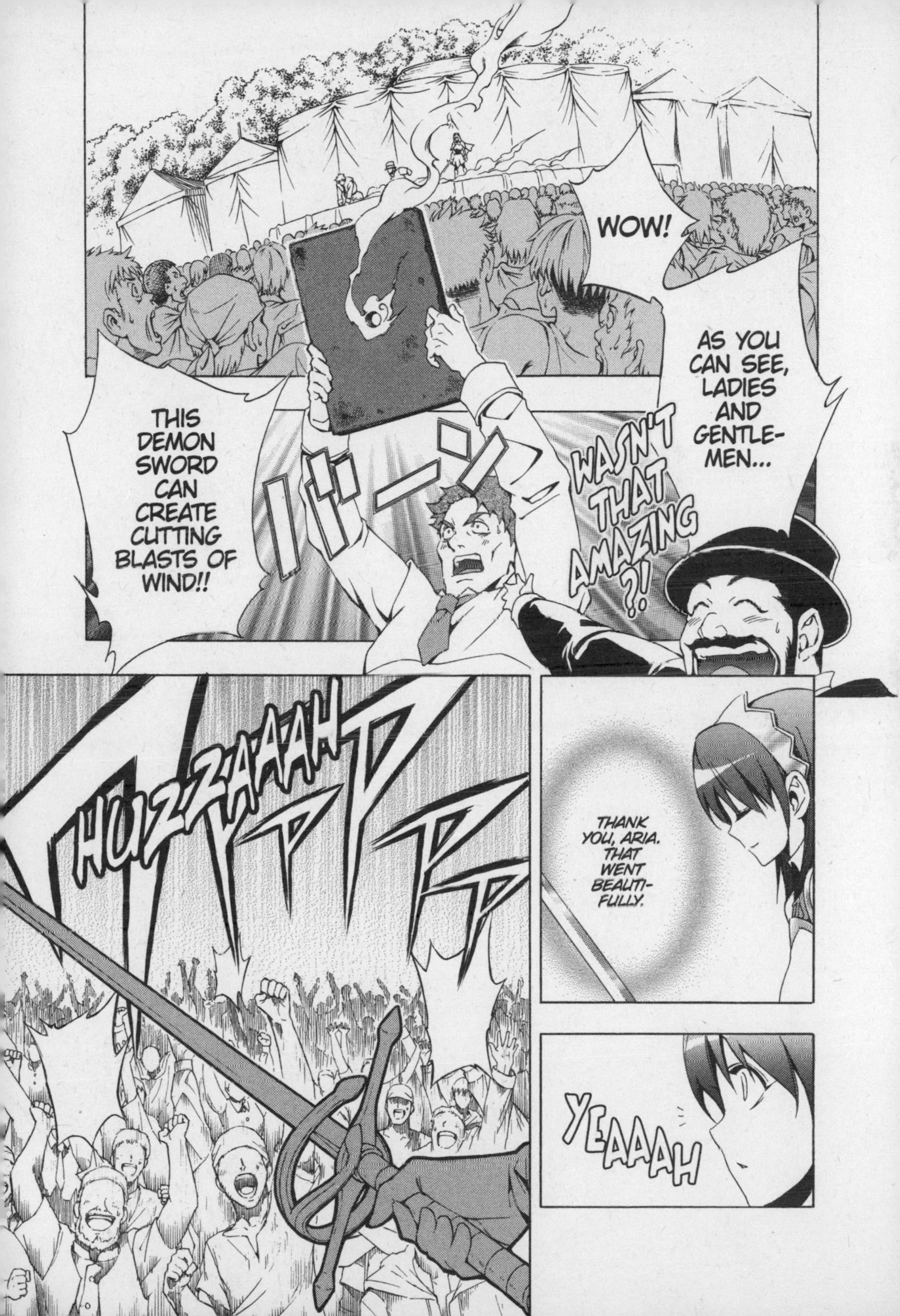
WOW!
AS YOU CAN SEE, LADIES AND GENTLEMEN...
WASN'T THAT AMAZING?!
THIS DEMON SWORD CAN CREATE CUTTING BLASTS OF WIND!!
THANK YOU, ARIA. THAT WENT BEAUTIFULLY.
YEAAAH
HUZZAAAH

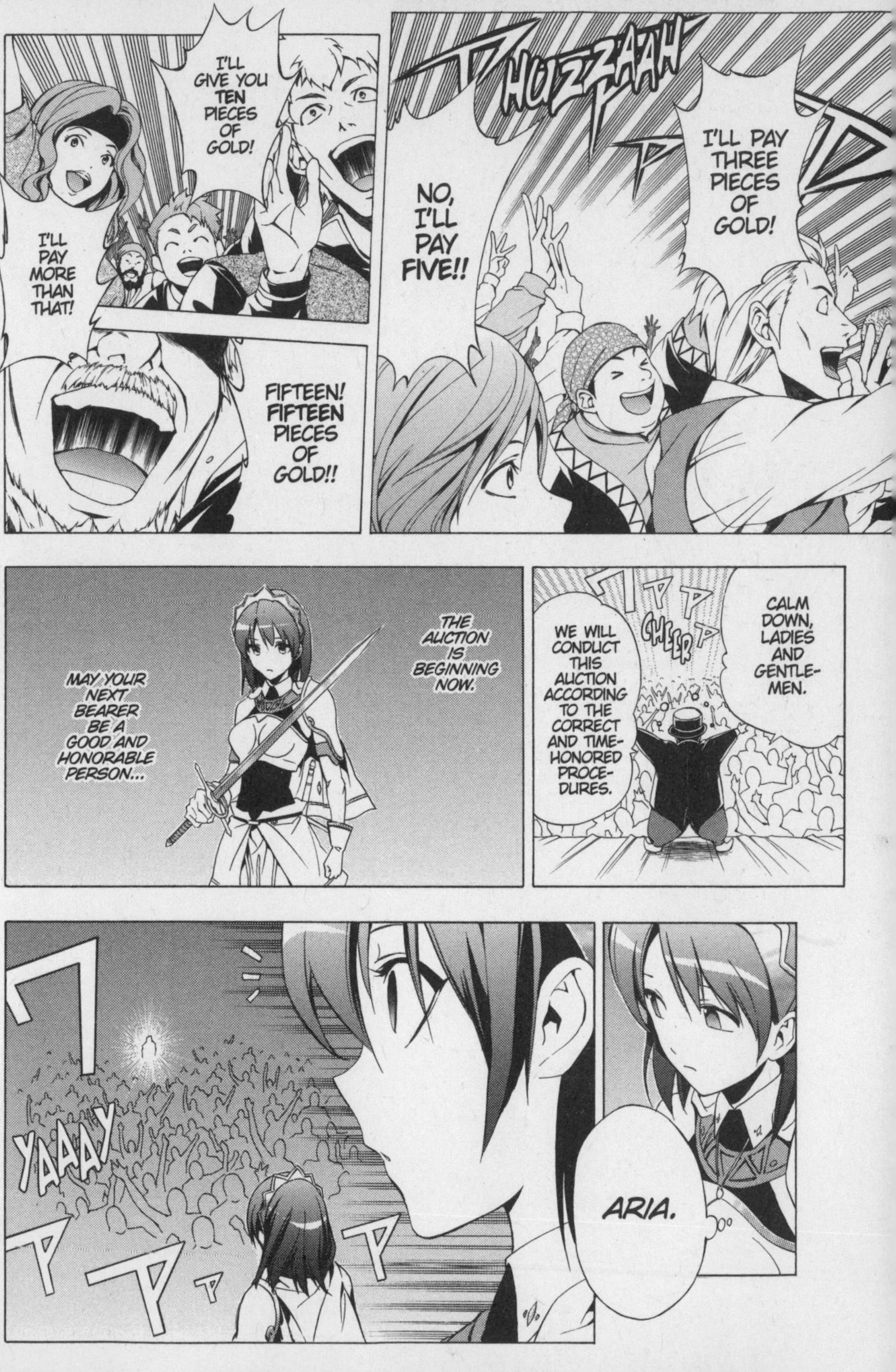
HUZZAAH
I'LL PAY THREE PIECES OF GOLD!
NO, I'LL PAY FIVE!!
I'LL GIVE YOU TEN PIECES OF GOLD!
I'LL PAY MORE THAN THAT!
FIFTEEN! FIFTEEN PIECES OF GOLD!!
CALM DOWN, LADIES AND GENTLE-MEN.
CHEER
WE WILL CONDUCT THIS AUCTION ACCORDING TO THE CORRECT AND TIME-HONORED PROCE-DURES.
THE AUCTION IS BEGINNING NOW.
MAY YOUR NEXT BEARER BE A GOOD AND HONORABLE PERSON...
ARIA.
YAAAY

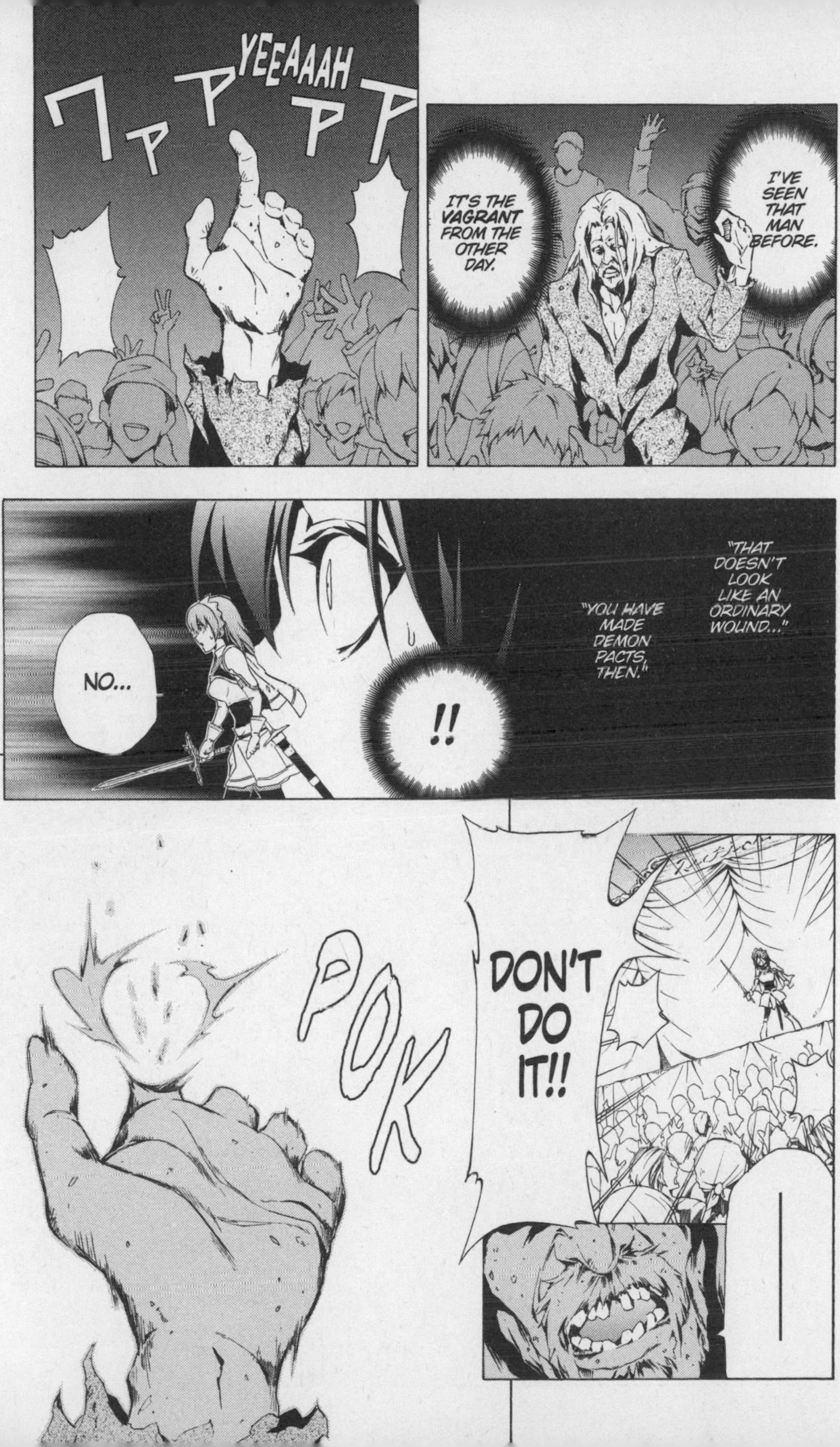
I'VE SEEN THAT MAN BEFORE.
IT'S THE VAGRANT FROM THE OTHER DAY.
YEEAAAH
"THAT DOESN'T LOOK LIKE AN ORDINARY WOUND..."
"YOU HAVE MADE DEMON PACTS, THEN."
!!
NO...
DON'T DO IT!!
POK

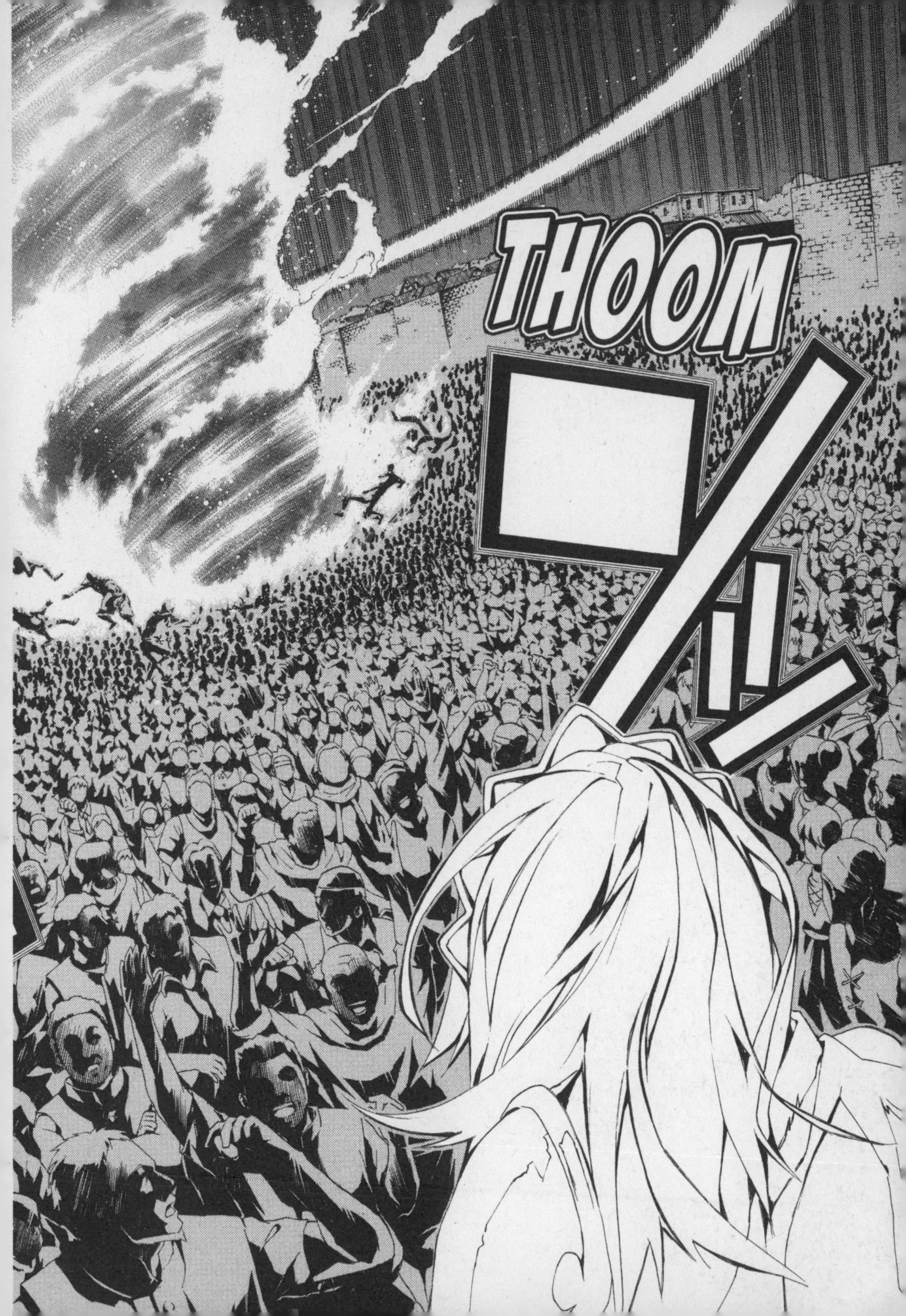
THOOM

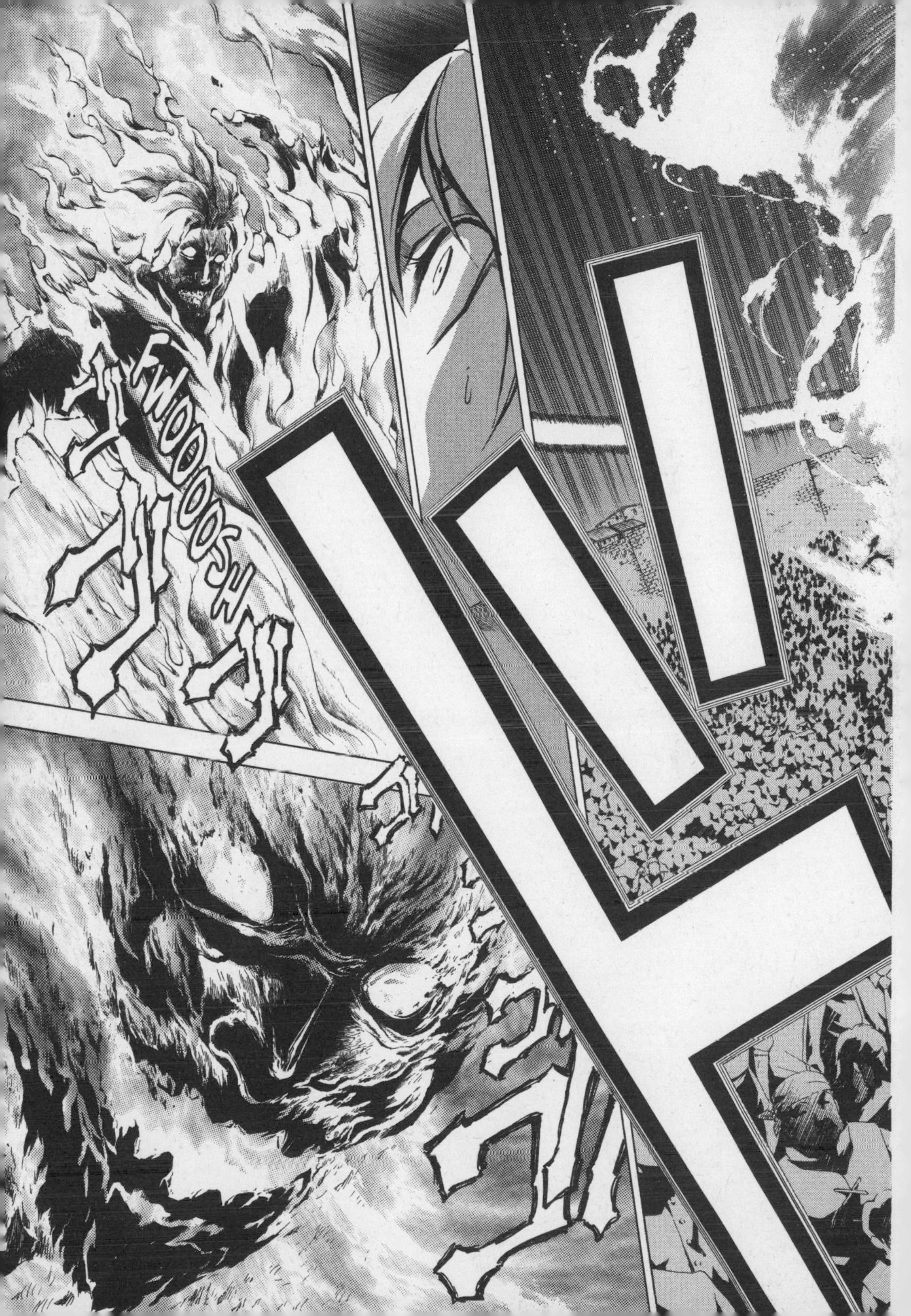
FWOOOOOSH

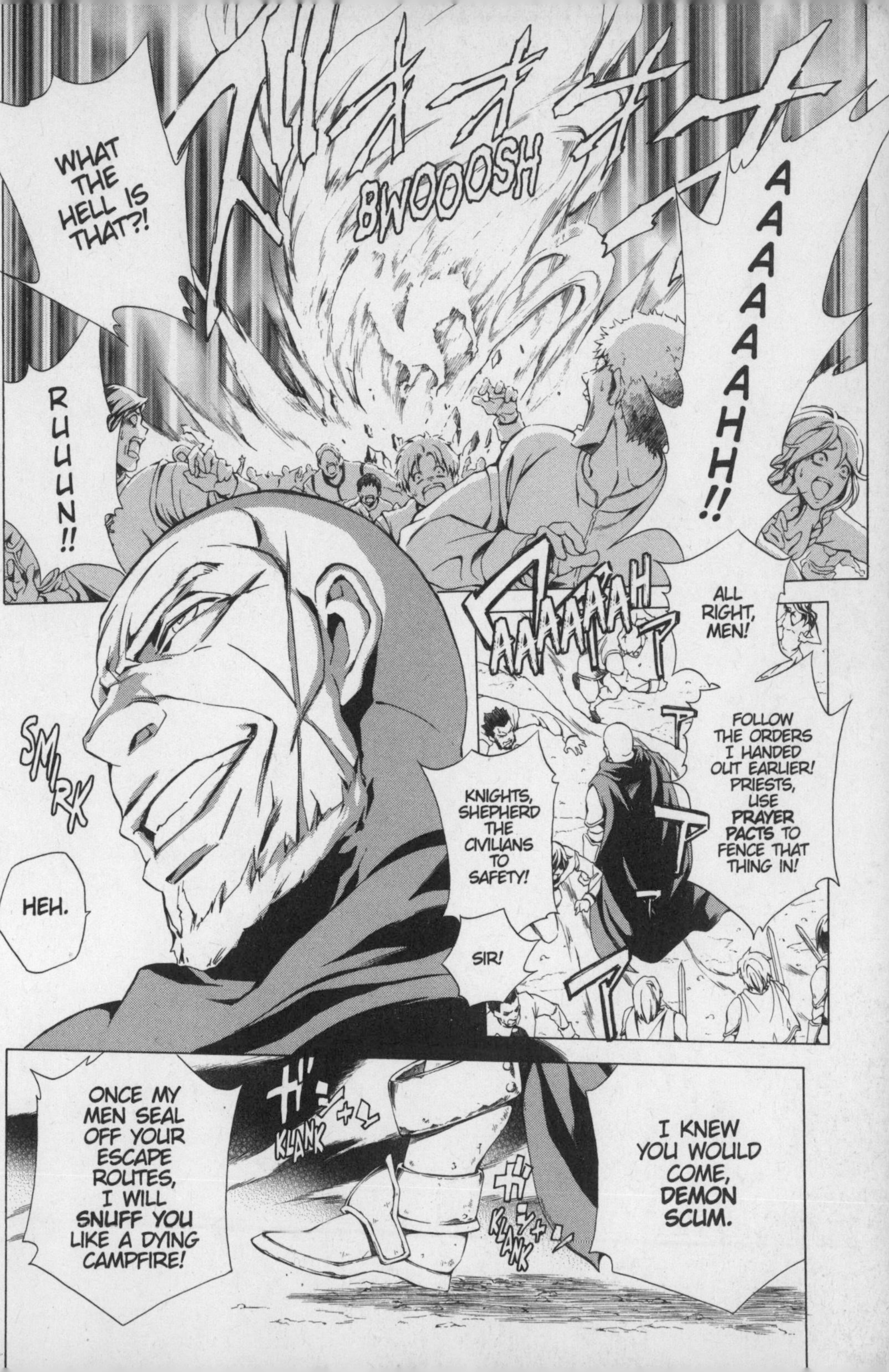
AAAAAAAAHH!!
BWOOOSH
WHAT THE HELL IS THAT?!
RUUUUN!!
AAAAAAAH
ALL RIGHT, MEN!
FOLLOW THE ORDERS I HANDED OUT EARLIER! PRIESTS, USE PRAYER PACTS TO FENCE THAT THING IN!
KNIGHTS, SHEPHERD THE CIVILIANS TO SAFETY!
SIR!
SMIRK
HEH.
I KNEW YOU WOULD COME, DEMON SCUM.
KLANK
KLANK
ONCE MY MEN SEAL OFF YOUR ESCAPE ROUTES, I WILL SNUFF YOU LIKE A DYING CAMPFIRE!

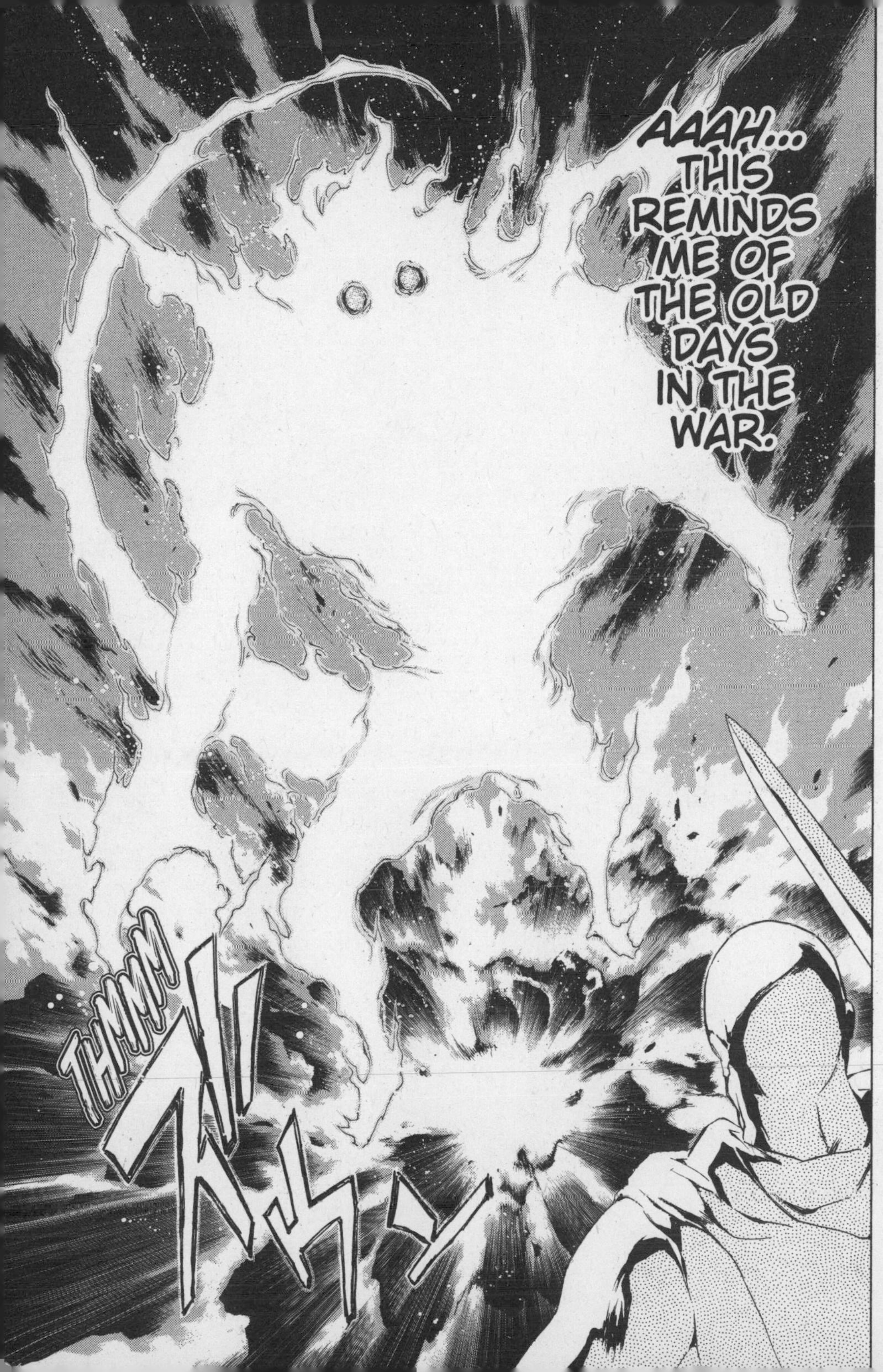
AAAH... THIS REMINDS ME OF THE OLD DAYS IN THE WAR.
THMMM

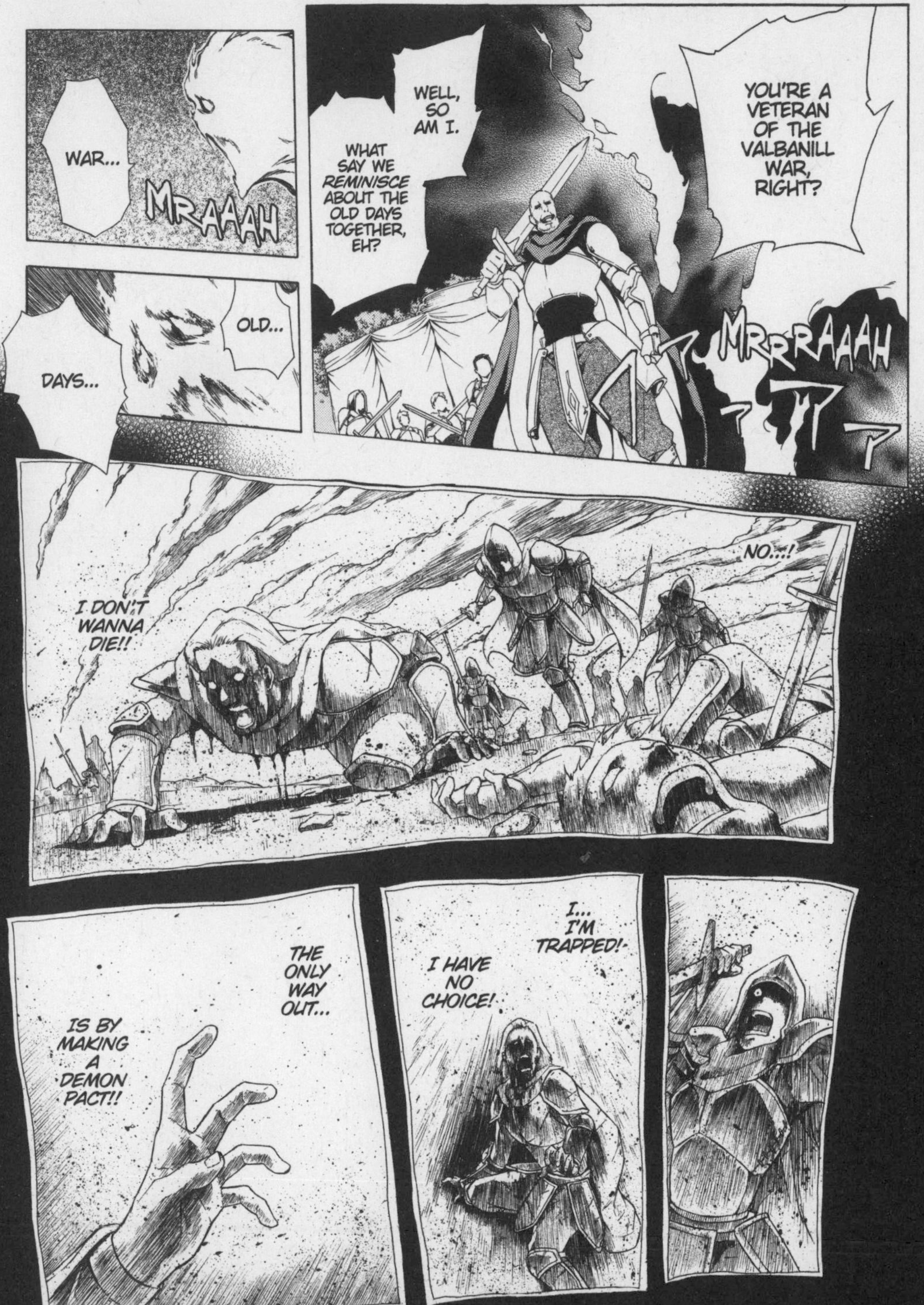
YOU'RE A VETERAN OF THE VALBANILL WAR, RIGHT?
WELL, SO AM I.
WHAT SAY WE REMINISCE ABOUT THE OLD DAYS TOGETHER, EH?
MRRRAAAH
WAR...
MRAAAH
OLD...
DAYS...
NO...!
I DON'T WANNA DIE!!
I... I'M TRAPPED!
I HAVE NO CHOICE!
THE ONLY WAY OUT...
IS BY MAKING A DEMON PACT!!

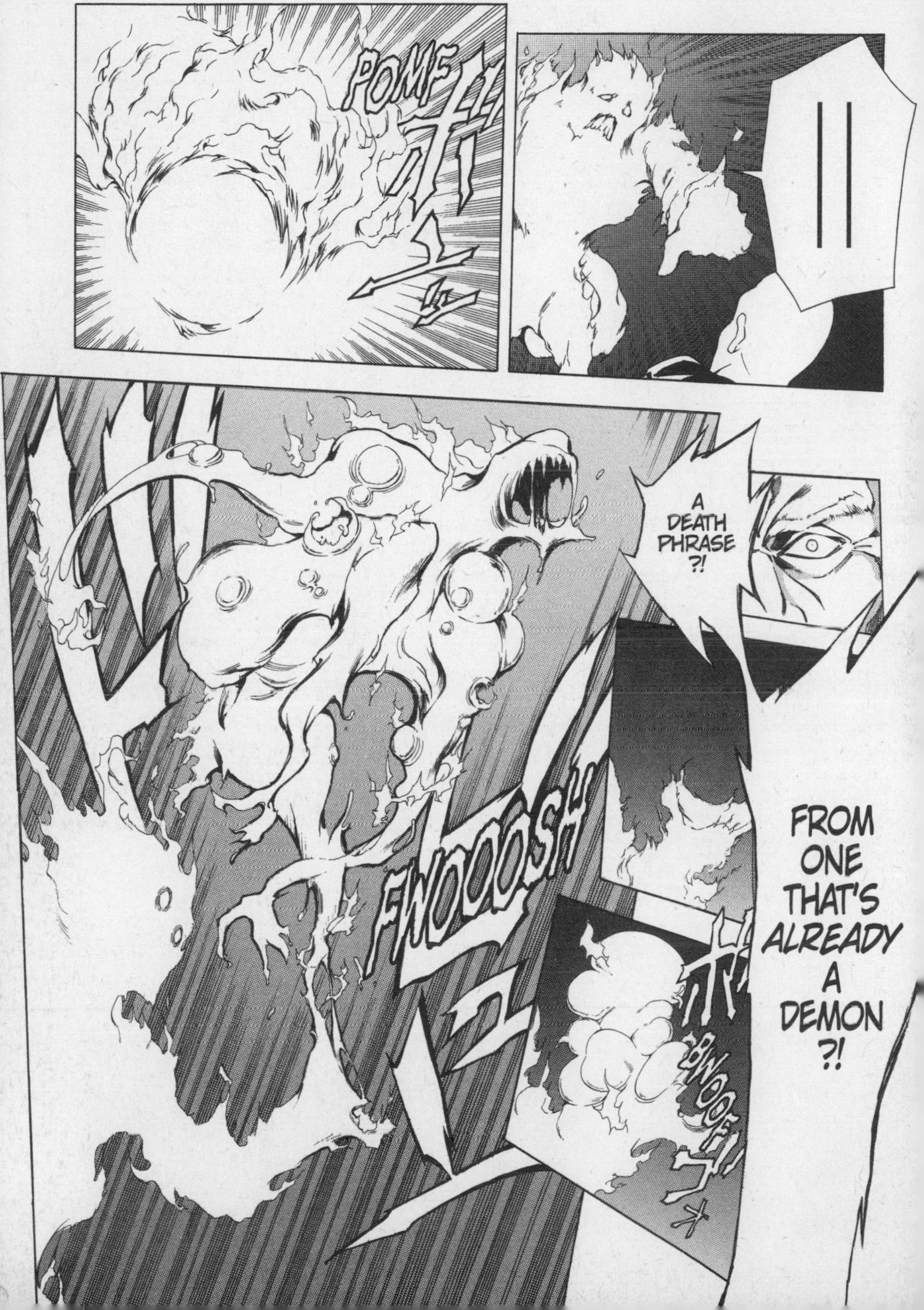

POMF
A DEATH PHRASE ?!
FROM ONE THAT'S ALREADY A DEMON ?!
BWOOF!!
FWOOOSH

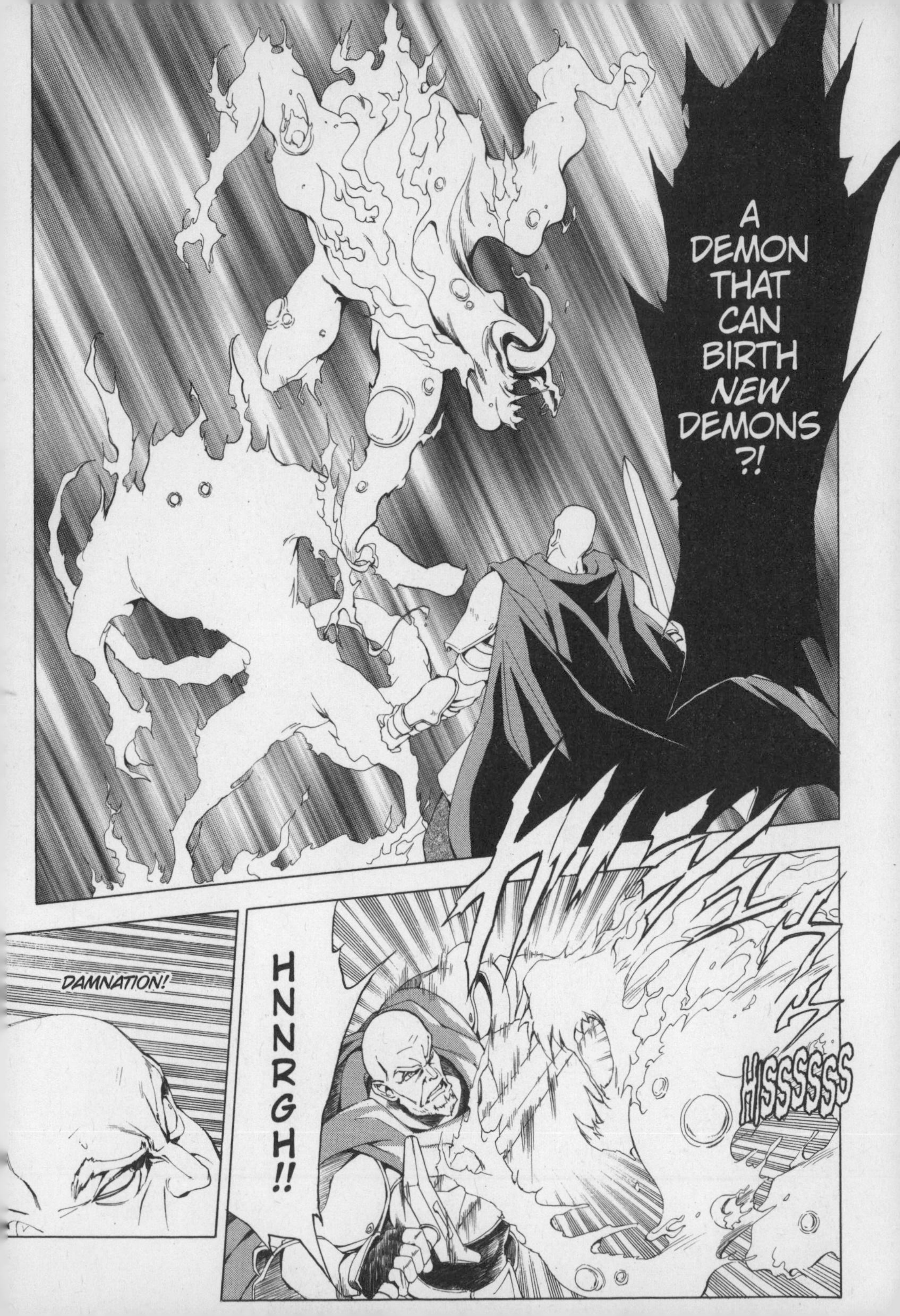
A DEMON THAT CAN BIRTH NEW DEMONS ?!
HISSSSSS
HNNRGH!!
DAMNATION!

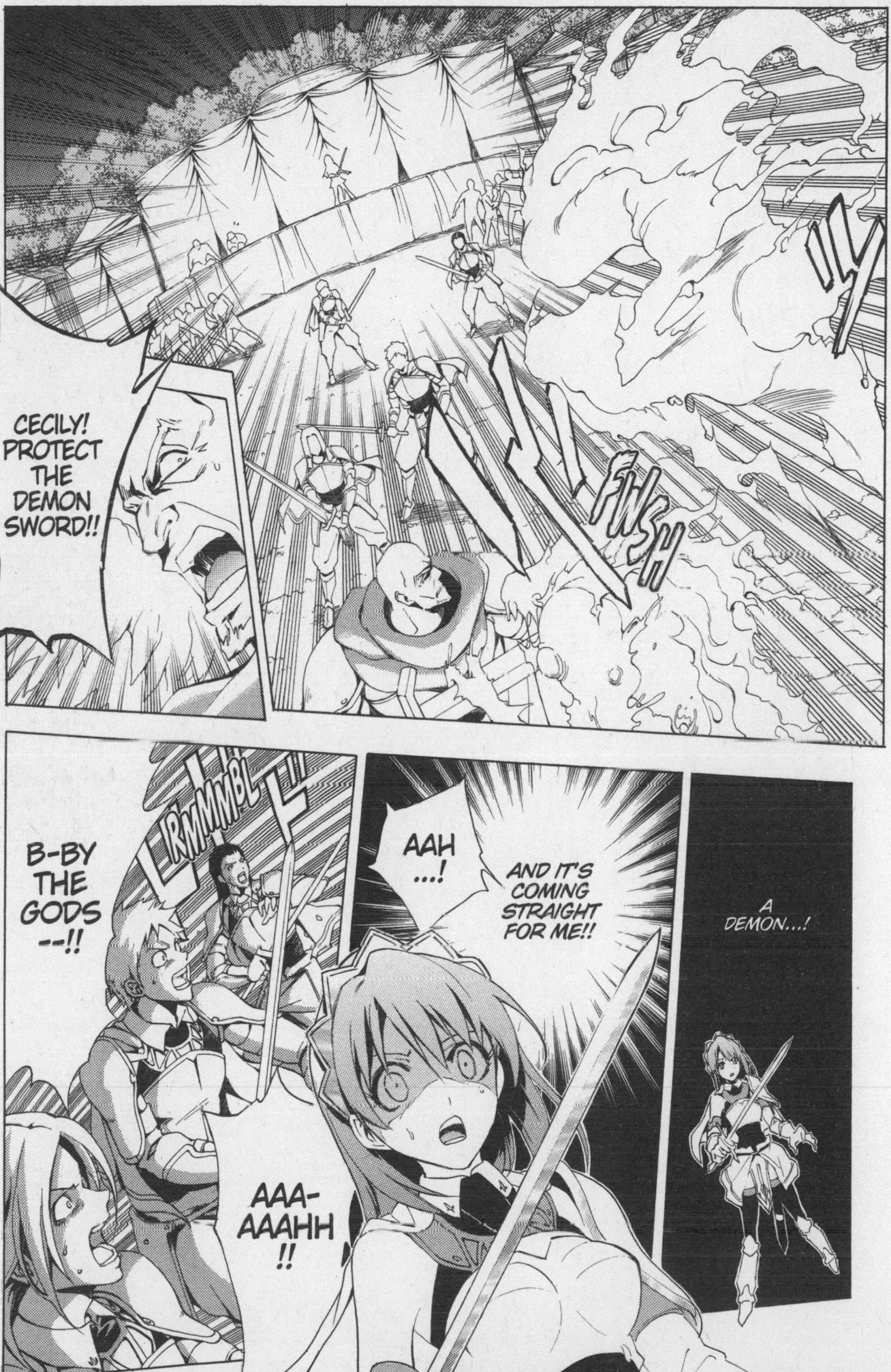

FWSH
CECILY! PROTECT THE DEMON SWORD!!
A DEMON...!
AAH ...!
AND IT'S COMING STRAIGHT FOR ME!!
RMMMBL
B-BY THE GODS --!!
AAA-AAAHH !!

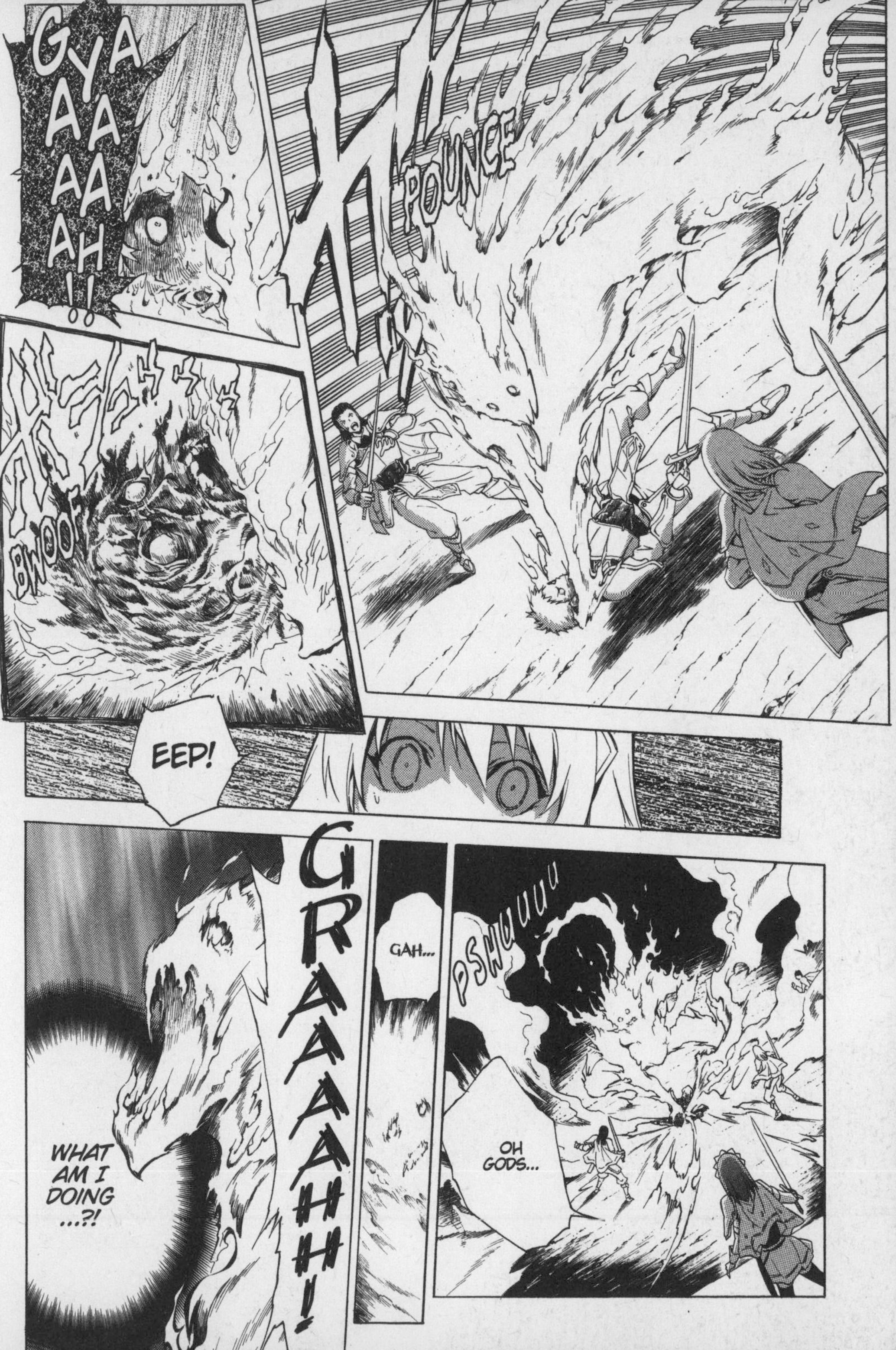
POUNCE
GYAAAAAH!!
BWOOF
EEP!
PSHUUUU
GAH...
OH GODS...
GRAAAAAH!
WHAT AM I DOING ...?!

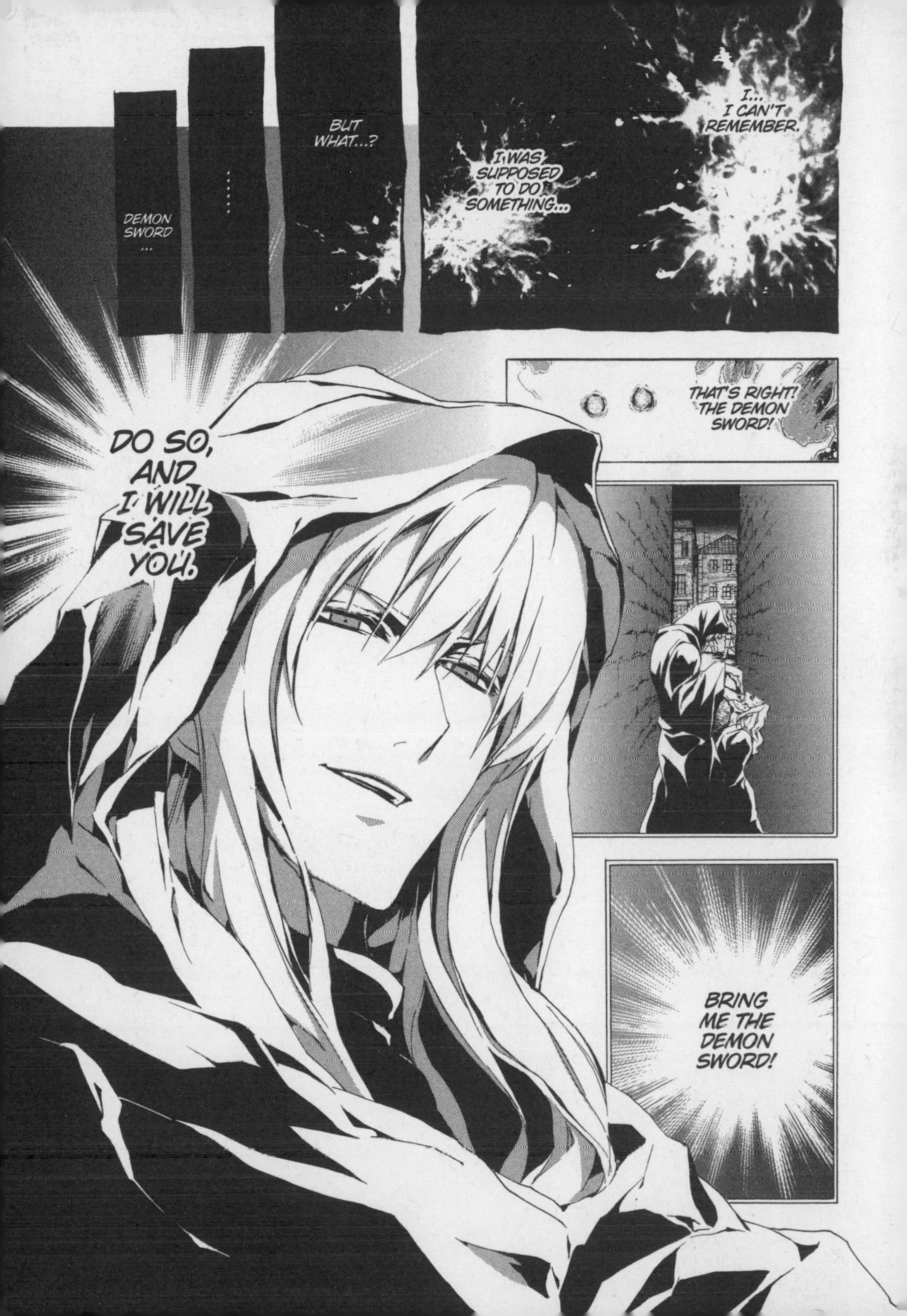
I... I CAN'T REMEMBER.
I WAS SUPPOSED TO DO SOMETHING...
BUT WHAT...?
......
DEMON SWORD ...
THAT'S RIGHT! THE DEMON SWORD!
BRING ME THE DEMON SWORD!
DO SO, AND I WILL SAVE YOU.

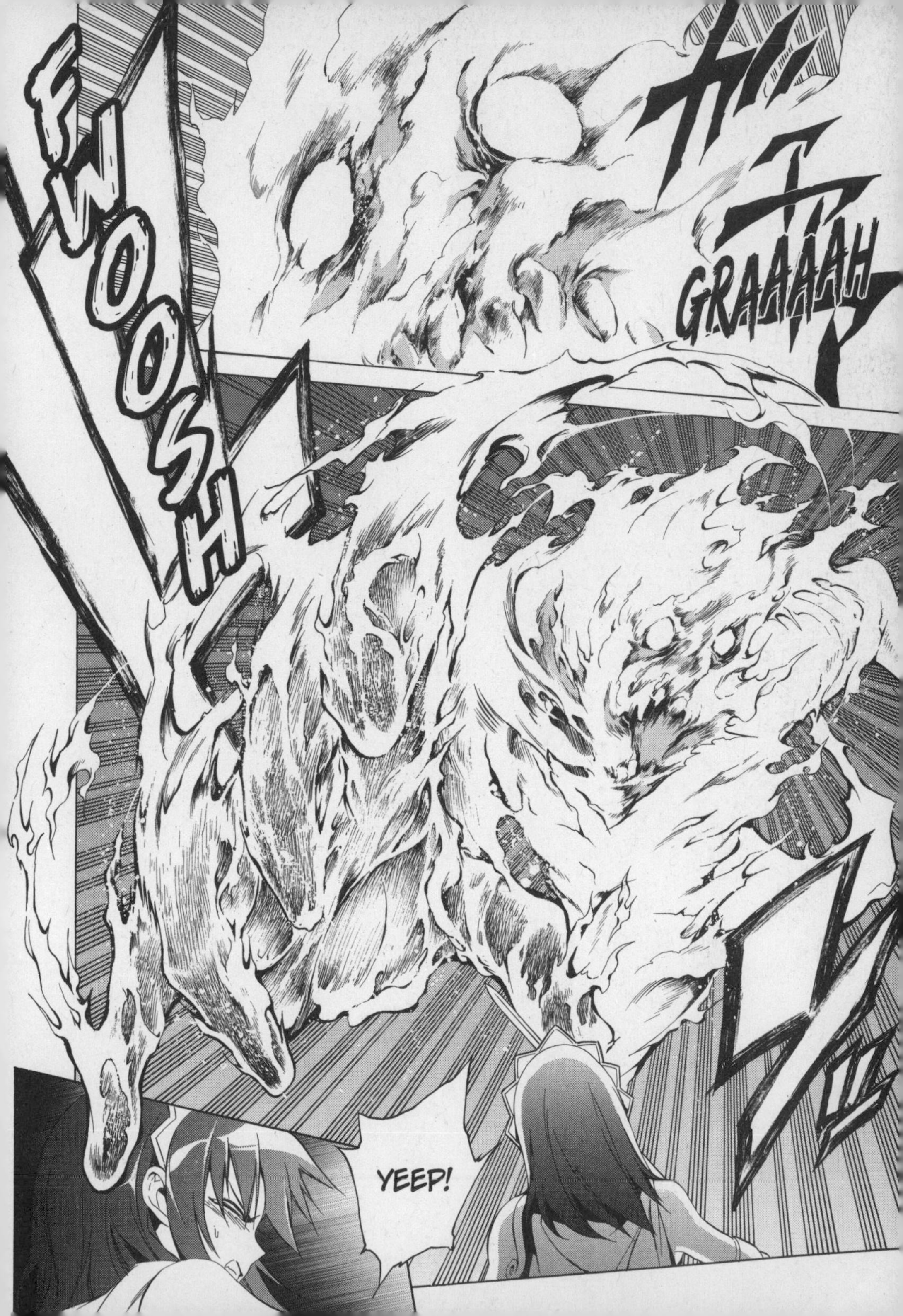
GRAAAAH
FWOOSH
YEEP!

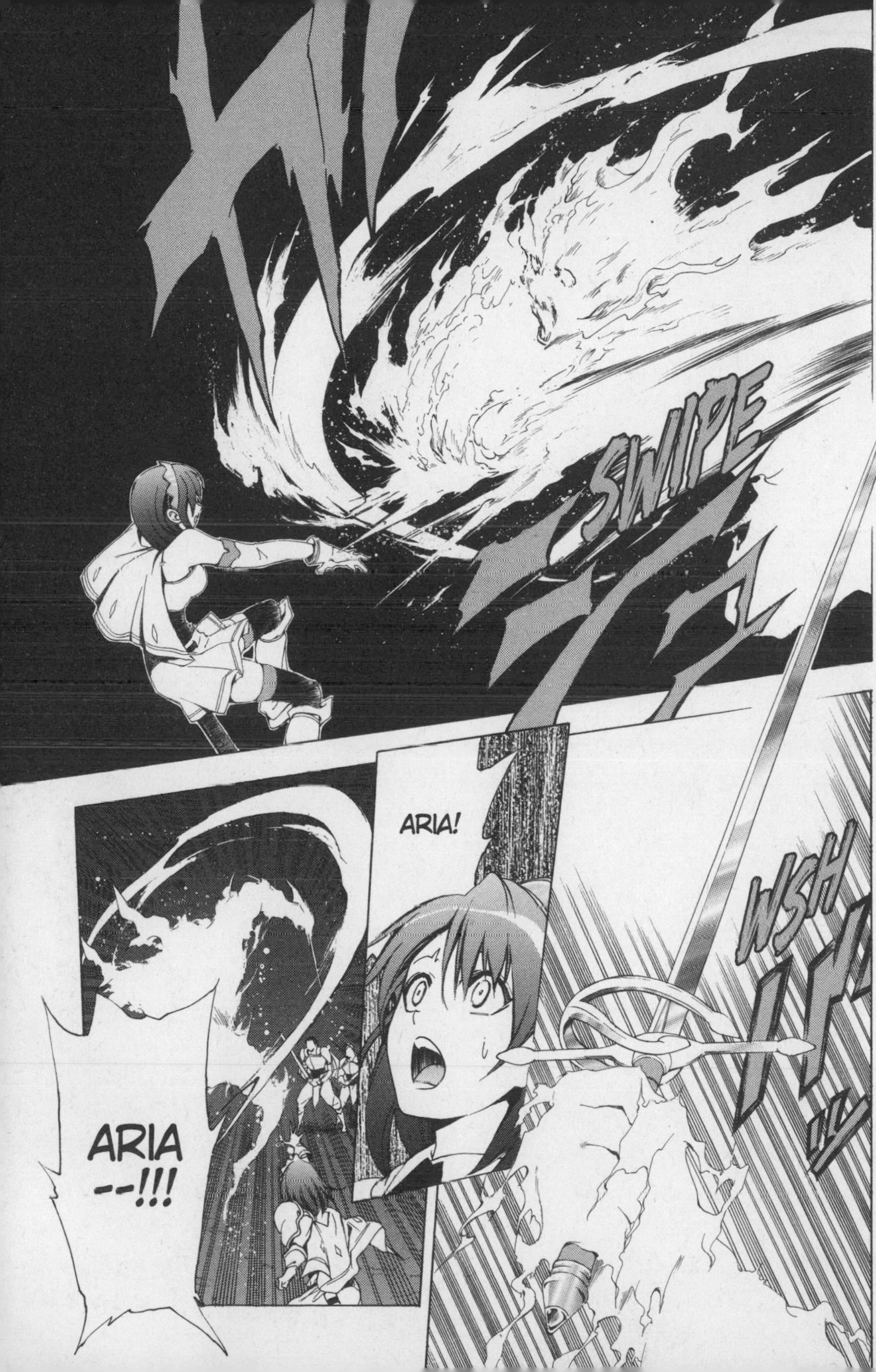
SWIPE
ARIA!
WSH
ARIA --!!!

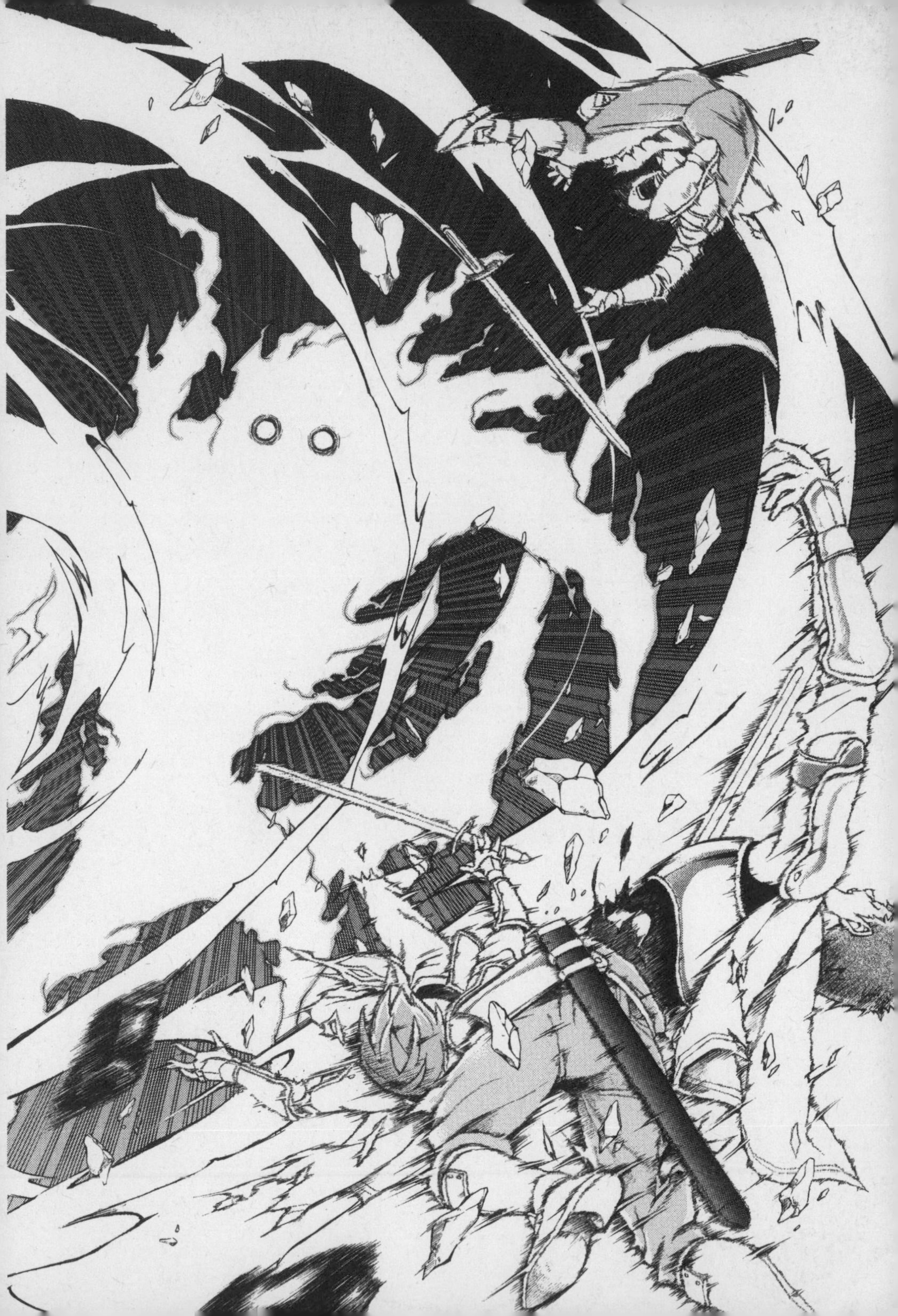

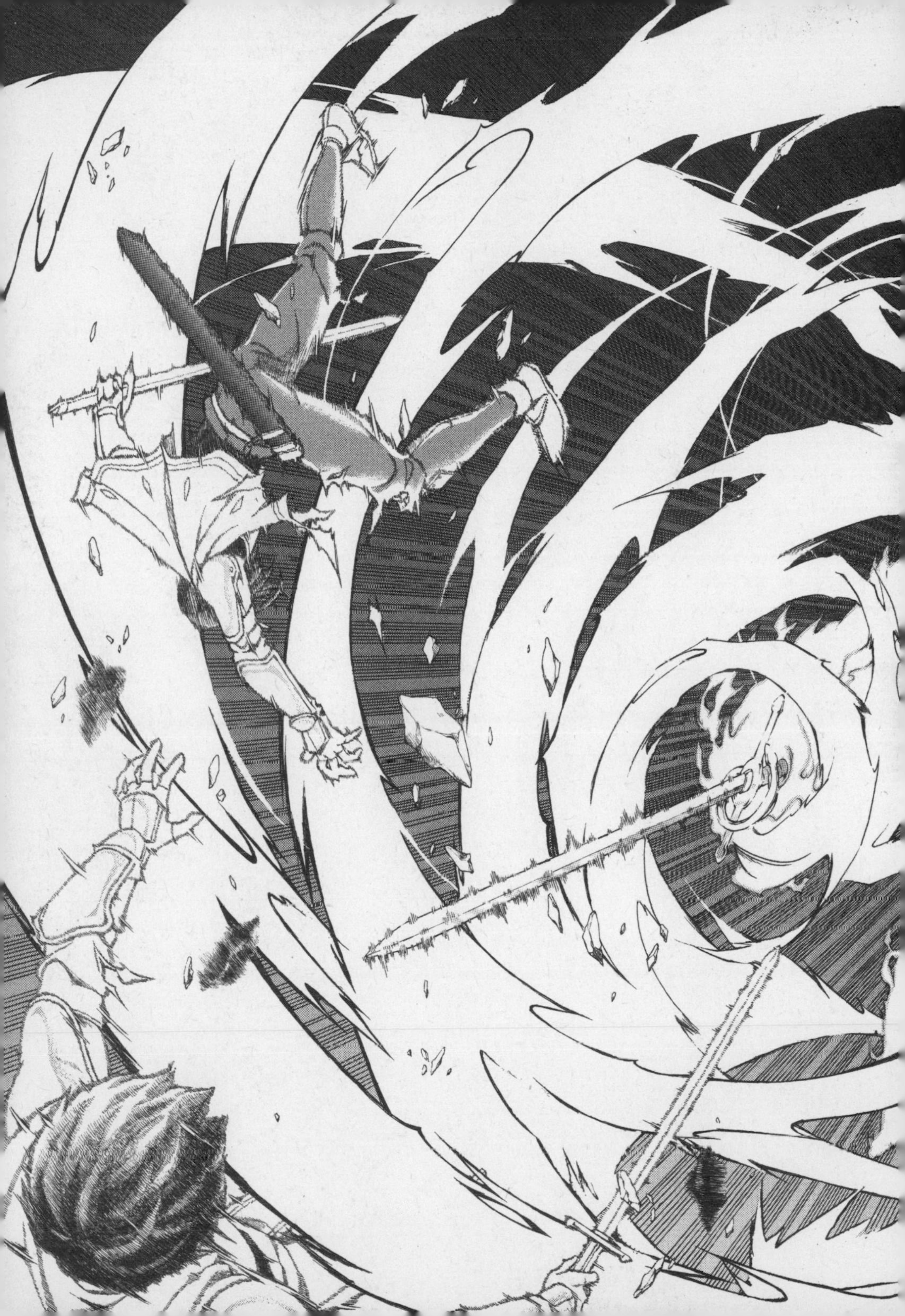

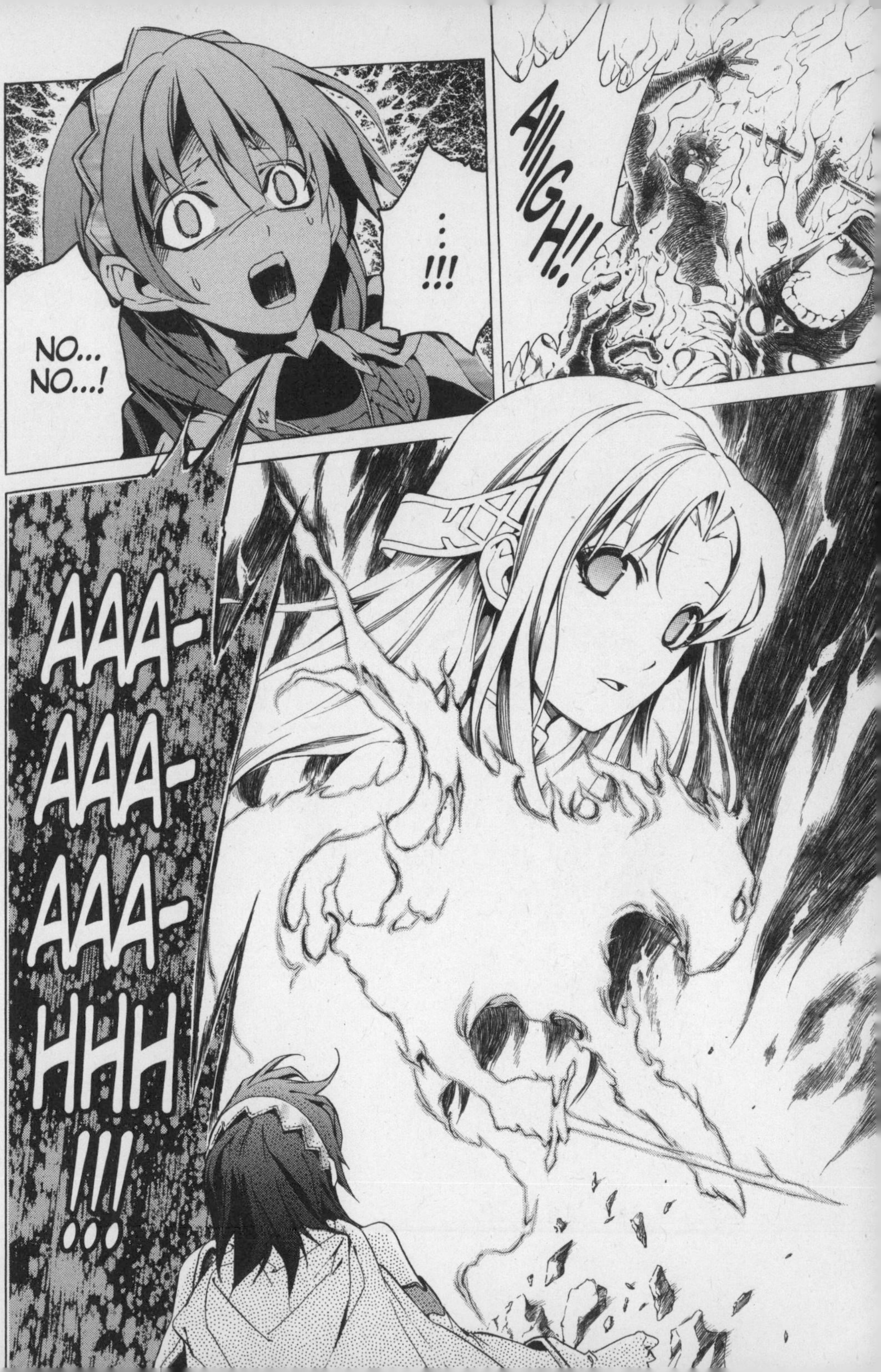
AIIGH!!
...!!!
NO... NO...!
AAA-AAA-AAA-HHH!!!

✳ *Aria* ✳

The Sacred Blacksmith

聖剣の刀鍛冶

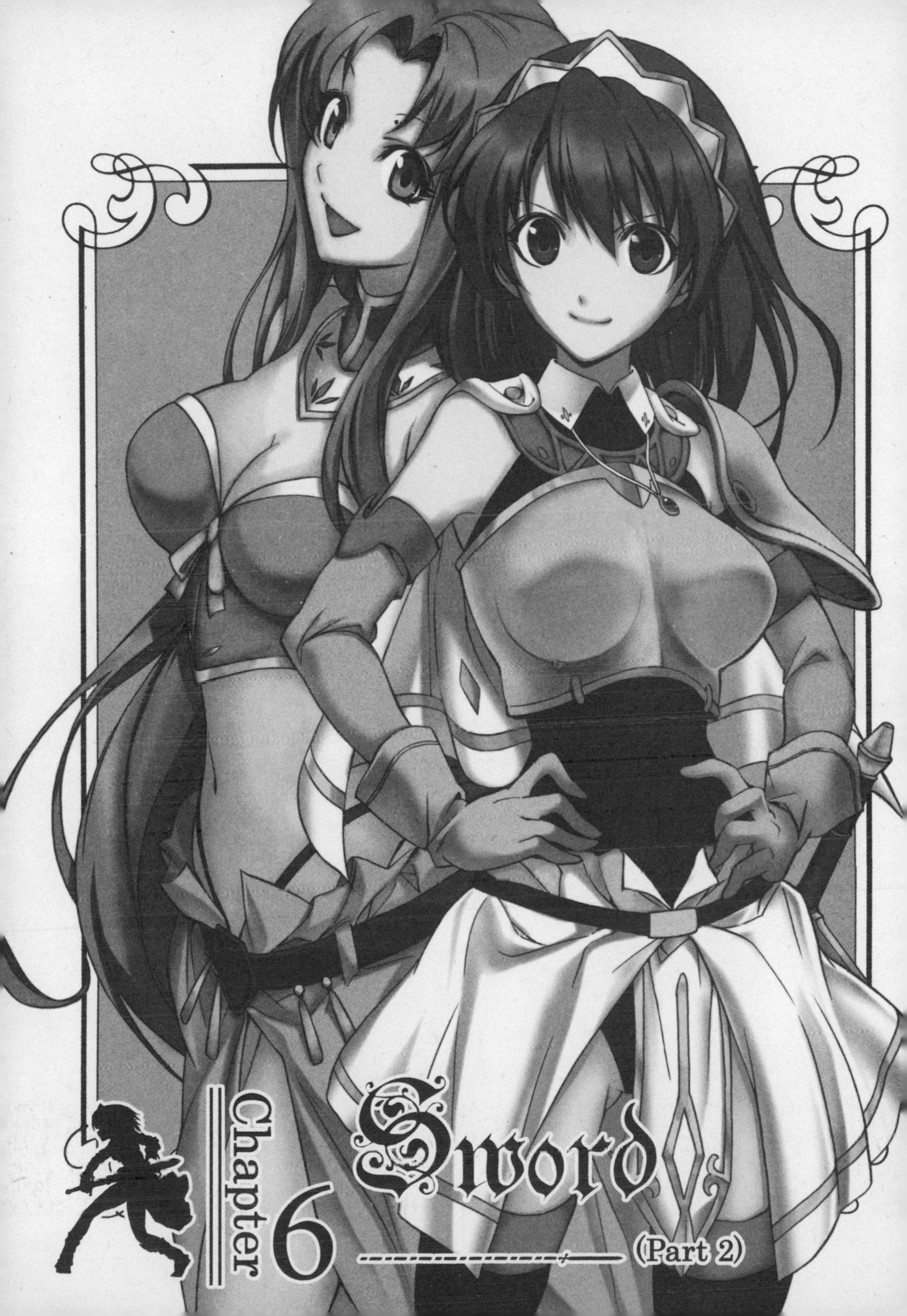

Chapter 6 Sword (Part 2)

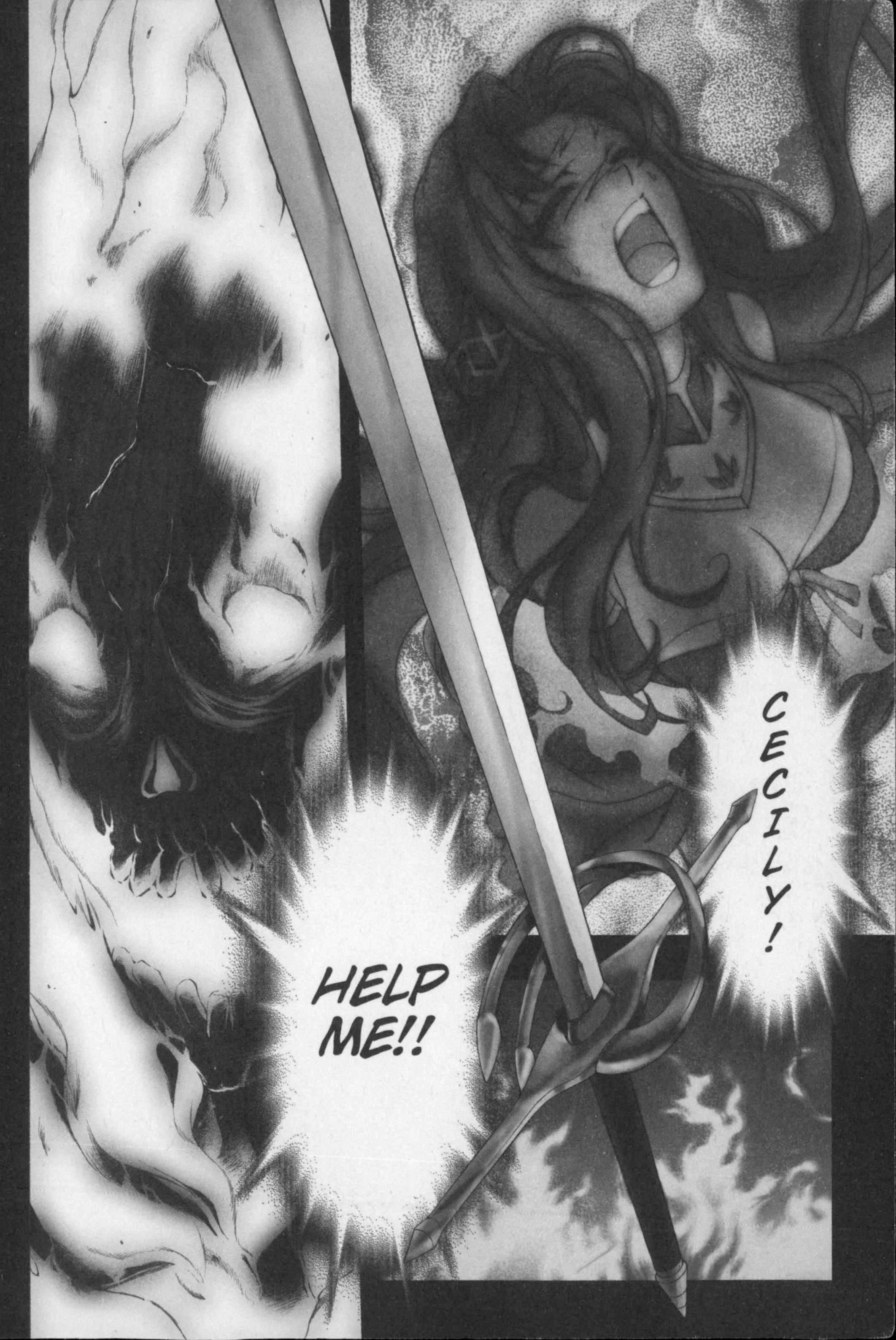
CECILY!
HELP ME!!

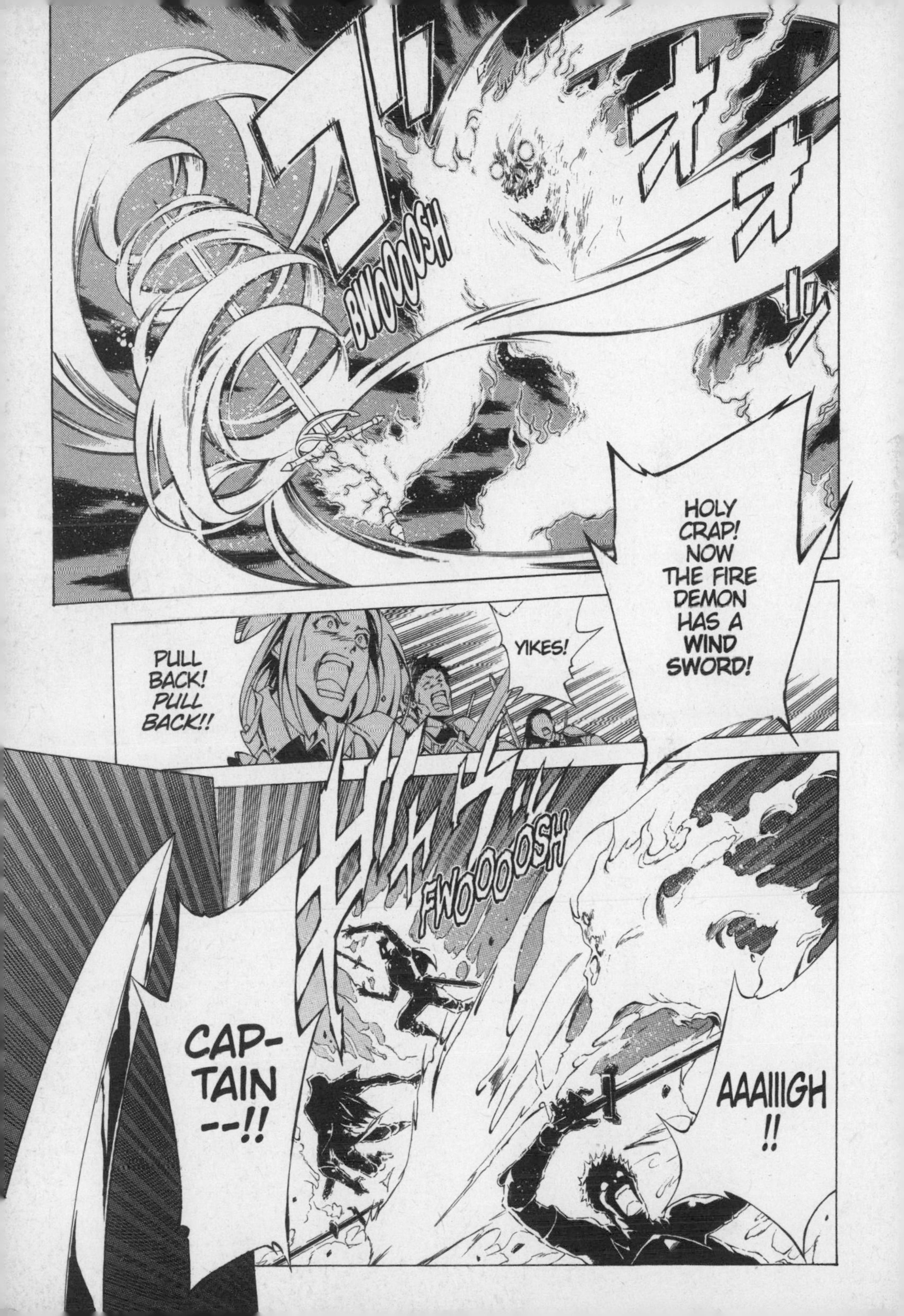
BWOOOOSH
HOLY CRAP! NOW THE FIRE DEMON HAS A WIND SWORD!
YIKES!
PULL BACK! PULL BACK!!
FWOOOOSH
AAAIIIGH!!
CAP-TAIN--!!

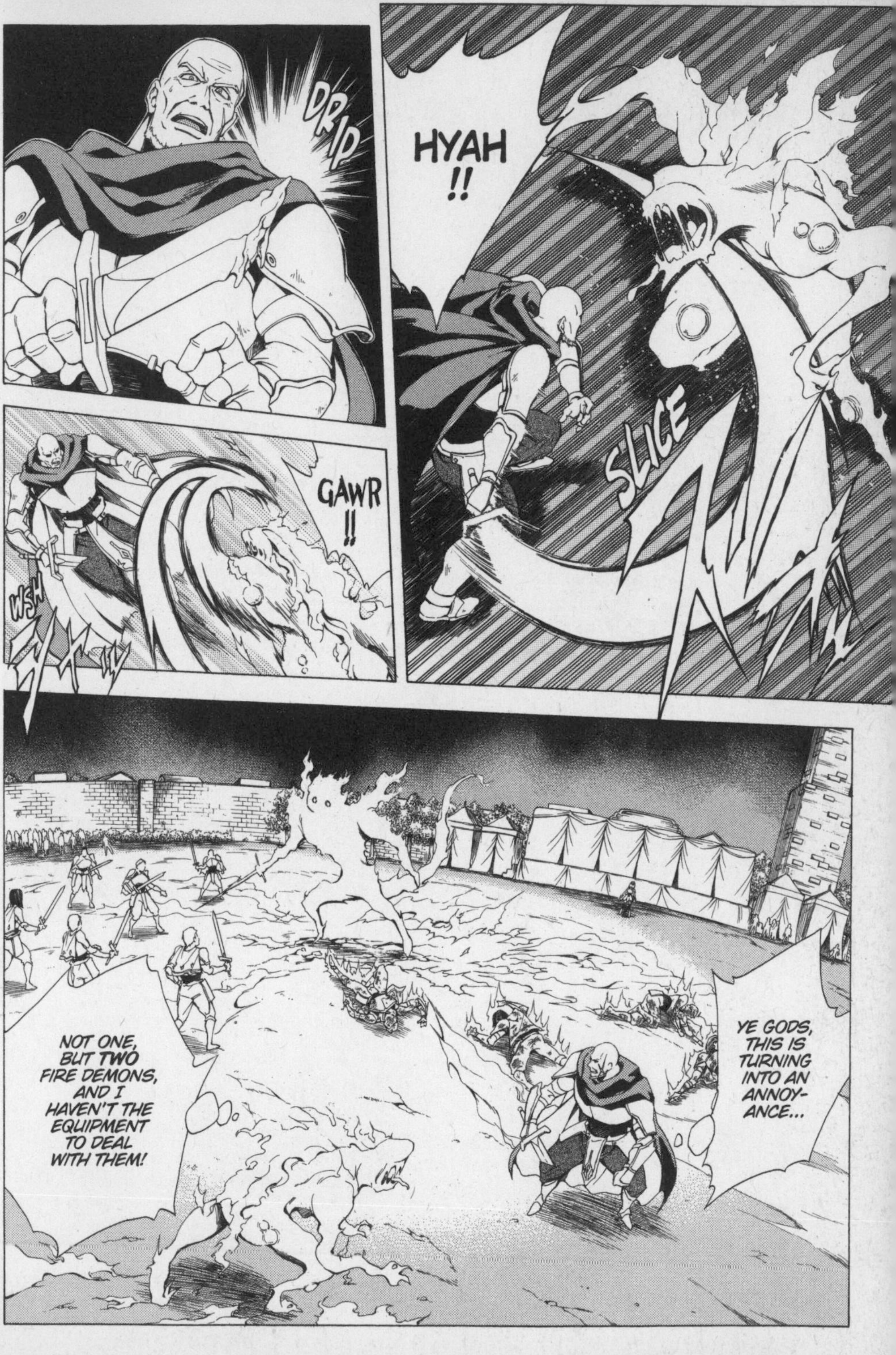
HYAH !!
SLICE
DRIP
GAWR !!
WSH
YE GODS, THIS IS TURNING INTO AN ANNOY-ANCE...
NOT ONE, BUT TWO FIRE DEMONS, AND I HAVEN'T THE EQUIPMENT TO DEAL WITH THEM!

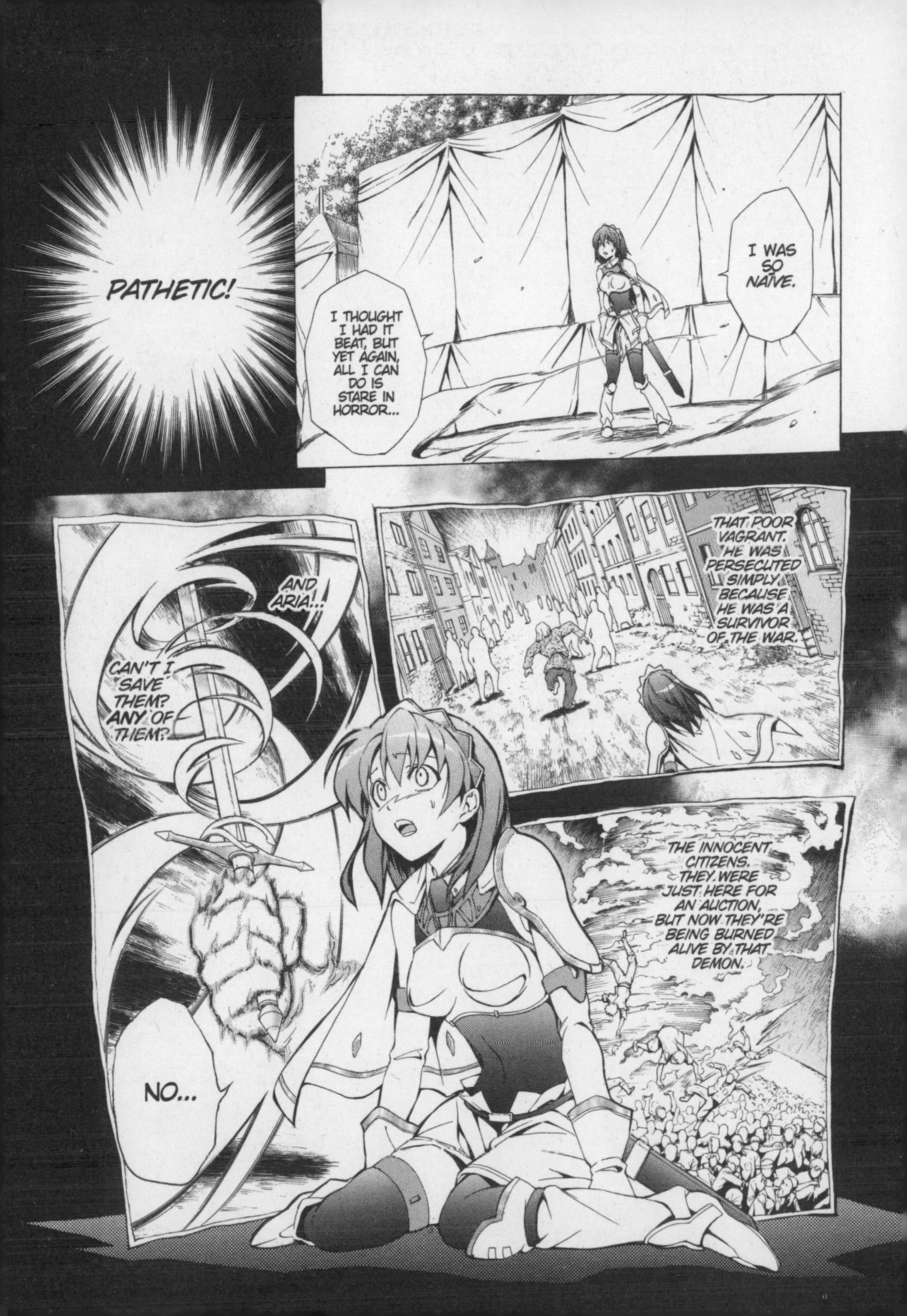
I WAS SO NAÏVE.
I THOUGHT I HAD IT BEAT, BUT YET AGAIN, ALL I CAN DO IS STARE IN HORROR...
PATHETIC!
THAT POOR VAGRANT. HE WAS PERSECUTED SIMPLY BECAUSE HE WAS A SURVIVOR OF THE WAR.
THE INNOCENT CITIZENS. THEY WERE JUST HERE FOR AN AUCTION, BUT NOW THEY'RE BEING BURNED ALIVE BY THAT DEMON.
AND ARIA...
CAN'T I SAVE THEM? ANY OF THEM?
NO...

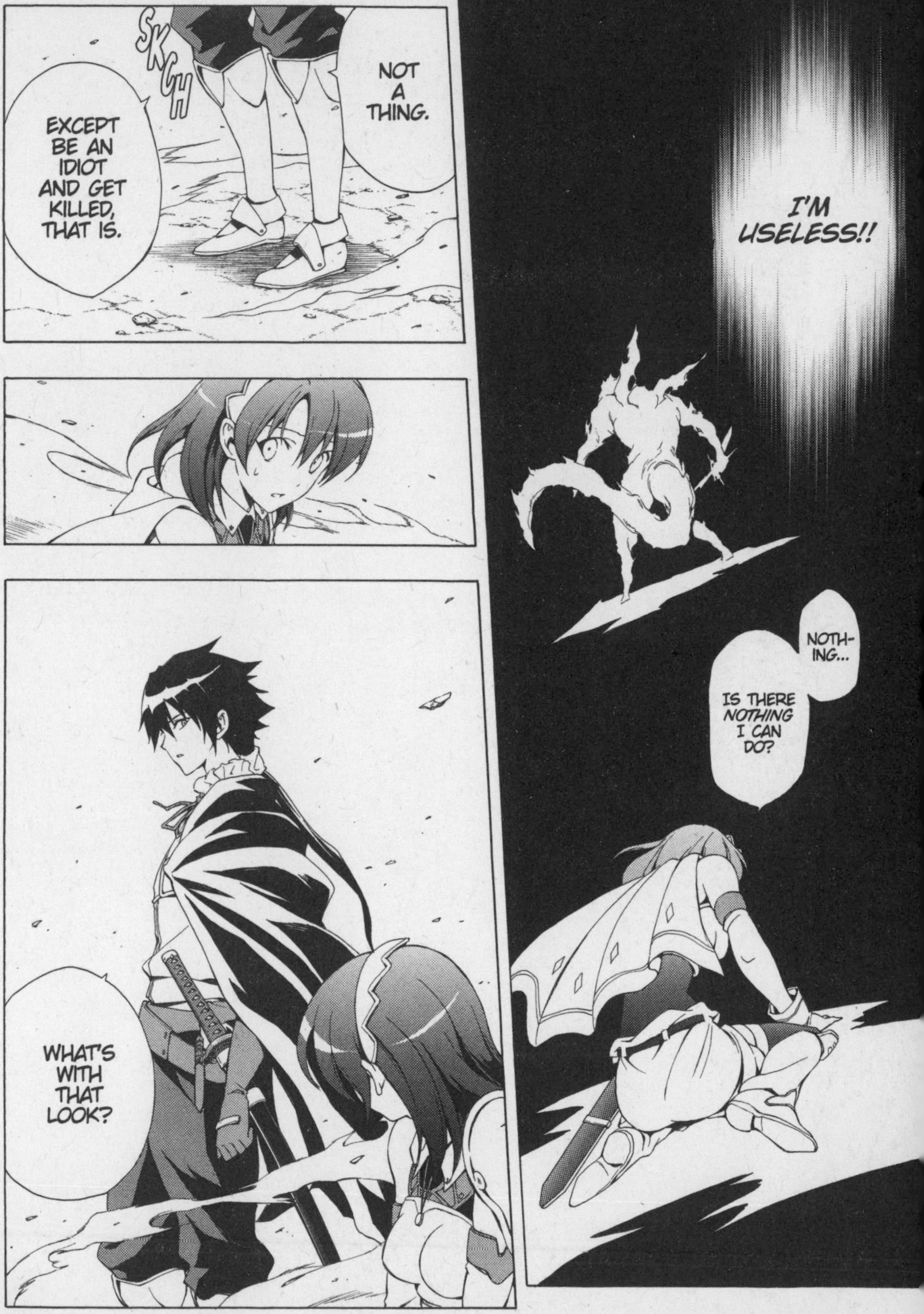

I'M USELESS!!
NOTHING...
IS THERE NOTHING I CAN DO?
NOT A THING.
SKCH
EXCEPT BE AN IDIOT AND GET KILLED, THAT IS.
WHAT'S WITH THAT LOOK?

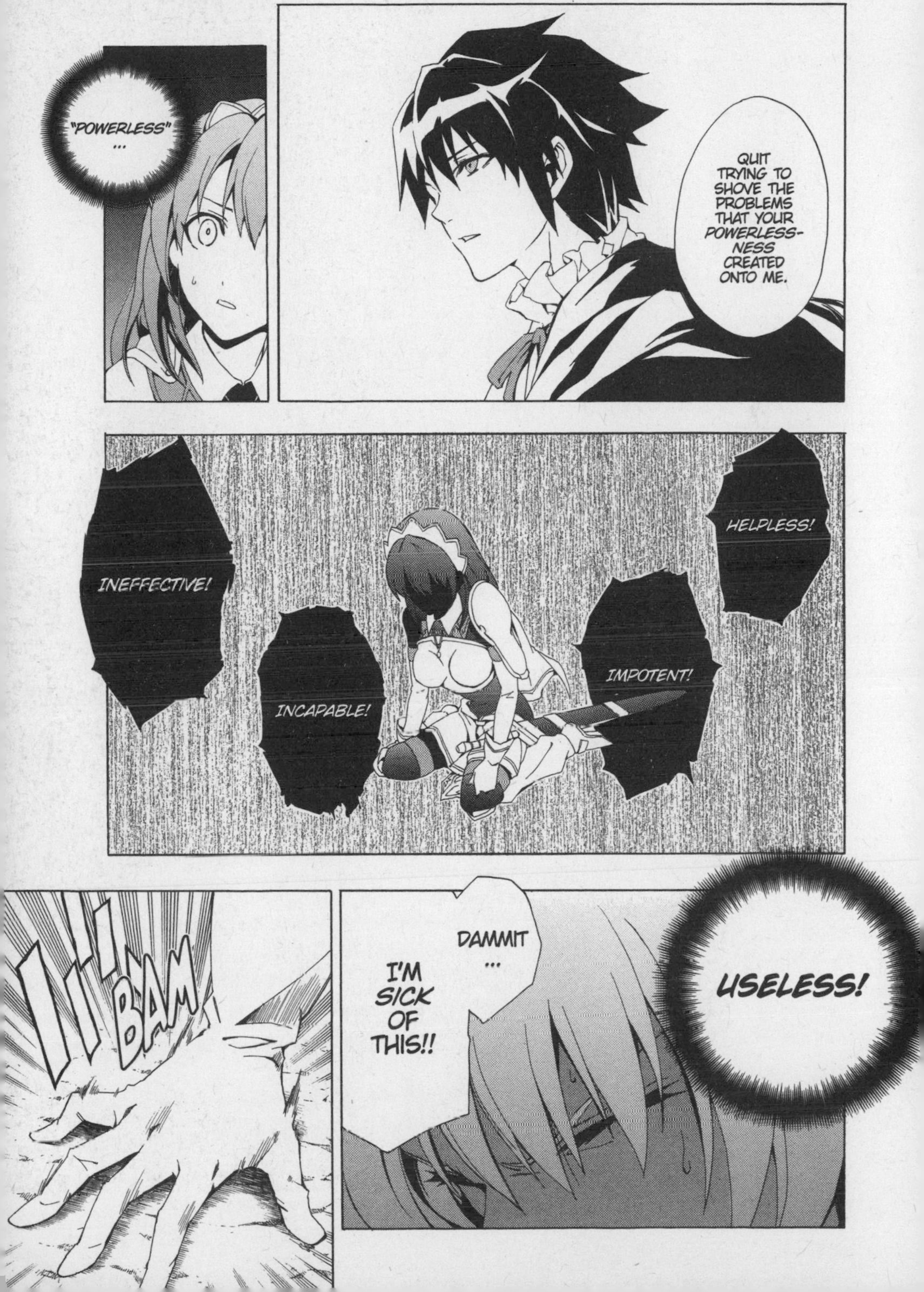
QUIT TRYING TO SHOVE THE PROBLEMS THAT YOUR POWERLESS-NESS CREATED ONTO ME.
"POWERLESS" ...
HELPLESS!
IMPOTENT!
INCAPABLE!
INEFFECTIVE!
USELESS!
DAMMIT ...
I'M SICK OF THIS!!
BAM

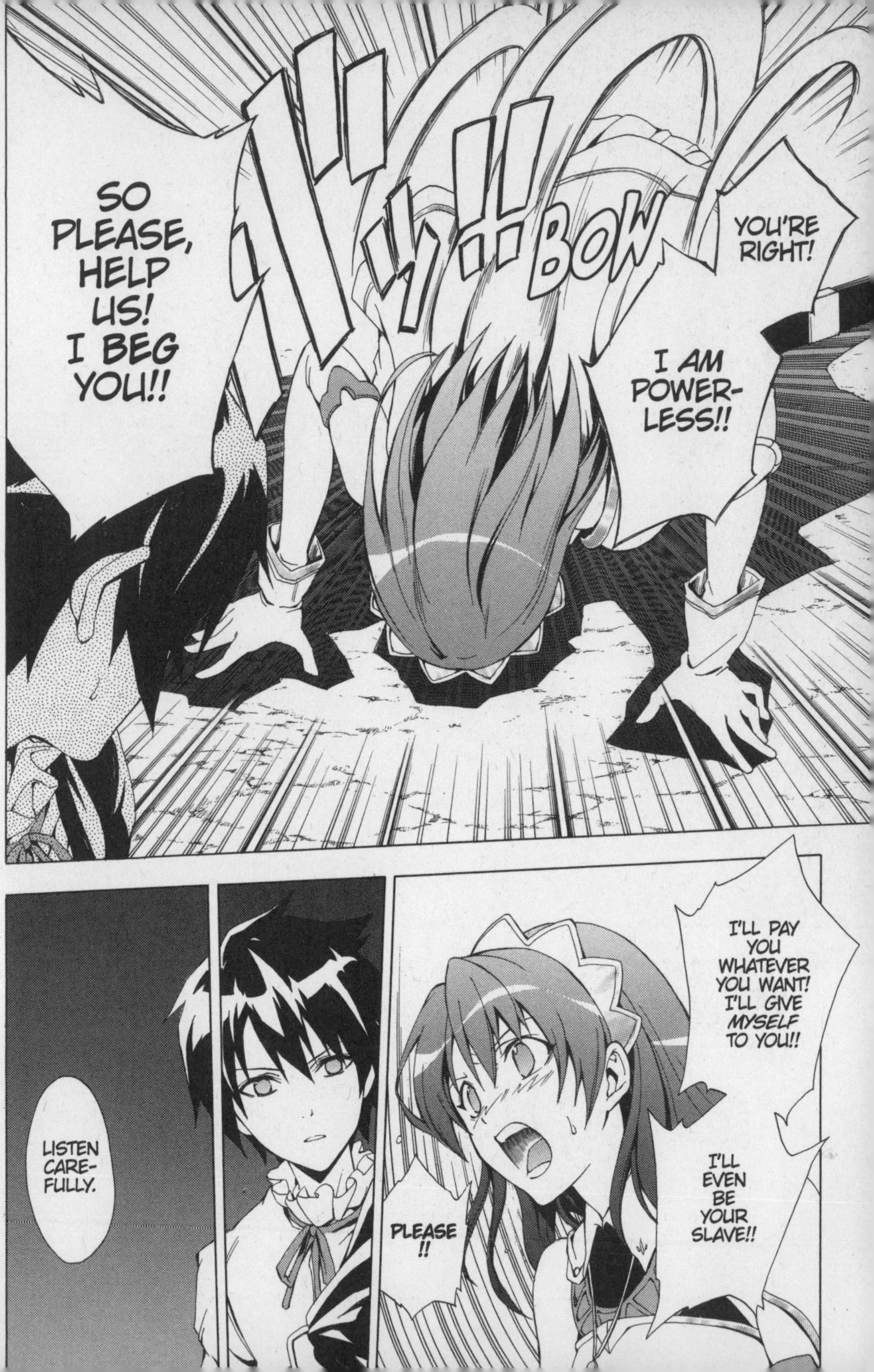
YOU'RE RIGHT!
I AM POWERLESS!!
BOW
SO PLEASE, HELP US! I BEG YOU!!
I'LL PAY YOU WHATEVER YOU WANT! I'LL GIVE *MYSELF* TO YOU!!
I'LL EVEN BE YOUR SLAVE!!
PLEASE!!
LISTEN CAREFULLY.

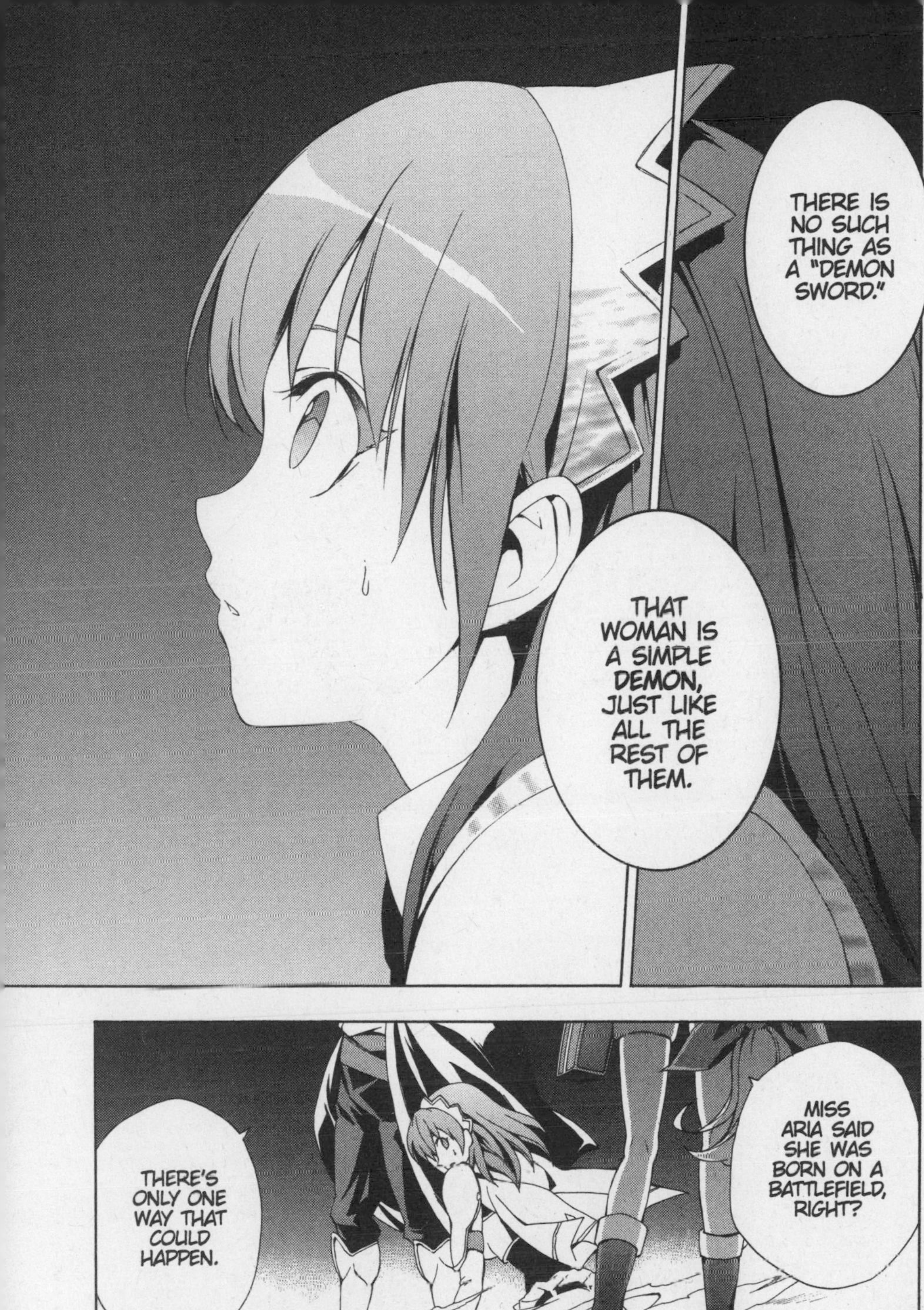
THERE IS NO SUCH THING AS A "DEMON SWORD."
THAT WOMAN IS A SIMPLE DEMON, JUST LIKE ALL THE REST OF THEM.
MISS ARIA SAID SHE WAS BORN ON A BATTLEFIELD, RIGHT?
THERE'S ONLY ONE WAY THAT COULD HAPPEN.

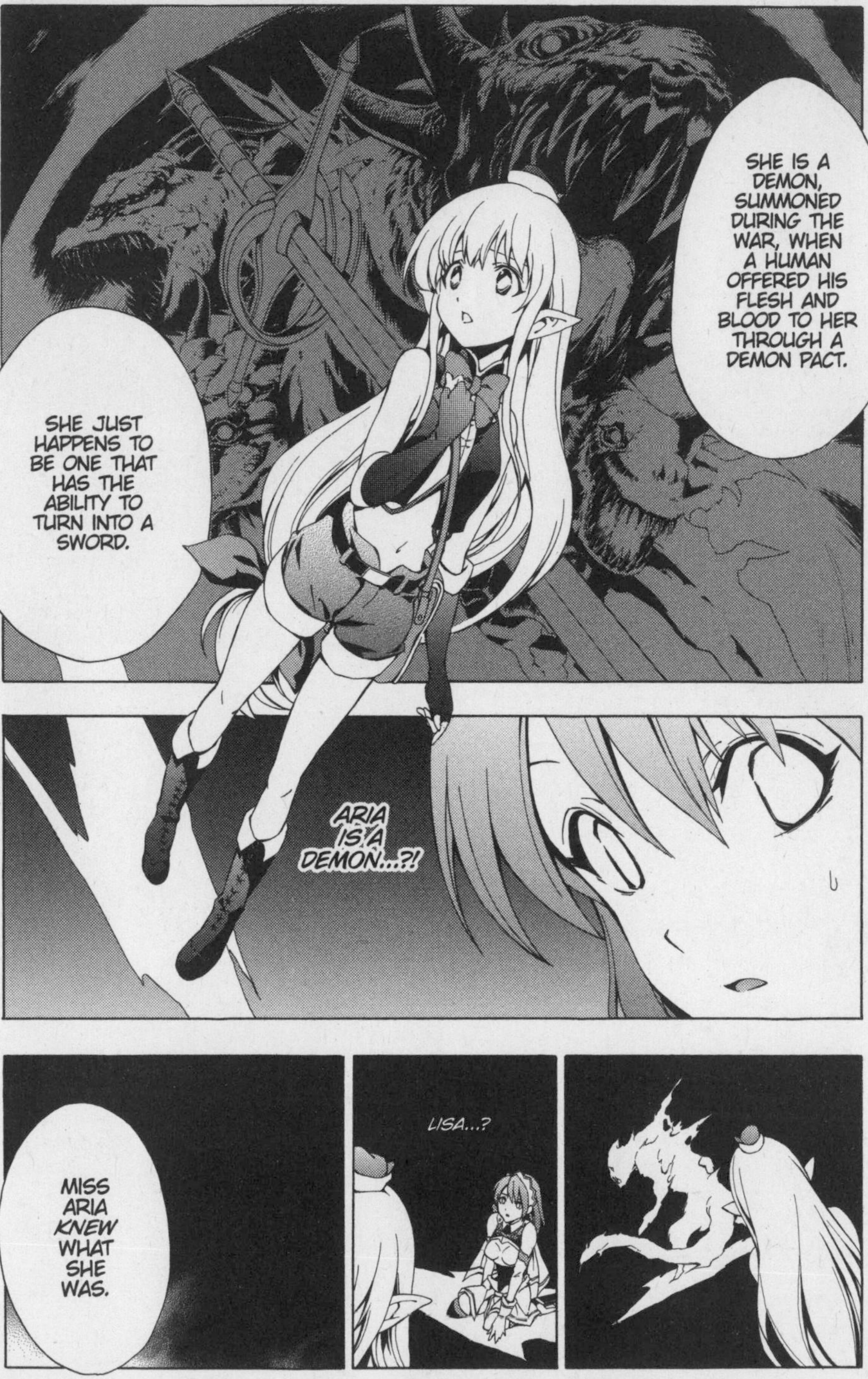
SHE IS A DEMON, SUMMONED DURING THE WAR, WHEN A HUMAN OFFERED HIS FLESH AND BLOOD TO HER THROUGH A DEMON PACT.
SHE JUST HAPPENS TO BE ONE THAT HAS THE ABILITY TO TURN INTO A SWORD.
ARIA IS A DEMON...?!
LISA...?
MISS ARIA *KNEW* WHAT SHE WAS.

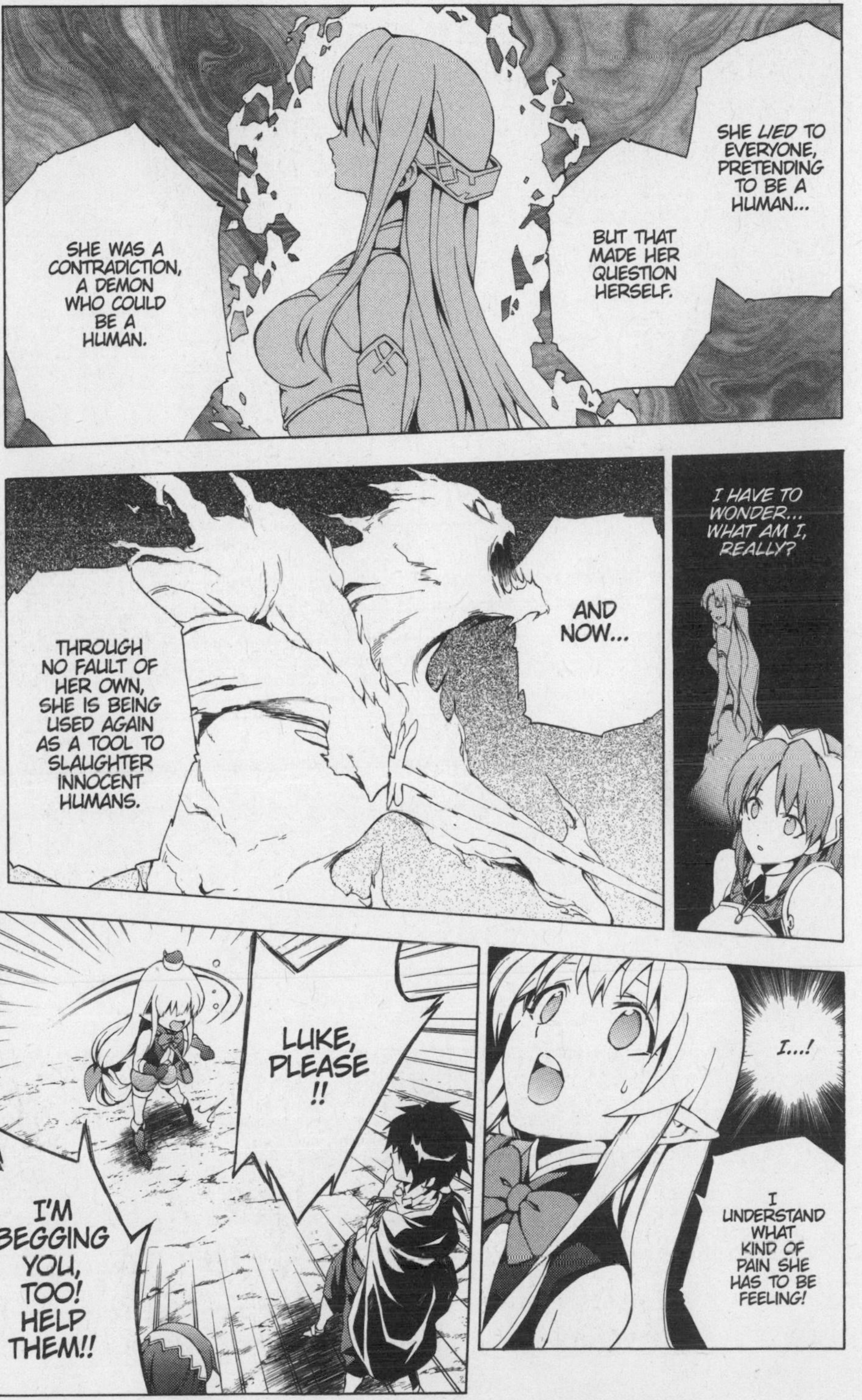
SHE *LIED* TO EVERYONE, PRETENDING TO BE A HUMAN...
BUT THAT MADE HER QUESTION HERSELF.
SHE WAS A CONTRADICTION, A DEMON WHO COULD BE A HUMAN.
I HAVE TO WONDER... WHAT AM I, REALLY?
AND NOW...
THROUGH NO FAULT OF HER OWN, SHE IS BEING USED AGAIN AS A TOOL TO SLAUGHTER INNOCENT HUMANS.
I...!
I UNDERSTAND WHAT KIND OF PAIN SHE HAS TO BE FEELING!
LUKE, PLEASE!!
I'M BEGGING YOU, TOO! HELP THEM!!

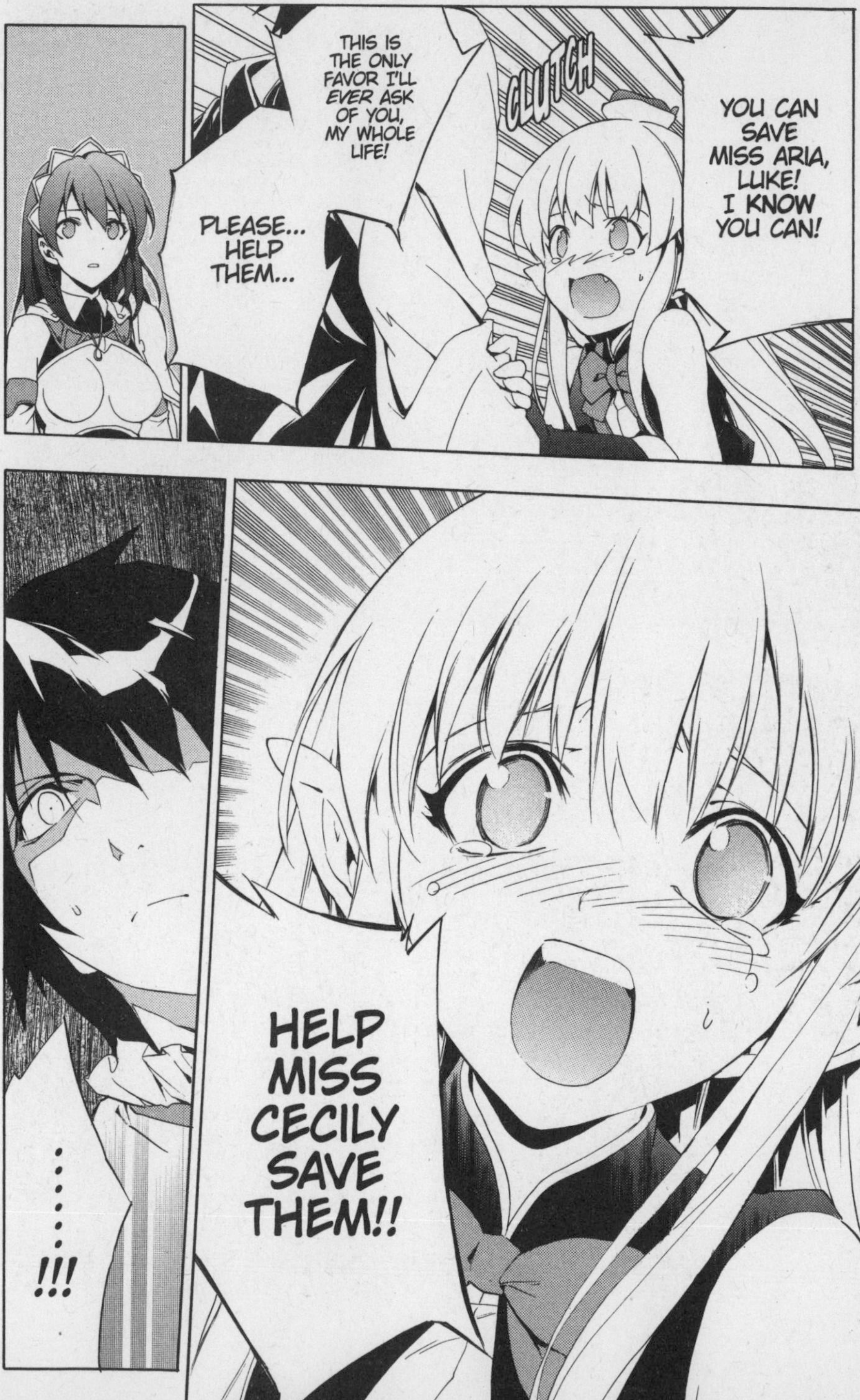
YOU CAN SAVE MISS ARIA, LUKE! I KNOW YOU CAN!
CLUTCH
THIS IS THE ONLY FAVOR I'LL EVER ASK OF YOU, MY WHOLE LIFE!
PLEASE... HELP THEM...
HELP MISS CECILY SAVE THEM!!
......!!!

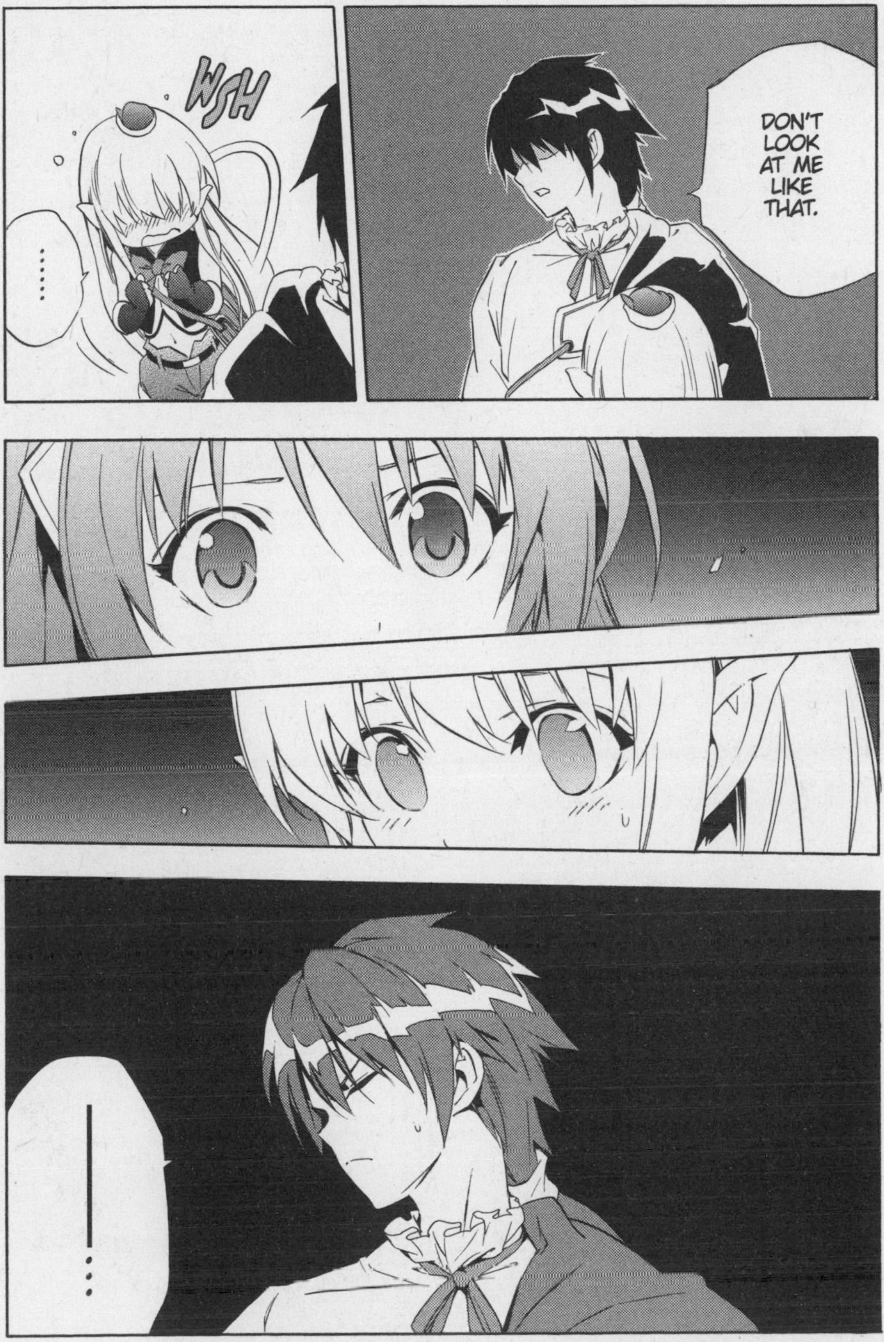
DON'T LOOK AT ME LIKE THAT.
WSH
......
—...

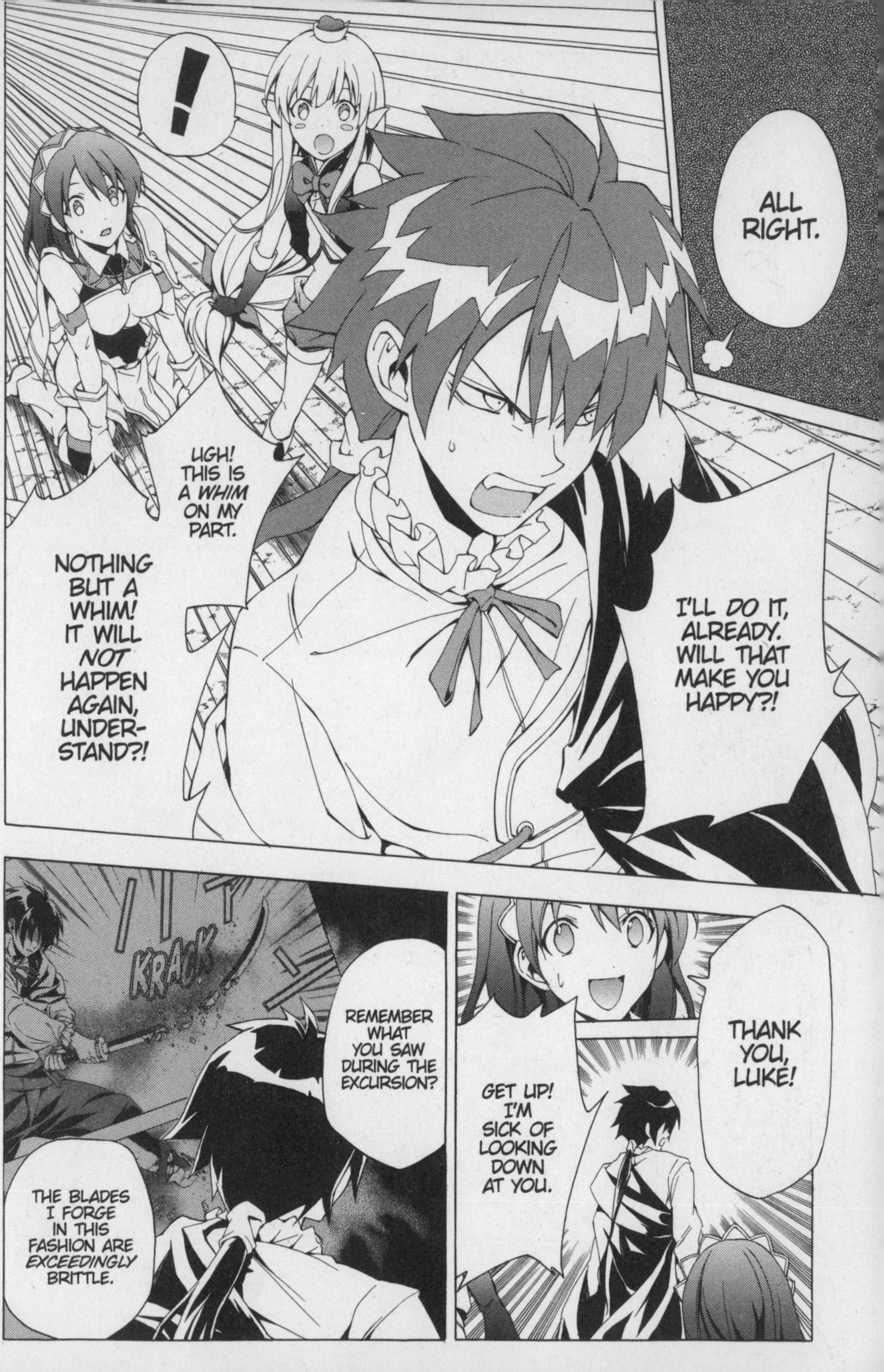
ALL RIGHT.
!
I'LL *DO* IT, ALREADY. WILL THAT MAKE YOU HAPPY?!
UGH! THIS IS A *WHIM* ON MY PART.
NOTHING BUT A WHIM! IT WILL *NOT* HAPPEN AGAIN, UNDER-STAND?!
THANK YOU, LUKE!
GET UP! I'M SICK OF LOOKING DOWN AT YOU.
KRACK
REMEMBER WHAT YOU SAW DURING THE EXCURSION?
THE BLADES I FORGE IN THIS FASHION ARE *EXCEEDINGLY* BRITTLE.

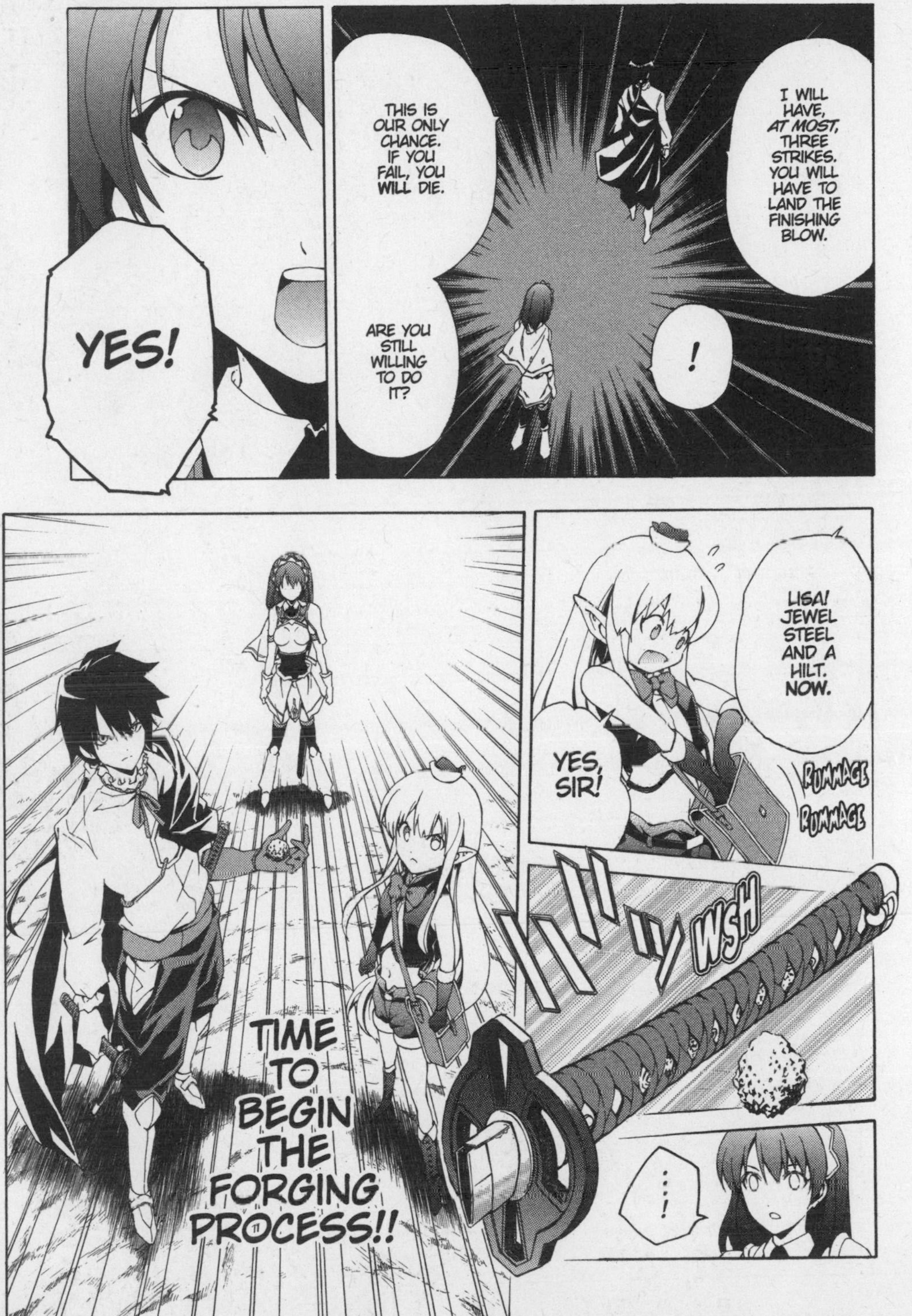
I WILL HAVE, *AT MOST,* THREE STRIKES. YOU WILL HAVE TO LAND THE FINISHING BLOW.
!
THIS IS OUR ONLY CHANCE. IF YOU FAIL, YOU WILL DIE.
ARE YOU STILL WILLING TO DO IT?
YES!
LISA! JEWEL STEEL AND A HILT. NOW.
YES, SIR!
RUMMAGE
RUMMAGE
WSH
...!
TIME TO BEGIN THE FORGING PROCESS!!

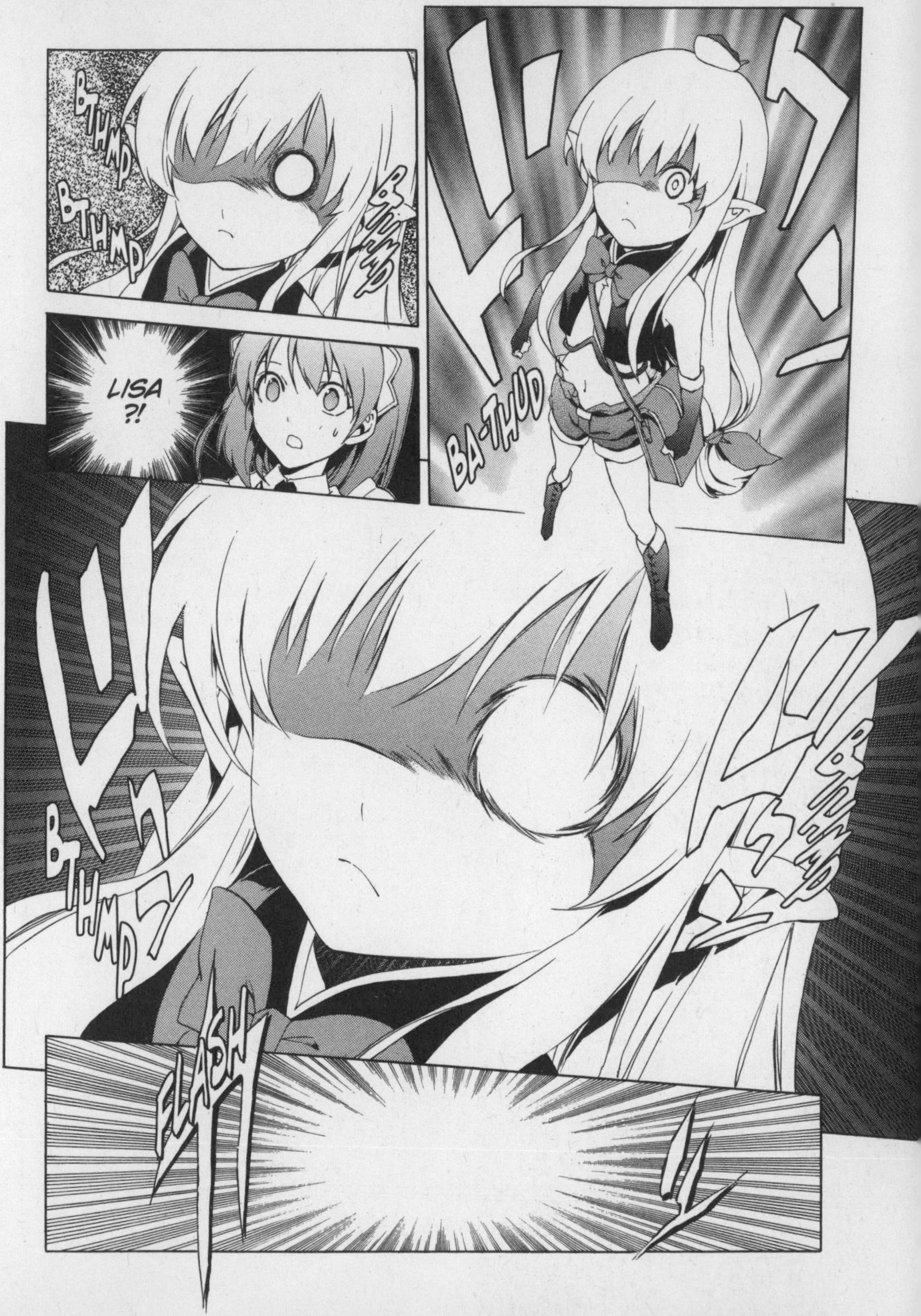
BA-THUD
BTHMP BTHMP
LISA ?!
BTHMP
FLASH

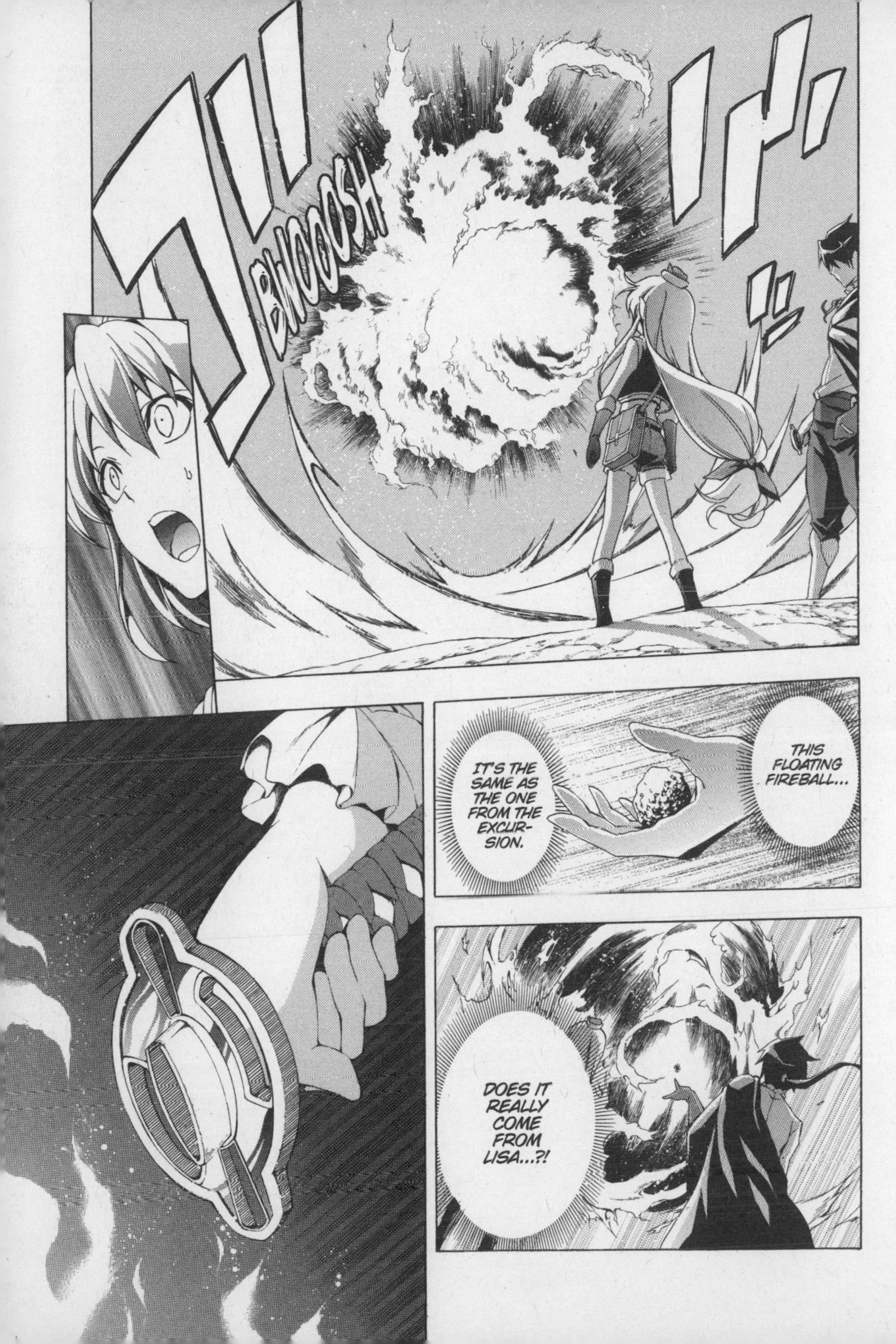
BWOOOSH
THIS FLOATING FIREBALL...
IT'S THE SAME AS THE ONE FROM THE EXCUR-SION.
DOES IT REALLY COME FROM LISA...?!

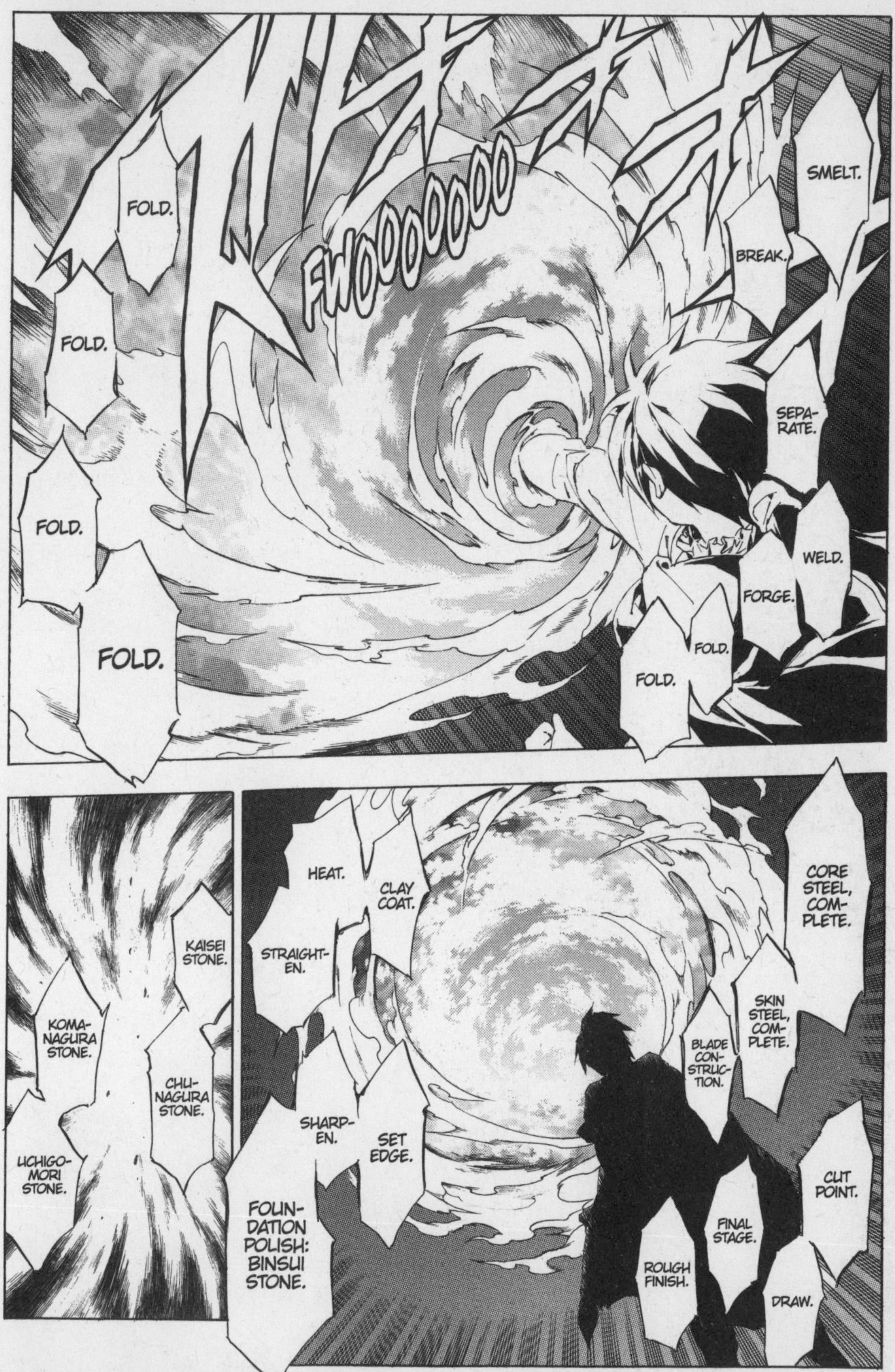
FWOOOOOOO
SMELT.
BREAK.
SEPARATE.
WELD.
FORGE.
FOLD.
FOLD.
FOLD.
FOLD.
FOLD.
FOLD.
CORE STEEL, COMPLETE.
SKIN STEEL, COMPLETE.
BLADE CONSTRUCTION.
DRAW.
ROUGH FINISH.
FINAL STAGE.
CUT POINT.
CLAY COAT.
HEAT.
STRAIGHTEN.
SET EDGE.
SHARPEN.
FOUNDATION POLISH: BINSUI STONE.
KAISEI STONE.
KOMANAGURA STONE.
CHUNAGURA STONE.
UCHIGOMORI STONE.

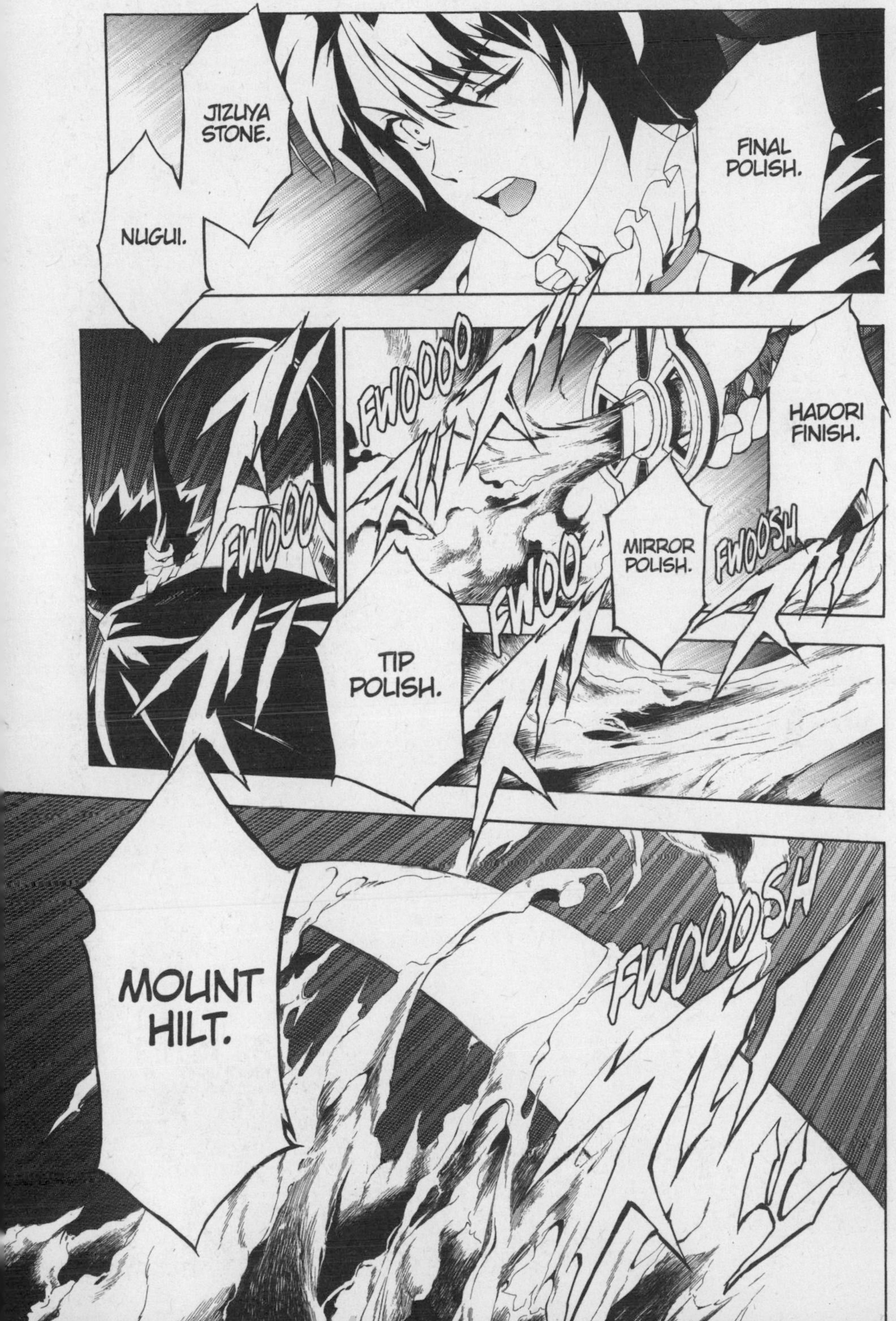
FINAL POLISH.
JIZUYA STONE.
NUGUI.
HADORI FINISH.
FWOOOO
FWOOSH
MIRROR POLISH.
FWOO
FWOOO
TIP POLISH.
FWOOOSH
MOUNT HILT.

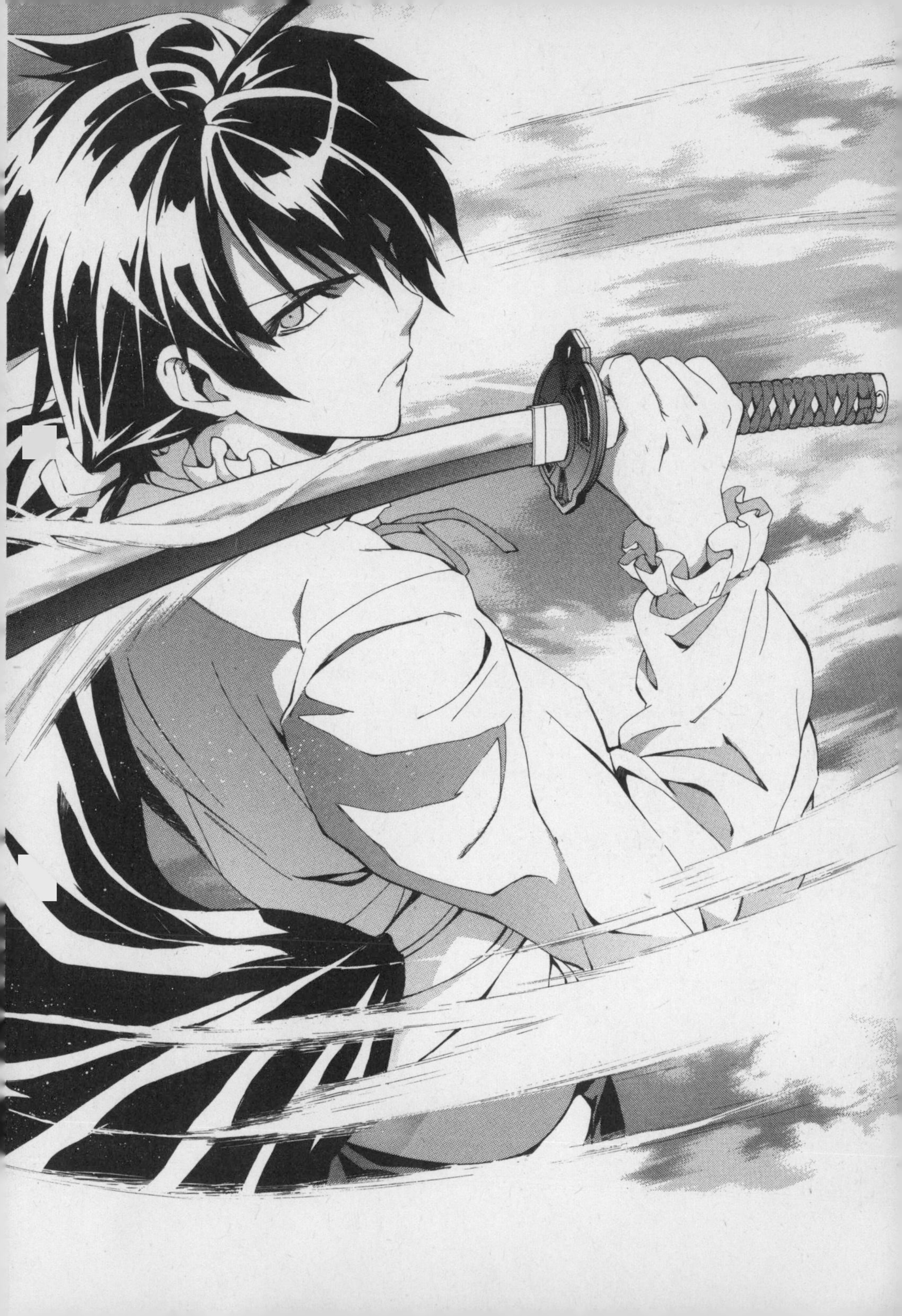

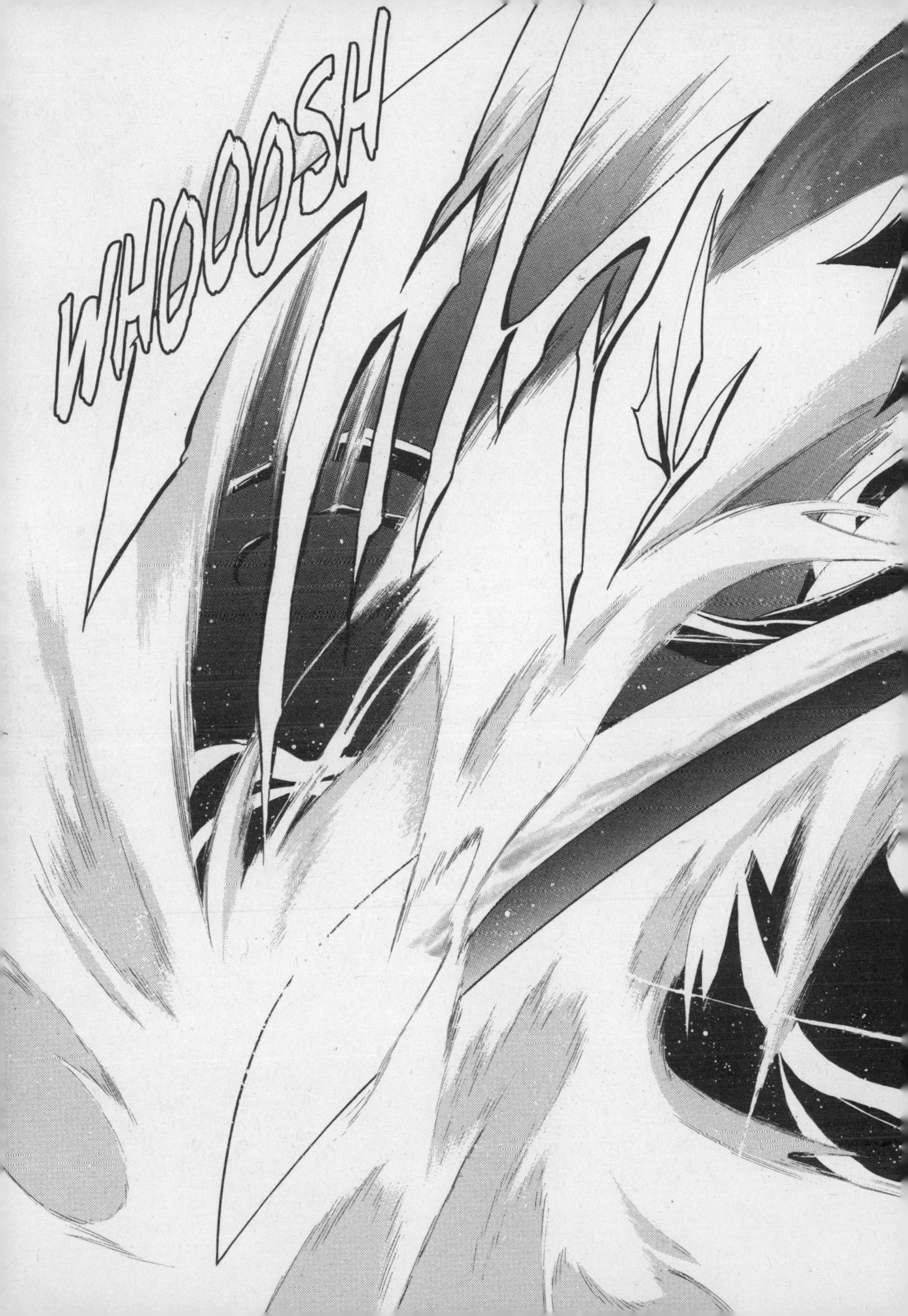
WHOOOSH

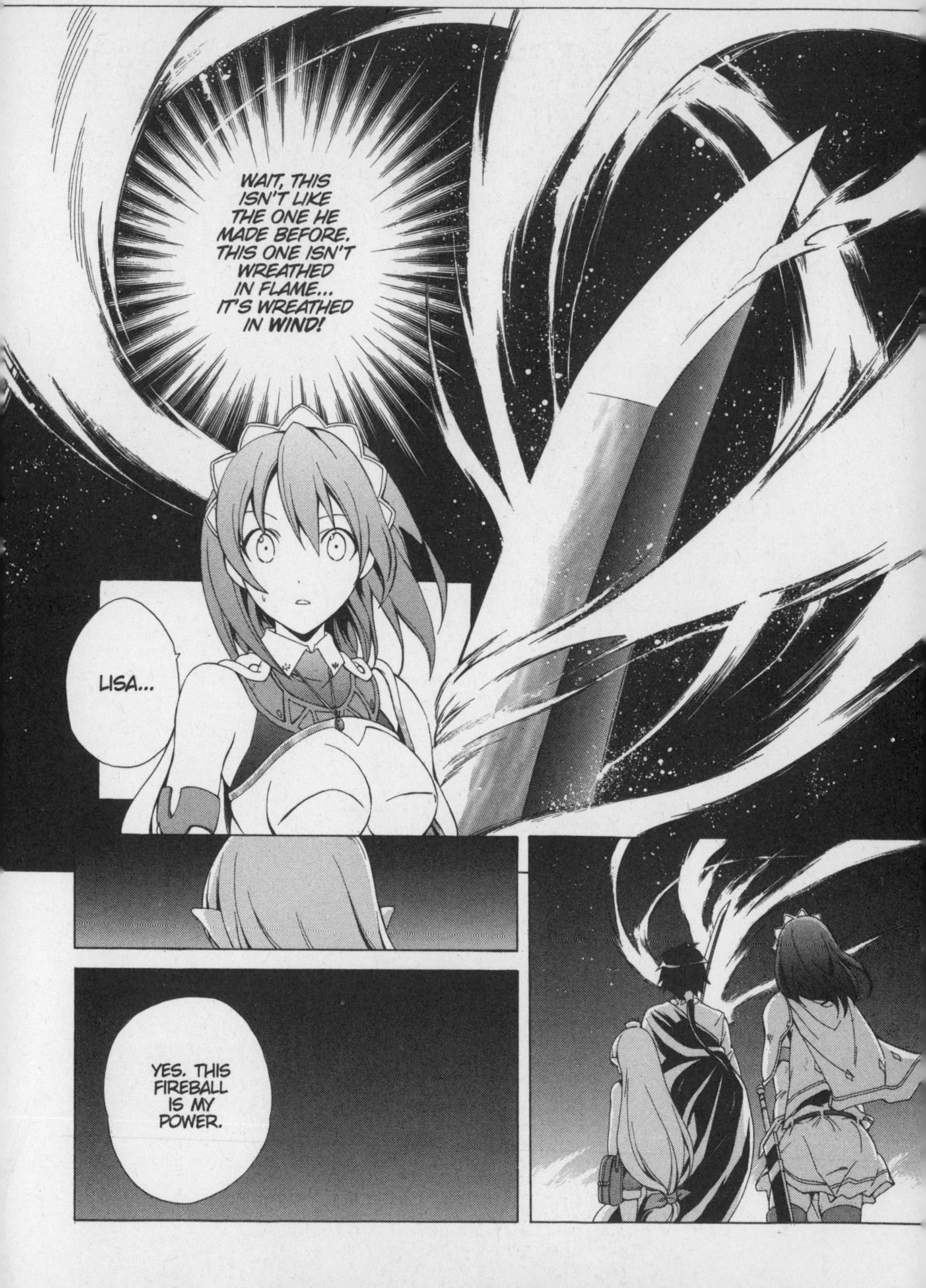
WAIT, THIS ISN'T LIKE THE ONE HE MADE BEFORE. THIS ONE ISN'T WREATHED IN FLAME... IT'S WREATHED IN WIND!
LISA...
YES. THIS FIREBALL IS MY POWER.

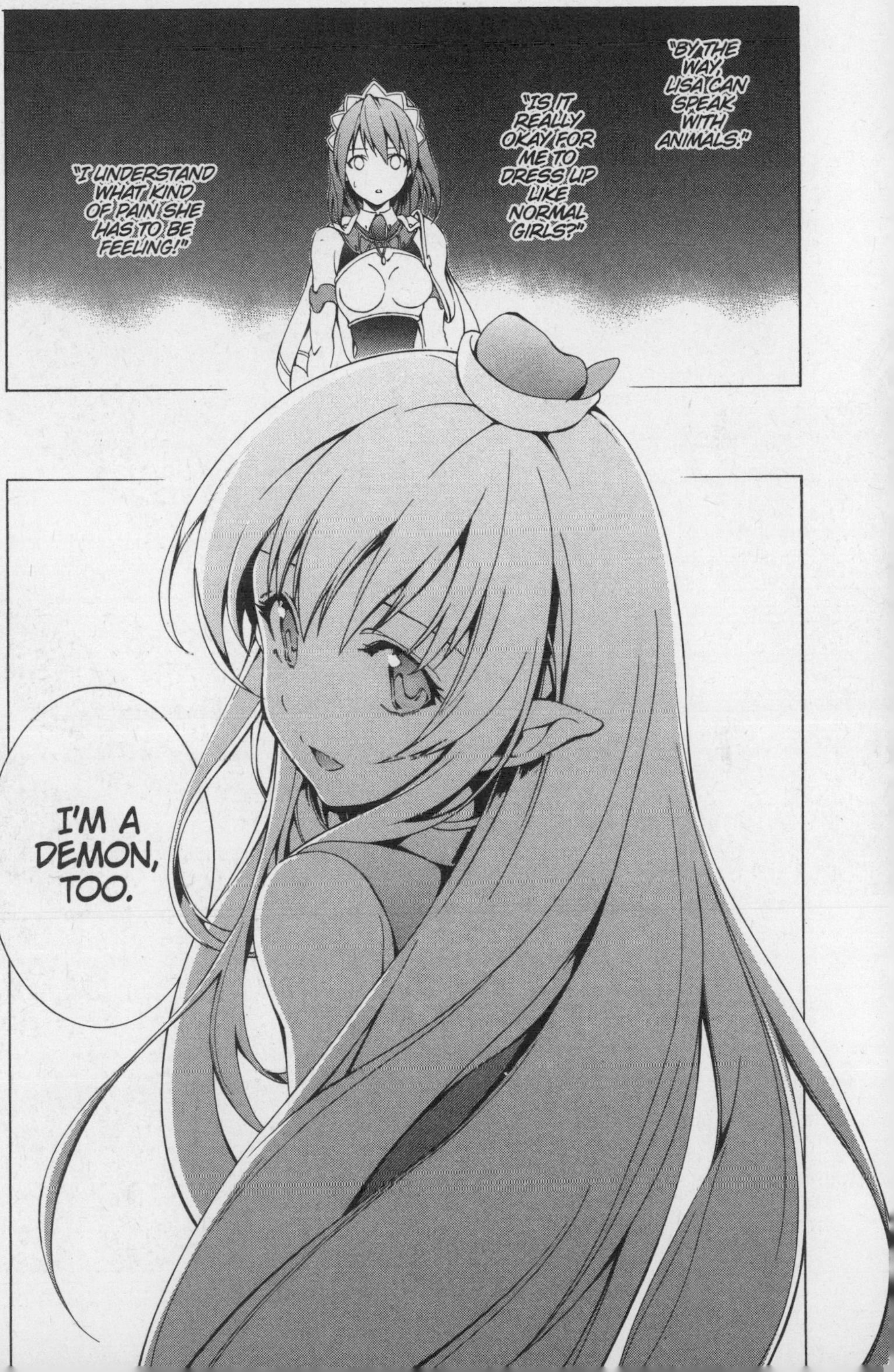
"BY THE WAY, LISA CAN SPEAK WITH ANIMALS."
"IS IT REALLY OKAY FOR ME TO DRESS UP LIKE NORMAL GIRLS?"
"I UNDERSTAND WHAT KIND OF PAIN SHE HAS TO BE FEELING!"
I'M A DEMON, TOO.

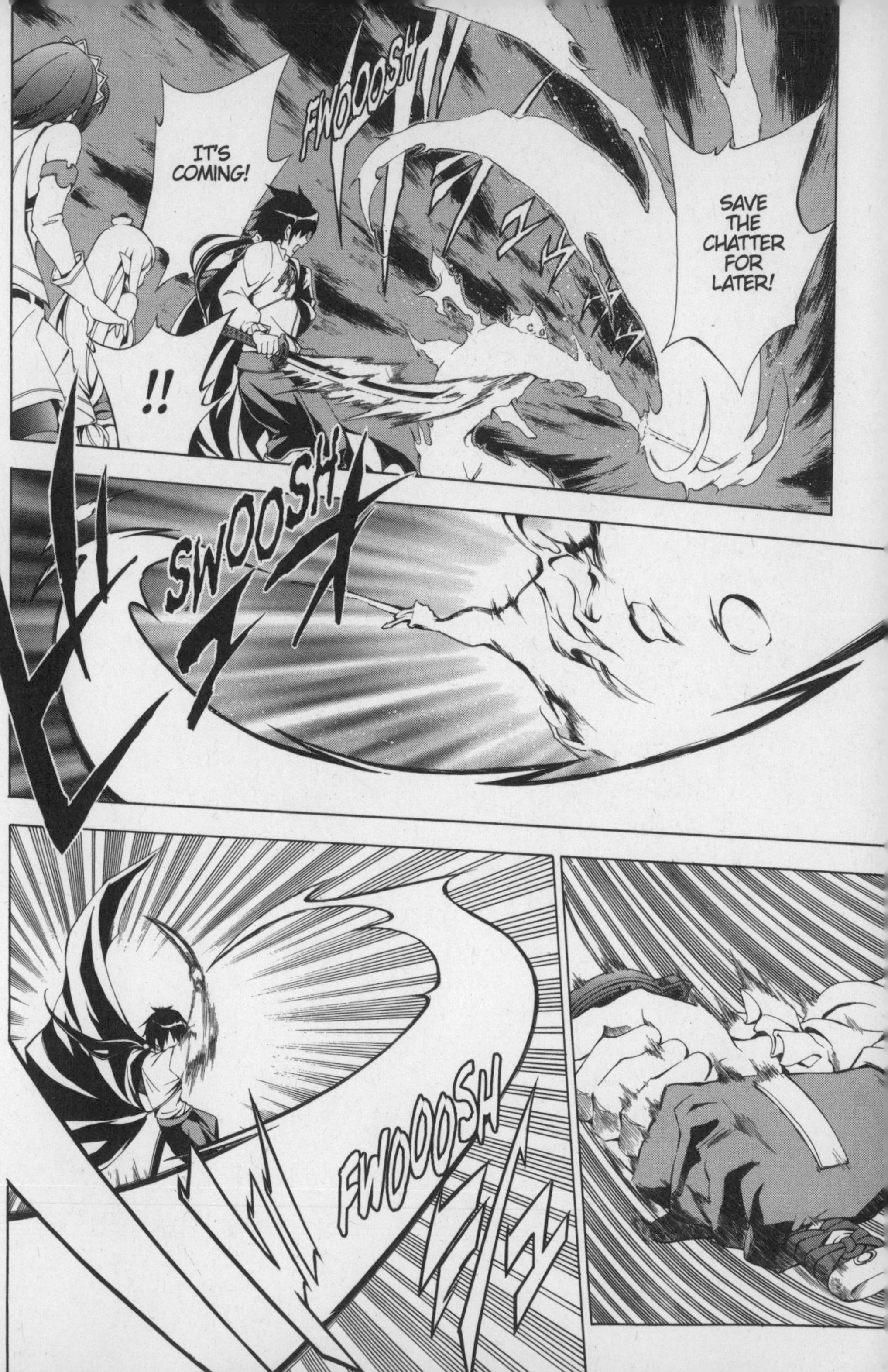
SAVE THE CHATTER FOR LATER!
FWOOOSH
IT'S COMING!
!!
SWOOSH
FWOOOSH

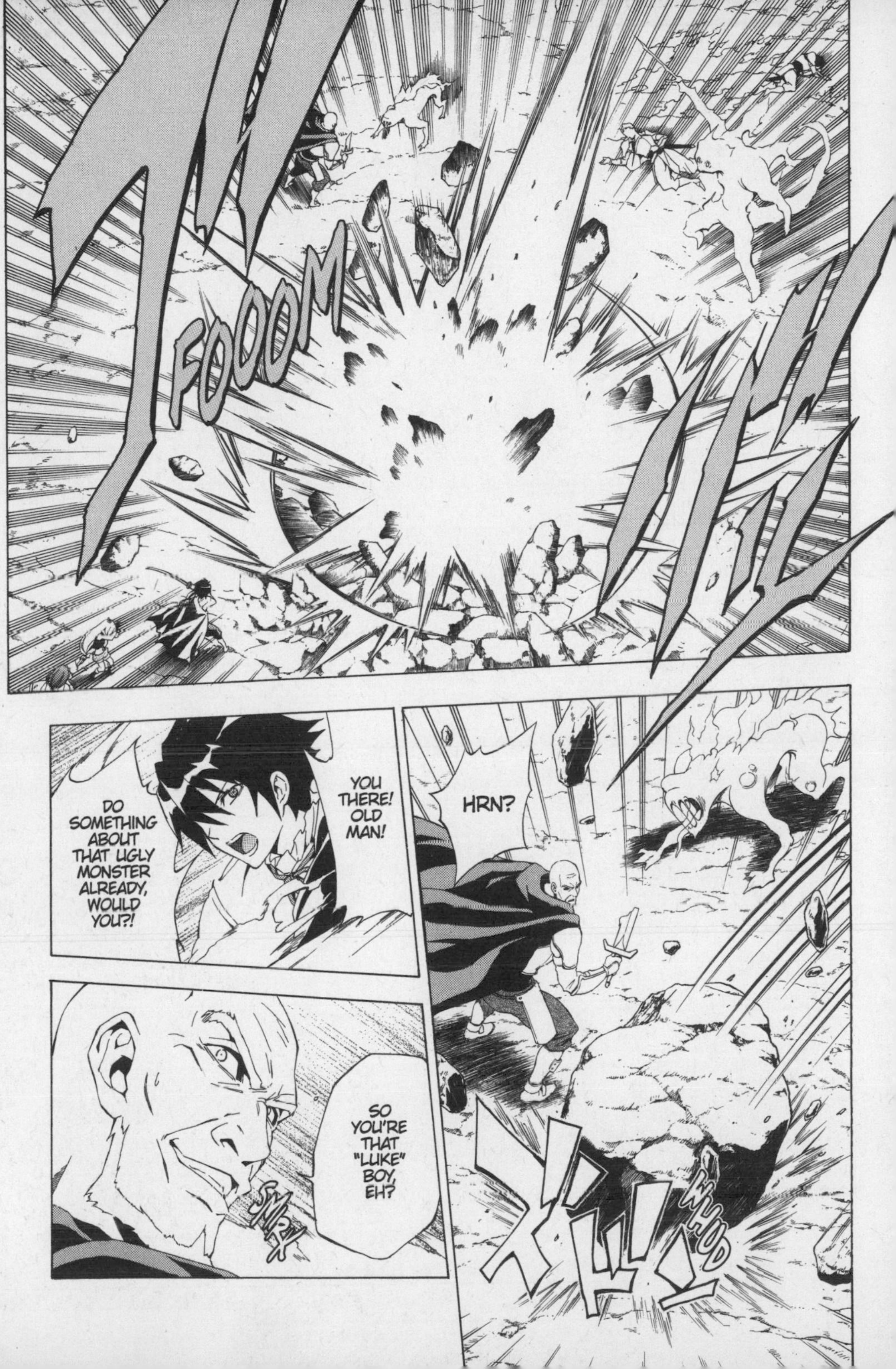
FOOOM
HRN?
WHUD
YOU THERE! OLD MAN!
DO SOMETHING ABOUT THAT UGLY MONSTER ALREADY, WOULD YOU?!
SO YOU'RE THAT "LUKE" BOY, EH?
SMRK

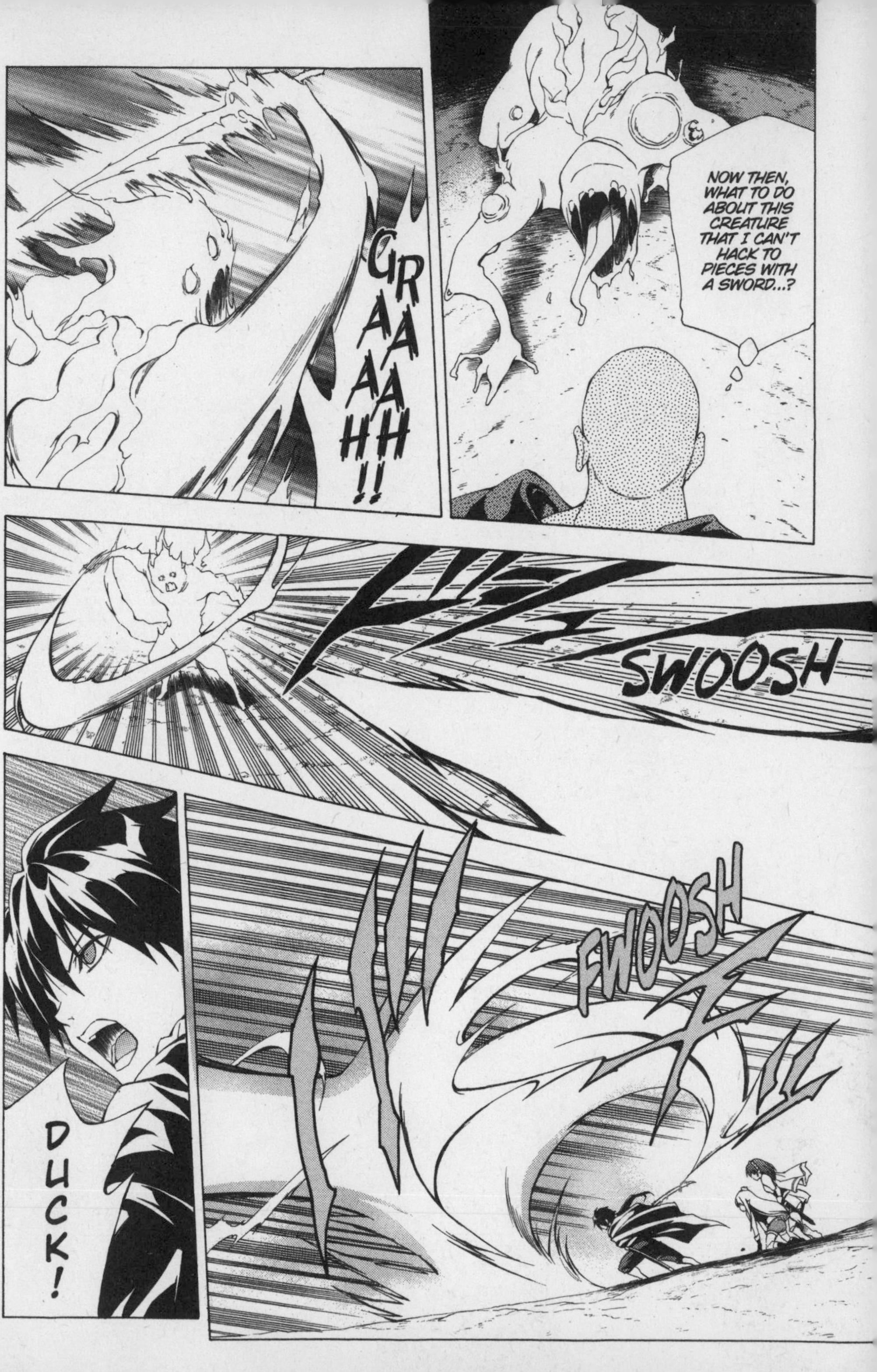
NOW THEN, WHAT TO DO ABOUT THIS CREATURE THAT I CAN'T HACK TO PIECES WITH A SWORD...?
GRAAAAHH!!
SWOOSH
FWOOSH
DUCK!

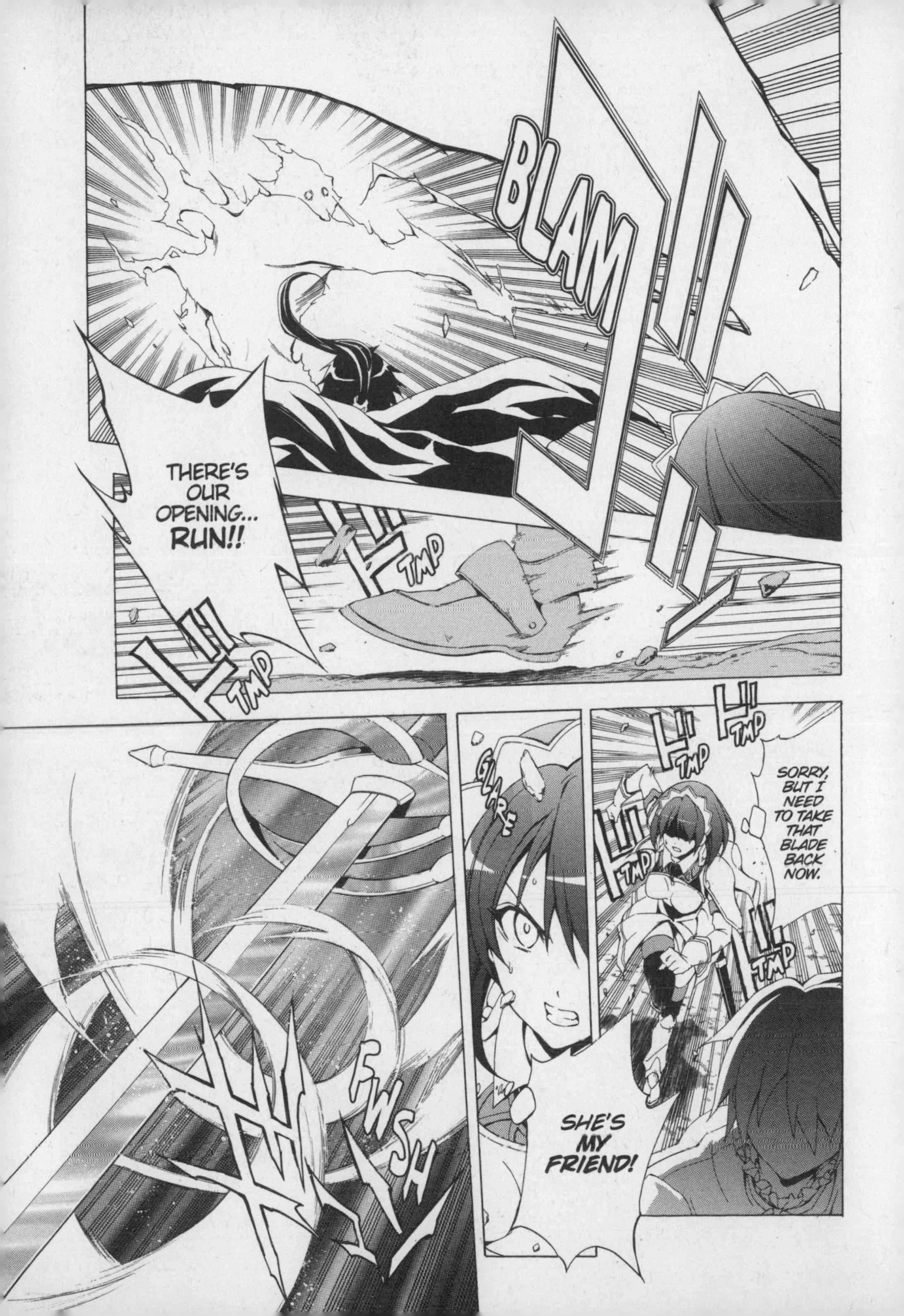
BLAM
THERE'S OUR OPENING... RUN!!
TMP
TMP
TMP
TMP
SORRY, BUT I NEED TO TAKE THAT BLADE BACK NOW.
TMP
TMP
GLARE
SHE'S MY FRIEND!
FWSH

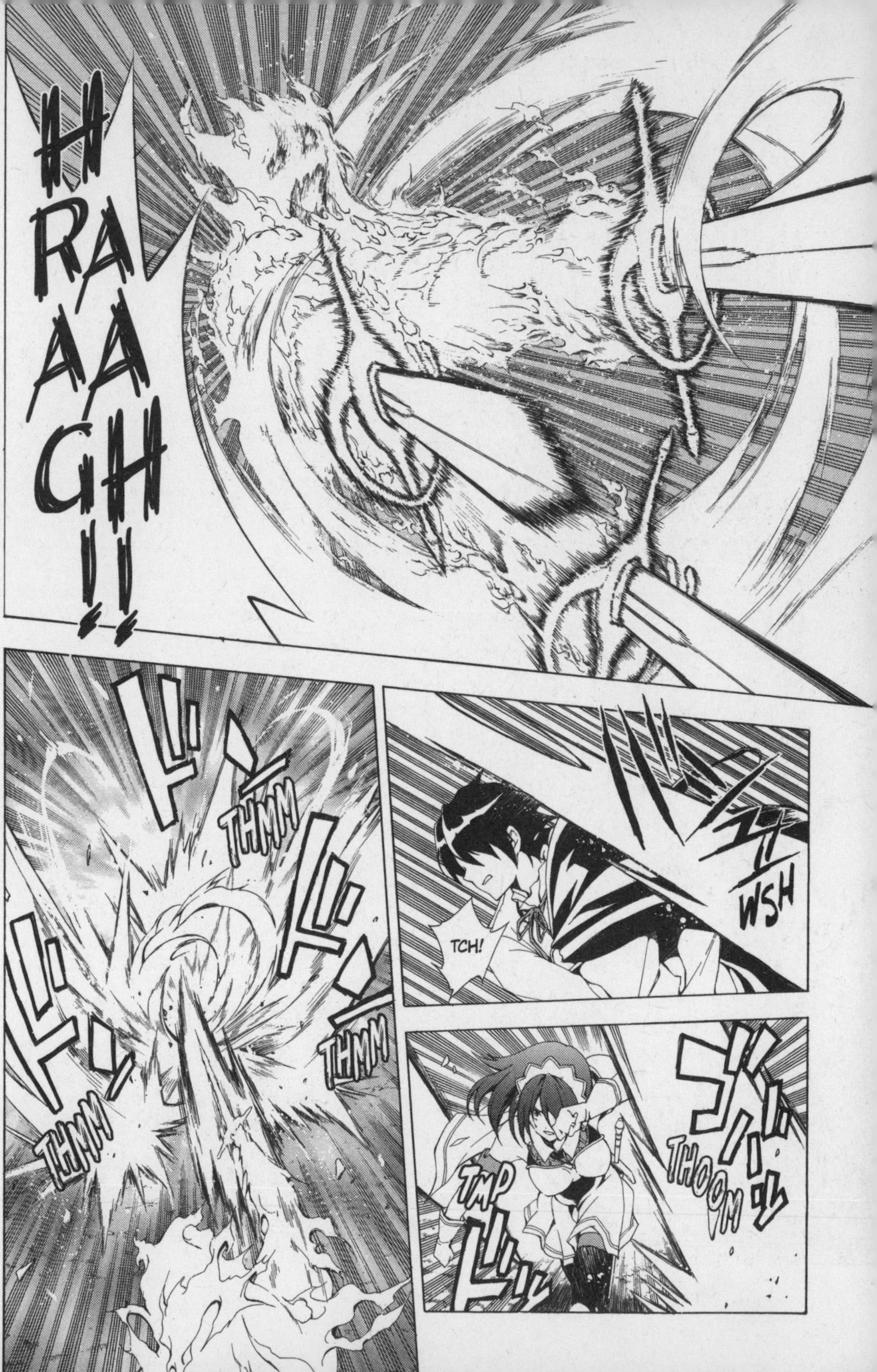
HRAAGH!!
WSH
TCH!
THOOM
TMP
THMM
THMM
THMM
THMM

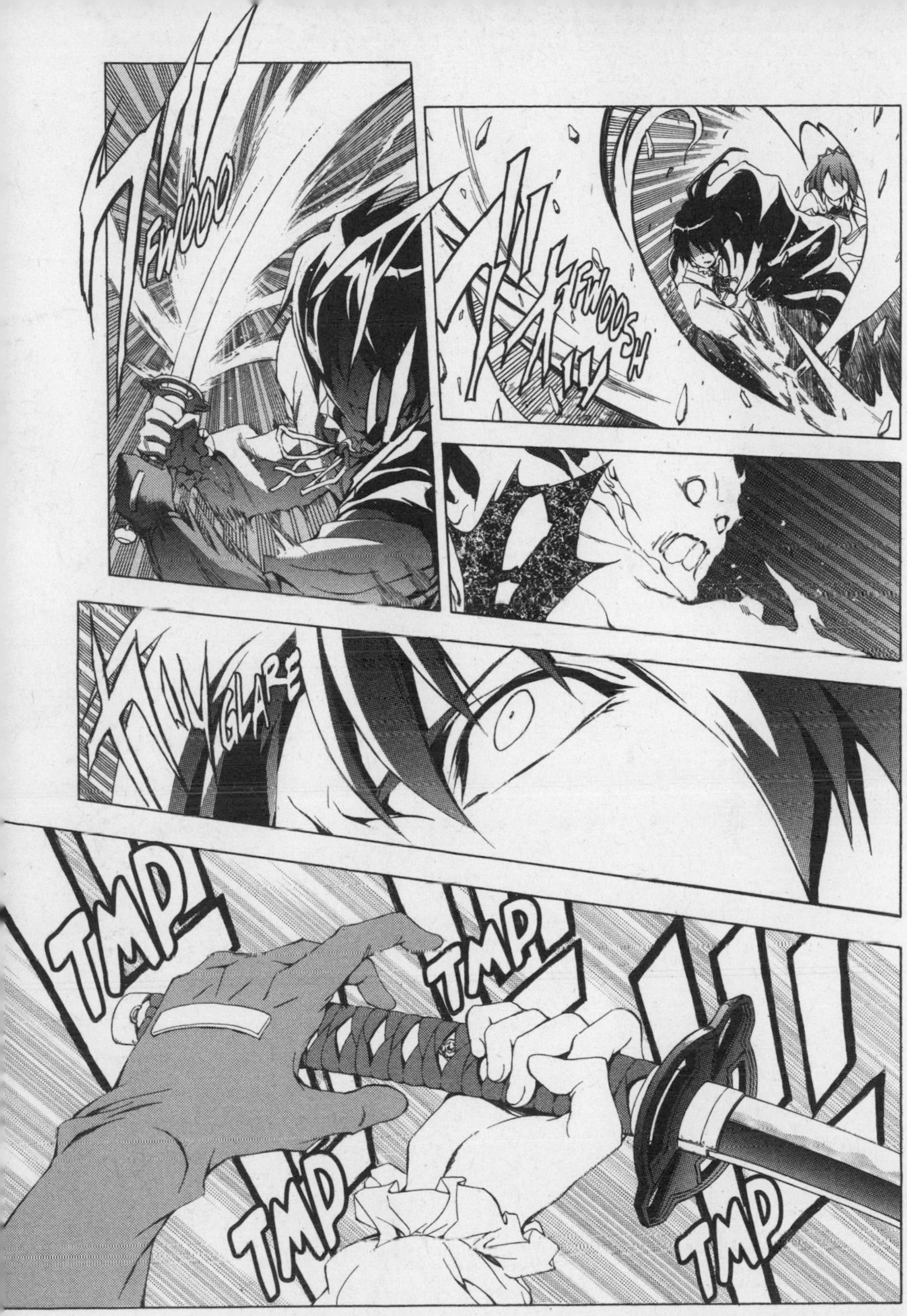
FWOOSH
FWOOO
GLARE
TMP
TMP
TMP
TMP

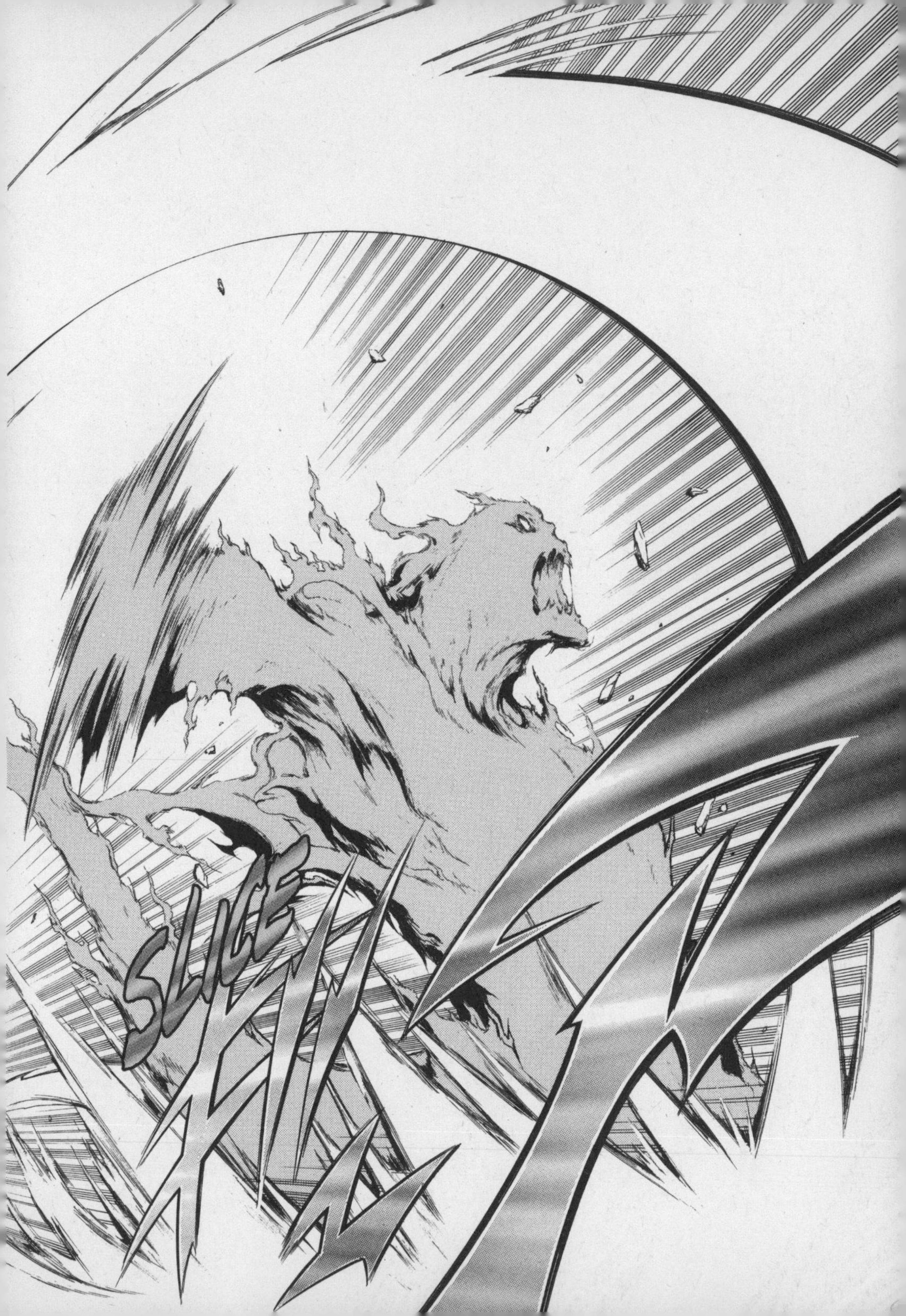
SLICE

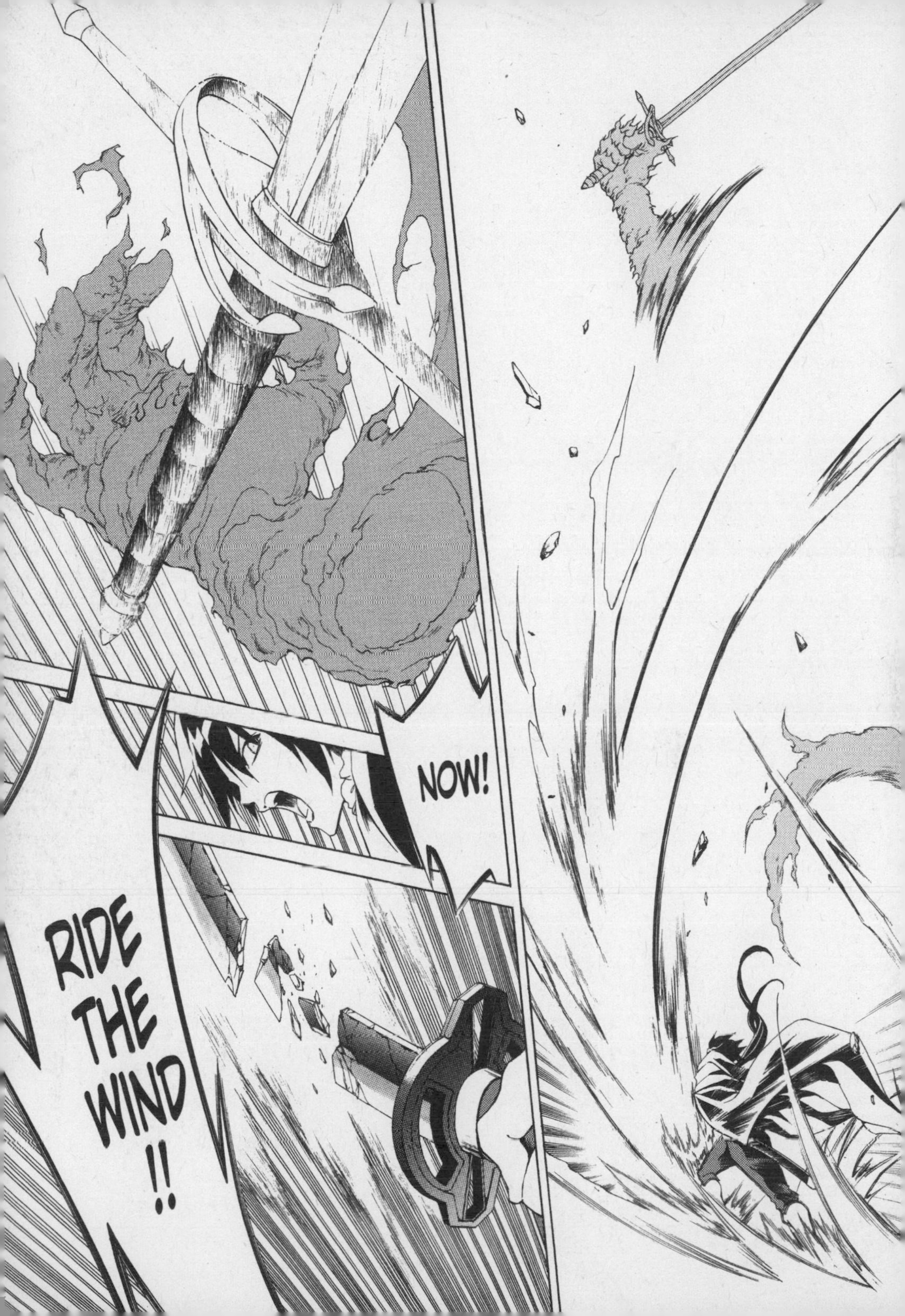
NOW!
RIDE THE WIND!!

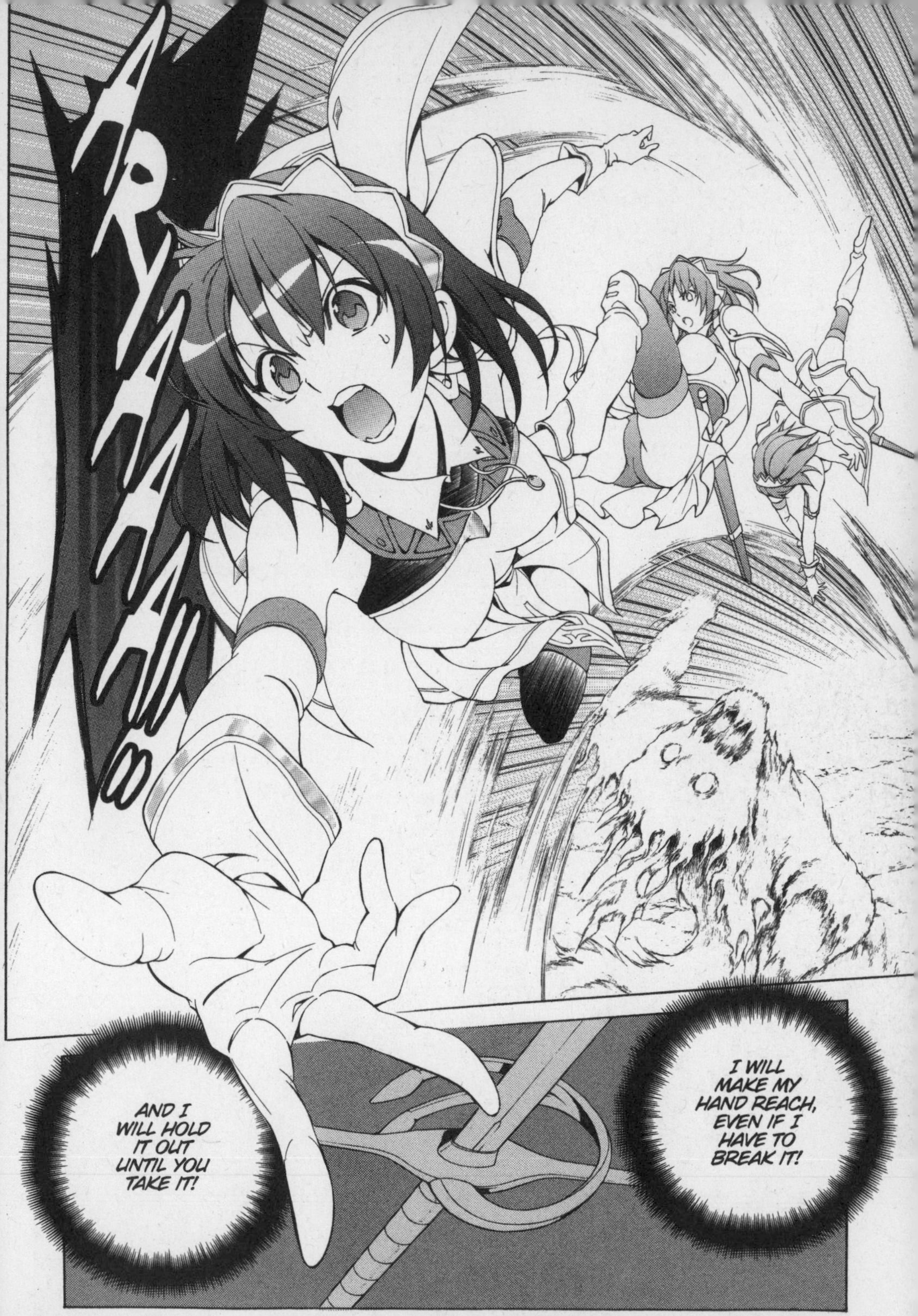
ARAAAA!!
I WILL MAKE MY HAND REACH, EVEN IF I HAVE TO BREAK IT!
AND I WILL HOLD IT OUT UNTIL YOU TAKE IT!

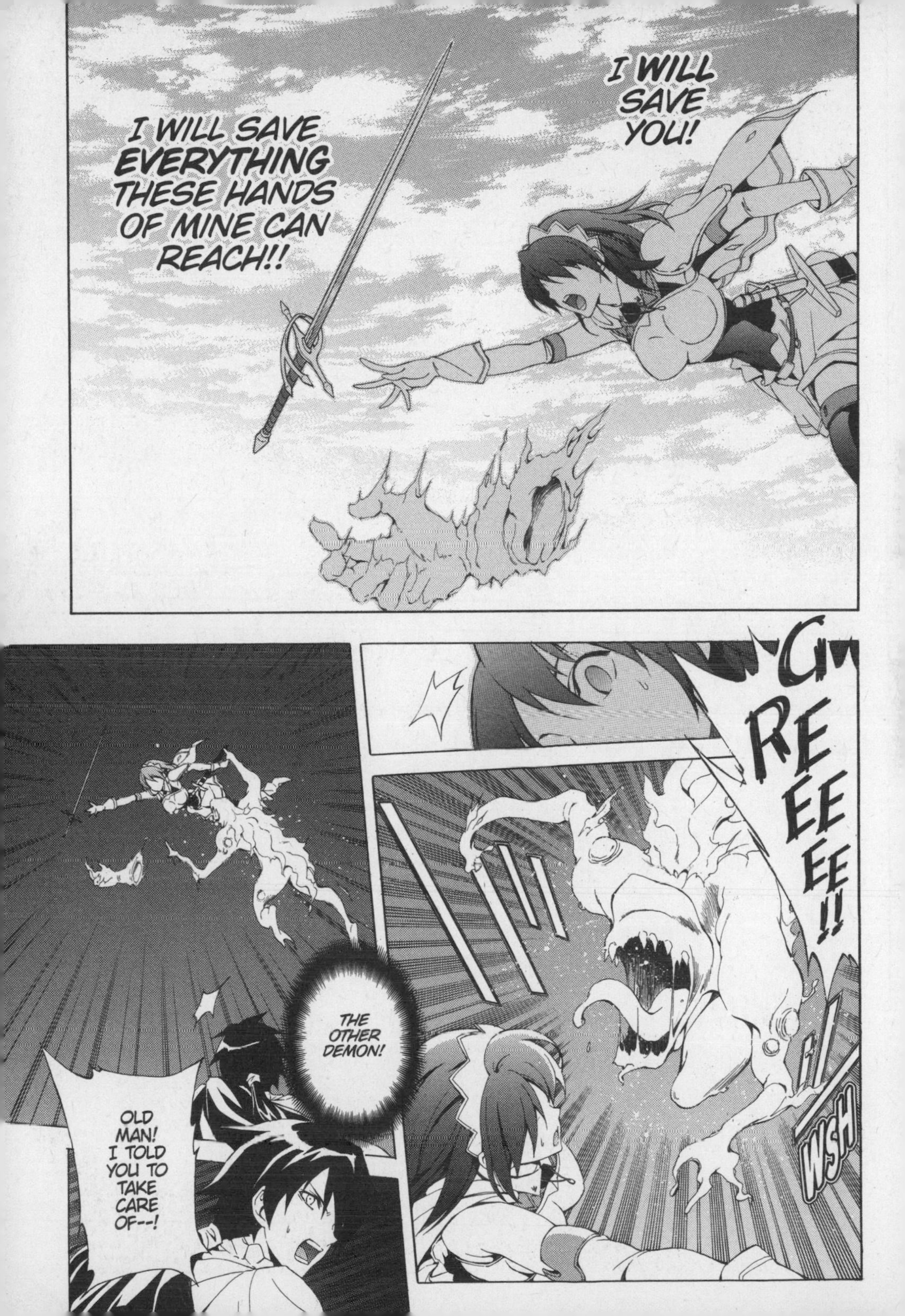
I WILL SAVE YOU!
I WILL SAVE EVERYTHING THESE HANDS OF MINE CAN REACH!!
GREEEE!!
WSH
THE OTHER DEMON!
OLD MAN! I TOLD YOU TO TAKE CARE OF--!

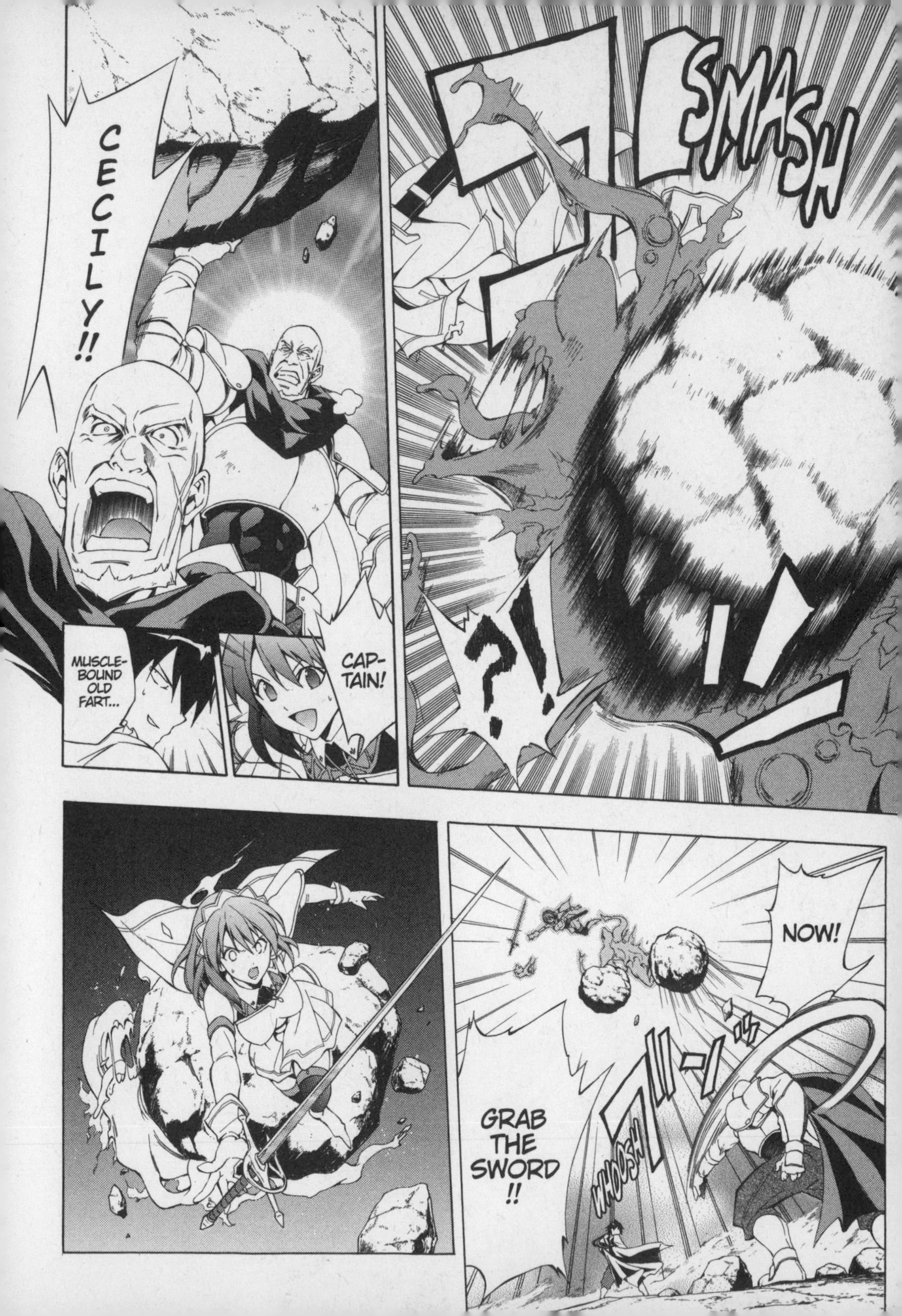
SMASH
?!
CECILY!!
CAP-TAIN!
MUSCLE-BOUND OLD FART...
NOW!
GRAB THE SWORD!!
WHOOSH

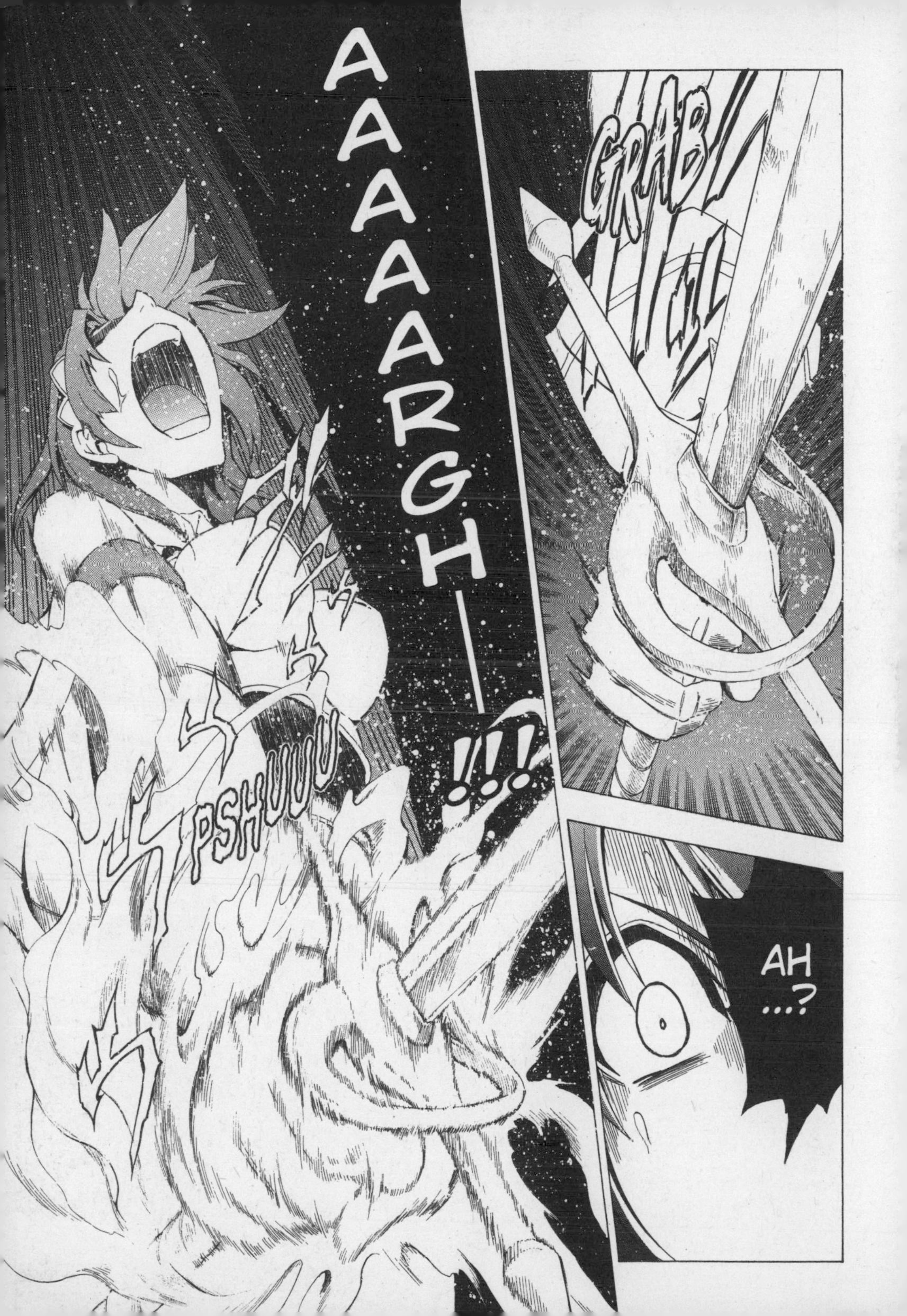
GRAB
AH ...?
AAAARGH—!!!
PSHUUU

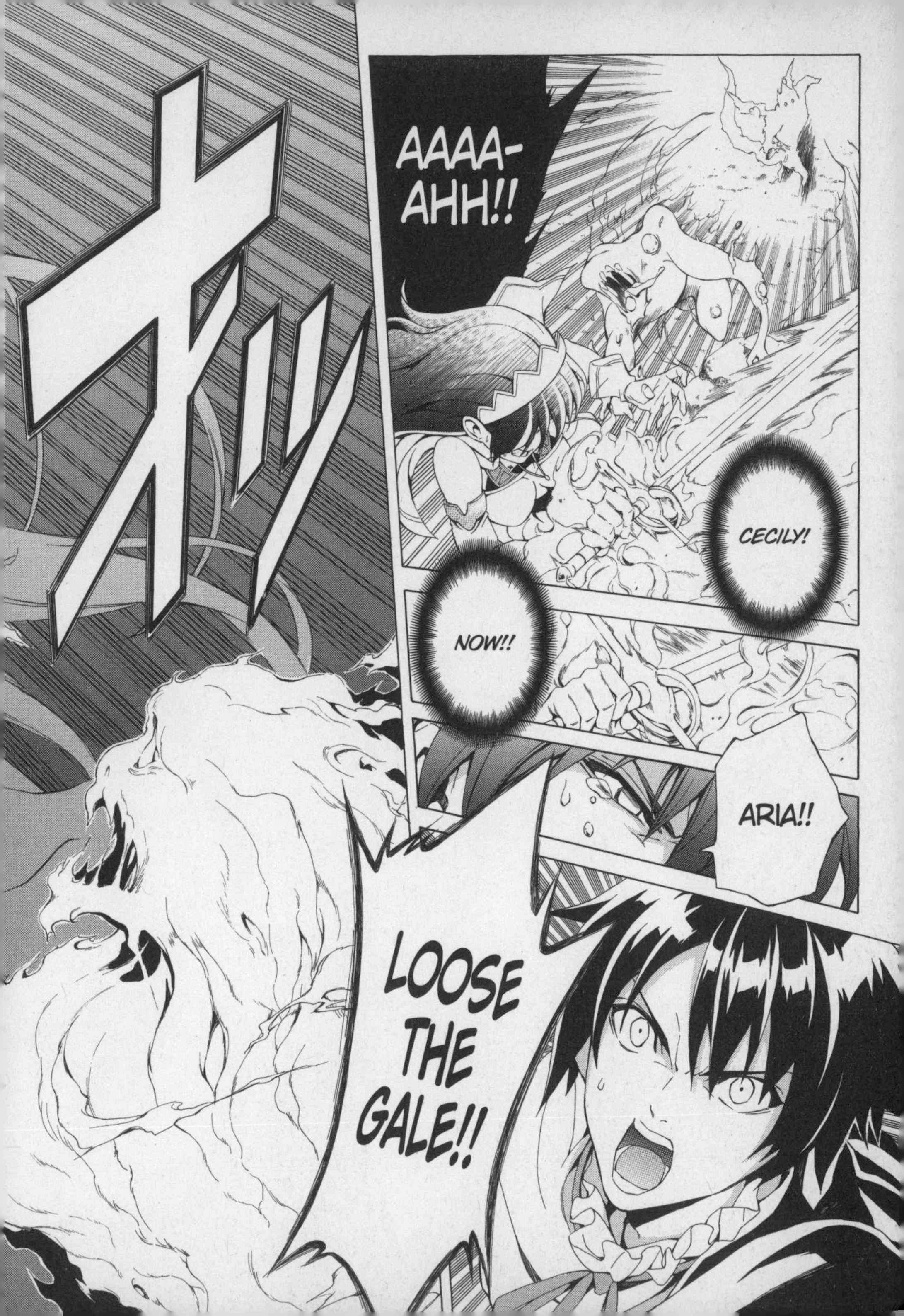
AAAA-AHH!!
CECILY!
NOW!!
ARIA!!
LOOSE THE GALE!!
オッ

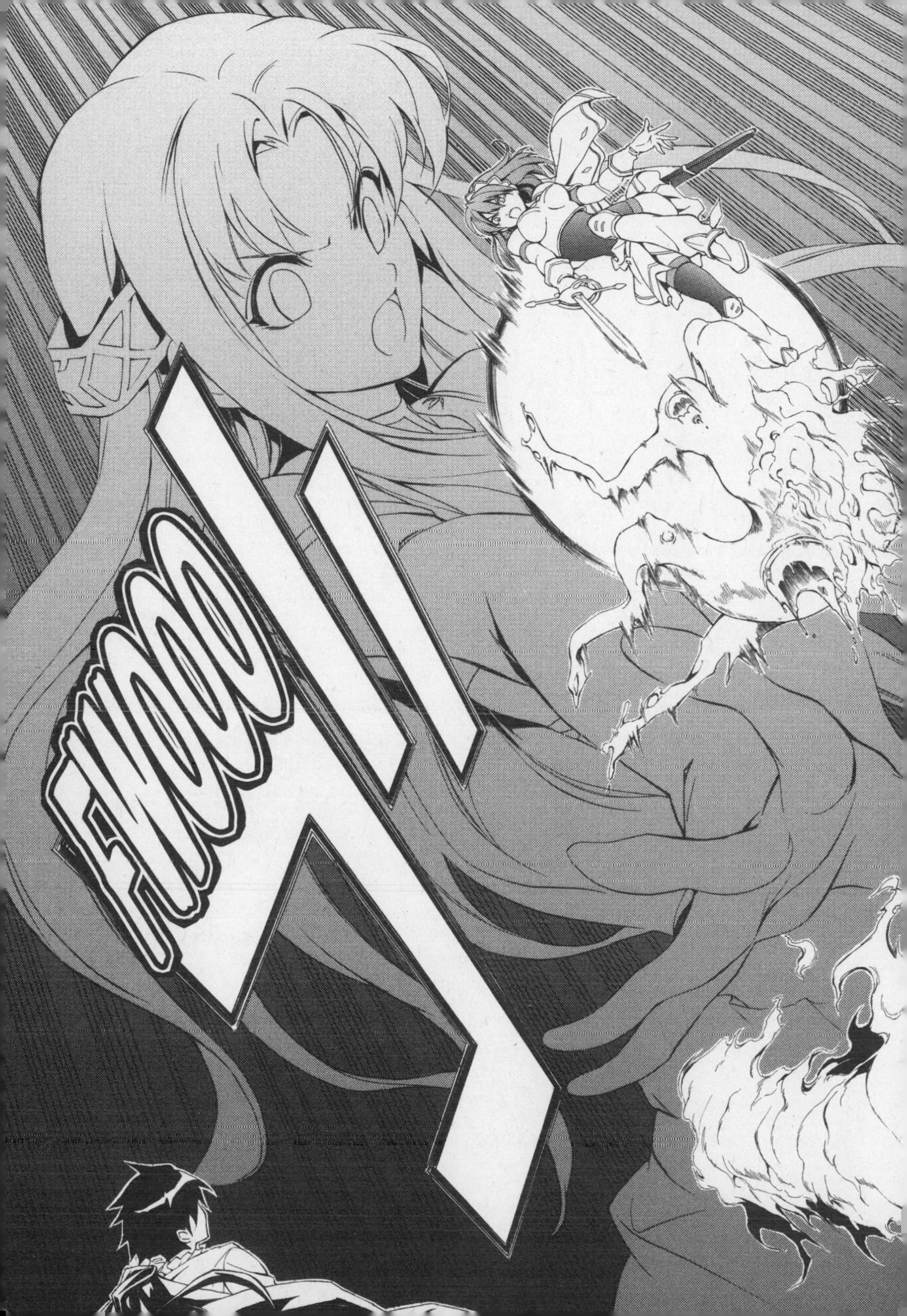
FWOOO!!

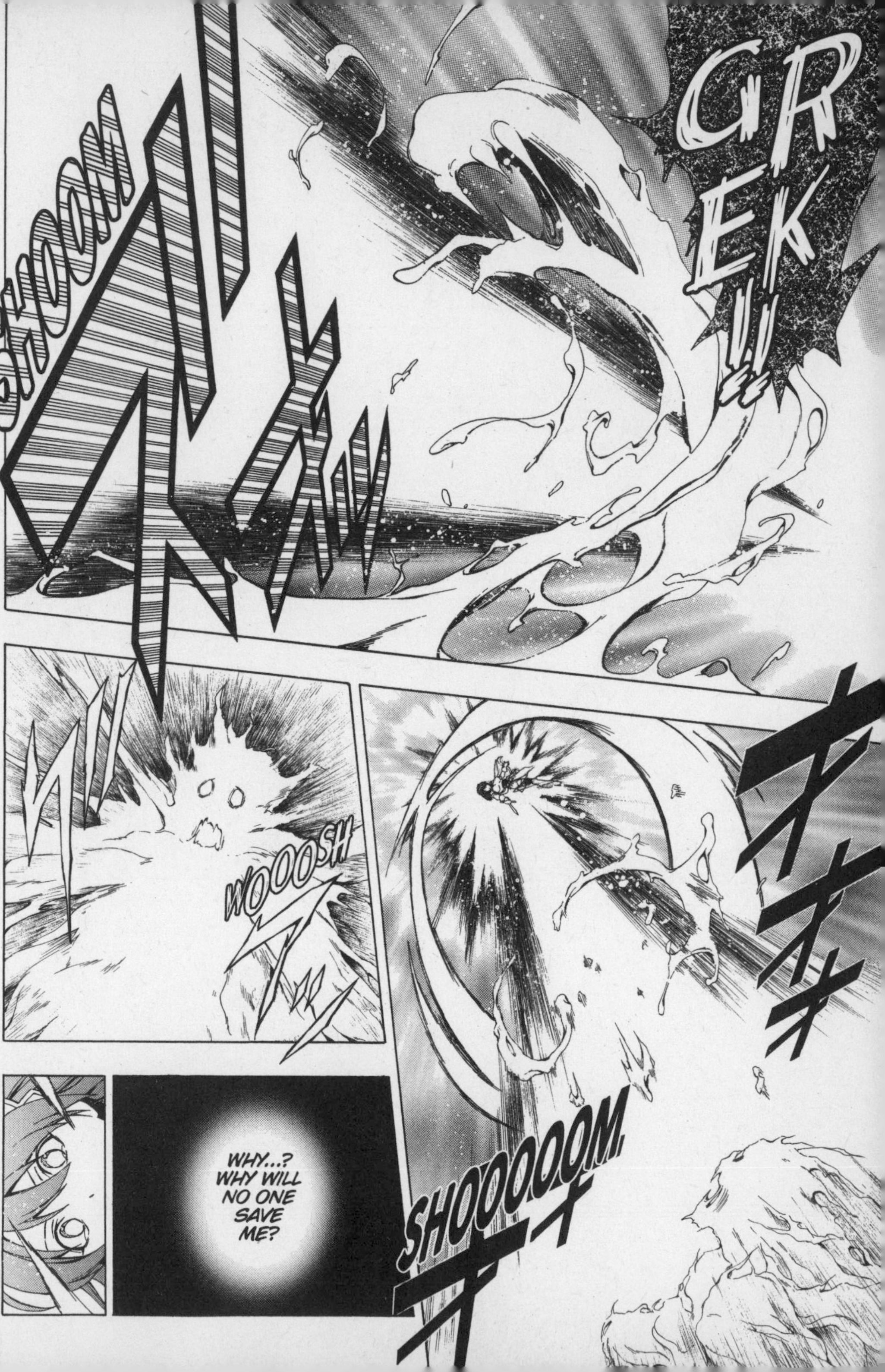
GREK!!
SHOOM
SHOOOOOM
WOOOSH
WHY...? WHY WILL NO ONE SAVE ME?

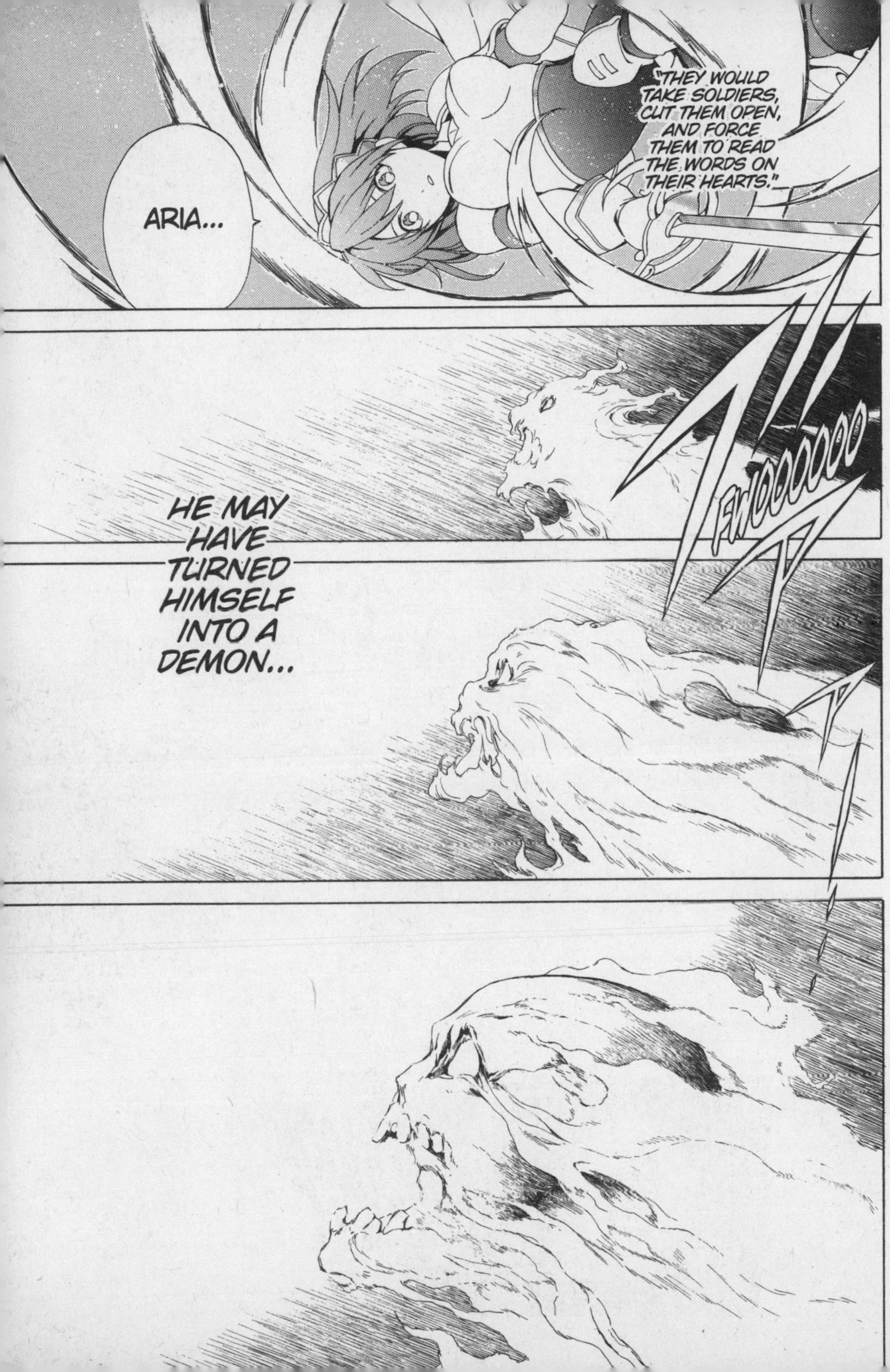

"THEY WOULD TAKE SOLDIERS, CUT THEM OPEN, AND FORCE THEM TO READ THE WORDS ON THEIR HEARTS."
ARIA...
FWOOOOOOO
HE MAY HAVE TURNED HIMSELF INTO A DEMON...

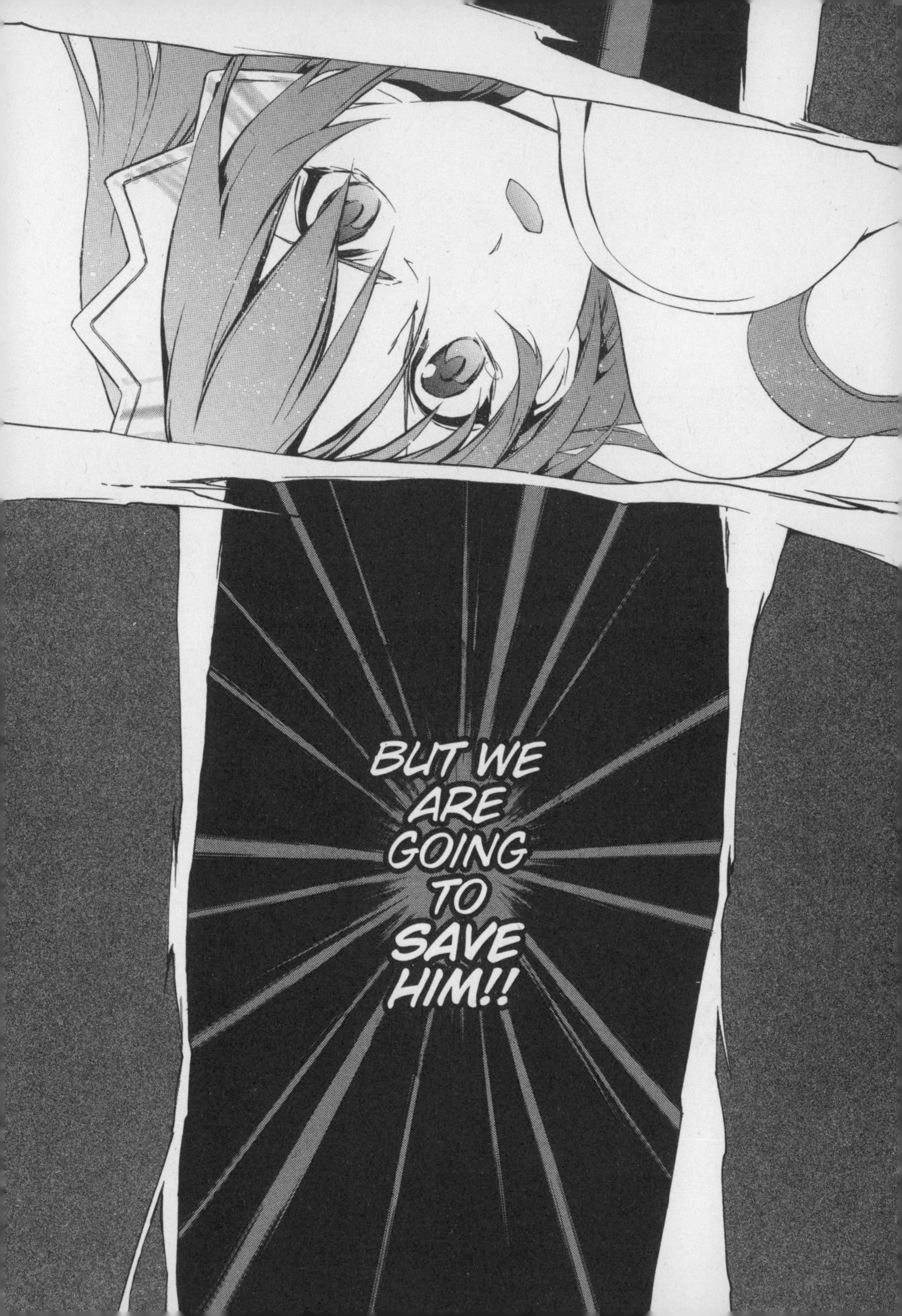
BUT WE ARE GOING TO SAVE HIM!!

The Sacred Blacksmith

聖剣の刀鍛冶

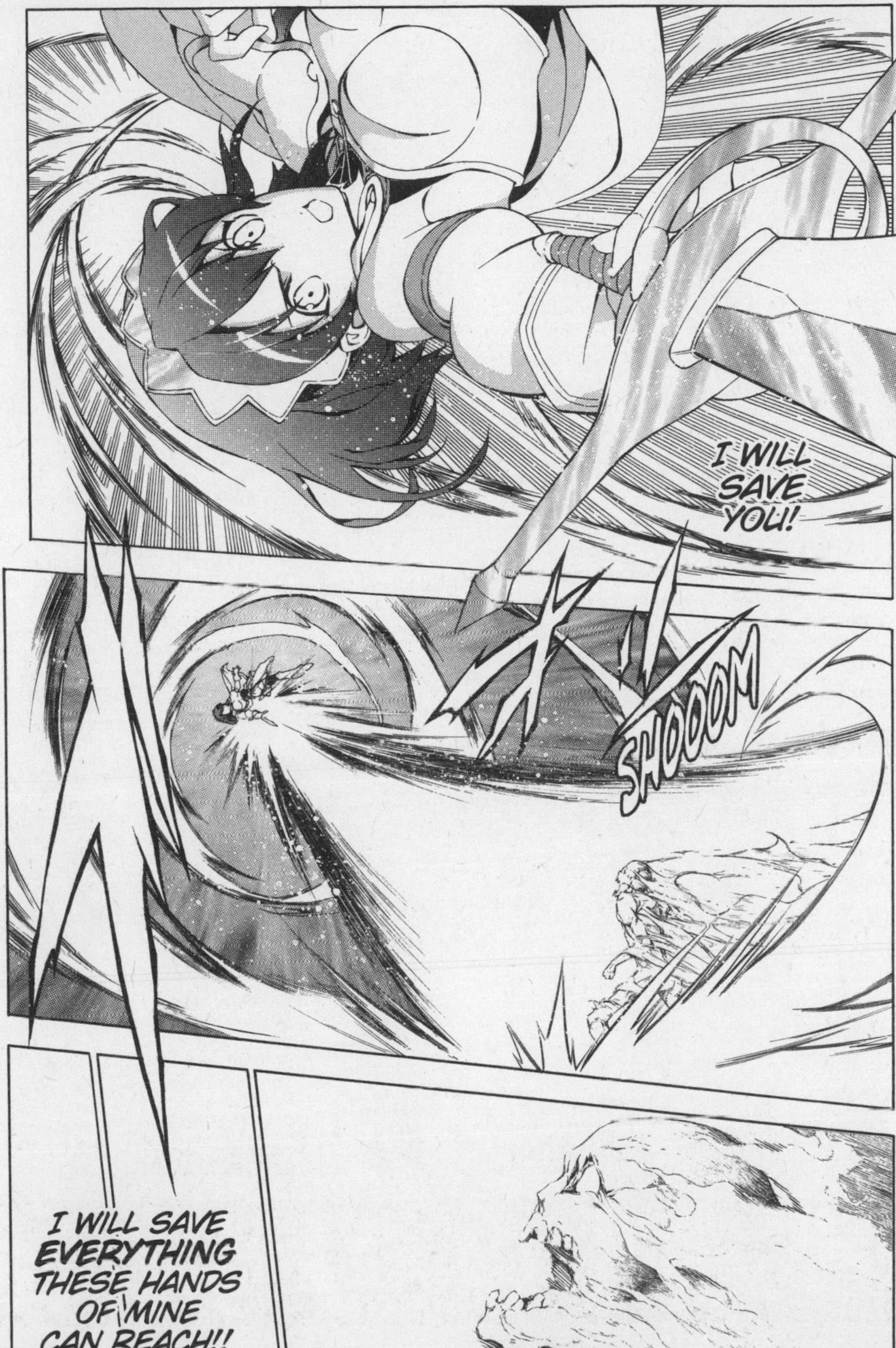
I WILL SAVE YOU!
SHOOOM
I WILL SAVE EVERYTHING THESE HANDS OF MINE CAN REACH!!

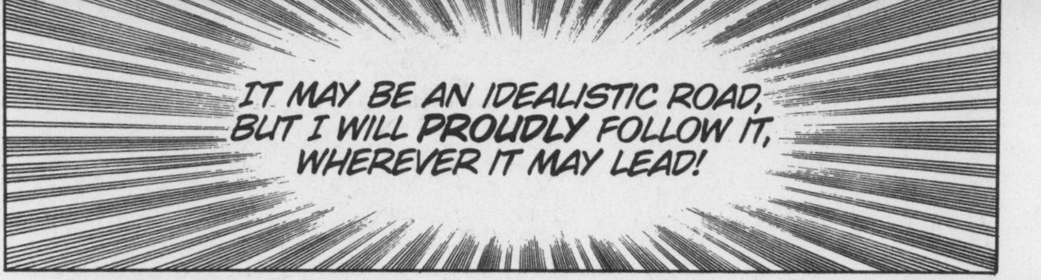
IT MAY BE AN IDEALISTIC ROAD, BUT I WILL **PROUDLY** FOLLOW IT, WHEREVER IT MAY LEAD!
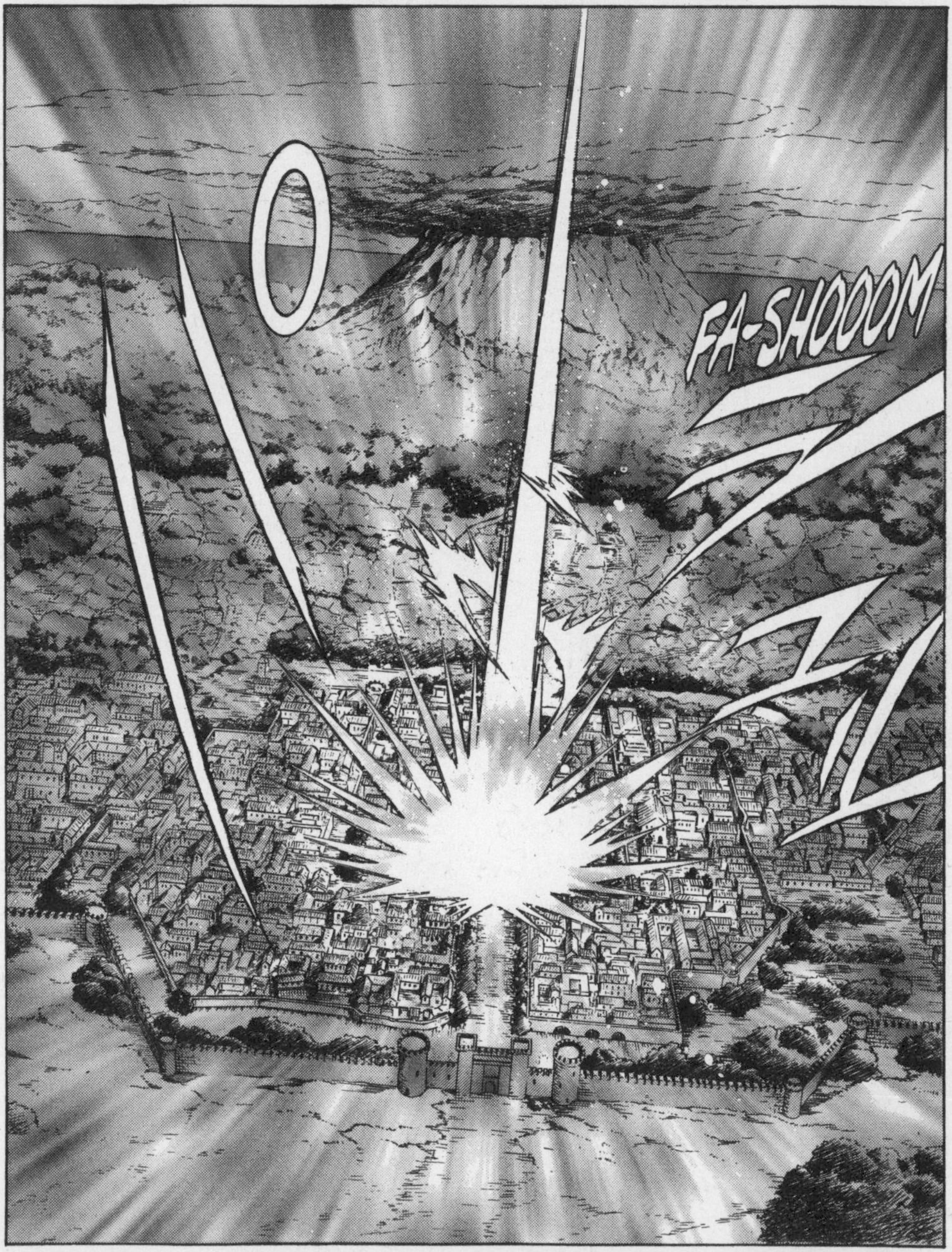
FA-SHOOOM

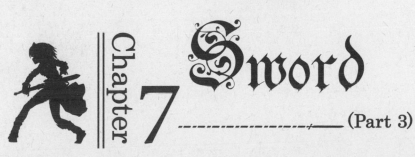

Chapter 7 **Sword** ———————————— (Part 3)

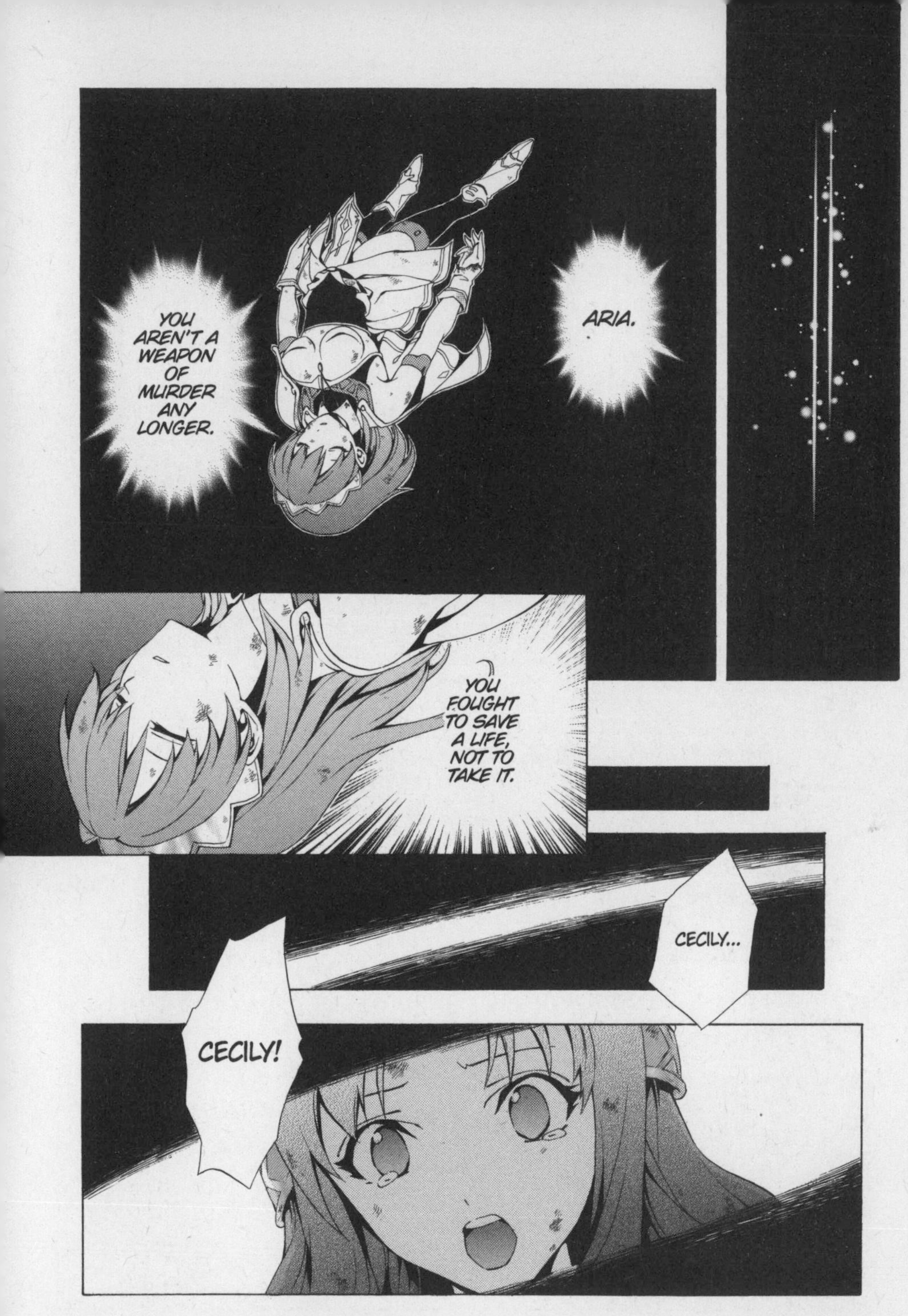
ARIA.
YOU AREN'T A WEAPON OF MURDER ANY LONGER.
YOU FOUGHT TO SAVE A LIFE, NOT TO TAKE IT.
CECILY...
CECILY!

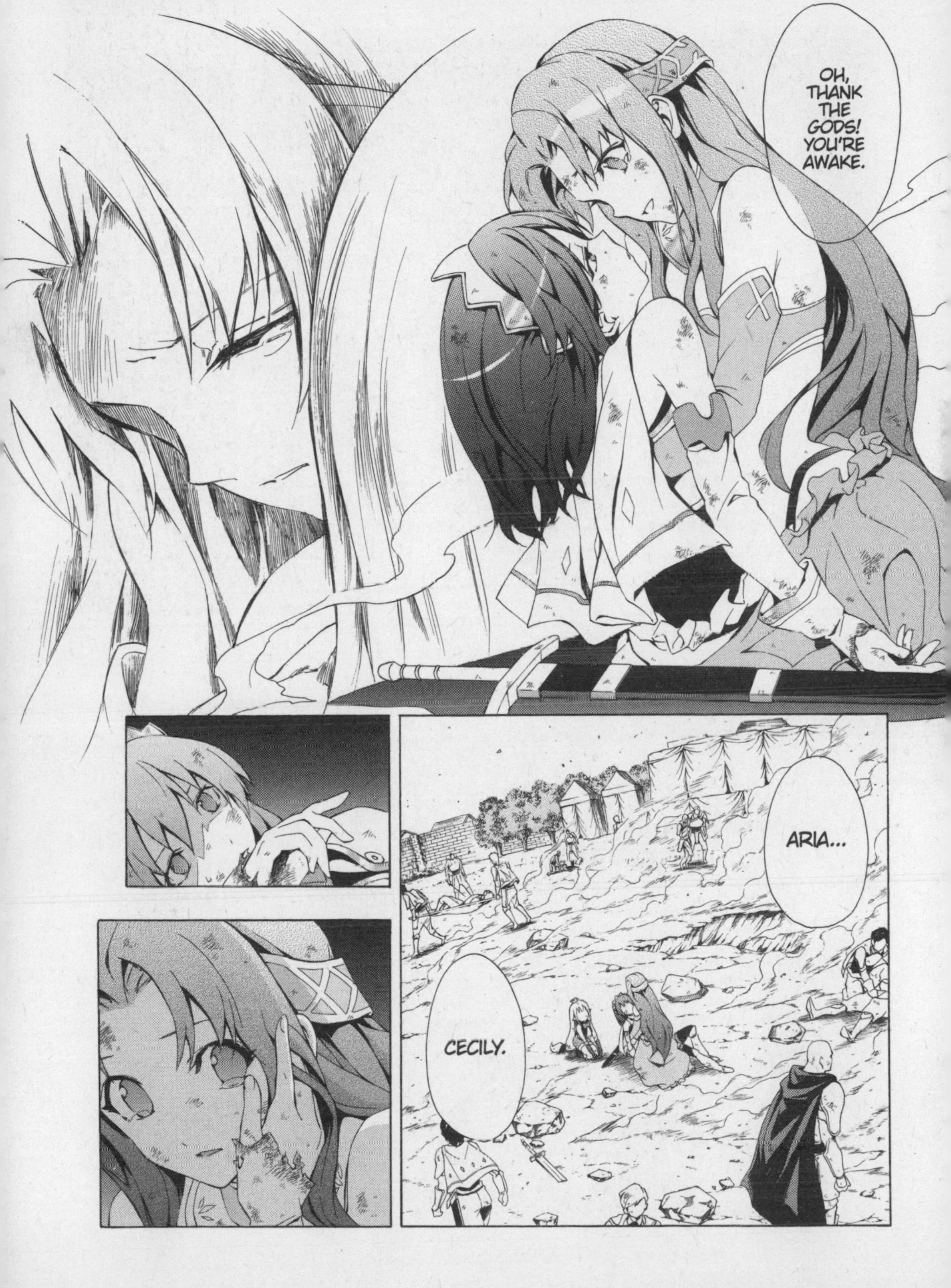
OH, THANK THE GODS! YOU'RE AWAKE.
ARIA...
CECILY.

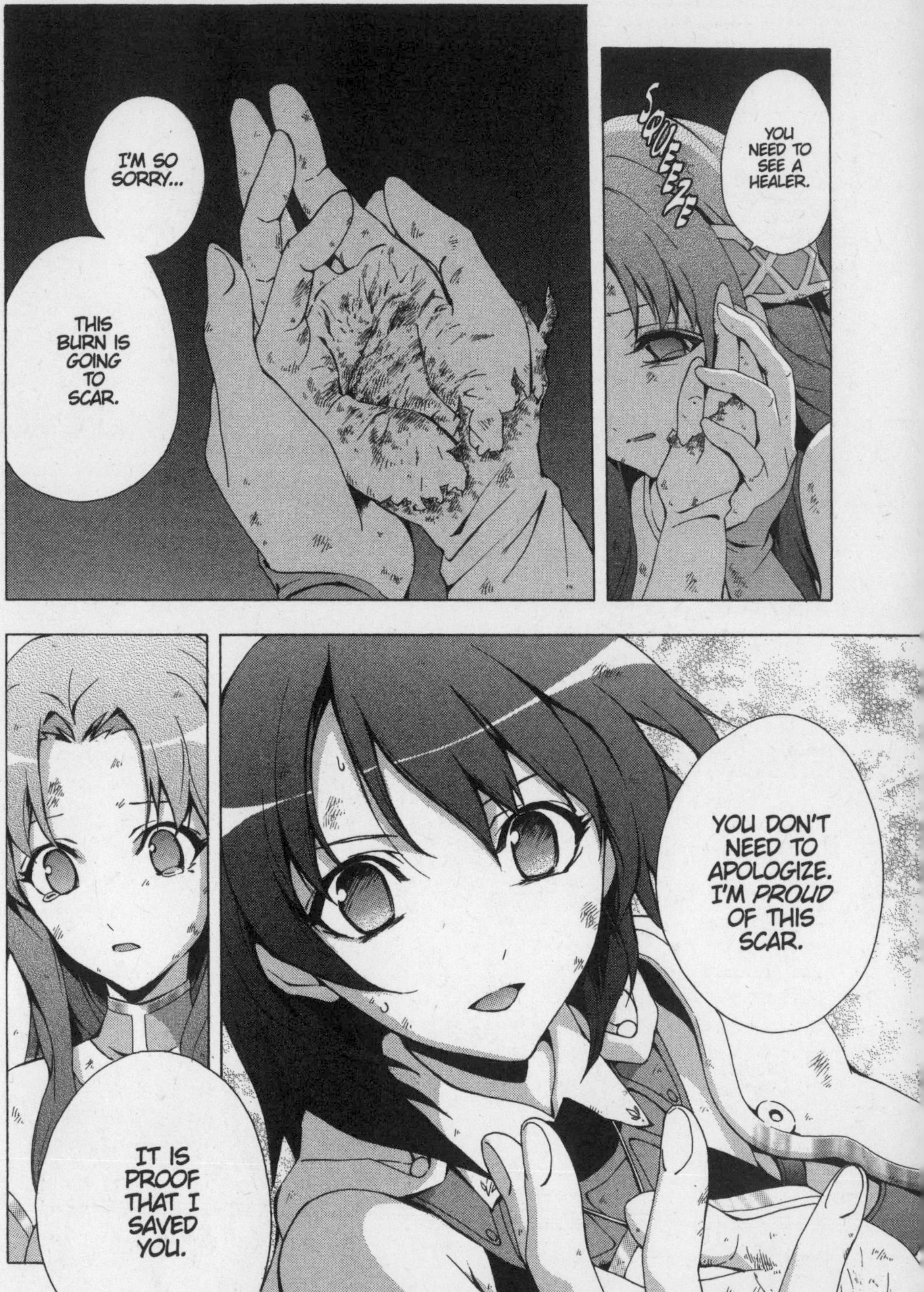
SQUEEEZE
YOU NEED TO SEE A HEALER.
I'M SO SORRY...
THIS BURN IS GOING TO SCAR.
YOU DON'T NEED TO APOLOGIZE. I'M *PROUD* OF THIS SCAR.
IT IS PROOF THAT I SAVED YOU.

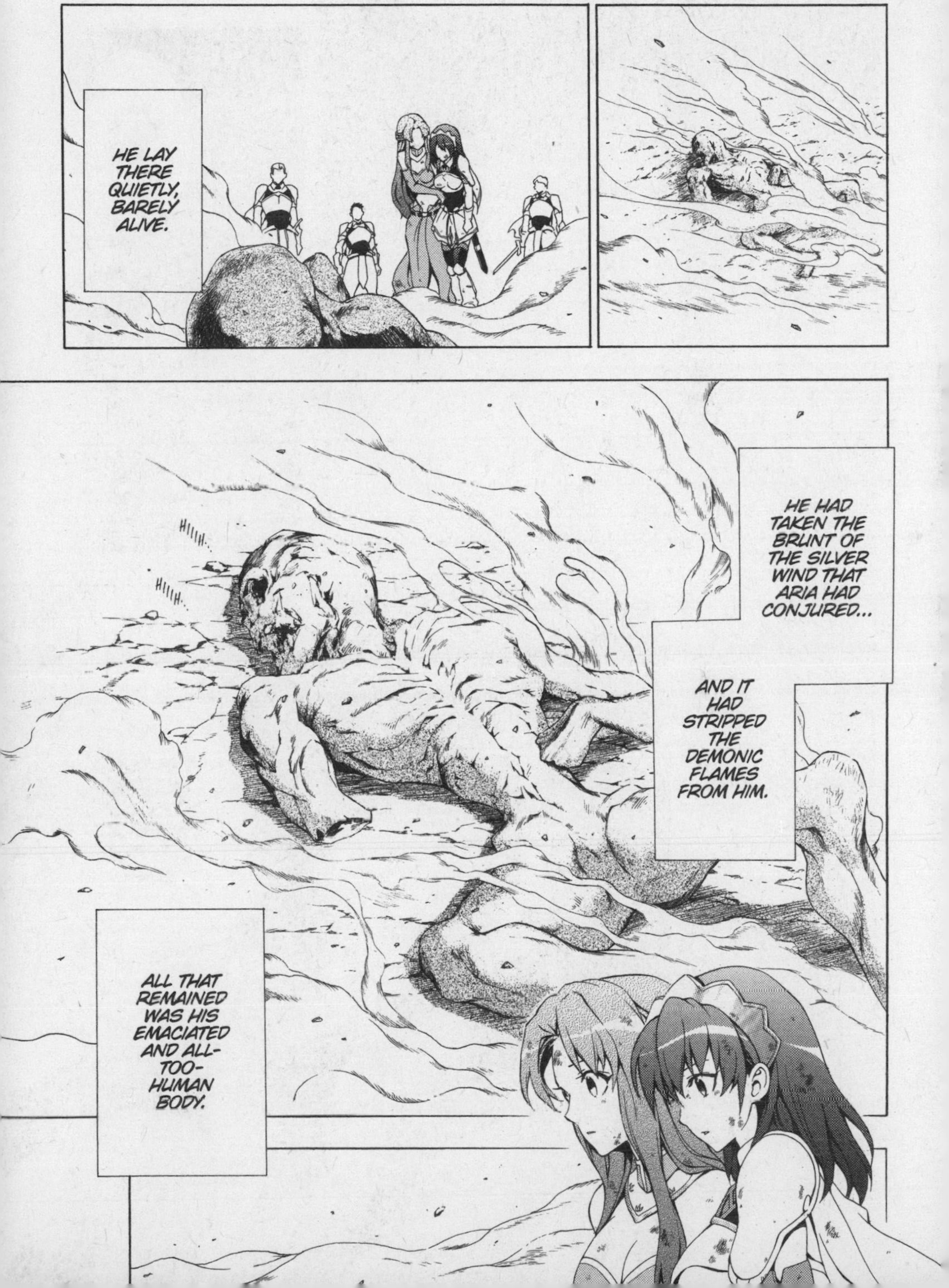
HE LAY THERE QUIETLY, BARELY ALIVE.
HE HAD TAKEN THE BRUNT OF THE SILVER WIND THAT ARIA HAD CONJURED...
AND IT HAD STRIPPED THE DEMONIC FLAMES FROM HIM.
HIIIH...
HIIIH...
ALL THAT REMAINED WAS HIS EMACIATED AND ALL-TOO-HUMAN BODY.

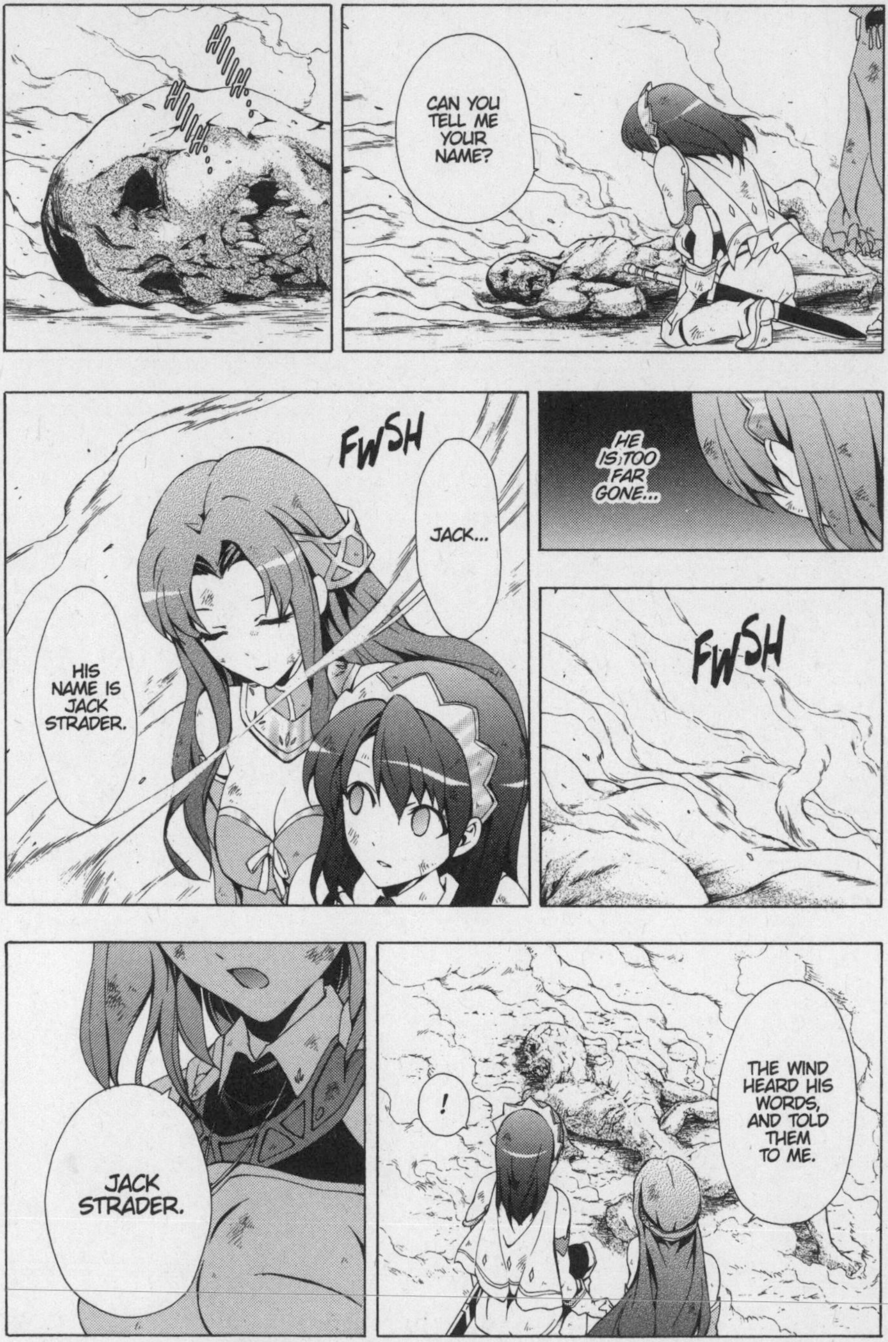
CAN YOU TELL ME YOUR NAME?
HIIIH
HIIIH
HE IS TOO FAR GONE...
FWSH
FWSH
JACK...
HIS NAME IS JACK STRADER.
THE WIND HEARD HIS WORDS, AND TOLD THEM TO ME.
!
JACK STRADER.

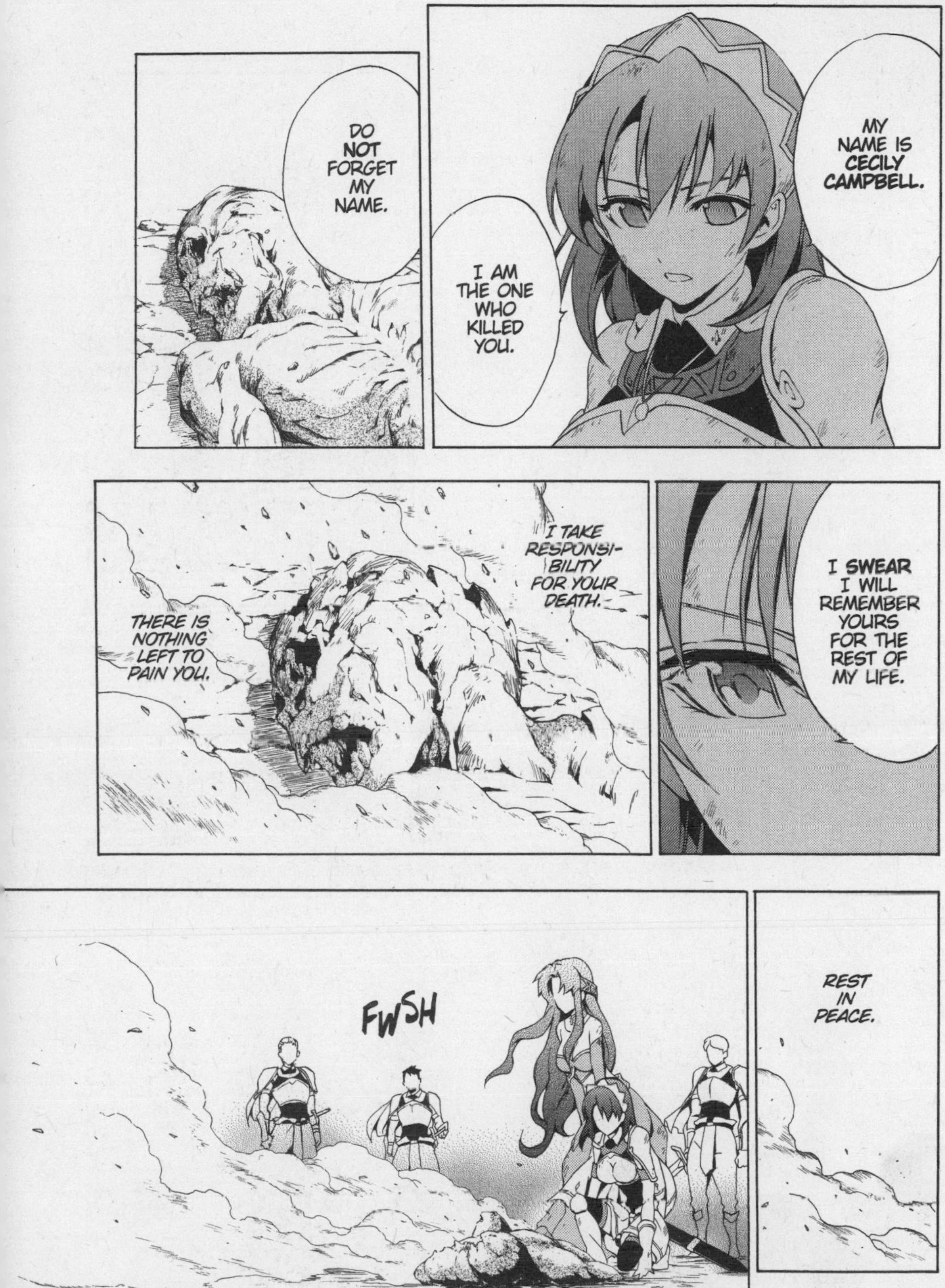
MY NAME IS CECILY CAMPBELL.
I AM THE ONE WHO KILLED YOU.
DO NOT FORGET MY NAME.
I SWEAR I WILL REMEMBER YOURS FOR THE REST OF MY LIFE.
I TAKE RESPONSIBILITY FOR YOUR DEATH.
THERE IS NOTHING LEFT TO PAIN YOU.
REST IN PEACE.
FWSH

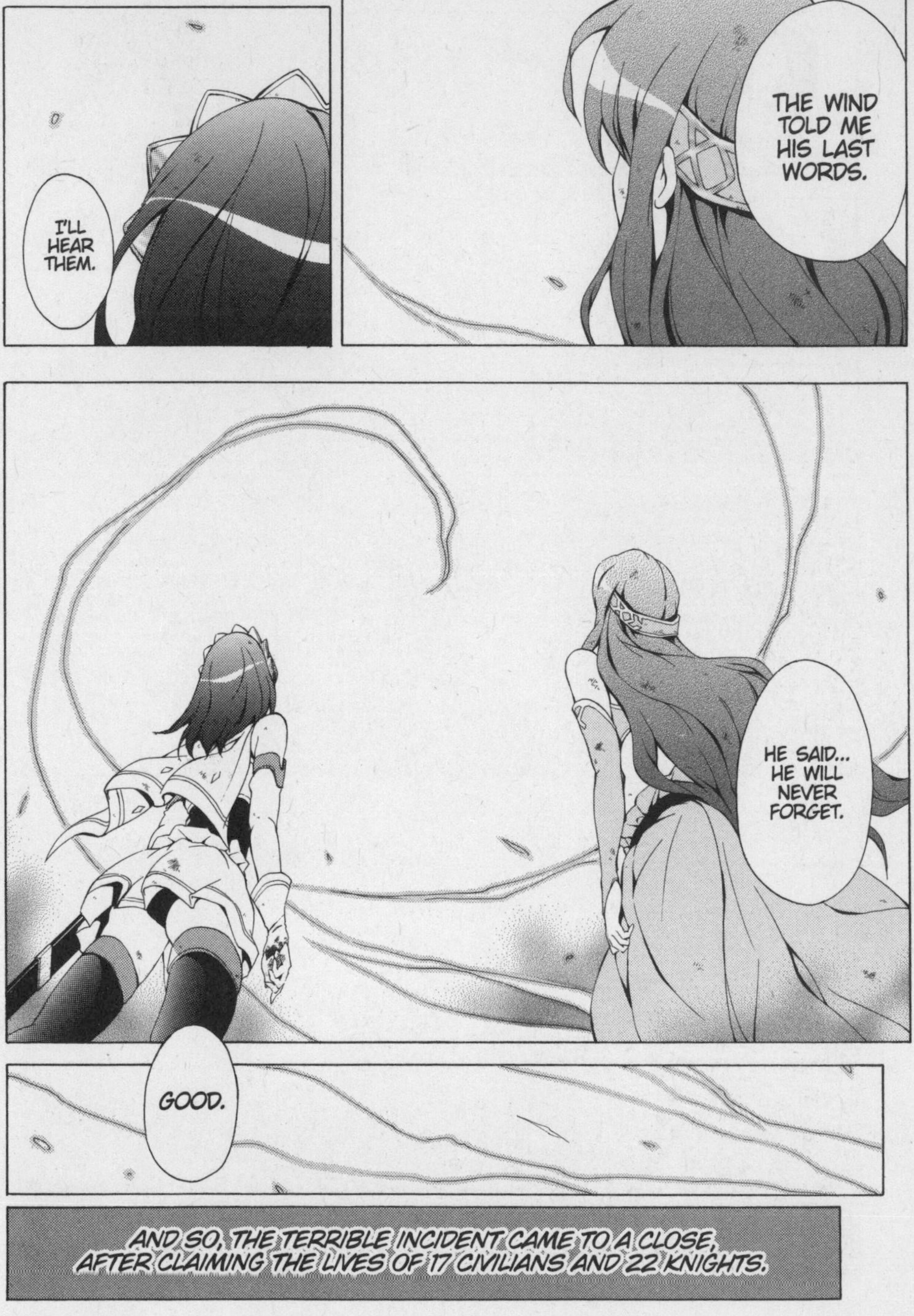
THE WIND TOLD ME HIS LAST WORDS.
I'LL HEAR THEM.
HE SAID... HE WILL NEVER FORGET.
GOOD.
AND SO, THE TERRIBLE INCIDENT CAME TO A CLOSE, AFTER CLAIMING THE LIVES OF 17 CIVILIANS AND 22 KNIGHTS.

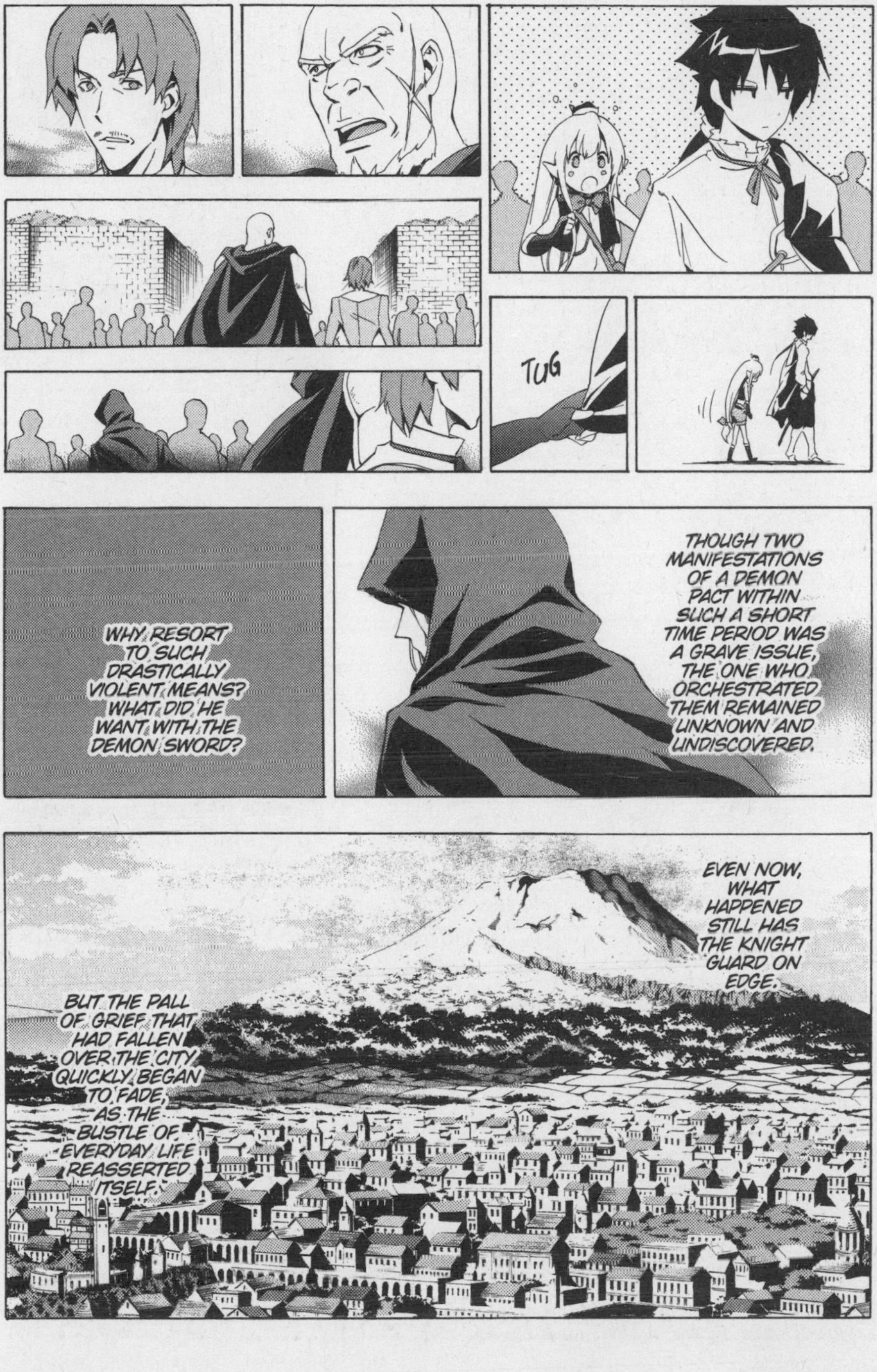

TUG
THOUGH TWO MANIFESTATIONS OF A DEMON PACT WITHIN SUCH A SHORT TIME PERIOD WAS A GRAVE ISSUE, THE ONE WHO ORCHESTRATED THEM REMAINED UNKNOWN AND UNDISCOVERED.
WHY RESORT TO SUCH DRASTICALLY VIOLENT MEANS? WHAT DID HE WANT WITH THE DEMON SWORD?
EVEN NOW, WHAT HAPPENED STILL HAS THE KNIGHT GUARD ON EDGE.
BUT THE PALL OF GRIEF THAT HAD FALLEN OVER THE CITY QUICKLY BEGAN TO FADE, AS THE BUSTLE OF EVERYDAY LIFE REASSERTED ITSELF.

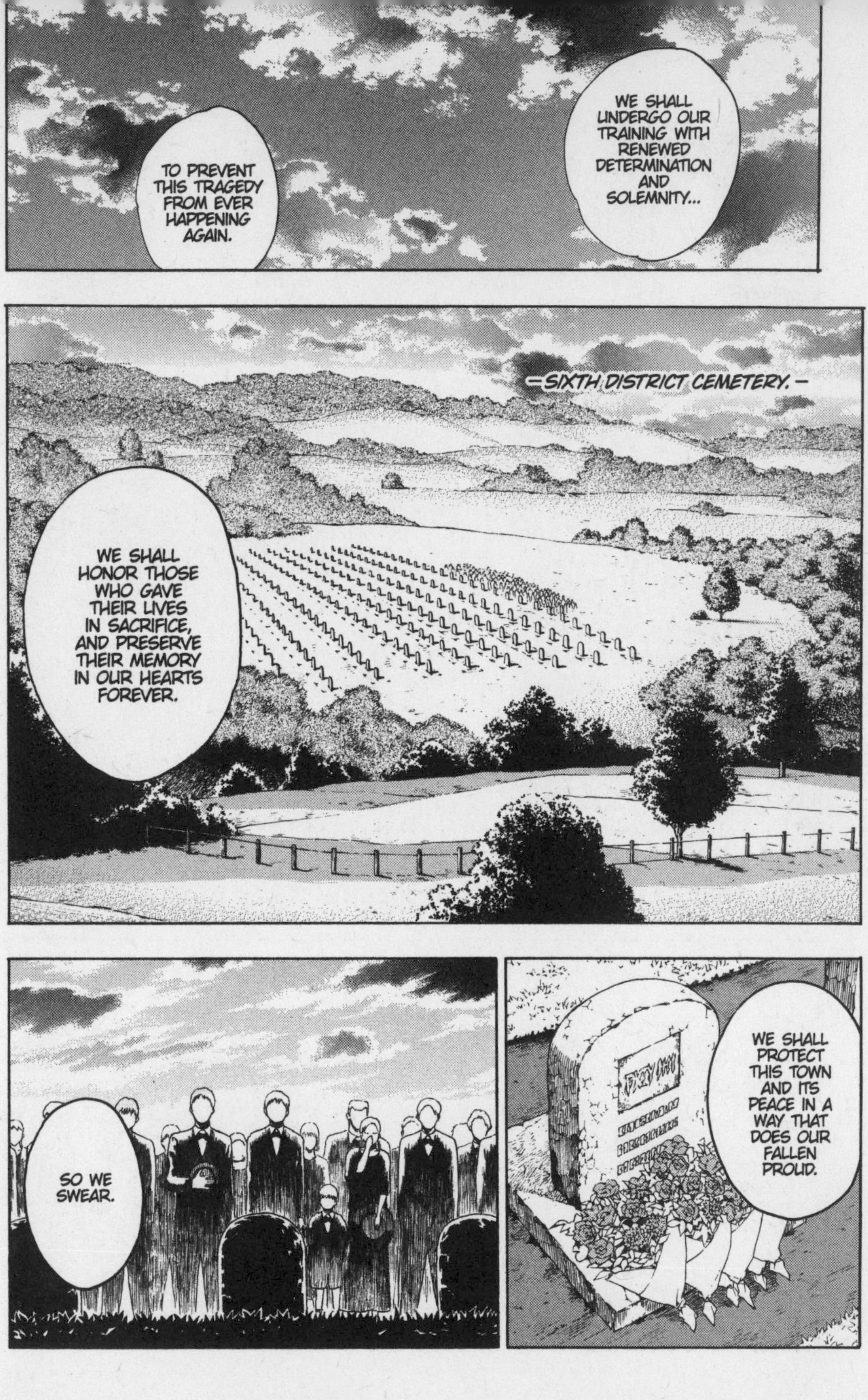
WE SHALL UNDERGO OUR TRAINING WITH RENEWED DETERMINATION AND SOLEMNITY...
TO PREVENT THIS TRAGEDY FROM EVER HAPPENING AGAIN.
—SIXTH DISTRICT CEMETERY.—
WE SHALL HONOR THOSE WHO GAVE THEIR LIVES IN SACRIFICE, AND PRESERVE THEIR MEMORY IN OUR HEARTS FOREVER.
WE SHALL PROTECT THIS TOWN AND ITS PEACE IN A WAY THAT DOES OUR FALLEN PROUD.
SO WE SWEAR.

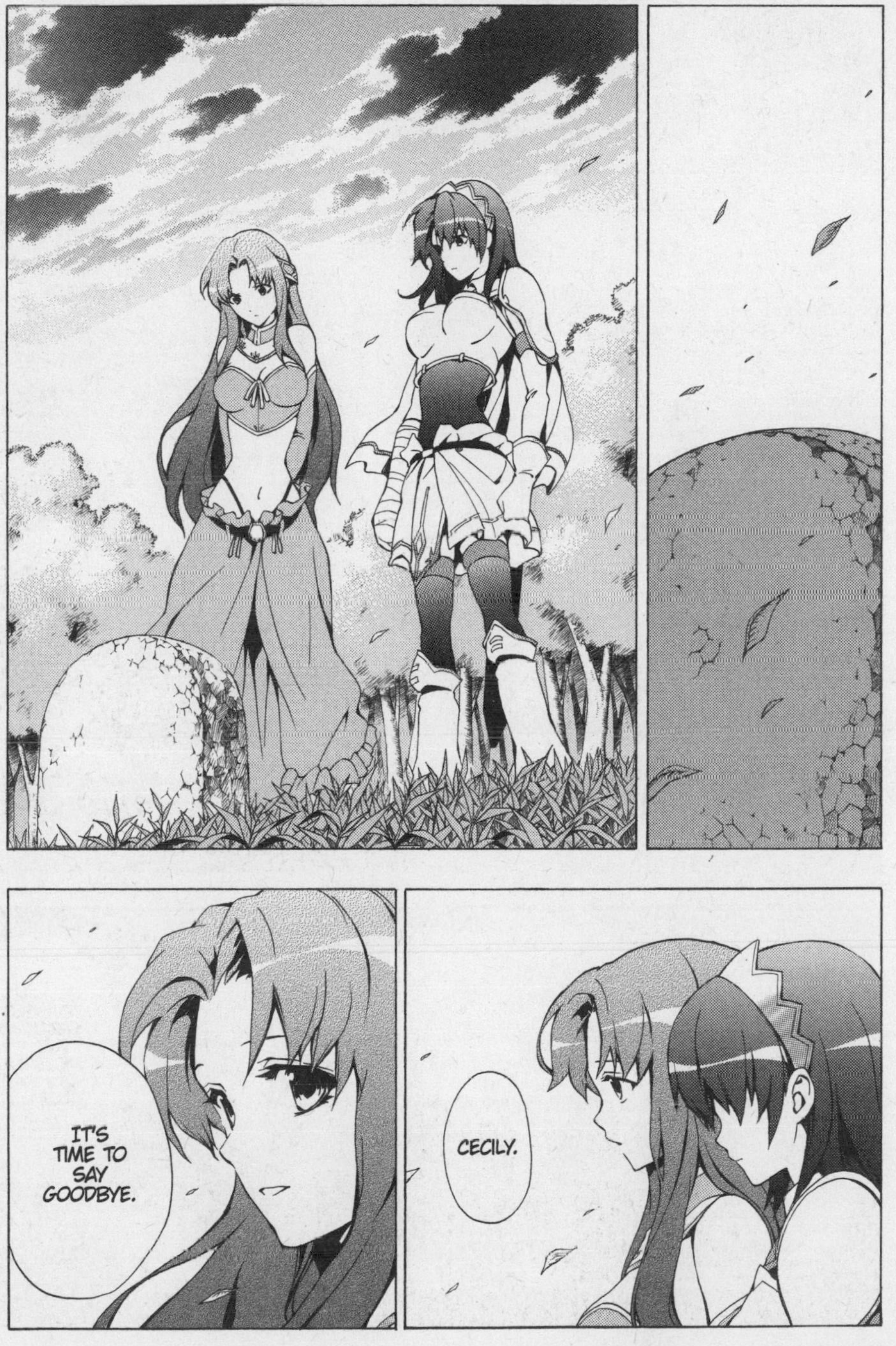
CECILY.
IT'S TIME TO SAY GOODBYE.

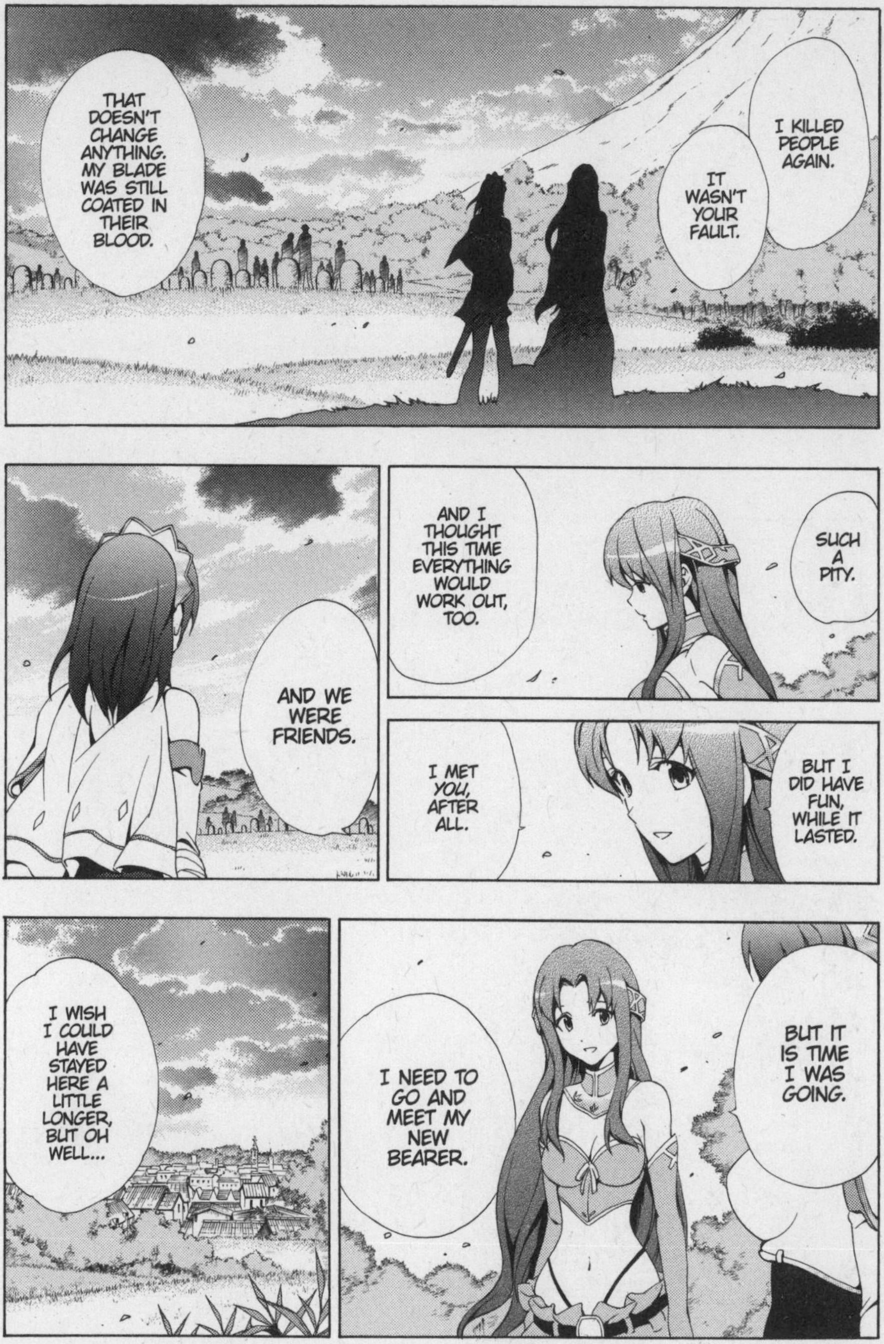
I KILLED PEOPLE AGAIN.
IT WASN'T YOUR FAULT.
THAT DOESN'T CHANGE ANYTHING. MY BLADE WAS STILL COATED IN THEIR BLOOD.
SUCH A PITY.
AND I THOUGHT THIS TIME EVERYTHING WOULD WORK OUT, TOO.
BUT I DID HAVE FUN, WHILE IT LASTED.
I MET *YOU*, AFTER ALL.
AND WE WERE FRIENDS.
BUT IT IS TIME I WAS GOING.
I NEED TO GO AND MEET MY NEW BEARER.
I WISH I COULD HAVE STAYED HERE A LITTLE LONGER, BUT OH WELL...

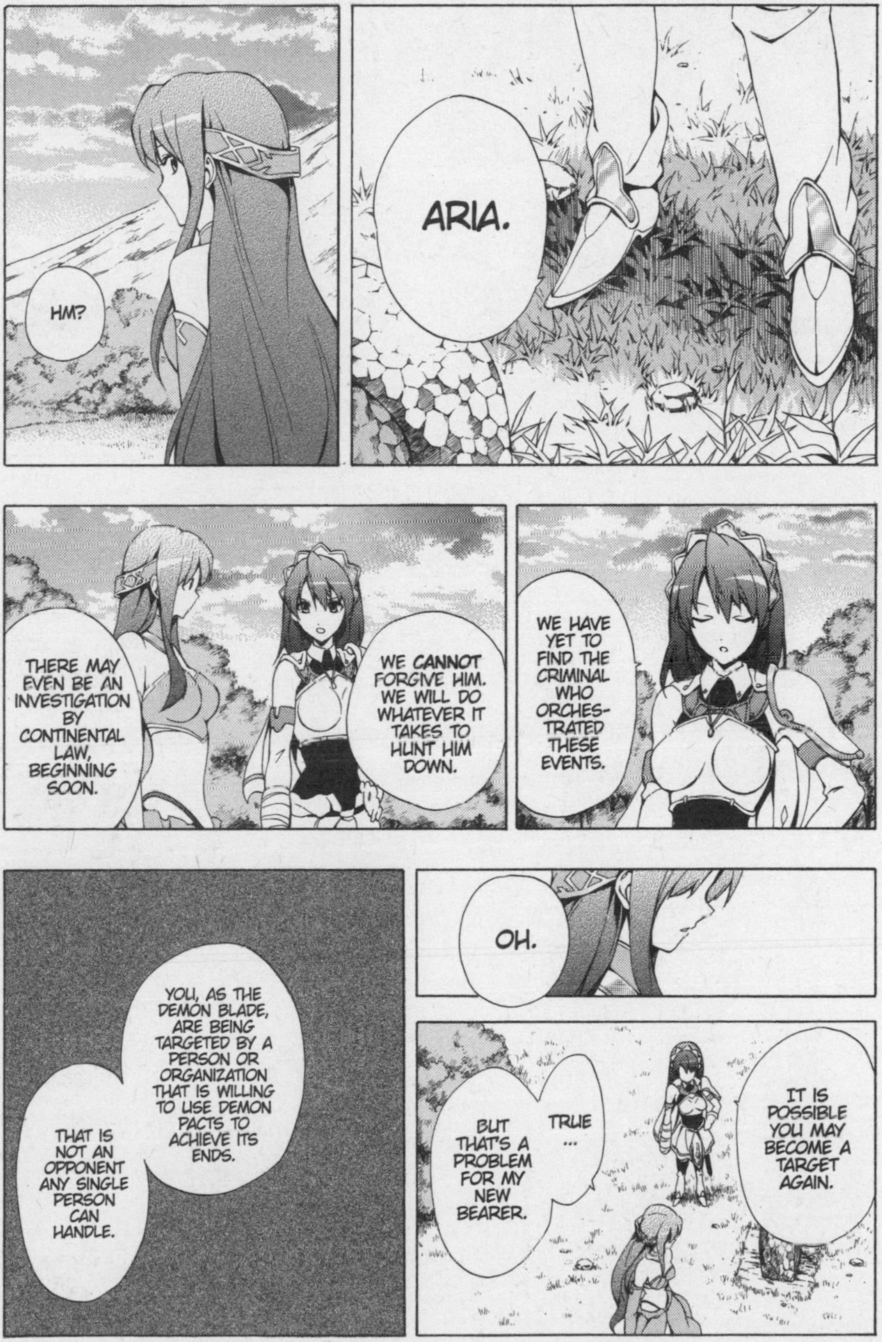
ARIA.
HM?
WE HAVE YET TO FIND THE CRIMINAL WHO ORCHES-TRATED THESE EVENTS.
WE CANNOT FORGIVE HIM. WE WILL DO WHATEVER IT TAKES TO HUNT HIM DOWN.
THERE MAY EVEN BE AN INVESTIGATION BY CONTINENTAL LAW, BEGINNING SOON.
OH.
IT IS POSSIBLE YOU MAY BECOME A TARGET AGAIN.
TRUE ...
BUT THAT'S A PROBLEM FOR MY NEW BEARER.
YOU, AS THE DEMON BLADE, ARE BEING TARGETED BY A PERSON OR ORGANIZATION THAT IS WILLING TO USE DEMON PACTS TO ACHIEVE ITS ENDS.
THAT IS NOT AN OPPONENT ANY SINGLE PERSON CAN HANDLE.

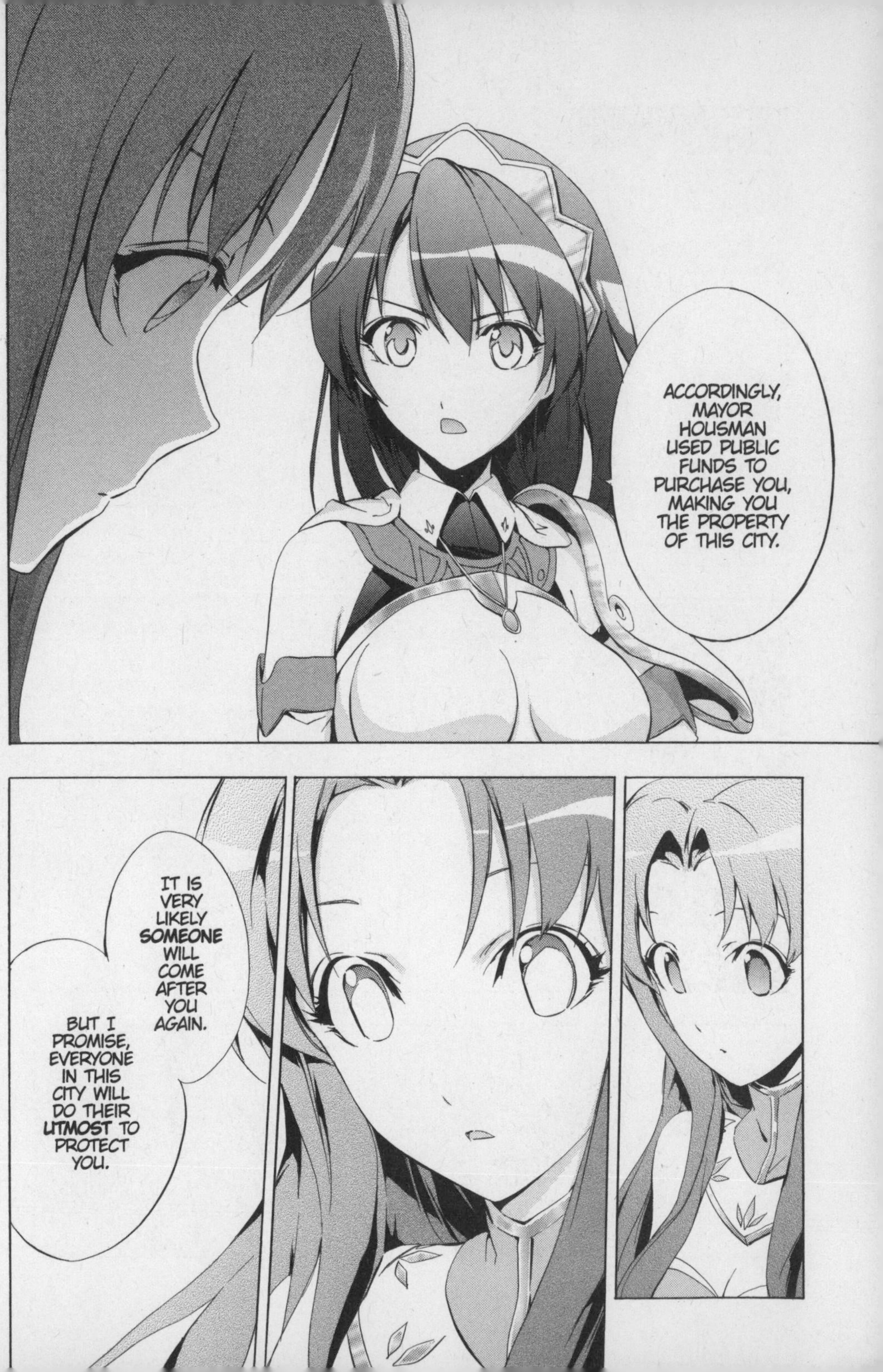
ACCORDINGLY, MAYOR HOUSMAN USED PUBLIC FUNDS TO PURCHASE YOU, MAKING YOU THE PROPERTY OF THIS CITY.
IT IS VERY LIKELY **SOMEONE** WILL COME AFTER YOU AGAIN.
BUT I PROMISE, EVERYONE IN THIS CITY WILL DO THEIR **UTMOST** TO PROTECT YOU.

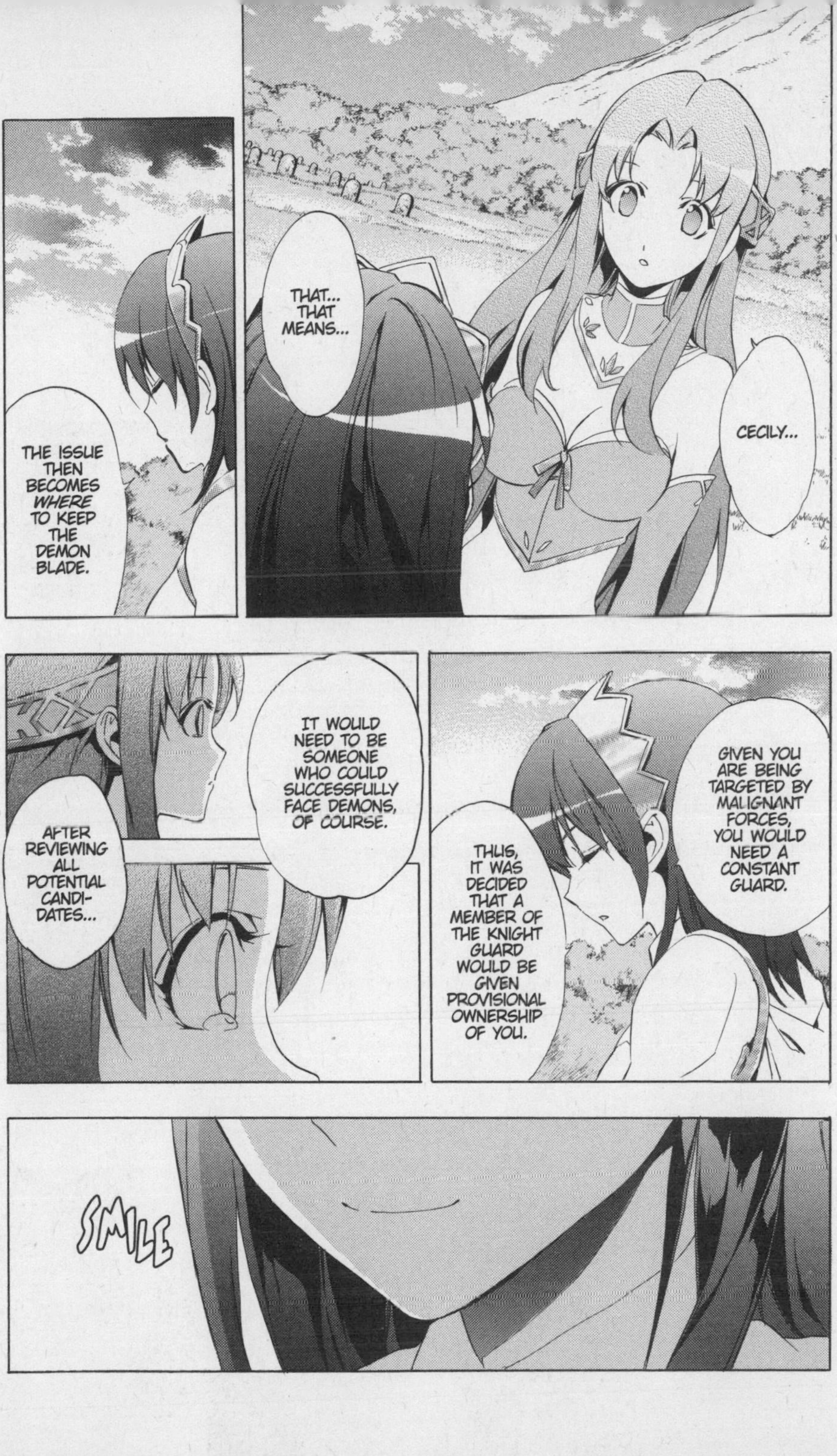
CECILY...
THAT... THAT MEANS...
THE ISSUE THEN BECOMES *WHERE* TO KEEP THE DEMON BLADE.
GIVEN YOU ARE BEING TARGETED BY MALIGNANT FORCES, YOU WOULD NEED A CONSTANT GUARD.
THUS, IT WAS DECIDED THAT A MEMBER OF THE KNIGHT GUARD WOULD BE GIVEN PROVISIONAL OWNERSHIP OF YOU.
IT WOULD NEED TO BE SOMEONE WHO COULD SUCCESSFULLY FACE DEMONS, OF COURSE.
AFTER REVIEWING ALL POTENTIAL CANDI-DATES...
SMILE

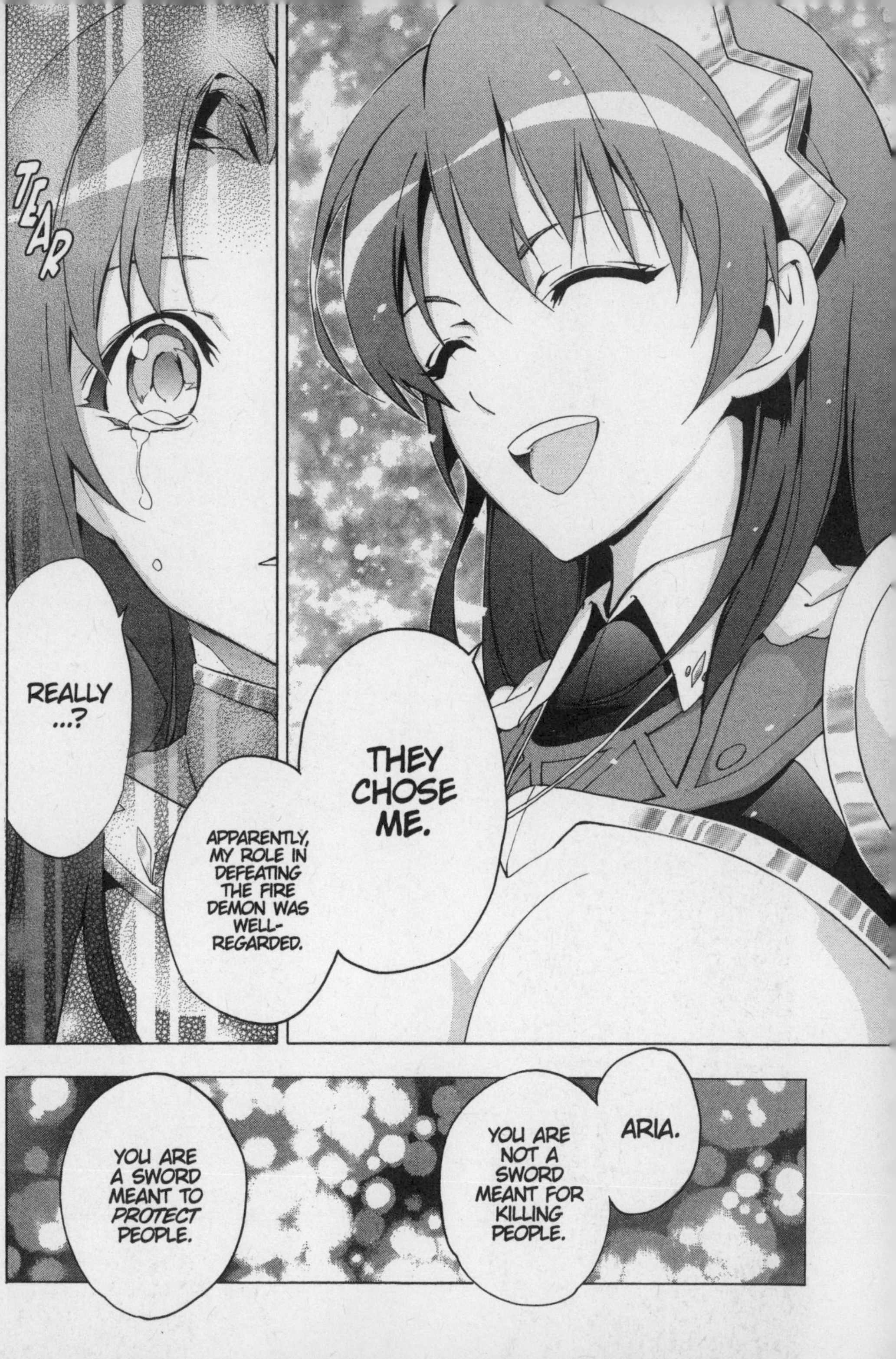
THEY CHOSE ME.
APPARENTLY, MY ROLE IN DEFEATING THE FIRE DEMON WAS WELL-REGARDED.
TEAR
REALLY ...?
ARIA.
YOU ARE NOT A SWORD MEANT FOR KILLING PEOPLE.
YOU ARE A SWORD MEANT TO *PROTECT* PEOPLE.

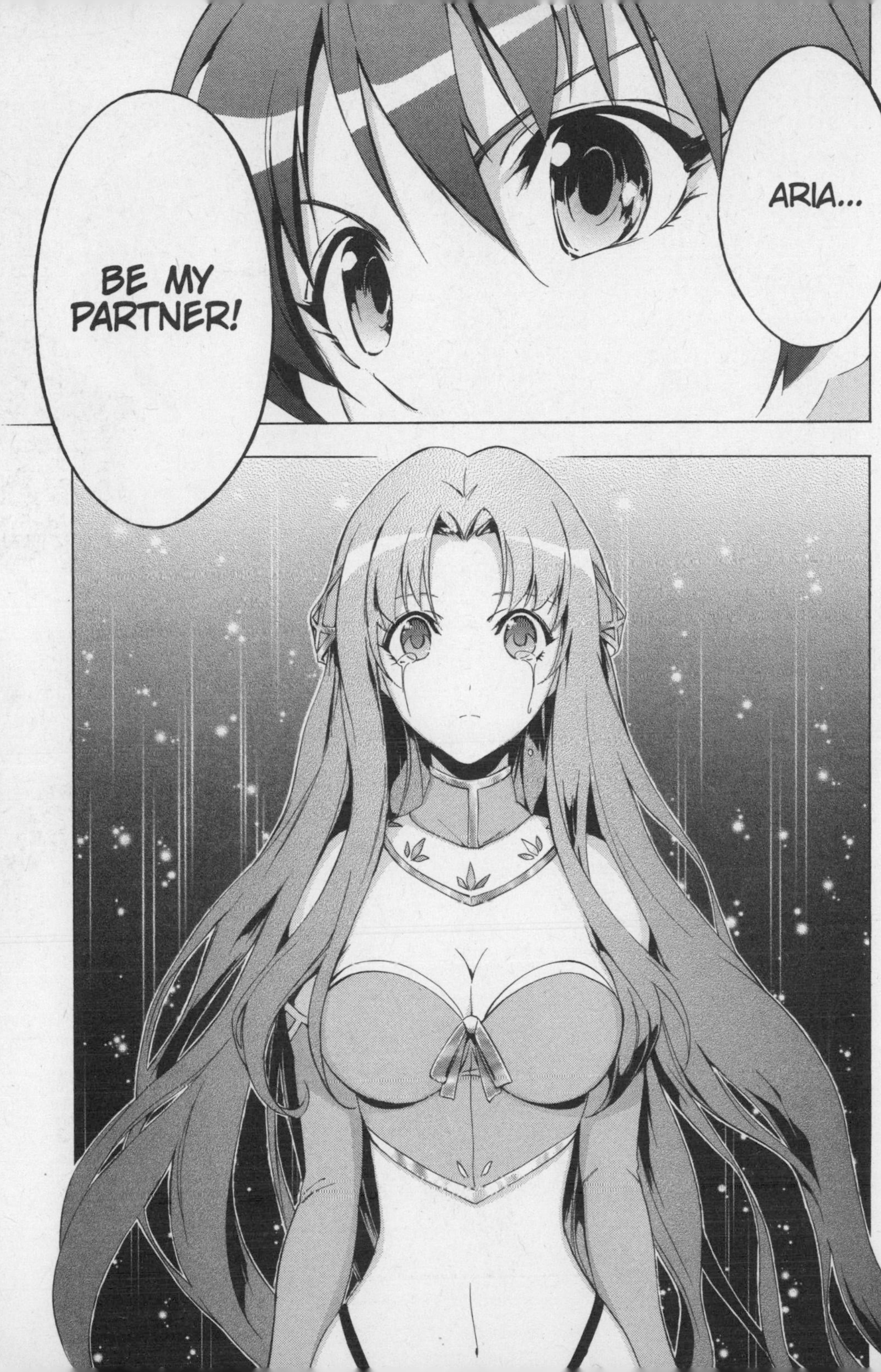
ARIA...
BE MY PARTNER!

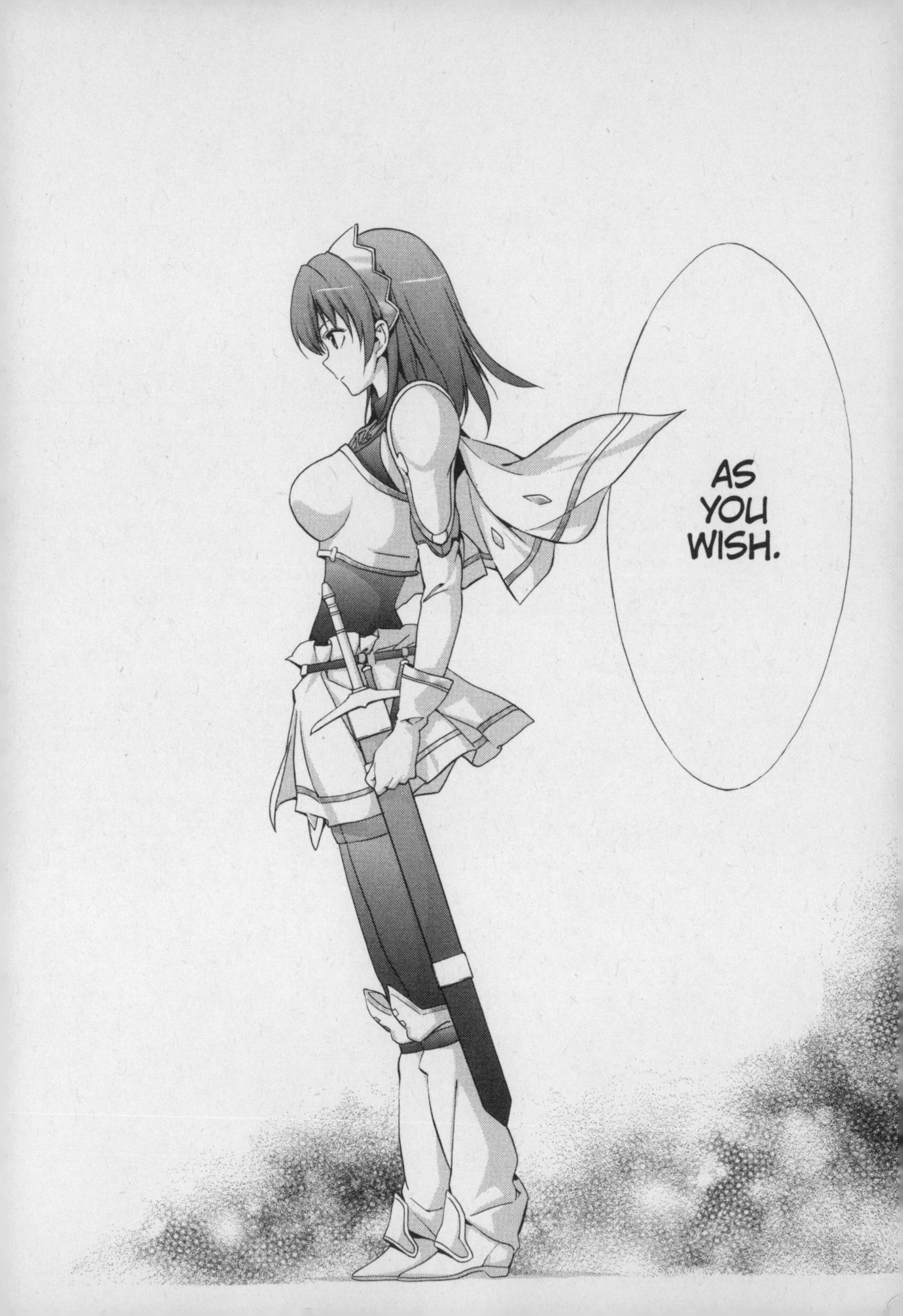
AS YOU WISH.

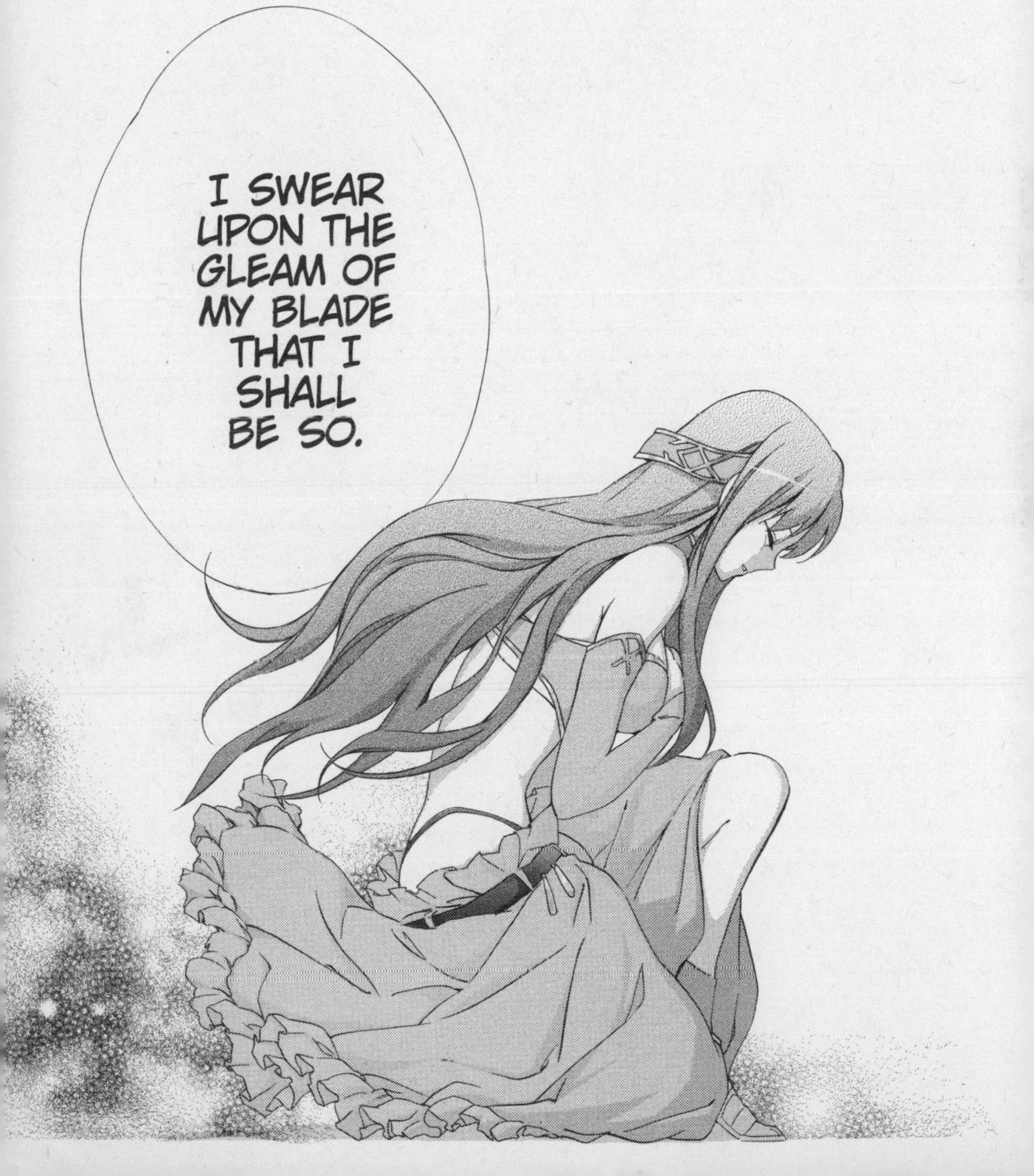
I SWEAR UPON THE GLEAM OF MY BLADE THAT I SHALL BE SO.

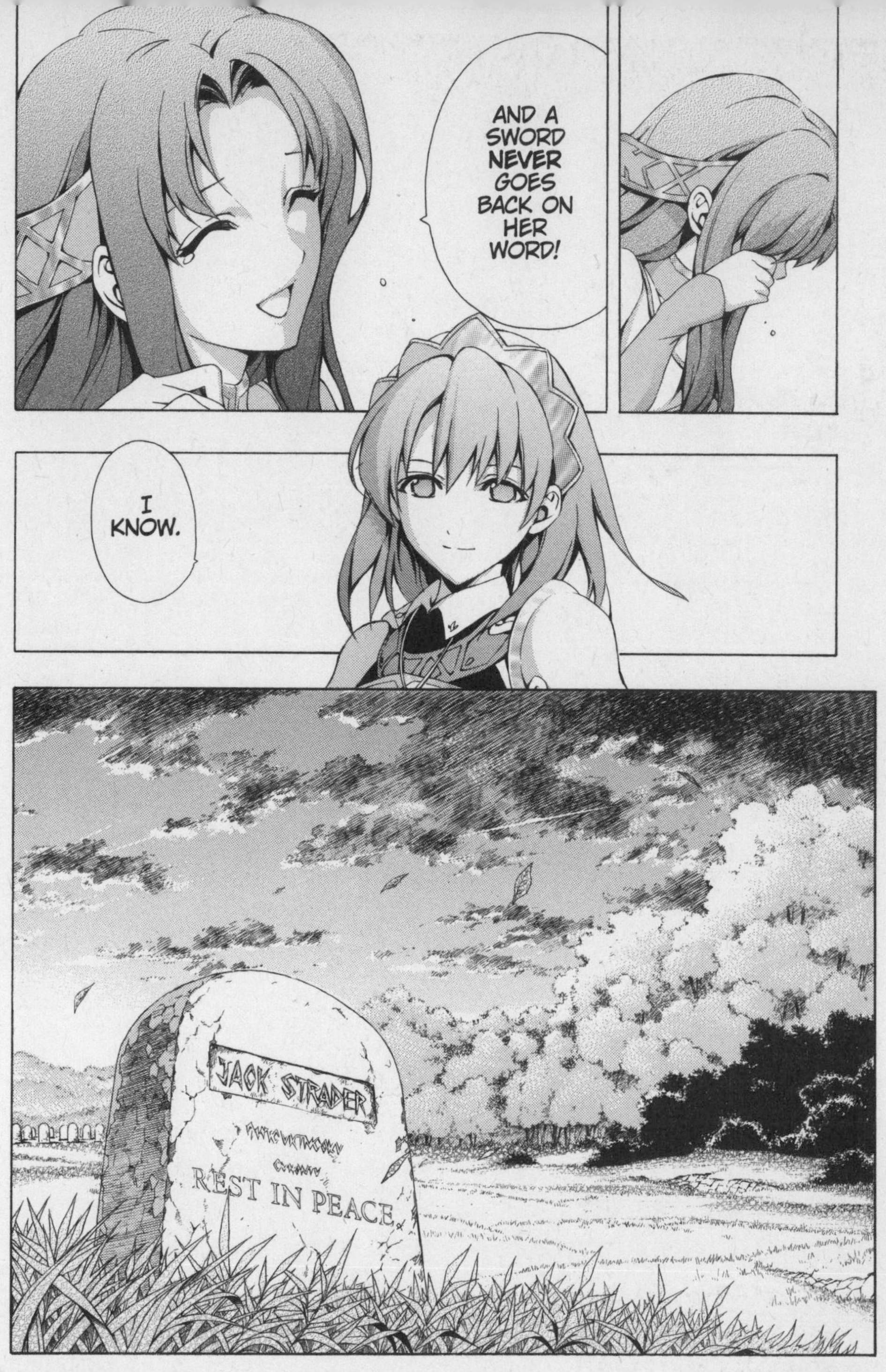
AND A SWORD NEVER GOES BACK ON HER WORD!
I KNOW.
JACK STRADER
REST IN PEACE

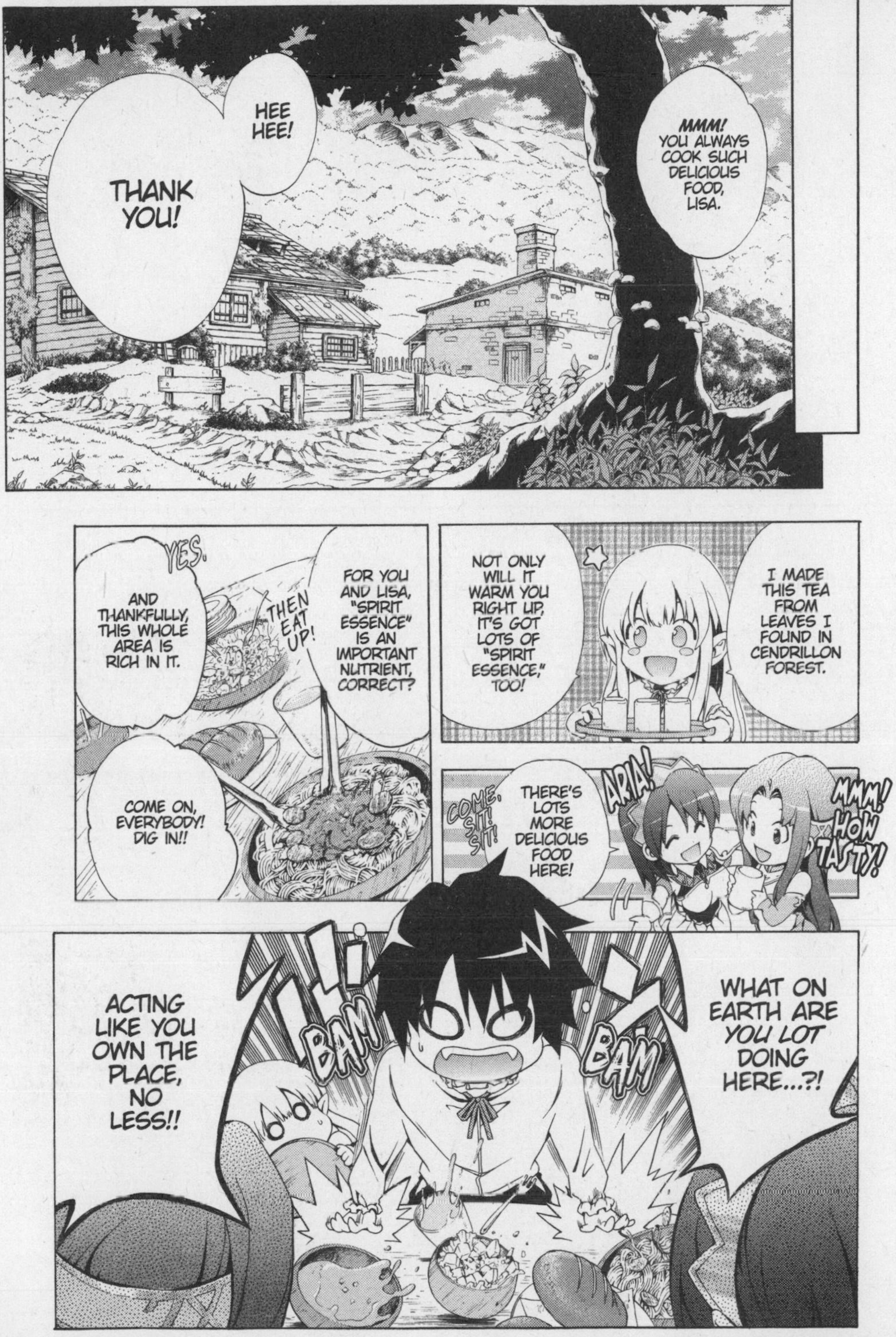
MMM! YOU ALWAYS COOK SUCH DELICIOUS FOOD, LISA.
HEE HEE!
THANK YOU!
I MADE THIS TEA FROM LEAVES I FOUND IN CENDRILLON FOREST.
NOT ONLY WILL IT WARM YOU RIGHT UP, IT'S GOT LOTS OF "SPIRIT ESSENCE," TOO!
MMM! HOW TASTY!
ARIA!
THERE'S LOTS MORE DELICIOUS FOOD HERE!
COME, SIT! SIT!
FOR YOU AND LISA, "SPIRIT ESSENCE" IS AN IMPORTANT NUTRIENT, CORRECT?
THEN EAT UP!
YES.
AND THANKFULLY, THIS WHOLE AREA IS RICH IN IT.
COME ON, EVERYBODY! DIG IN!!
BAM
BAM
WHAT ON EARTH ARE YOU LOT DOING HERE...?!
ACTING LIKE YOU OWN THE PLACE, NO LESS!!

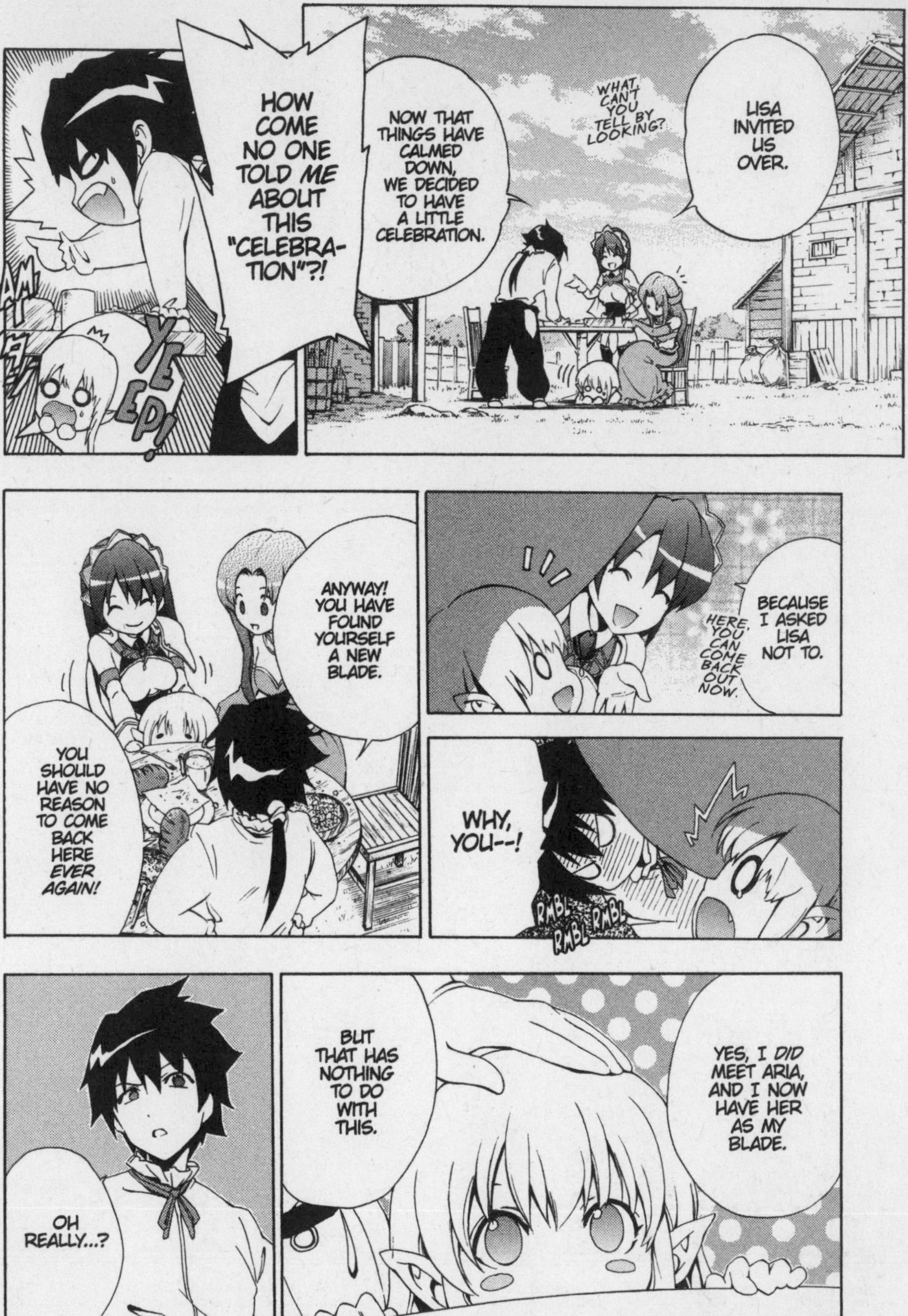
LISA INVITED US OVER.
WHAT, CAN'T YOU TELL BY LOOKING?
NOW THAT THINGS HAVE CALMED DOWN, WE DECIDED TO HAVE A LITTLE CELEBRATION.
HOW COME NO ONE TOLD *ME* ABOUT THIS "CELEBRATION"?!
BAM
YEEP!
BECAUSE I ASKED LISA NOT TO.
HERE, YOU CAN COME BACK OUT NOW.
WHY, YOU--!
RMBL RMBL RMBL
ANYWAY! YOU HAVE FOUND YOURSELF A NEW BLADE.
YOU SHOULD HAVE NO REASON TO COME BACK HERE *EVER* AGAIN!
YES, I *DID* MEET ARIA, AND I NOW HAVE HER AS MY BLADE.
BUT THAT HAS NOTHING TO DO WITH THIS.
OH REALLY...?

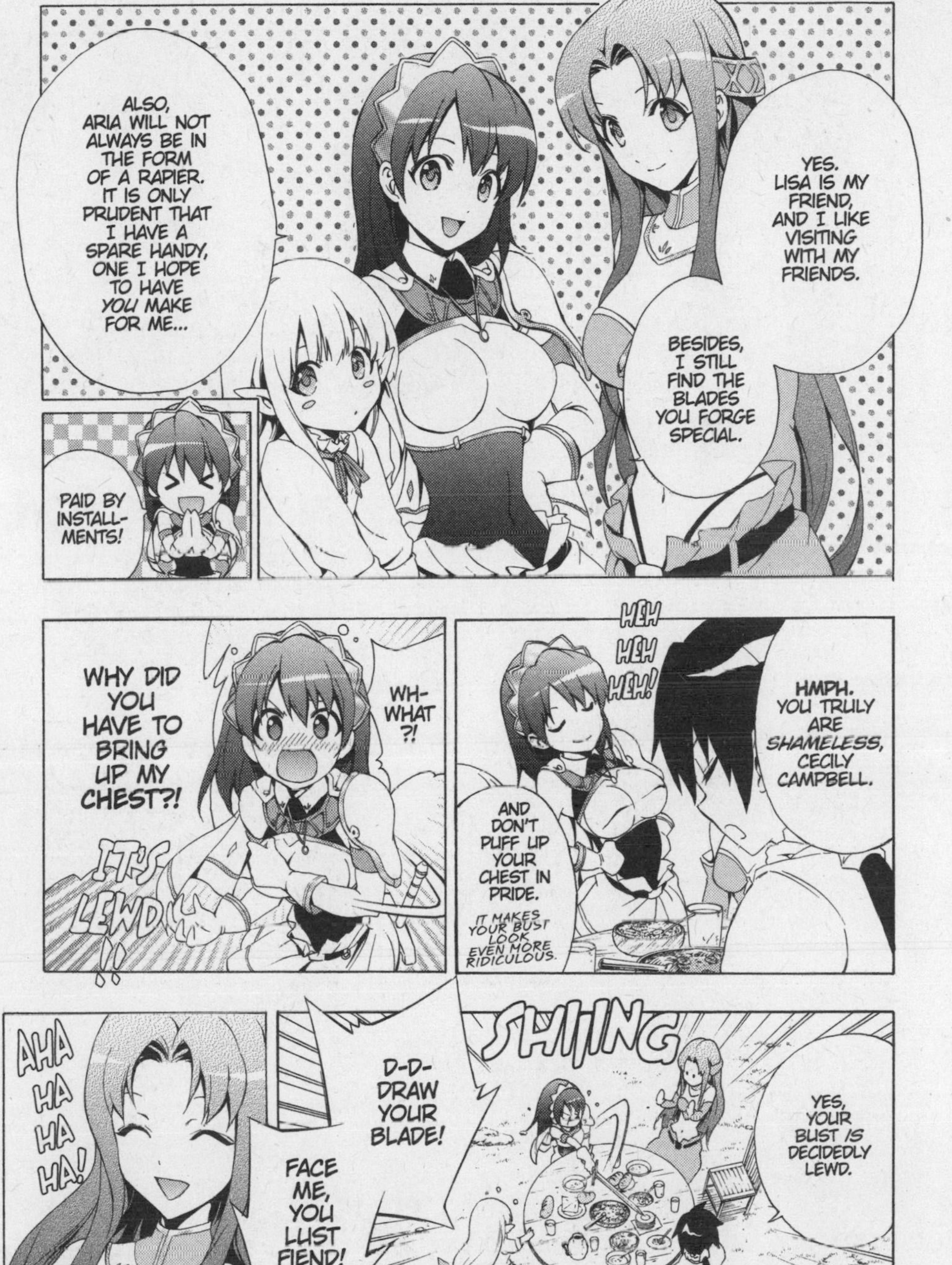
YES. LISA IS MY FRIEND, AND I LIKE VISITING WITH MY FRIENDS.
BESIDES, I STILL FIND THE BLADES YOU FORGE SPECIAL.
ALSO, ARIA WILL NOT ALWAYS BE IN THE FORM OF A RAPIER. IT IS ONLY PRUDENT THAT I HAVE A SPARE HANDY, ONE I HOPE TO HAVE YOU MAKE FOR ME...
PAID BY INSTALL-MENTS!
HEH HEH HEH!
HMPH. YOU TRULY ARE SHAMELESS, CECILY CAMPBELL.
AND DON'T PUFF UP YOUR CHEST IN PRIDE.
IT MAKES YOUR BUST LOOK EVEN MORE RIDICULOUS.
WH-WHAT?!
WHY DID YOU HAVE TO BRING UP MY CHEST?!
IT'S LEWD!!
YES, YOUR BUST IS DECIDEDLY LEWD.
SHIIING
D-D-DRAW YOUR BLADE!
FACE ME, YOU LUST FIEND!
AHA HA HA HA!

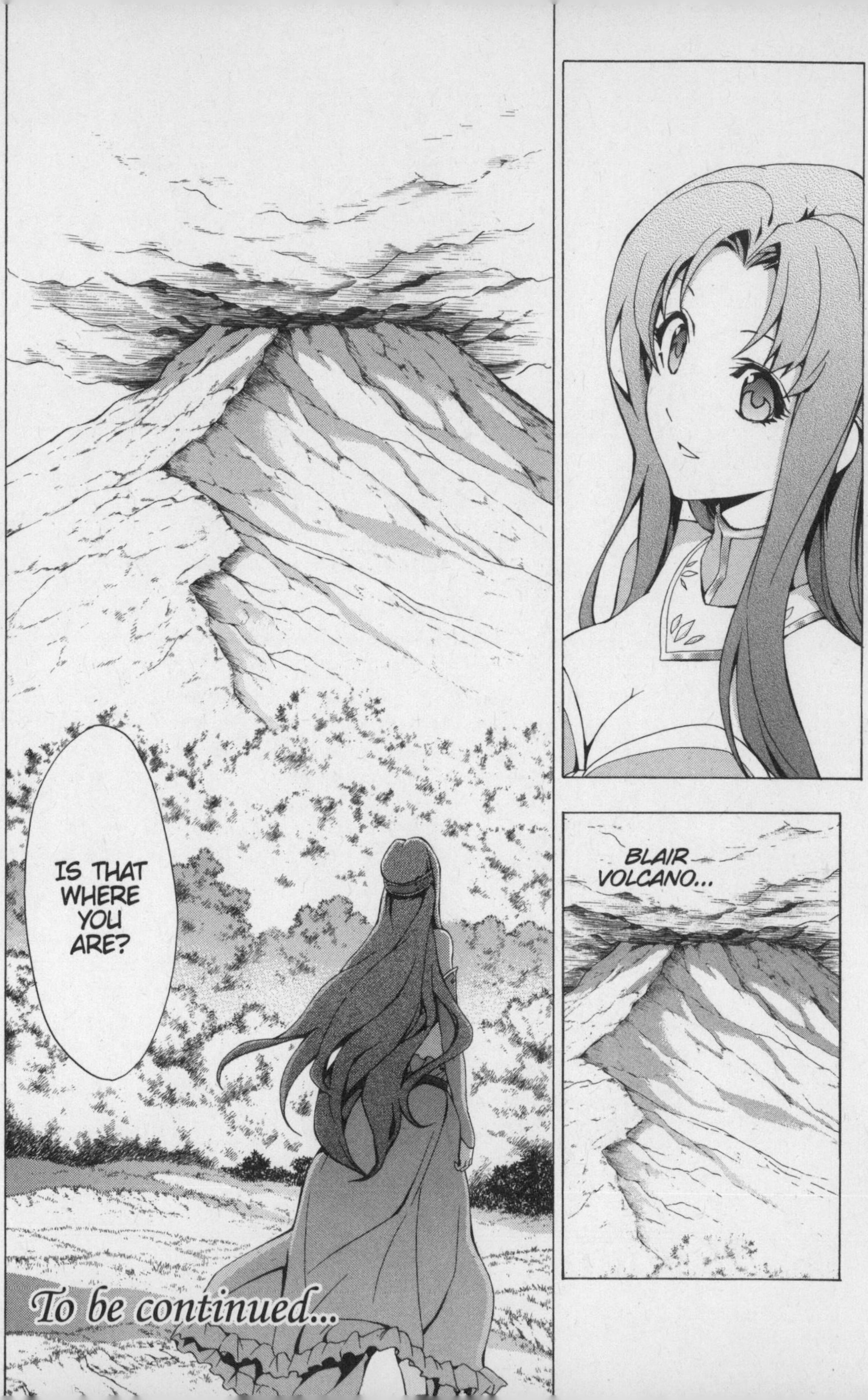
BLAIR VOLCANO...
IS THAT WHERE YOU ARE?
To be continued...

✳ *Hannibal Quasar* ✳

The Sacred Blacksmith

聖剣の刀鍛冶

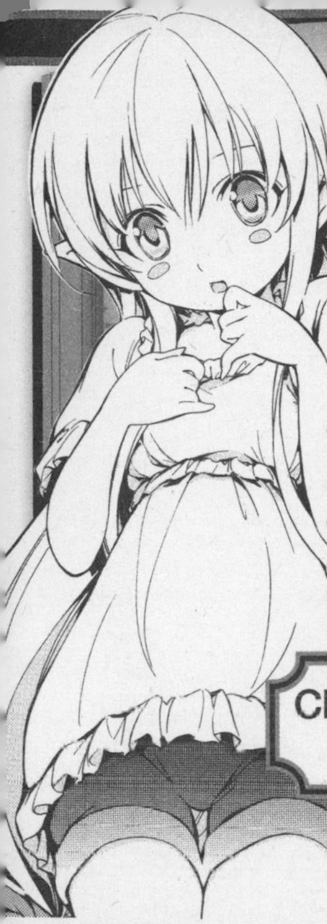

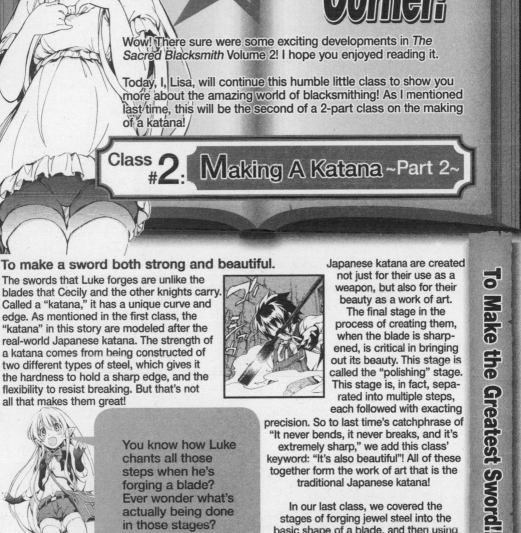

Lisa's Let's Learn Blacksmithing Corner!

Wow! There sure were some exciting developments in *The Sacred Blacksmith* Volume 2! I hope you enjoyed reading it.

Today, I, Lisa, will continue this humble little class to show you more about the amazing world of blacksmithing! As I mentioned last time, this will be the second of a 2-part class on the making of a katana!

Class #2: Making A Katana ~Part 2~

To Make the Greatest Sword!!

To make a sword both strong and beautiful.

The swords that Luke forges are unlike the blades that Cecily and the other knights carry. Called a "katana," it has a unique curve and edge. As mentioned in the first class, the "katana" in this story are modeled after the real-world Japanese katana. The strength of a katana comes from being constructed of two different types of steel, which gives it the hardness to hold a sharp edge, and the flexibility to resist breaking. But that's not all that makes them great!

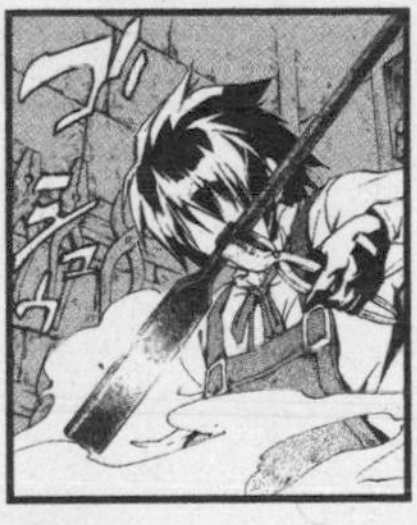

Japanese katana are created not just for their use as a weapon, but also for their beauty as a work of art. The final stage in the process of creating them, when the blade is sharpened, is critical in bringing out its beauty. This stage is called the "polishing" stage. This stage is, in fact, separated into multiple steps, each followed with exacting precision. So to last time's catchphrase of "It never bends, it never breaks, and it's extremely sharp," we add this class' keyword: "It's also beautiful"! All of these together form the work of art that is the traditional Japanese katana!

In our last class, we covered the stages of forging jewel steel into the basic shape of a blade, and then using a special heating and quenching process to give the blade its distinctive curve. Today, let's move on to the next step in the process.

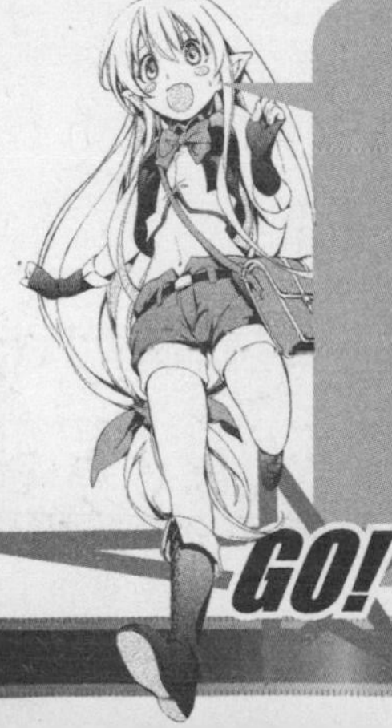
GO!

You know how Luke chants all those steps when he's forging a blade? Ever wonder what's actually being done in those stages? Turn the page, and I'll explain! ♪

It doesn't break! It doesn't bend! It's super sharp!

+ It's beau-tiful!!

Part 2 How To Forge A Japanese Katana

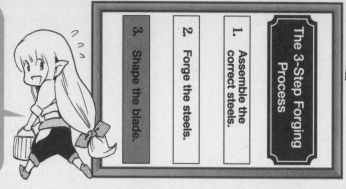

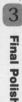

Every step of the katana forging process is followed with exacting precision. Now that the basic shape of the blade is done, it's time to work on the detail! ♪

The 3-Step Forging Process

1. Assemble the correct steels.
2. Forge the steels.
3. Shape the blade.

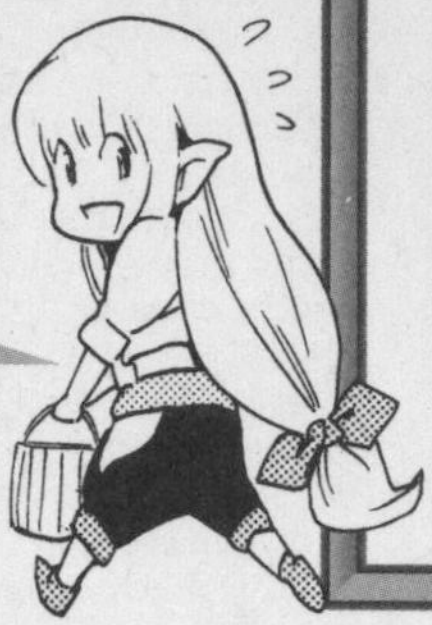

Those are the three major steps in making a katana. Today, we're looking at the final step.

1 Kaji-Oshi

Now that the base blade is forged, the smith will adjust the finer details of its shape until he is satisfied. This is the stage where the general condition of the blade is examined, and how the polishing steps will proceed is determined. The blade's curve is neatened, the edge is very roughly sharpened, and any scrapes or imperfections on the blade are hammered out.

2 Foundation Polishing

Foundation polishing neatens the basic geometry of the blade, and involves the use of multiple types of polishing stones. Soft stones are used at first, progressing to harder and harder stones.

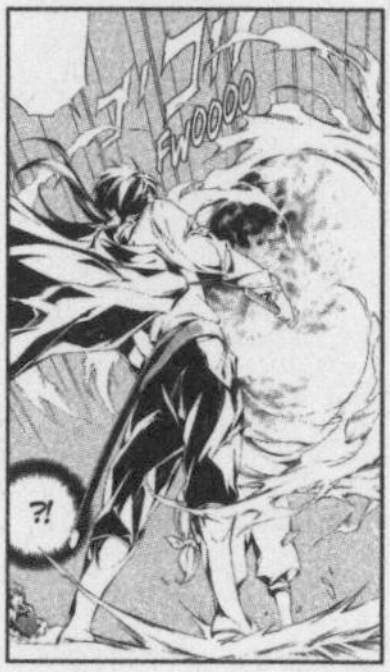

?!

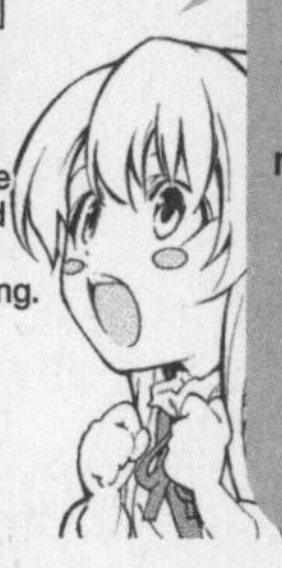

These are the stones used, in order from the roughest to the finest grade. If you mess up in the middle of polishing, you've gotta go *all* the way back to the beginning, so polishers concentrate *real hard* on what they're doing!

Binsui ← **Kaisei** ← **Chu-nagura** ← **Koma-nagura** ← **Uchigumori**

Binsui: The first stone used in polishing.

Kaisei: This stone is used to remove the marks made on the blade by the binsui stone.

Chu-nagura: From binsui to this stone, the polisher is still setting the general shape of the edge.

Koma-nagura: Of all the polishing stones that are cut from nagura stones, this one has the finest grade.

Uchigumori: There are two types of uchigumori stone: *uchigumori-hado* to polish the edge, and *uchigumori-jido* to polish the rest of the blade. Both are the same grade.

3 Final Polish

In this stage, the jigane (the bulk of the blade that has yet to be polished) and the hamon (the wavy pattern on the edge, made when the blade was clay-coated and heated) are polished. Jizuya stone is used to polish the jigane, and hazuya stone to polish the hamon.

Hazuya: These are actually very fine chips of uchigumori stone.

Jizuya: These are often fine chips of narutaki stone, but some polishing styles crush those chips further into 1mm pieces. Those are called kudaki-jizuya.

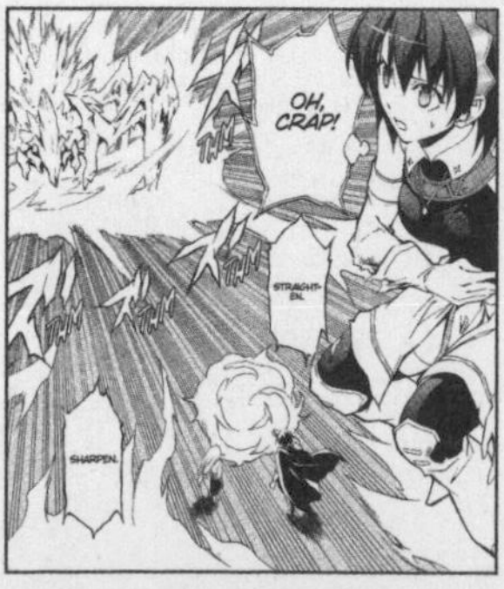

OH, CRAP!
SHARPEN

4 Nugui

In this step, the blade is polished using cotton balls and paper dipped in a mixture of oil and metal chips from when the blade was first forged. It got the name "nugui" from the Japanese word "to wipe" (nuguu), because it looks like the polisher is simply wiping the blade. This step gives the blade its shine, though if you aren't careful, you could wind up making it as shiny and reflective as a mirror!

5 Hadori

During the nugui step, the wavy "hamon" pattern on the blade's edge is darkened. The hadori step is designed to lighten it back up and to make it look neater. A mixture of hazuya stone chips and uchigumori stone chips in oil is carefully wiped along the line of the hamon, to make it stand out.

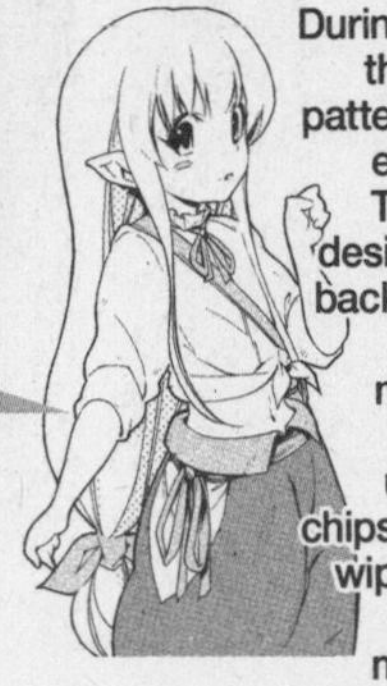

Doing this gives the blade a clear light and dark contrast. This is where various modern and classical styles, as well as the polisher's own personal touch come into play.

6 Polishing

A slim, round metal rod about 15cm long is used to polish the ridge and sides of the blade. This gives the katana its unique dark shine.

7 Tip Polish

Hazuya stone is used to polish the tip area to a light shine. The polisher needs to have perfectly steady hands to smooth out any rough patches and give the tip a bright white finish.

8 Engraving

After all the many sharpening and polishing steps are done, the maker deliberately adds some scratches to either the tip or the base of the blade as his "signature." Mess this up and it's all the way back to the Koma-nagura stage, so it's a really nerve-wracking step!

And with that, the hilt, tsuba, and other things which make the blade easy to hold and use are added, and the katana is finished!

Luke does all this by himself, but real-world katana are made by many different specialists: the blacksmith who forges the blade, the polisher, the sheath-maker, the metal smith, the painter, and lots more!

YAAAY♪

FWOOOSH

Now I get it! With all that work that goes into Luke's katana, it's no wonder they're both beautiful and hard to break!

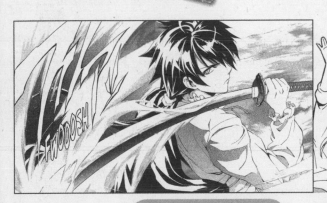

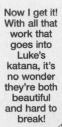

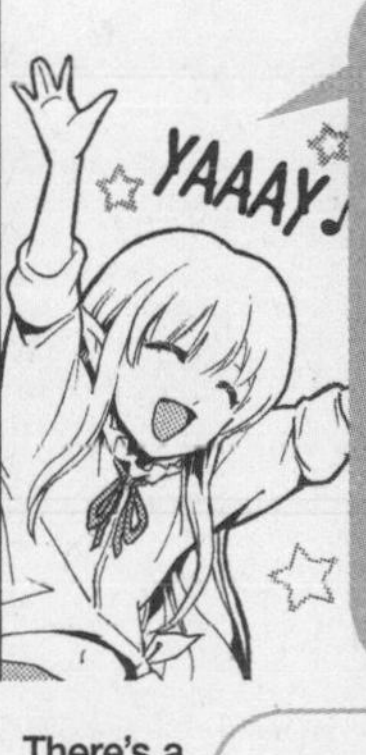

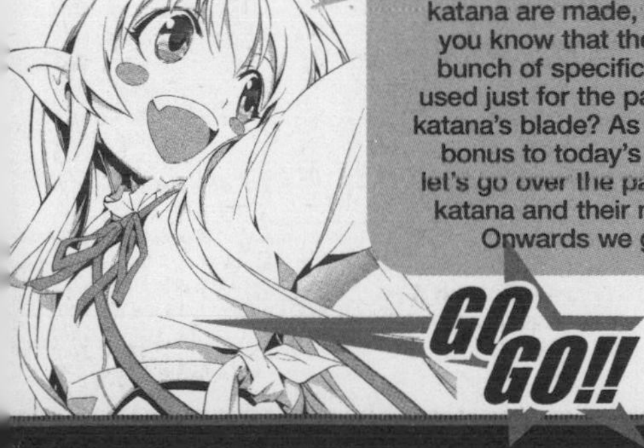

There's a forging scene in this very volume, so now that you know what goes on in each stage of the process, it could be interesting to go back and re-read that section with a new understanding!

So far, I've given a really general explanation of how katana are made, but did you know that there's a bunch of specific terms used just for the parts of a katana's blade? As an extra bonus to today's class, let's go over the parts of a katana and their names. Onwards we go!

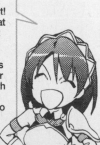

GO GO!!

Katana: A List of Terms

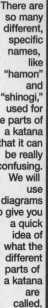

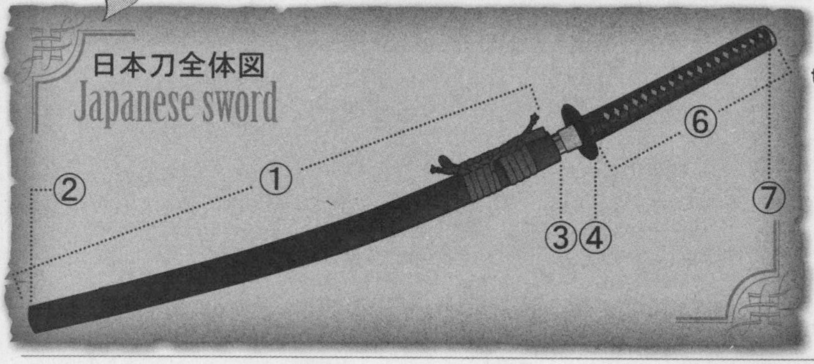

There are so many different, specific names, like "hamon" and "shinogi," used for the parts of a katana that it can be really confusing. We will use diagrams to give you a quick idea of what the different parts of a katana are called.

A Well-Known Vocabulary?

During the "How to Forge A Japanese Katana" class, several unique names related to specific parts of a katana were mentioned. Some of them probably sounded familiar. Several of them have found their way into commonly used Japanese sayings. Below, we will explain not only the terms themselves, but some of the sayings that have come from them.

The numbers in the explanation match up with the numbers in the diagrams. Look for the ★ mark to read about well-known katana-related sayings!

日本刀全体図
Japanese sword
①
②
③④
⑥
⑦

⑤
⑧
⑨
Close-Up of the Tsuba

① 鞘 [Saya]

② 鐺／小尻 [Kojiri]

The butt-end of the saya. Also the name of any decorative cap added there.

③ 鯉口 [Koikuchi]

The mouth of the saya. The phrase "Koikuchi wo kiru" (to cut the koi's mouth) actually means loosening the katana from the koikuchi, making it easier to draw.

④ 鍔 [Tsuba]

The oval guard, set between the base of the blade and the top of the hilt, to protect the hand.

★ 鍔迫り合い [Tsuba zeri'ai]

"To lock swords." From when two people clash blades by their hilts, leading to pushing back and forth. Means intense competition.

⑤ 切羽 [Seppa]

Part of the tsuba, it is the metal part that presses the tsuka (hilt) firmly to the saya (sheath).

★ 切羽つまる [Seppa tsumaru]

"To be packed to the hilt." This saying comes from the image of a well-made seppa, which holds the katana in its sheath snuggly, with no rattling.

⑥ 柄 [Tsuka]

⑦ 柄頭／頭 [Tsuka-kashira]

The metal cap at the end of the tsuka.

⑧ 目貫 [Menuki]

The metal decoration on the side of the tsuka, atop the bolt that holds the blade and hilt together.

★ 目抜き通り [Menuki-doori]

"Main street." The menuki is a decorative, yet important part of a katana. It came to be used to describe high-traffic, yet fancy town districts or streets.

⑨ 柄巻 [Tsuka-maki]

The wrapping around the tsuka. It is usually not cloth, but the hide of a salmon shark.

刀身図
Japanese sword

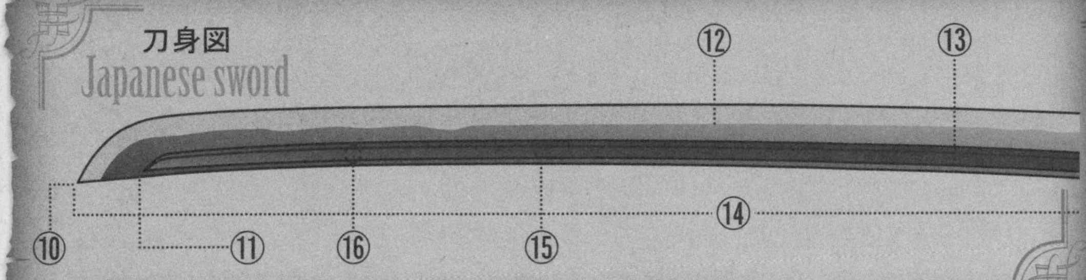

⑫
⑬
⑩
⑪
⑯
⑮
⑭

⑩ 切先 [Kissaki]

⑪ 帽子 [Boushi]

⑫ 刃文 [Hamon] The pattern on the blade, made during the clay-coat and firing step. This pattern determines where the white portion of the edge begins.

⑬ 鎬 [Shinogi] The line that runs the length of the blade, between the edge and the ridge.

★ 鎬を削る [Shinogi wo kezuru] "To compete ruthlessly." When dueling katana to katana, you block with the shinogi, not the edge of the blade. In a stiff fight, these parts will scrape together often, leading to a phrase that means competing roughly.

⑭ 反り [Sori] The part of the blade that curved during quenching.

⑮ 棟 [Mune] The unsharpened side of the blade.

⑯ 鎬地 [Shinogichi] The space between the shinogi and the mune.

There's lots more sayings that come from the katana!

★ 地金が出る [Jigane ga deru] "Showing one's true (ugly) character." Polishing a katana too much will reveal its ugly jigane core. Accordingly, this came to be a euphemism for unmasking someone's unsavory character.

★ なまくら [Namakura] "A blunt blade." This happens when a blade isn't fired long enough, giving it a poor edge. It means a person who is only half-trained, or is lazy and unambitious. "Not the sharpest knife in the drawer."

★ 焼きがまわる [Yaki ga mawaru] "To lose your edge." Conversely, firing a blade too long will give it a bad edge. Thus, the saying means to grow so old, you lose your skill.

★ 付け焼き刃 [Tsukeyake yaiba] "A thin veneer." Covering a blunt blade with a shiny steel edge barely makes it useable. That led to this saying, which means that something has been jerry-rigged, thus it only barely passes muster.

So, as you can see, even the tiniest parts of a katana have their own special names. Some of them were undoubtedly new, but others were probably familiar, thanks to well-known sayings. I hope that the two How-To classes and this lesson in katana vocabulary have given you a better idea about the Japanese katana, and what's so cool about them!

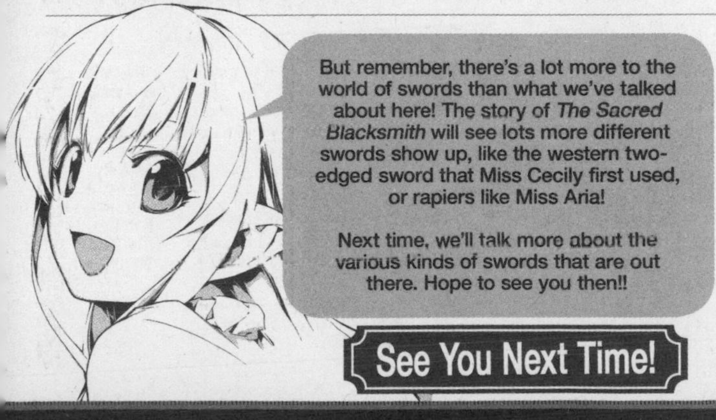

But remember, there's a lot more to the world of swords than what we've talked about here! The story of *The Sacred Blacksmith* will see lots more different swords show up, like the western two-edged sword that Miss Cecily first used, or rapiers like Miss Aria!
Next time, we'll talk more about the various kinds of swords that are out there. Hope to see you then!!
See You Next Time!

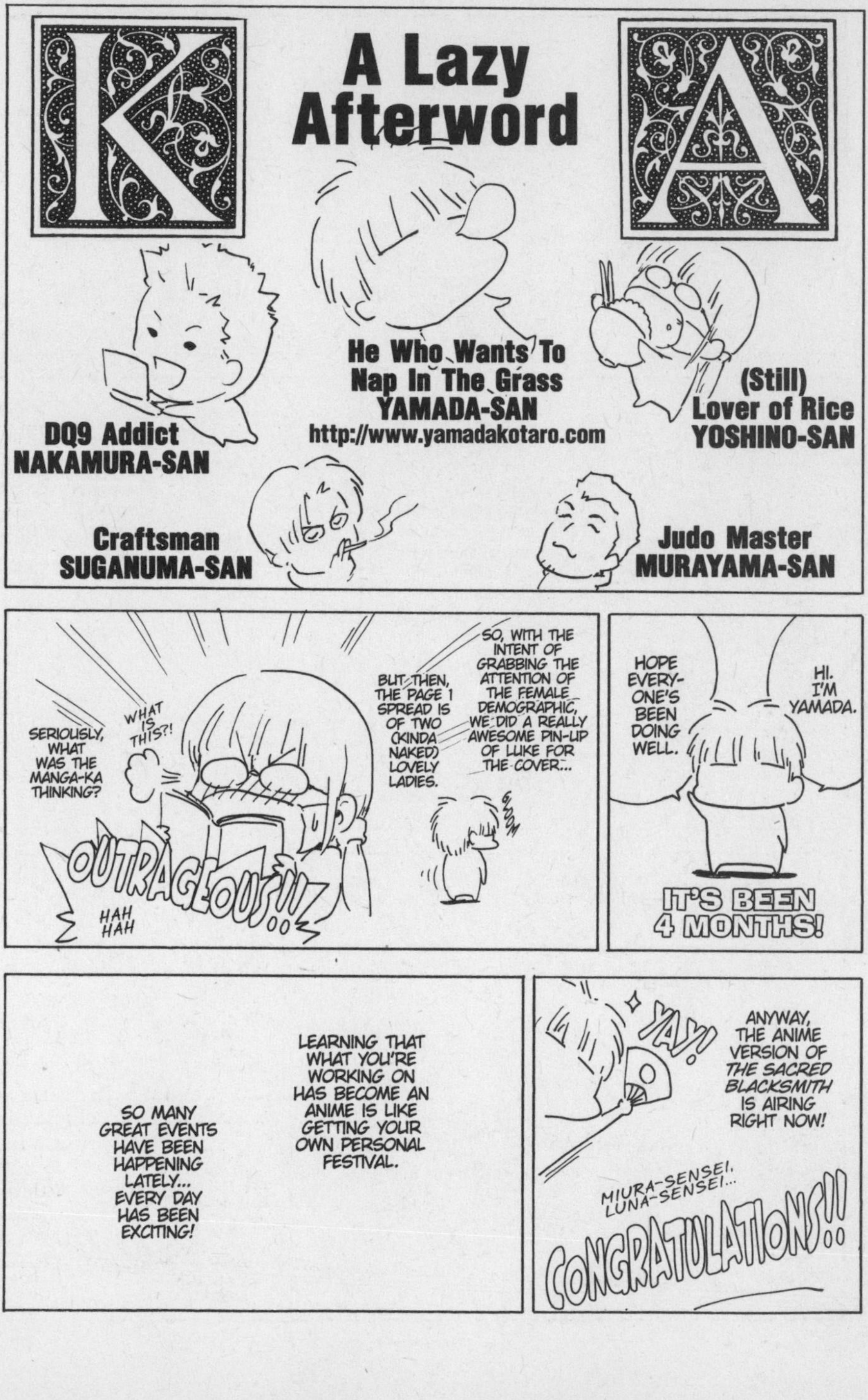
K
A Lazy Afterword
A
He Who Wants To Nap In The Grass YAMADA-SAN
http://www.yamadakotaro.com
(Still) Lover of Rice YOSHINO-SAN
DQ9 Addict NAKAMURA-SAN
Judo Master MURAYAMA-SAN
Craftsman SUGANUMA-SAN
HI. I'M YAMADA.
HOPE EVERYONE'S BEEN DOING WELL.
IT'S BEEN 4 MONTHS!
SO, WITH THE INTENT OF GRABBING THE ATTENTION OF THE FEMALE DEMOGRAPHIC, WE DID A REALLY AWESOME PIN-UP OF LUKE FOR THE COVER...
BUT THEN, THE PAGE 1 SPREAD IS OF TWO (KINDA NAKED) LOVELY LADIES.
WHAT IS THIS?!
SERIOUSLY, WHAT WAS THE MANGA-KA THINKING?
OUTRAGEOUS!!
HAH HAH
ANYWAY, THE ANIME VERSION OF THE SACRED BLACKSMITH IS AIRING RIGHT NOW!
YAY!
MIURA-SENSEI, LUNA-SENSEI...
CONGRATULATIONS!!
LEARNING THAT WHAT YOU'RE WORKING ON HAS BECOME AN ANIME IS LIKE GETTING YOUR OWN PERSONAL FESTIVAL.
SO MANY GREAT EVENTS HAVE BEEN HAPPENING LATELY... EVERY DAY HAS BEEN EXCITING!

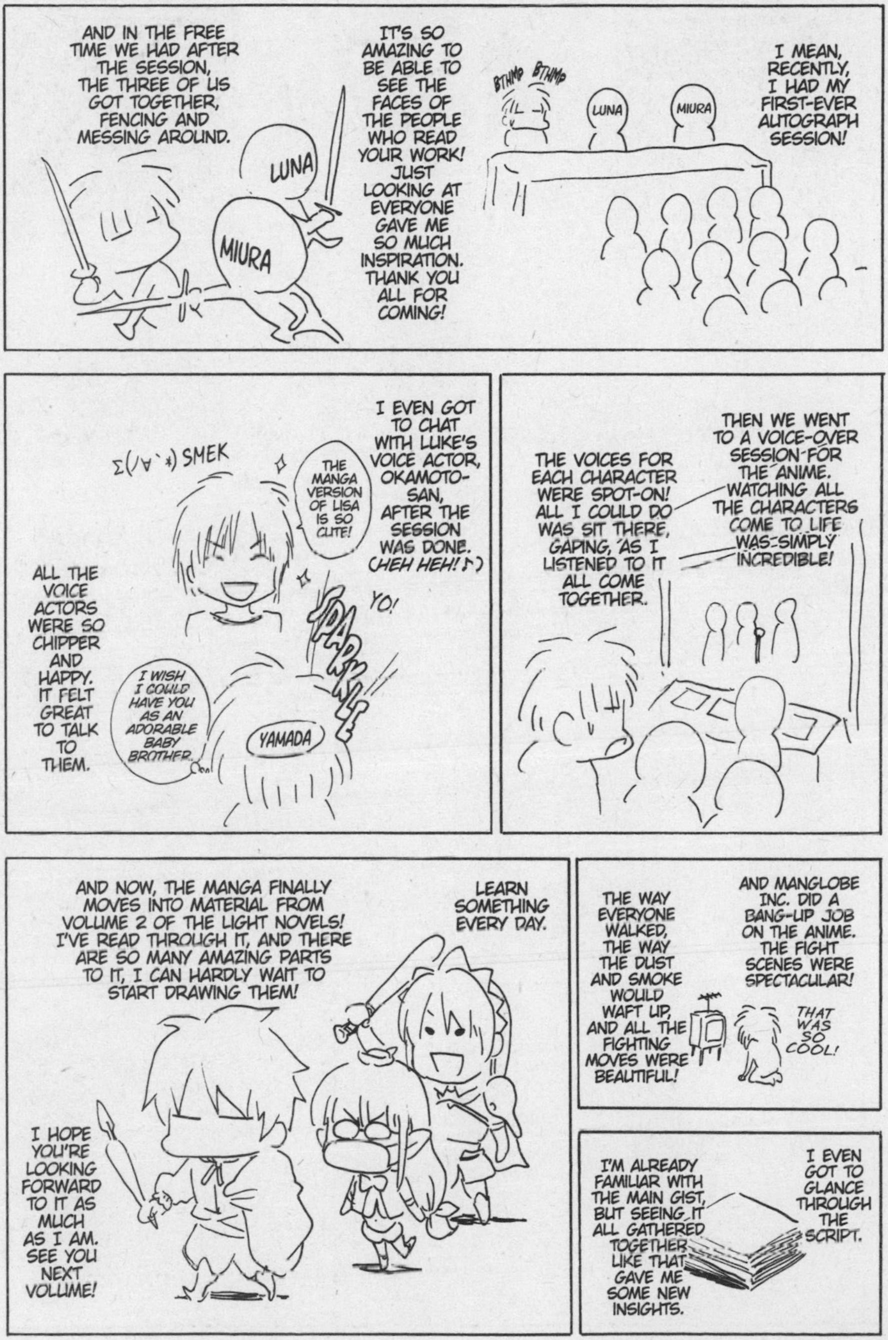

I MEAN, RECENTLY, I HAD MY FIRST-EVER AUTOGRAPH SESSION!
MIURA
LUNA
BTHMP BTHMP
IT'S SO AMAZING TO BE ABLE TO SEE THE FACES OF THE PEOPLE WHO READ YOUR WORK! JUST LOOKING AT EVERYONE GAVE ME SO MUCH INSPIRATION. THANK YOU ALL FOR COMING!
LUNA
MIURA
AND IN THE FREE TIME WE HAD AFTER THE SESSION, THE THREE OF US GOT TOGETHER, FENCING AND MESSING AROUND.
THEN WE WENT TO A VOICE-OVER SESSION FOR THE ANIME. WATCHING ALL THE CHARACTERS COME TO LIFE WAS SIMPLY INCREDIBLE!
THE VOICES FOR EACH CHARACTER WERE SPOT-ON! ALL I COULD DO WAS SIT THERE, GAPING, AS I LISTENED TO IT ALL COME TOGETHER.
I EVEN GOT TO CHAT WITH LUKE'S VOICE ACTOR, OKAMOTO-SAN, AFTER THE SESSION WAS DONE. (HEH HEH!♪)
THE MANGA VERSION OF LISA IS SO CUTE!
Σ(ﾉ∀`*) SMEK
YO!
SPARKLE
YAMADA
I WISH I COULD HAVE YOU AS AN ADORABLE BABY BROTHER.
ALL THE VOICE ACTORS WERE SO CHIPPER AND HAPPY. IT FELT GREAT TO TALK TO THEM.
AND MANGLOBE INC. DID A BANG-UP JOB ON THE ANIME. THE FIGHT SCENES WERE SPECTACULAR!
THAT WAS SO COOL!
THE WAY EVERYONE WALKED, THE WAY THE DUST AND SMOKE WOULD WAFT UP, AND ALL THE FIGHTING MOVES WERE BEAUTIFUL!
I EVEN GOT TO GLANCE THROUGH THE SCRIPT.
I'M ALREADY FAMILIAR WITH THE MAIN GIST, BUT SEEING IT ALL GATHERED TOGETHER LIKE THAT GAVE ME SOME NEW INSIGHTS.
LEARN SOMETHING EVERY DAY.
AND NOW, THE MANGA FINALLY MOVES INTO MATERIAL FROM VOLUME 2 OF THE LIGHT NOVELS! I'VE READ THROUGH IT, AND THERE ARE SO MANY AMAZING PARTS TO IT, I CAN HARDLY WAIT TO START DRAWING THEM!
I HOPE YOU'RE LOOKING FORWARD TO IT AS MUCH AS I AM. SEE YOU NEXT VOLUME!

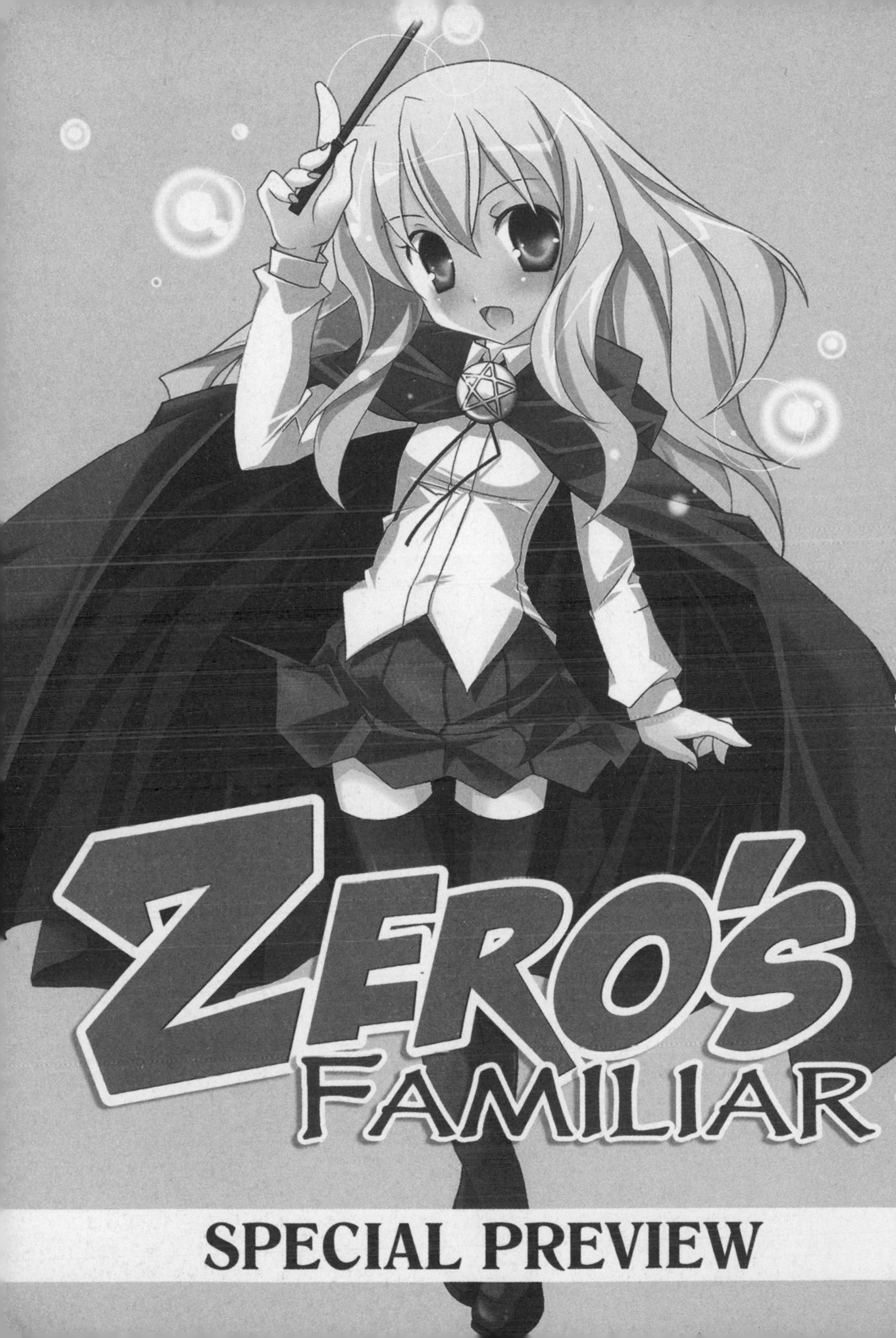
ZERO'S
FAMILIAR
SPECIAL PREVIEW

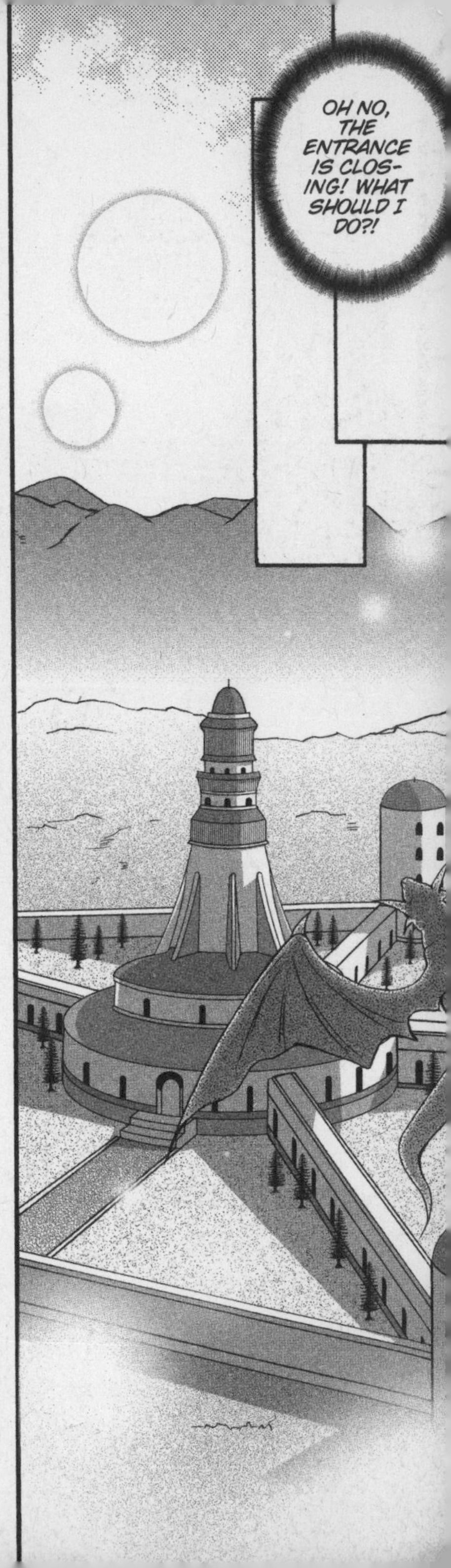
OH NO, THE ENTRANCE IS CLOSING! WHAT SHOULD I DO?!

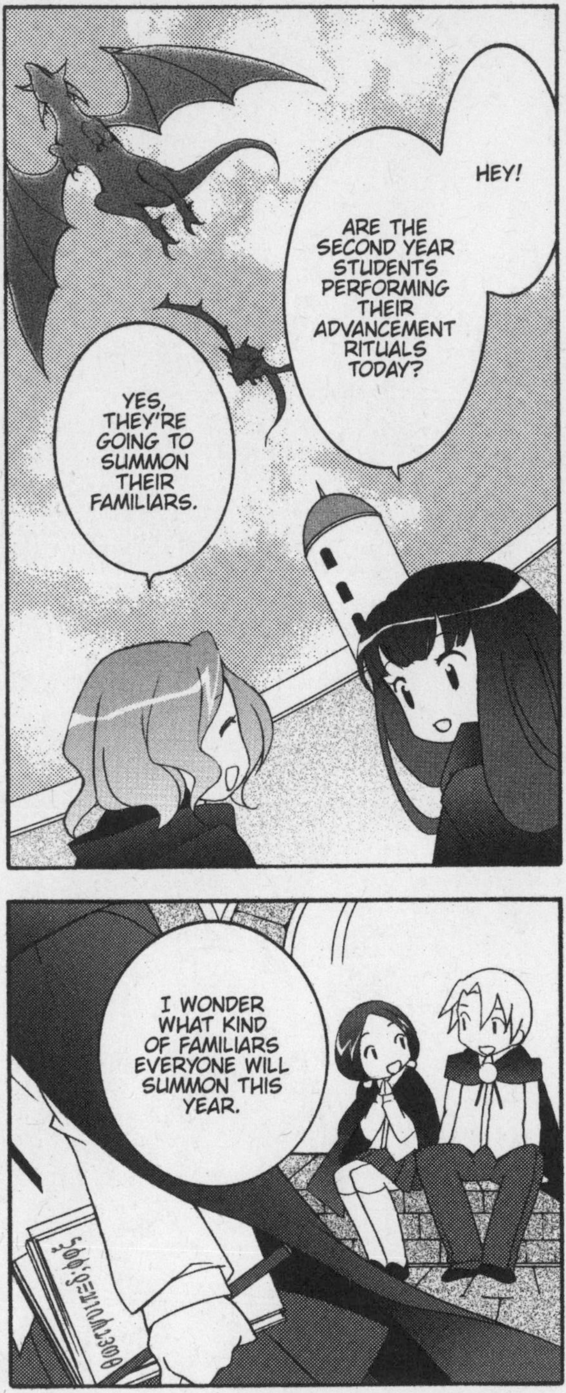
HEY!
ARE THE SECOND YEAR STUDENTS PERFORMING THEIR ADVANCEMENT RITUALS TODAY?
YES, THEY'RE GOING TO SUMMON THEIR FAMILIARS.
I WONDER WHAT KIND OF FAMILIARS EVERYONE WILL SUMMON THIS YEAR.

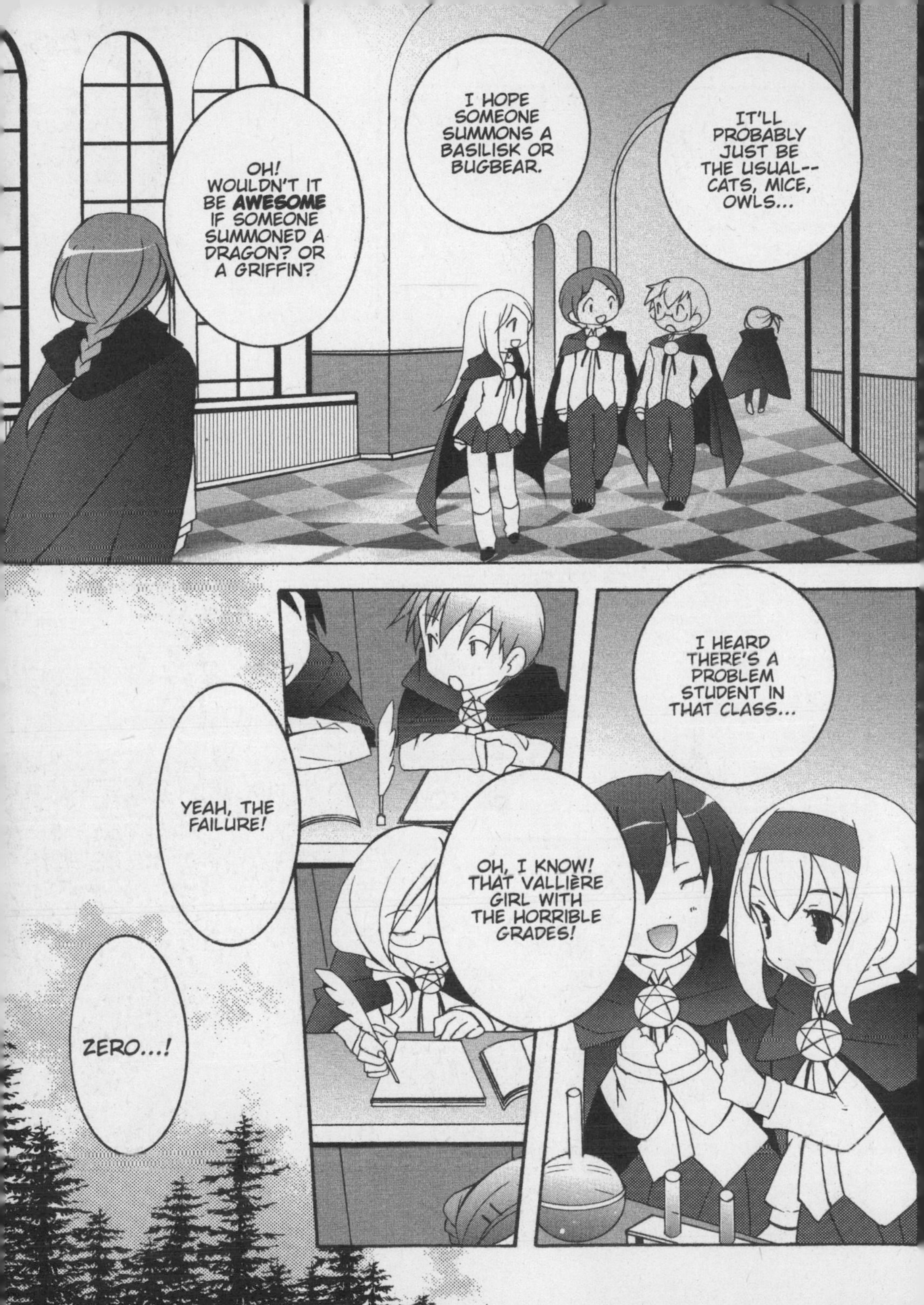
IT'LL PROBABLY JUST BE THE USUAL-- CATS, MICE, OWLS...
I HOPE SOMEONE SUMMONS A BASILISK OR BUGBEAR.
OH! WOULDN'T IT BE **AWESOME** IF SOMEONE SUMMONED A DRAGON? OR A GRIFFIN?
I HEARD THERE'S A PROBLEM STUDENT IN THAT CLASS...
OH, I KNOW! THAT VALLIÈRE GIRL WITH THE HORRIBLE GRADES!
YEAH, THE FAILURE!
ZERO...!

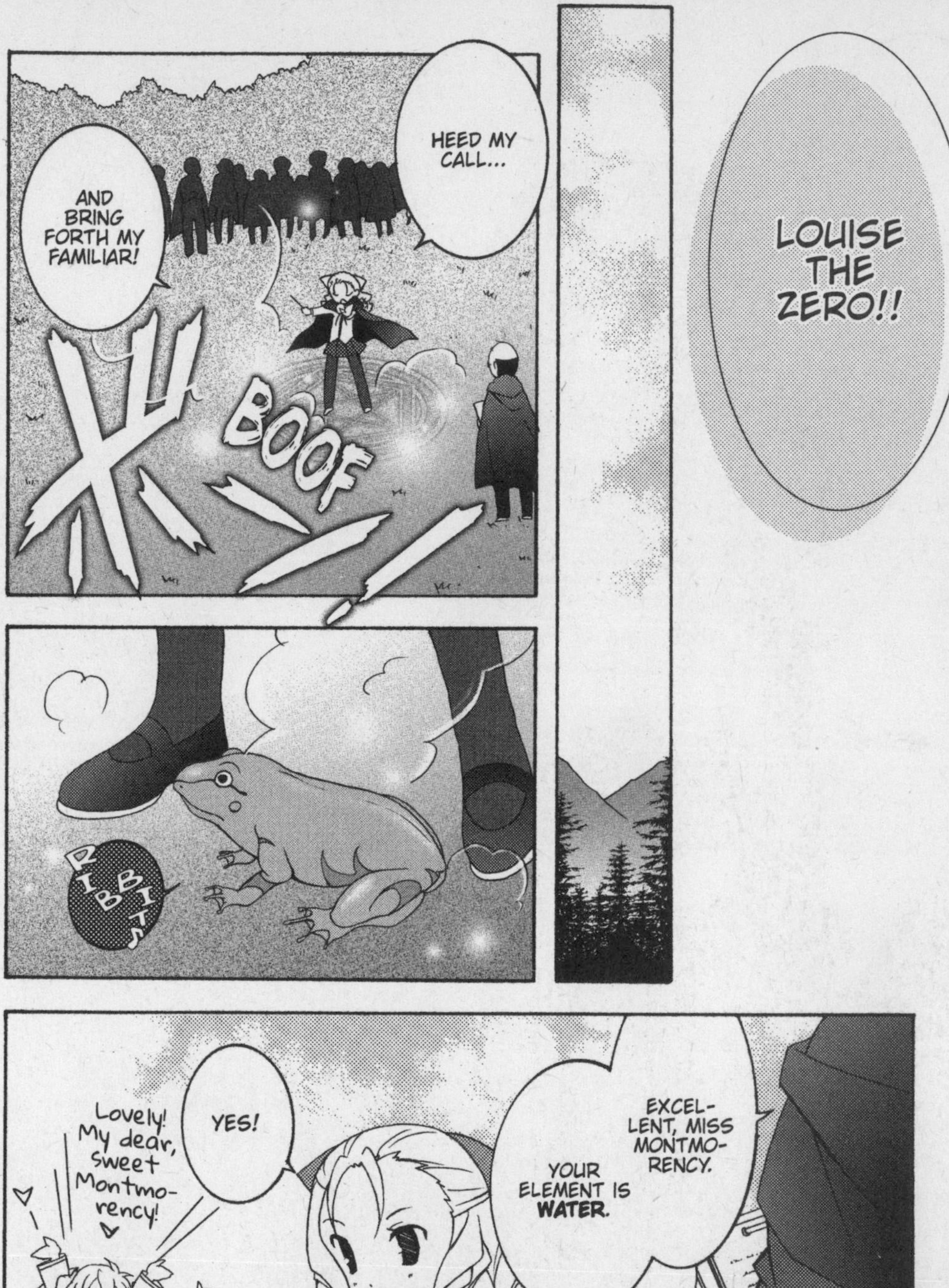
LOUISE THE ZERO!!
HEED MY CALL...
AND BRING FORTH MY FAMILIAR!
BOOF
RIBBIT♪
EXCEL-LENT, MISS MONTMO-RENCY.
YOUR ELEMENT IS **WATER**.
YES!
Lovely! My dear, sweet Montmo-rency!

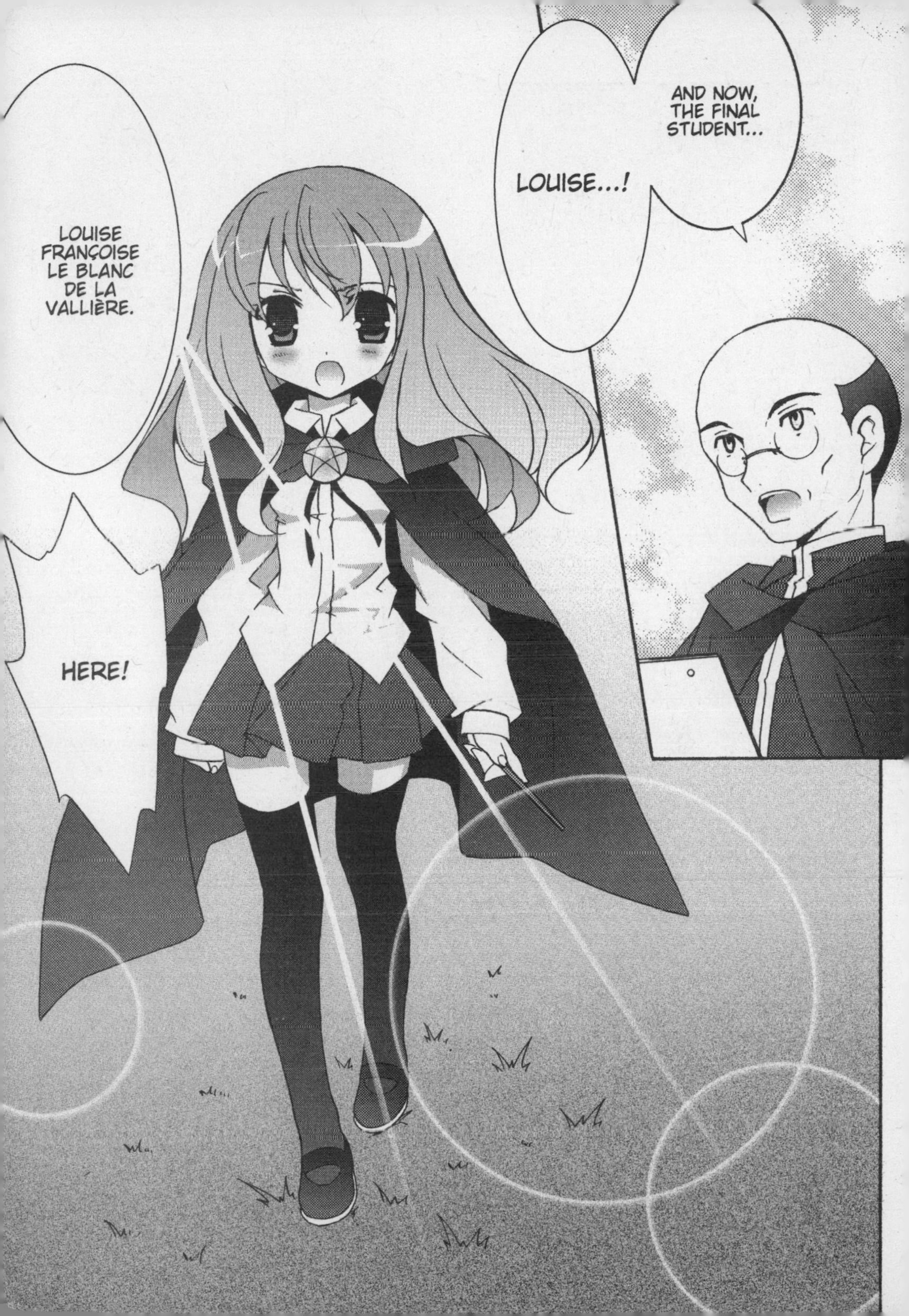
AND NOW, THE FINAL STUDENT...
LOUISE...!
LOUISE FRANÇOISE LE BLANC DE LA VALLIÈRE.
HERE!

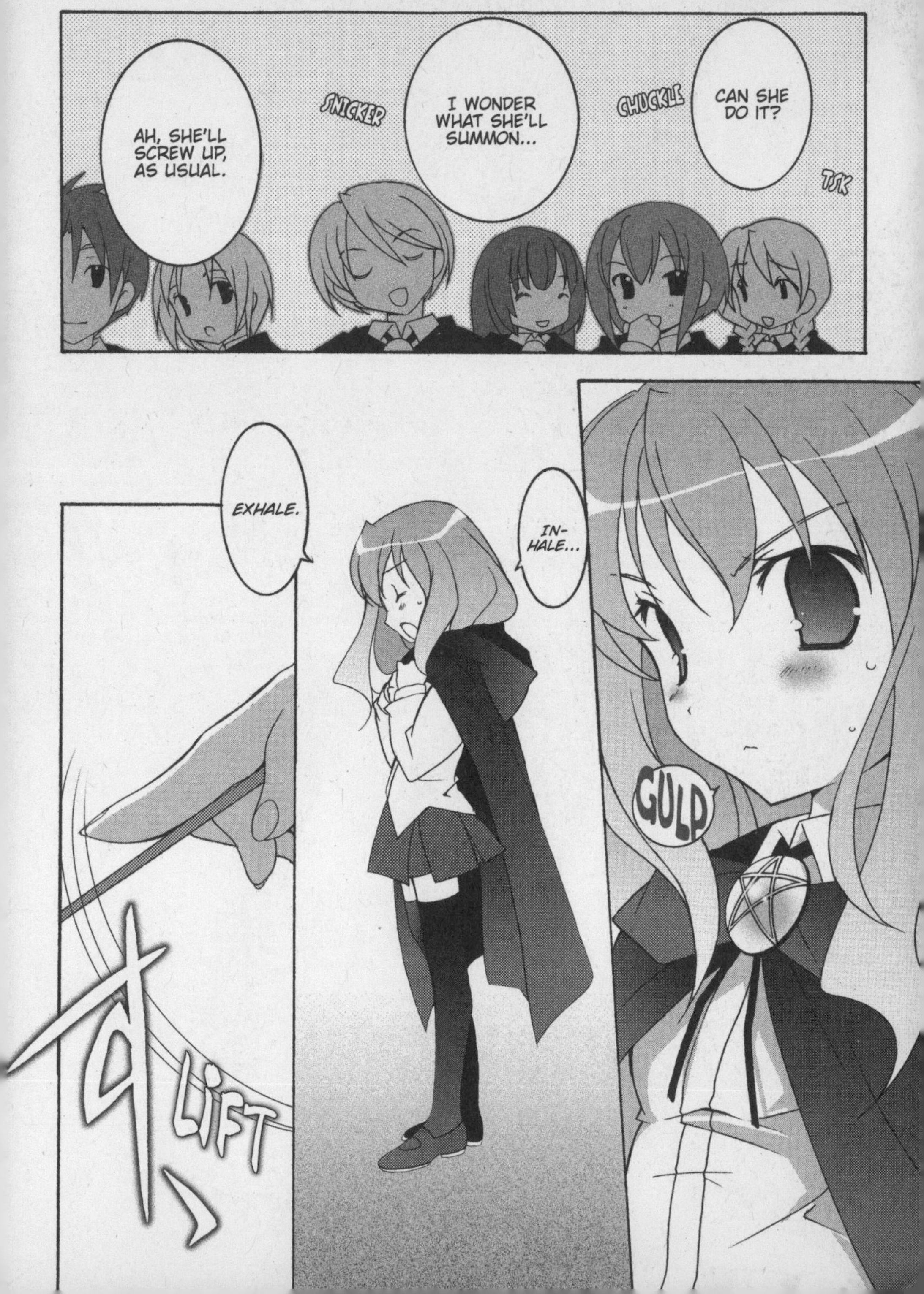
TSK
CAN SHE DO IT?
CHUCKLE
I WONDER WHAT SHE'LL SUMMON...
SNICKER
AH, SHE'LL SCREW UP, AS USUAL.
GULP
IN-HALE...
EXHALE.
LIFT

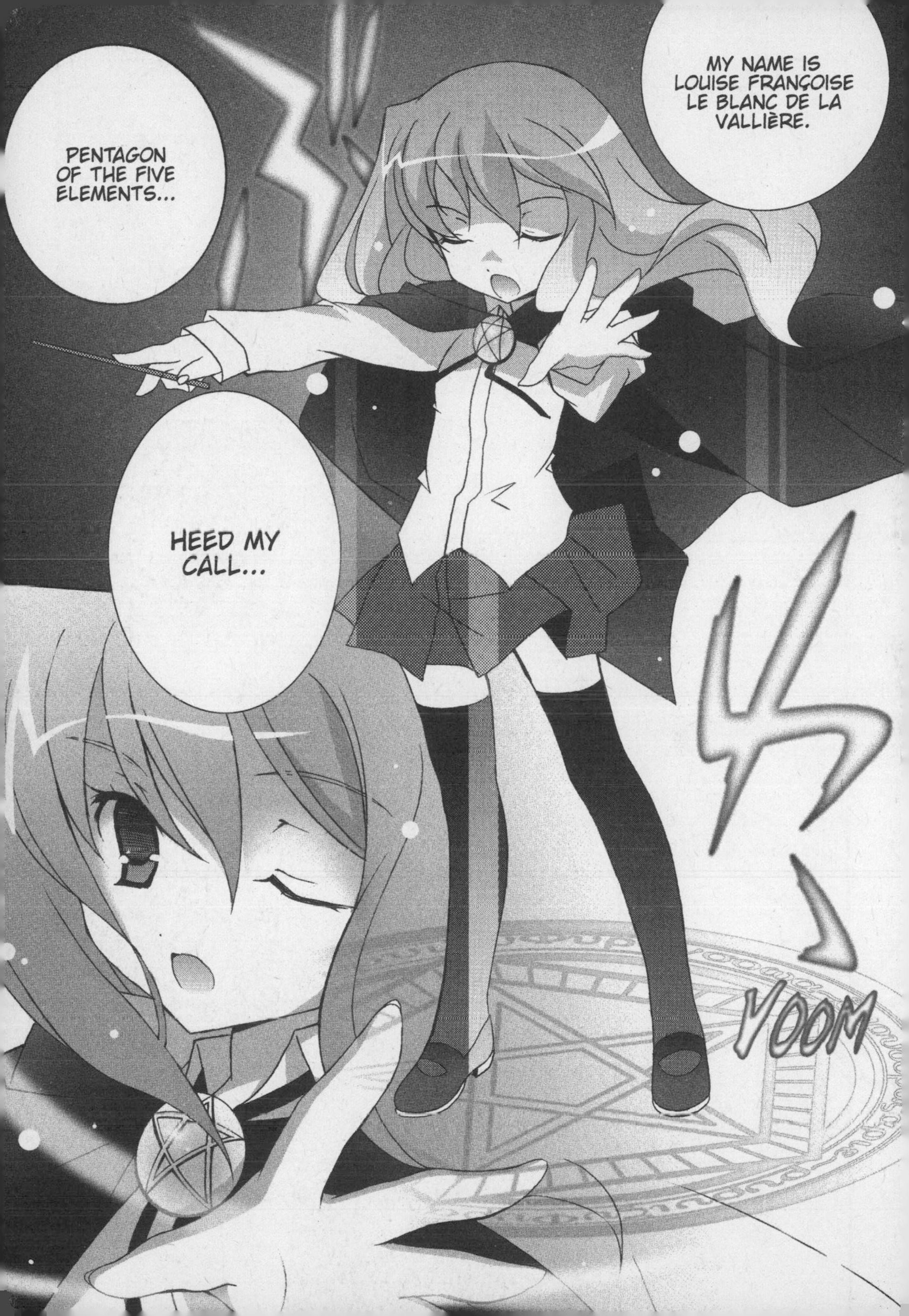
MY NAME IS LOUISE FRANÇOISE LE BLANC DE LA VALLIÈRE.
PENTAGON OF THE FIVE ELEMENTS...
HEED MY CALL...
YOOM

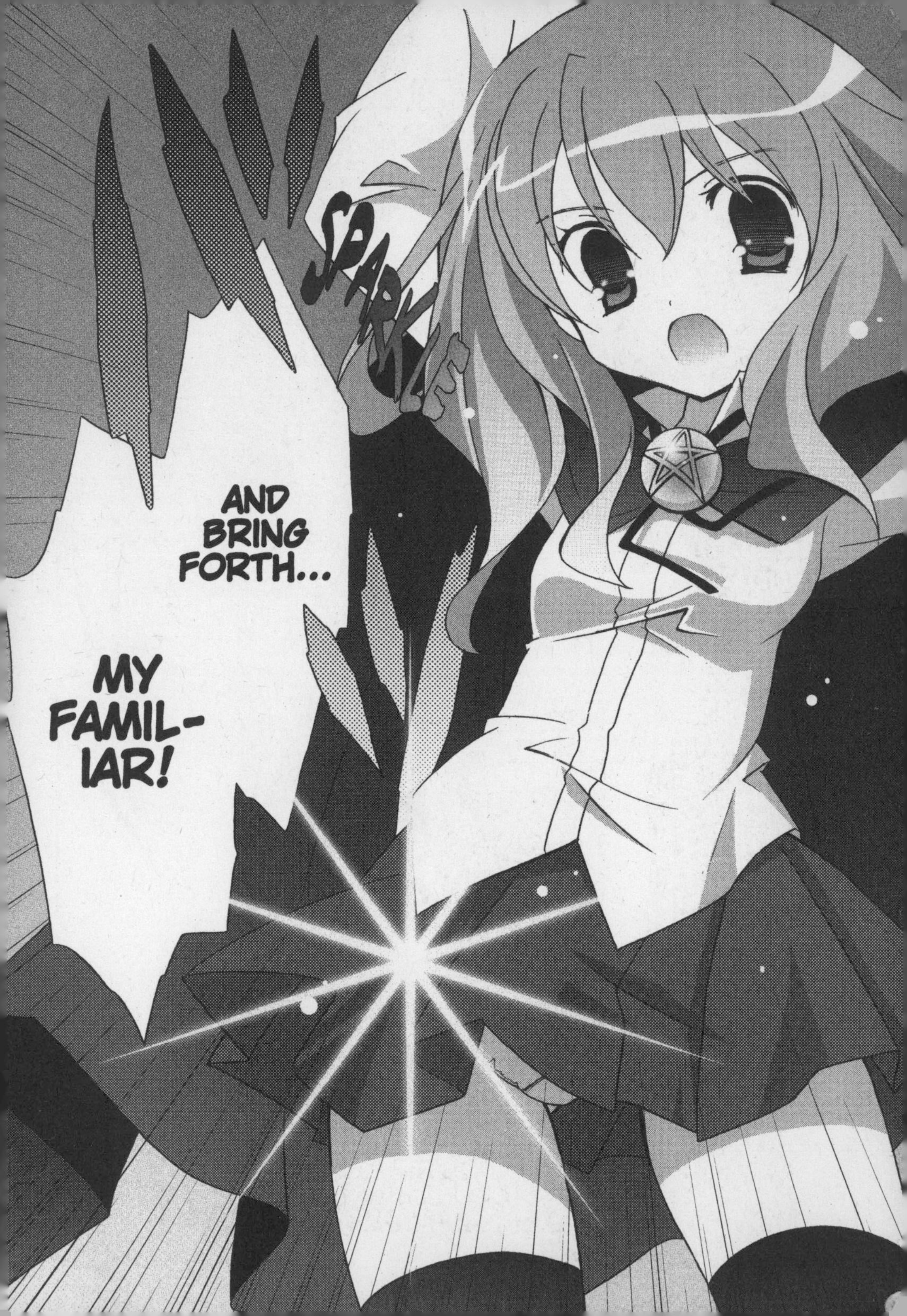
SPARKLE
AND BRING FORTH...
MY FAMIL-IAR!

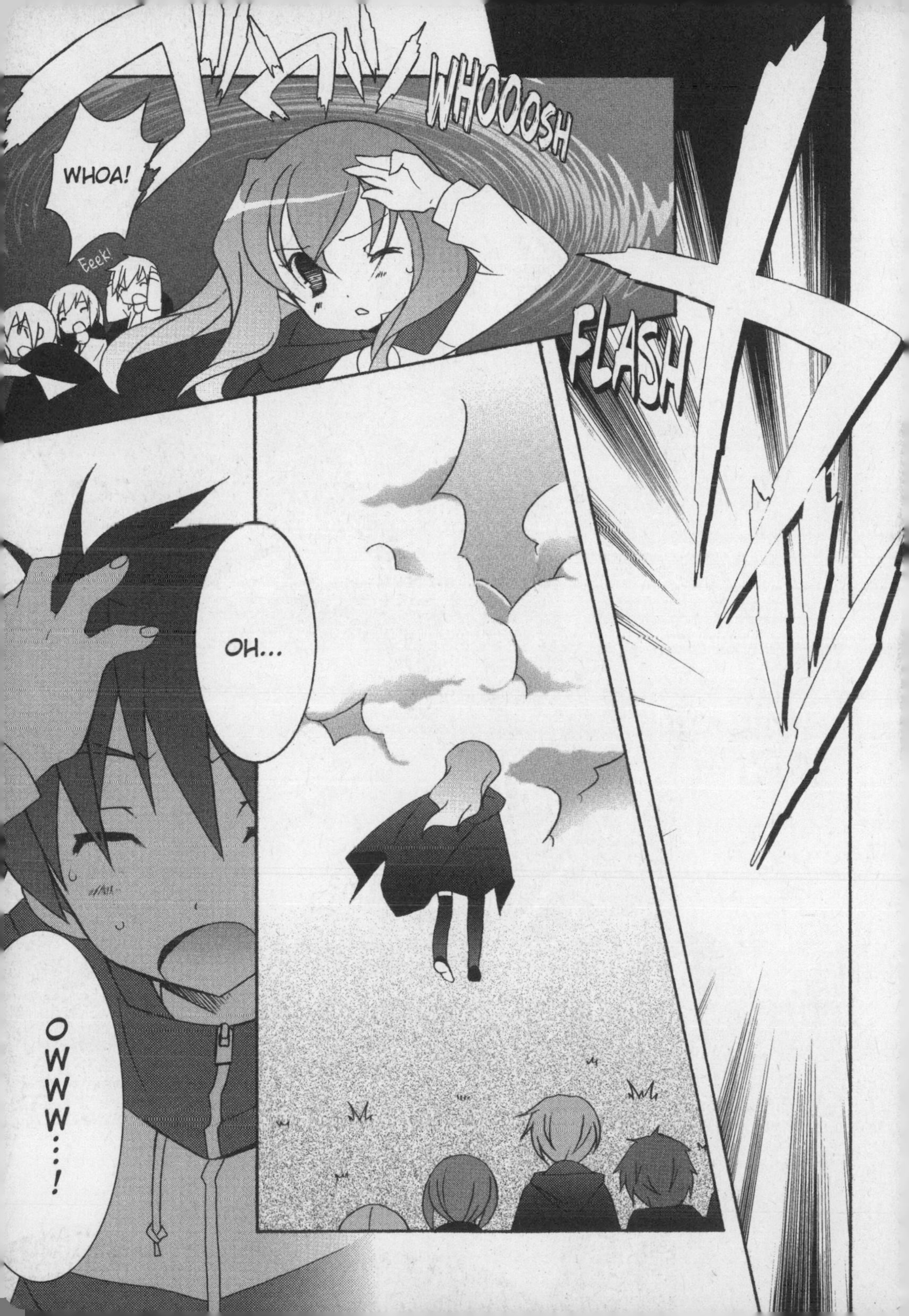
WHOOOSH
WHOA!
Eeek!
FLASH
OH...
OWWW...!

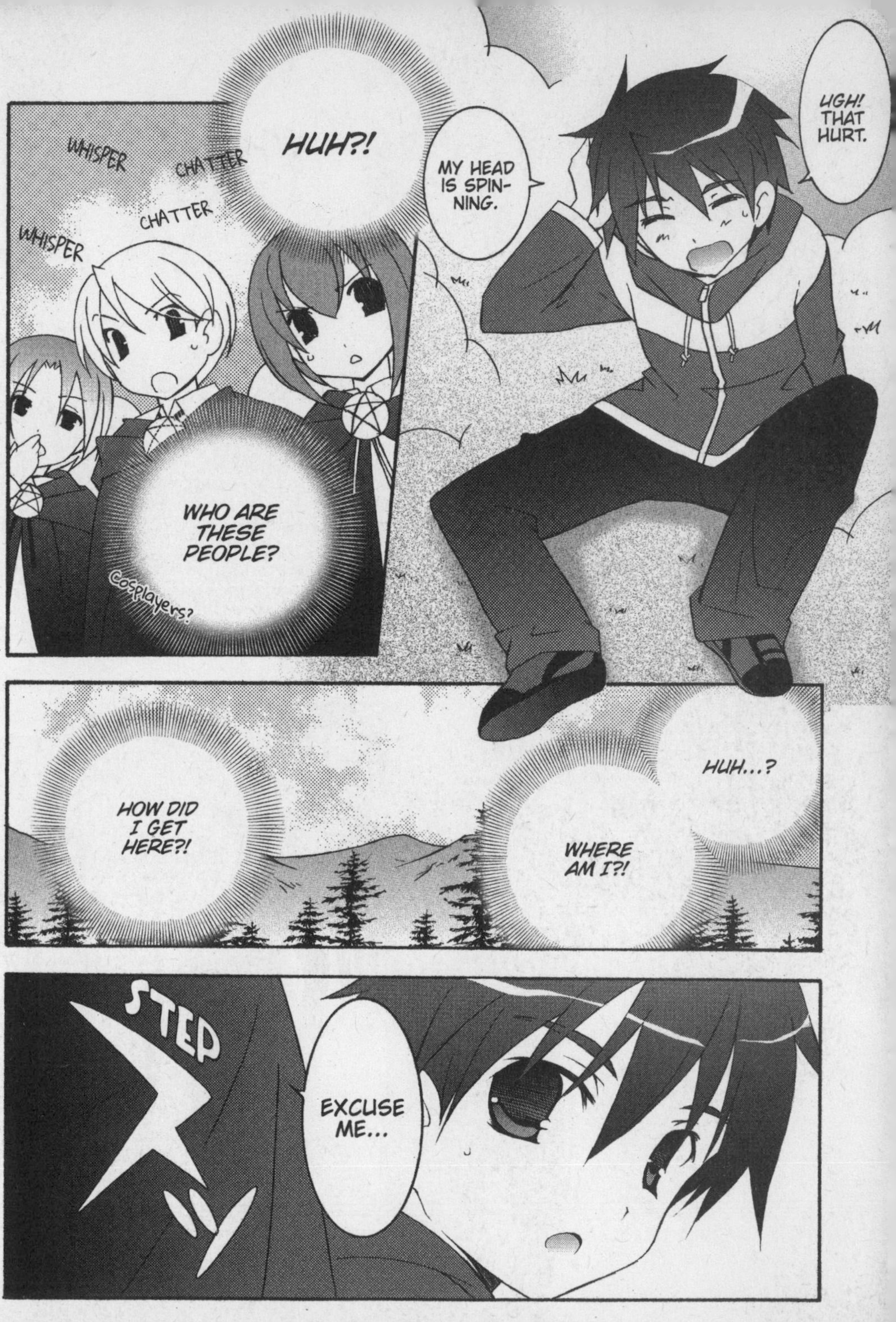
UGH! THAT HURT.
MY HEAD IS SPIN-NING.
HUH?!
WHISPER
CHATTER
CHATTER
WHISPER
WHO ARE THESE PEOPLE?
Cosplayers?
HUH...?
WHERE AM I?!
HOW DID I GET HERE?!
EXCUSE ME...
STEP

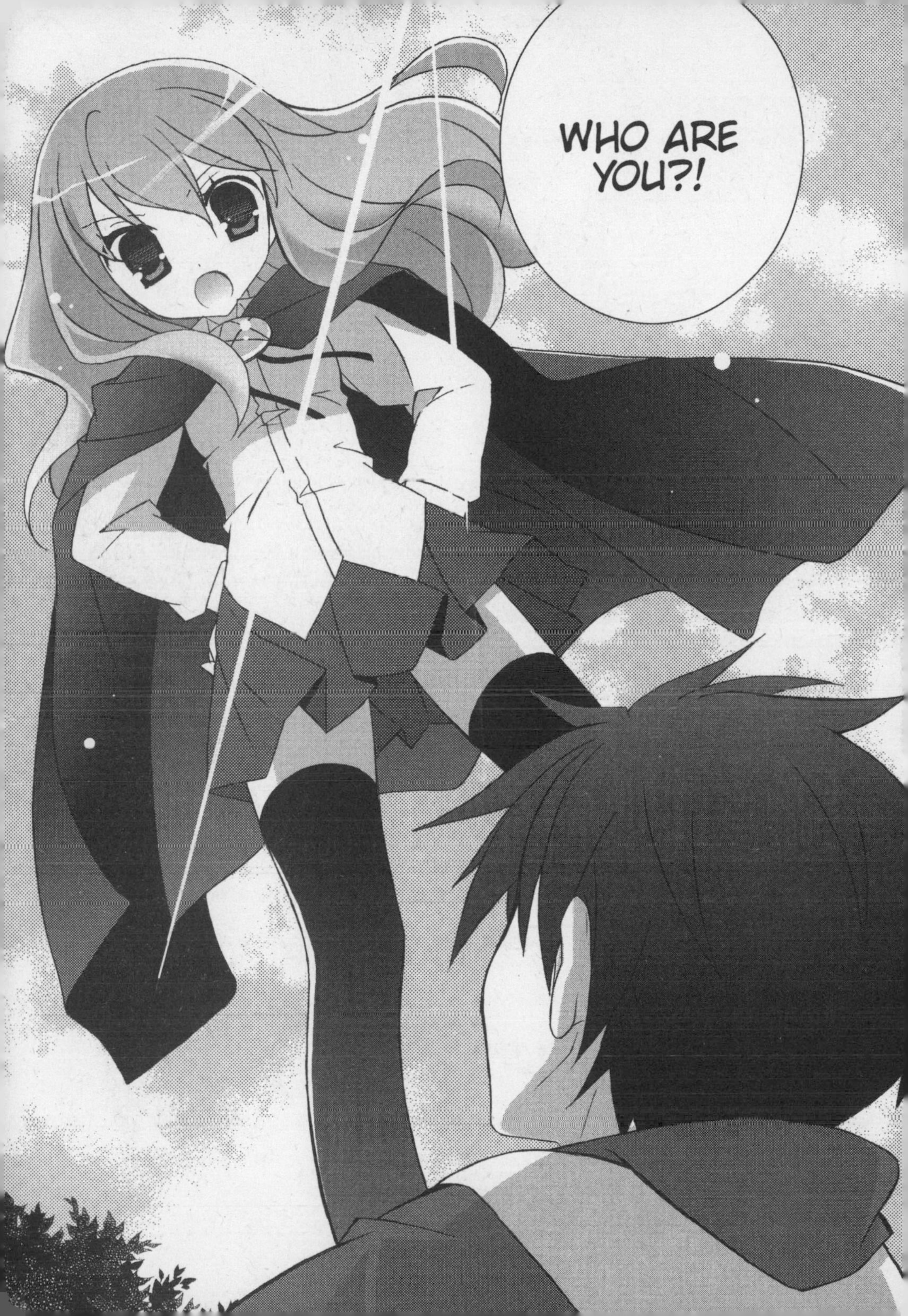
WHO ARE YOU?!

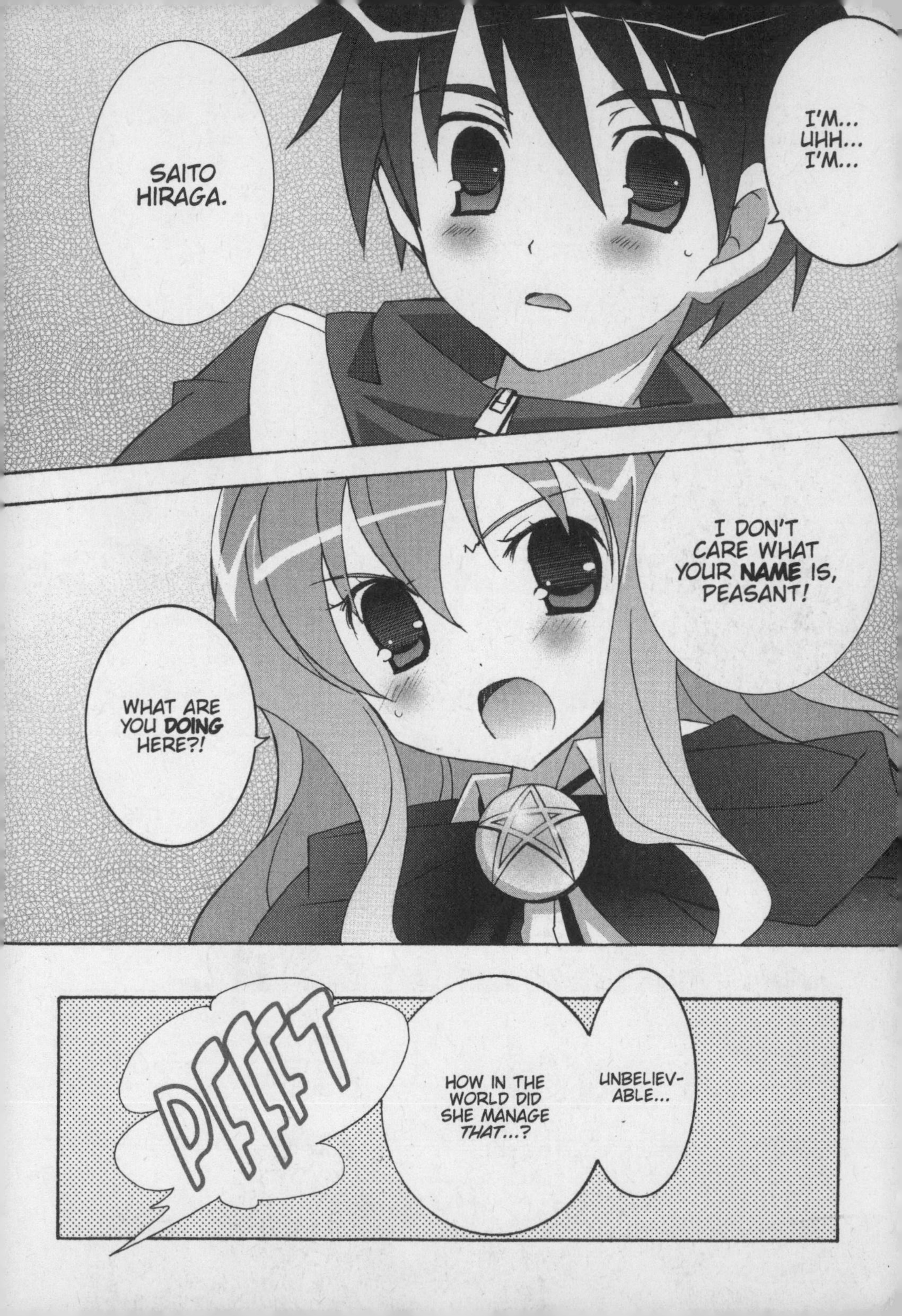
I'M... UHH... I'M...
SAITO HIRAGA.
I DON'T CARE WHAT YOUR **NAME** IS, PEASANT!
WHAT ARE YOU **DOING** HERE?!
UNBELIEV-ABLE...
HOW IN THE WORLD DID SHE MANAGE *THAT*...?
PFFFT